CONCEPCION

CONCEPCION

AN IMMIGRANT
FAMILY'S FORTUNES

❧

ALBERT SAMAHA

Riverhead Books   New York   2021

RIVERHEAD BOOKS
An imprint of Penguin Random House LLC
penguinrandomhouse.com

Library of Congress Cataloging-in-Publication Data
Names: Samaha, Albert, author.
Title: Concepcion : an immigrant family's fortunes / Albert Samaha.
Other titles: Immigrant family's fortunes
Description: New York : Riverhead Books, 2021. | Includes bibliographical references.
Identifiers: LCCN 2021013641 (print) | LCCN 2021013642 (ebook) |
ISBN 9780593086087 (hardcover) | ISBN 9780593086100 (ebook)
Subjects: LCSH: Concepcion family. | Samaha, Albert—Family. |
Filipino Americans—California—San Francisco—Biography. |
Filipino Americans—California—San Francisco—History—20th century. |
Immigrants—California—San Francisco—Biography. |
San Francisco (Calif.)—Biography. | Mindanao Island (Philippines)—Biography. |
Mindanao Island (Philippines)—Politics and government.
Classification: LCC F869.S39 F436 2021 (print) |
LCC F869.S39 (ebook) | DDC 929.20973—dc23
LC record available at https://lccn.loc.gov/2021013641
LC ebook record available at https://lccn.loc.gov/2021013642

International edition ISBN: 9780593421222

Printed in the United States of America
1   3   5   7   9   10   8   6   4   2

BOOK DESIGN BY LUCIA BERNARD

For Tia, Chloé, Bella, and Maïa

꧁꧂

Without willing it, I had gone from being ignorant of being ignorant, to being aware of being aware. And the worst part of my awareness was that I didn't know what I was aware of.

—MAYA ANGELOU, *I Know Why the Caged Bird Sings*

Why was America so kind and yet so cruel?

—CARLOS BULOSAN, *America Is in the Heart*

Good or evil, it is yours, you belong to it, and this side of the grave you will never get away from the marks that it has given you.

—GEORGE ORWELL, "England Your England"

You who are to see the dawn, welcome it, and do not forget those who fell during the night.

—JOSÉ RIZAL, *Noli Me Tángere*

꧁꧂

CONTENTS

CONCEPCION

CHAPTER I

THE SCORE

My mom almost got scammed this one time, not long ago. She'd met a guy who seemed promising, a white dude who prayed with her over the phone and talked about business deals he was making all over the world. She had been struggling for a while. She'd bounced across a half-dozen cities over the past decade, started and ended a bunch of jobs, sometimes grinding two or three gigs at a time to keep the rent paid and the lights on, and life was only getting harder. By the end of 2018, she hadn't broke even in months. Her credit card debt rose to sums she would only whisper to me, even when nobody else was around. The temp agency she was working for hadn't given her an assignment in weeks. On the last, filing papers for a property management company at a Section 8 apartment complex, a tenant had threatened to shoot up the place after learning he was getting evicted. My mom was so scared that her boss let her go home early. "OMG, what a stress," she had texted me, punctuating the message with an emoji of a frowning face with a bead of sweat dripping from its forehead.

She was living in San Francisco now, in the cramped ground-floor unit of a creaky two-story duplex that had been in our family for decades.

Her landlord, her cousin-in-law, kept the rent at a family discount. The space had once been a doctor's office, and it was drafty and narrow. When I visited from New York, as I did once or twice a year, I slept on the couch bundled in a hoodie, nodding off to the Gregorian chants coming from the boom box in my mom's bedroom.

The neighborhood used to be known as the Fillmore District, or the Western Addition, but newcomers call it NoPa, for "north of the Panhandle," because the developers buying up the housing stock and the brokers writing the listings want to distance their increasingly valuable buildings from the area's reputation as a historically Black community. In recent years the area began sprouting the amenities you might expect from a place with a name like NoPa: a café serving seven-dollar toast, a bar decorated with surrealist art available for purchase, a three-floor entertainment center featuring vintage arcade games, one-bedroom condos going for $700,000—a world of luxury just outside my mom's door, but tauntingly out of reach. The contrast was disconcerting. As the neighborhood's prospects brightened, hers only dimmed.

She always assured me she was doing fine. She described her days to me as simple and peaceful, and as evidence sent me photos from her early morning walks on Ocean Beach—dogs splashing in the tide, jellyfish washed ashore, messages she wrote in the sand, like "Happy Birthday, Jesus!" with a heart dotting the exclamation point. She collected shells, stones, and sand dollars, some for their unusual colors, some for their smooth, perfect form, some because they bore marks in which she saw the face of Christ. My mother saw miracles everywhere.

When she was a kid back in the Philippines, her own mother would wake her and her brothers and sisters at three a.m. on each of the nine days leading up to Christmas, to walk thirty minutes in the dark to a packed church where they would pray the novenas; by the fourth or fifth day, my mom was the only one of the children who could be gotten out of bed. Anytime something good happens, my mom says, "Praise the

Lord!" and anytime something bad happens, she says it's part of God's plan. She goes to church six days a week, and on Good Friday she hibernates in prayer from noon to three, the hours Christ hung on the cross. Every time she moves, she has a priest bless her new home with holy water, and when she drives, she listens to a Catholic AM radio station or Christian rock CDs. The background on her cell phone is a portrait of Jesus—not a Renaissance classic or an image of suffering, but a handsome, square-jawed, smiling white Jesus with romance-novel hair. Whenever I express concern or apprehension about anything big or small, her response is, "Don't worry, God will take care of us."

There was a time when I shared that certainty. Over the years I'd come to doubt that tribulations have greater purpose, that justice awaits the righteous, that misfortune is the product of anything but human malevolence or sheer chance. But I kept this to myself. Why undermine my mother's hope if I had no alternative to offer? Instead, I concentrated on solutions. More and more, our phone calls and texts focused on ways to address her money problems. More and more, I worried about her. Sometimes, shamefully and selfishly, I took out my frustration on her, hardening my voice as if I were the parent and she were a wayward child. Why had she quit a job that seemed stable, even if the boss was an asshole? Why had she left her purse in the backseat of her car, for someone to steal? One Christmas morning when I was back visiting her in California, I saw her put a fifty-dollar bill in the collection plate at church. I shot her a harsh look. "Dang, Mom! You don't gotta give 'em all that!" She countered my show of disapproval with an icy glare of true parental force, the one that says, Boy, you better check yourself, although all she said was, "Albert, it's Christmas."

Maybe it was her trust in a fair and merciful greater power that kept her so relentlessly optimistic. She schemed and hustled, certain she was but a winning move away from the life to which she aspired. If she could just patch together the funds to put a down payment on an investment property, or buy her mother's old coconut farm in the Philippines, or fix up her tiny living room so she could put it on Airbnb without her land-lord knowing. But the opportunities never came close enough to snatch.

So I was more relieved than anything when she told me she'd been talking to this guy who apparently had a lot of money. I wasn't surprised such good fortune had come her way. My mom sparkles with energy, carries conversations with playfulness and curiosity, her eyes big and hands like fireworks when she gets on a thread you really should know about, like the ingredients in her homemade smoothies, or the benefits of a credit union, or the Illuminati. She's a former model who dresses in pink or black chic, fully accessorized, like she's got a daily meeting with Anna Wintour, and she looks—swear to God—half of her sixty-one years. I've lost count of the times some stranger assumed she was my girlfriend or my wife, to my embarrassment and my mother's flattered, still-got-it amusement. She has never been short on suitors. The surpris-ing thing was that she'd become enamored enough to tell me about this one; most didn't last long before she dropped them, unimpressed. The last love interest I'd heard about had turned out to be a priest, news I met with a reflexive chuckle of incredulity, less at the situation's absurdity than at how it made more sense than anything I'd ever heard. Would it be wrong, she'd asked, if this man of God relinquished his sacred vocation for her? I suggested that maybe God made him a priest so that the two of them could meet, and absolutely they should go forth and live devoutly together. Alas, they discussed the possibility but never felt comfortable with it, and the priest transferred out of the parish to escape the temptation. I think I took it harder than my mom did, or at least more than she let on.

She'd met the international developer on LinkedIn, her preferred so-cial media platform at the time. In photos he sported short gray hair and hip glasses with red frames. He told her he lived in Los Angeles but was frequently in the Bay Area for work. I never got a chance to meet him myself. Whenever I was in town, he happened to be out of the country. My mom kept trying to get him to talk to me on the phone, but he was always running to a meeting or to catch a flight. Once, he called her while we were in the car. She put the call on the speaker system, and after some pleasantries told him I was there too. The line went silent, but not dead. My mom said "Hello?" a few times before we heard him hang up. I figured he was just embarrassed, caught off guard by the sudden prospect of chopping it up with the grown son of a woman he'd been courting for not even four months.

Some weeks later, I came back to town for the holidays. When my mom picked me up from the airport, she announced that she had wonderful news: The guy she was sort of dating had just closed a big business deal, and he wanted to use a chunk of his new cash to partner with her on a real estate investment.

"How much does he want to put in?" I asked.

"Five hundred thousand!" my mom said, giddy, holding her mouth open in exaggerated shock.

For months, she had been trying to raise money to buy, renovate, and flip a house in San Francisco. It was her latest plan to make everything right—erase the debts, pay off the car, build up some savings, pull herself back to stability in one big windfall.

"That's great, Mom."

"Praise the Lord!"

It wasn't totally implausible. I mean, what's half a mil to a truly wealthy person? Let's welcome the blessings when they come, I figured.

IT HADN'T ALWAYS BEEN like this for my mother. The memory of the prosperous years she'd had in this country was still so strong that she believed she could retrace her steps back up the mountain. The further behind she fell, the more certain she seemed that a turnaround was imminent, overdue. To her eyes, there were always boom times on the American horizon. She'd been raised on stories of the nation's exceptionalism and the idea of the ever-upward trajectory it fueled.

From her earliest memories, her parents, Manuel and Rizalina Concepcion, had been drawing up plans to bring their eight children to the United States. Unlike many other immigrants, they hadn't had a pressing need to come. Indeed, the family had thrived in the Philippines in the years of my mother's childhood, the mid-1960s, moving up in a fast-developing nation with the second strongest economy in Asia. As young adults, they'd left their ancestral home on the southernmost island, Mindanao, and moved to Quezon City, then a sleepy suburb just inland from Manila. Rizalina was an accountant at the Philippine Central Bank and also managed a coconut farm that her family owned back in Mindanao. Manuel was a prominent civil attorney who often defended poor tenants in land disputes.

They built a big house on an empty corner lot in a neighborhood of tall tropical thickets, grassy fields, and newly paved roads. The family called the house Scout Reyes, after the street it was on, which would not stay sleepy for much longer. As other Filipinos left the agricultural provinces over the next two decades, the population of Quezon City tripled, eventually surpassing Manila's, subdivisions sprawling where jungles had once stood. By the time my mom was four, the family had maids and a driver and a boat, and her older siblings attended top private schools. Yet even at that point, when the family's comfort seemed most secure, Rizalina and Manuel saw a brighter future away from the Islands. "They didn't want to stay there forever," my mom's oldest sister, my auntie Ging, recalled years later. "America was the dreamland."

Manuel's sister, Caridad, had migrated to the States in 1949, when her job in the U.S. Army logistics department transferred her to San Francisco, securing her a visa, a valuable ticket then available to few—that year just 1,068 people from the Philippines were admitted into the country. She married a Filipino chiropractor who'd served in the U.S. Navy during World War II, and in 1957 the couple bought the Fillmore duplex and turned the bottom floor into a clinic for his practice. On her visits back to the Philippines, Caridad would parade into the Scout Reyes house to much fanfare, her nieces and nephews gathering around her and her bulging suitcase filled with pasalubong, including candies they'd never seen before and bags of caramel popcorn. She described the cable cars and jazz joints, the wide roads and giant steel bridges, the clean sidewalks and summers so temperate she didn't even own an electric fan. "Such a wonderful place to live," Ging remembers thinking. "Everyone can eat steak. If you have a job, you can eat whatever you want, buy whatever you want."

After visiting Caridad in the United States, Manuel and Rizalina returned to Scout Reyes with their own tales of wonder. More than once, Manuel recounted to his children his sidewalk encounter with a fellow Filipino, a humble elevator man just getting off work in downtown San Francisco. Catching glances in the magnetic pull of racial recognition, the men struck up a conversation as Manuel walked him to his car, which—Manuel would pause before the punch line—turned out to be a gleaming new Cadillac. My mother remembers her father saying, "In America, there is that dignity of labor."

The trouble, at first, was how to get in on that privilege. American borders, once open to all, had closed with racist fury long before my mother was born; since the 1880s, laws had severely limited which immigrants were welcome, and how many. Making it into the country was a moon shot of a dream, a lottery draw of astronomical odds, the winners arbitrary and few, an exclusivity that seemed almost fitting for a destination so desirable. Manuel and Rizalina had built the house on Scout Reyes without knowing if they'd ever have a chance to leave it for the American home they could only imagine.

Naturally, right after the family moved in, a clear path across the ocean suddenly materialized, as if the spirit of Uncle Sam was testing their faith, measuring just how much they were willing to leave behind. In 1965, when my mom was five, the United States passed a law erasing the race-based immigration quotas that had blocked new arrivals from nearly every part of the world except northern and western Europe. The old policy was "un-American in the highest sense, because it has been untrue to the faith that brought thousands to these shores even before we were a country," President Lyndon Johnson declared upon signing the bill. But under the new law, "those who do come will come because of what they are, and not because of the land from which they sprung."

Two years later, my grandparents, Rizalina and Manuel, were each approved for a U.S. permanent residency visa, which was not yet known as a green card. The game plan was clear to the whole family: once the parents could save enough money to secure a home and stable jobs in the United States, the children would follow. "They wanted all of us to go," Auntie Ging said. "They wanted to give us roots here." They didn't know how long it would be until the whole family was settled across the ocean, but they set their sights.

MANY OTHERS AROUND THE GLOBE had the same idea, forming a wave of migration to the country unprecedented in its scope. In the 1960s, for the first time in the country's history, the majority of immigrants came from non-European countries. From 1970 to 1999, around 20 million immigrants came to the United States, 90 percent of them from Asia, Africa, Central America, and South America. Some were refugees driven from countries long ravaged by colonizing empires and convulsing amid the proxy battles of the Cold War. Some, like my family, chose to leave all they'd built in their homeland, drawn by the allure of what they believed America to be.

When the United States began blocking immigration based on race, the first radio broadcast was two decades away, much of South America, Africa, and Asia were still under the rule of European colonizers, and it took about a week to cross the Atlantic Ocean by ship. By the time quotas were lifted, the first moon landing was four years away, liberation movements had bloomed across the colonies, and it took less than a day to cross the Pacific by airplane. The world had come to feel smaller and more open, the distance between leaving and arriving less daunting than it ever had been. Those who had been locked out of the United States began to pour in.

In the wake of the Korean War, the number of Korean immigrants entering the United States went from less than 5,000 in 1960 to nearly 275,000 in 1979, the biggest portion landing in Los Angeles. From 1970 to 1989, spurred by another American war, the annual influx of Vietnamese immigrants grew from around 3,000 to 320,000, many settling in San Jose, San Diego, and Houston. Laotians congregated in Sacramento, Cambodians in Stockton.

Following the revolution that overthrew the shah, the number of new arrivals from Iran tripled from the 1970s to the 1980s, many settling in Southern California. In the 1990s, following a debt crisis and ensuing recession, around 2.8 million people from Mexico became permanent residents of the U.S., more than four times as many as had come in the 1970s, spreading across the southwest and Texas and into Chicago. In the two decades after the fall of the Berlin Wall marked the ceremonial end of the Cold War, nearly a million new residents arrived from China, five times as many as in the prior two decades, filling growing enclaves in San Francisco, Los Angeles, New York City, and other metropolises. Following their nation's war with neighboring Eritrea, the number of new arrivals from Ethiopia rose from around 13,000 in the 1980s to nearly 90,000 in the 2000s, many landing in Washington, D.C. The number of Nigerian immigrants to the U.S. more than quadrupled, from around 60,000 in 1990—the year of a failed coup in their homeland and amid falling wages—to 280,000 in 2017, the largest shares of them settling in and around Houston and D.C. Over that same span, the number of immigrants from India—some fleeing religious persecution, others the stagnant economy—rose from around 450,000 to 2.3 million, with half a million ending up in the greater New York City area and more than 100,000 in and around San Jose.

All over the country, the immigrants of the great wave built communities and support systems, pooling resources, sharing roofs, sending dollars back to relatives who stayed behind. Migrants of Arab descent formed enclaves in Detroit and its surrounding suburbs. Arrivals from the Dominican Republic and the territory of Puerto Rico settled in Harlem and the Bronx, while those from Haiti and Jamaica landed in Brooklyn and southeast Queens. Cubans found homes in Miami, Somalis in Minneapolis. Overall, the United States took in around 250,000 immigrants a year in the 1950s, rising to 330,000 a year in the 1960s, 450,000 in the 1970s, 735,000 in the 1980s, and more than a million a year from the 1990s on. Diasporas spread wide, bringing languages, foods, traditions, and ways of thinking that wove into the social tapestries of blocks, neighborhoods, cities. The new land returned the favor, and when the immigrants had children, those children talked like Americans, dressed like Americans, and complained like Americans: a generation born to vindicate the hardships of migration by soaking in all there was to offer.

By 2017, America's foreign-born population neared 14 percent, five times higher than it had been in 1970, but right around what it had been at the turn of the previous century, before most of the immigration restrictions had been put in place. Unlike their immigrant predecessors from Europe, however, most of those who arrived in the second half of the twentieth century couldn't so easily blend in to the country's white mainstream—couldn't Anglify a name or nub down an accent, couldn't hide that they were, in fact, not only of a different place but of a different race. America's population, more than 80 percent white for two centuries, was 76 percent white by 1990, and 64 percent by 2010, the wave of new arrivals challenging any assurance that the U.S. was forever bound to be a majority white country.

In 1989, the year after my mom, pregnant with me, joined her mother and older sister in San Francisco, more immigrants arrived from the Philippines than from any other country except Mexico. The exodus kept up for another three decades, and today Filipino immigrants and their American-born descendants make up the fourth-largest diaspora in the United States, though it might not seem that way at passing glance, with so few Manilatowns and movie characters to mark our presence, and so many ethnicities for people to confuse us with. Masters of assimilation, a skill honed by our ancestors for centuries, we molded ourselves into the American image to which we aspired. To be of this place—that was the hope.

THE MIGRATING GENERATION takes the brunt of the transition, and my elders set me up well. Without having to do anything, I was born into the empire of the age, just one of many breaks to swing in my favor. The youngest among my American-raised cohort of cousins, I entered a world crafted for my benefit, a social infrastructure built by those who came before me. My family had enough money to soften the landing. My parents covered all my needs and then some—sports camps, a drum set, trips to Disneyland. As a child, I had no reason to question whether my elders had chosen the right place. Where else but America? I viewed the Philippines as among a wide swath of nations whose defining characteristic was that they were inferior to my country in most ways that mattered. Whatever game had unfolded over the course of human civilization, the Philippines had lost and the United States of America had

won. Its wealth and power were the logical result of free-market principles and a popularly elected government crafted from the lessons of the
Enlightenment. The sins of its past receded from view with each new
law bending U.S. policy toward equality. So went the march of American progress, was the belief. The United States, land of the winners,
seemed an obvious destination for anyone with the means to get there,
and by virtue of my family's migration, we could consider ourselves victorious as well.

America played the role of savior, while the immigrant protagonists
stood as shining examples of savvy and work ethic. From that lens, the
sacrifices were vindicated, indisputably, by default. We embraced our
ties to the colonizer, pledged fealty, took pride in being a part of it. The
empire keeps the records, builds the monuments, dictates the terms of
survival. The empire tells the stories. In another time and place, we
might have sought favor from the Mayans or the Ottomans, but as it
happened we were born into the American Century, the era of capitalist
democracy, and so it was the American gods that we worshipped.

I went to good schools, and emerged into adulthood without debt,
knowing that if I ever slipped up, my people would catch me. The empire has been good to me, just as the migrating elders had hoped. That
was what they sacrificed for, they'd say without hesitation, rattling off
the achievements of my American-bred cousins and me with our stable
careers, enjoying financial trajectories that surpassed their own.

The cost of my comfort got clearer with time. As I reached the age my
mother had been when she moved to the United States, there was no
more denying that her toil wasn't just a toll to pay on the road to easier
days but a permanent struggle. The thought filled me with sadness and
urgency. How to ensure that such a sacrifice wasn't wasted, I didn't know.
My cousin Jed, who is older than me and figured out the score long before I did, couldn't shake the angst either. More and more, our discussions about sneaker drops and basketball rosters detoured into soliloquies

on the burdens our elders still carried, the two of us soft and serious with our noses in our beers, looking all kawawa. Jed's parents, Auntie Ging and Uncle Spanky, had reached their seventies with bills and debts that seemed destined to keep them from ever retiring. The same year my mom almost got scammed, a burglar broke into their house, stole a few electronics, and ransacked the place. They couldn't afford to fix the busted door, knocked clean off its hinges, so they nailed plywood over the threshold and entered and exited through the garage for weeks.

One sappy night that December, Jed and I pondered the unspeakable question of whether our family would have been better off staying in the Philippines. "Life was much easier there," Jed said. "We had fuckin' maids." All that our ancestors had built there had been abandoned in the exodus, leaving only fantasies of parallel lives.

Unlike the ancestors of Native and Black Americans, ours had signed up of their own will, chasing dreams and stability only to slam into the walls of a stubbornly stratified and segregated nation. Maybe, having grown up here, I found it easier to see what my elders could not: the height of the climb and the length of the fall. I learned early on to take stock of the trade-offs, of the costs written as if in invisible ink on my elders' green cards, accruing like the interest due on their maxed-out credit lines. Perhaps it was my lack of roots, growing up as the initial cohort in a new place, that made me sensitive to the fragility of the world as I knew it. To me, it felt as if we were holding closed a broken door in the middle of an eternal blizzard; if we let up an inch, the wind might surge in and the snow bury us.

The next morning, Jed and I got brunch at one of the fancy spots down the street from the duplex. In the sobriety of daylight, the unspeakable question sounded nothing short of preposterous. Hell no, I didn't want to run it back and try my luck on the Islands, trade in the life my mom had gifted me at the top of the world for an infinite range of alternatives. It was my duty to indulge in the fruits of the empire; it was what my elders had worked for. To live in peace, thanks to the military might keeping war away from our borders. To wander well-lit neighborhoods served by police forces quick to squelch even the slightest disturbance. To buy food, clothes, and phones at cheaper prices because they were picked, stitched, and built by workers paid as poorly as their employers could get away with. To exist freely and securely in the rarefied air of the colonist class, to which just a minuscule slice of the world's population gains admittance.

The exclusivity explained the cost. For millennia, empires have jostled for supremacy, rising to hold the top spot in their known world for as long as they could before relinquishing it like a championship belt. Born into the age of imperialist conquest, America played the game well, a prodigy of a superpower that doubled in size within a century and established global hegemony not long after its bicentennial. For generations, my ancestors navigated the wakes of distant empires, adapting to distant whims, imprinted with the knowledge that their homeland served the needs of distant people, stuck on the wrong side of the colonized world until America invited us in. It seemed intuitive to me that as outsiders we had to pay an entry fee, prove ourselves worthy additions to the empire, deserving of the comforts it boasted. As triumphant products of immigrant investment, Jed and I validated our country's mythology. I understood that my mother's sacrifice was necessary long before I ever wondered why.

TWO NIGHTS after the excitement of the half-million-dollar investment offer, my mom walked out of her bedroom with a worried look on her face, phone in hand. She joined me on the couch, where we sat beneath a caramel-brown ceiling stain left by a leak from a recent downpour.

"Guess what," she said, her face showing the impact of a hit of bad news. The international developer was having trouble with his bank. The bank

wasn't letting him transfer money from his account without paying out-
rageous fees, and for some reason he couldn't use the money in his account to pay the fees; he needed my mom to send him $20,000 so he could
send her the $500,000.

My jaw tensed. This fucker.

My mom was despairing about the poor guy and his terrible bank.
She quoted her father: "You know the best way to rob a bank? Own one."
I told her I thought the whole thing was probably a scam.

"Nooo!" she countered. "He's a good man. We pray together."

She said that he had given her his account log-in information, and
she'd seen for herself that he had $1.5 million in there. I asked her to
show me on my laptop. My mom had been a late adapter to the internet,
and wasn't so fluent in its nuances. The website for the alleged bank was
janky as hell, with warped photos and page links that went nowhere, like
a high school kid had designed it for a school project in 2006. The
browser showed that the website was not secure, an impossibility for a
legitimate bank. The URL itself didn't contain the alleged bank's name
but an abbreviation of it. Clinking around the internet, I found that the
name, address, and color scheme of the website had been copied from a
UK-based bank that did exist (on its own verified, secure website). I
looked up the guy's alleged name on the databases I use in my work as a
journalist and found a match—to a thirty-seven-year-old in Texas, not
a fiftysomething in California. I reverse-searched the guy's LinkedIn
profile picture, and it turned out that at least one other name was using
the same photo. My mom observed silently as the contours of the scam
emerged, frowning, her brow furrowed.

"I don't know, Albert," she said, her voice soft. "Really? I don't think
so. We pray together."

I was scared. Over the years, our worldviews had diverged to such a
degree that I had little confidence in my ability to persuade my mother on
any meaningful matter. I'd gotten used to her meeting any fact I presented

with skepticism, mistrusting any opinion I could craft. I'd come to realize, with horror, that we held wholly different understandings of reality, and I had no idea how to bridge the gap, which was only growing wider with time.

At first I'd thought our parting was merely ideological, her social conservatism clashing with my liberal tendencies. Though she'd supported Barack Obama in 2008, she turned against him soon after, when she learned that the Affordable Care Act, a policy she otherwise liked, covered abortions. In my childhood, she'd been an avid follower of *The 700 Club,* echoing Pat Robertson's prophecies about the impending reckoning for the culture of immorality coursing through America, the satanic messages said to be coded into contemporary music, the president facing impeachment proceedings for relations with an intern. By the late aughts, she preferred Fox News over other stations but was beginning to get most of her news from highly partisan websites. By the start of Obama's second term, she was sending me links to wildly false articles and YouTube videos claiming to have evidence that Obama was Muslim, or wanted to remove "In God We Trust" from U.S. currency, or was part of a global cabal committed to eliminating the Catholic Church. It happened quickly, as if she'd been swept up into a current pulling her further and further out of reach. Soon she was hitting all the far-right-wing conspiracy checkpoints: birtherism, George Soros's new world order, murders ordered by the Clintons, QAnon. If she could do it over again, she told me, she wouldn't have gotten me vaccinated.

She attributed my objections to the corrupting influence of my profession: she mourned that I was becoming, in her words, "part of the liberal media." We had extensive, passionate, well-meaning arguments on the phone, talking in circles, always ending in stalemate. *What has this country done to her?* I often found myself thinking when we hung up.

Her preferred candidate in the 2016 presidential election was Texas senator Ted Cruz. She found Donald Trump vulgar and tacky, and when he won the Republican nomination, she said she'd vote for him only to preserve a conservative Supreme Court. But when my mom picks a side, she really holds the line. She sees the world in stark terms: right and wrong, saints and heathens. Encouraged by the voices she trusted, she planted her loyalty. Two years after the election, a framed photo of the forty-fifth president sat on the bookshelf in her bedroom, just below a figurine of Pope Francis.

One night around that time, after we debated the merits of a big news story about Trump, she texted me:

I pray you will not be a journalist for the deep state, cuz these journalists believe in their evil agenda.

U have to realize it's between good and evil. Which side are you???

If you're protecting the deep state, I can't accept any of your money no matter how I may be needing help. I have to be on the side of Trump.

I love you but I have to be on the side of good.

May God bless you, Albert.

May the holy spirit enlighten your understanding.

Now we sat silently on the couch as she processed what I'd revealed, weighing all she'd known before against all she knew now. It was a lot for her to take in, and I wasn't sure where she'd land.

It occurred to me to ask: "Did you put any important information into the fake bank website?"

"No," she said quickly. "Just the log-in he gave me."

Social security number? Passwords? She shook her head, eyes staring at the ground in concentration. Bank account info? She looked up at me, and I could tell from her face, frozen in dread, that she was indeed giving credence to the possibility that the man she'd been seeing had targeted her in an elaborate deception. She told me that she'd entered her account and routing numbers to initiate the sham transfer. We stared at each other with big eyes for a long second. I imagined the many hours this man had devoted to orchestrating his con, picking the color schemes for his shitty little website, lying awake in bed crafting his cover story, cropping photos and revising details on his fake-ass social media accounts, excitement building as he drew closer to looting the hard-earned capital of my innocent, God-fearing mother. Her circumstances were precarious enough without this bullshit.

Mind swirling, trying to steady myself, almost too terrified to ask, I managed to breathe out, "How much do you have in your bank account?"

My mom's face softened at the question, as if she hadn't expected it, and I caught the slightest hint of a smirk. "Like, seventy dollars." I felt a surge rising in my chest. Our smiles widened in tandem before erupting into laughter. We roared, tears in our eyes, slapping knees, huffing and puffing until we had to catch our breath.

CHAPTER 2

DEPARTURES

Santo Niño was but a humble passenger when the ships set sail from Seville on September 20, 1519. At a mere eleven inches tall, wearing a red velvet cape over a white ruffled blouse and a red velvet bonnet over his chestnut curls, he kept a regal bearing. In his left hand, he held a gold cross. His chubby-cheeked face, the color of burnished oak, stayed calm through the long journey, with the hint of a smile. Across his waist glimmered a double-headed eagle emblazoned in green and red gems, the coat of arms of the House of Habsburg.

Santo Niño had been born in Flanders, which in 1482 came under the rule of the House of Habsburg, then the largest empire in Central Europe. Fourteen years later, a Habsburg prince married a Castilian princess, who soon became Queen of Spain. Their child, Charles, ascended to the throne at age sixteen, overseeing a sprawling European empire well-positioned to compete in the scramble for overseas conquest.

For years, Spain had jostled with Portugal for control of maritime commerce. Pressed against the edge of the known world, on a peninsula beyond the reach of the Silk Road, the dueling Iberian kingdoms saw opportunity in the vast western sea, seeking routes to the east that bypassed the lands of rival powers. In the 1440s, Portugal's shipbuilders designed a caravel suited for sailing into the wind, allowing crews to travel farther south than any Europeans before them. Portugal established the first European outpost in equatorial Africa and controlled shipping routes to China with coastal settlements along the Southeast Asian peninsula. Patrolling surrounding waters, Portuguese fleets pilfered goods and detained crews from Spanish ships crossing the Indian Ocean.

While Spain had beaten its European rivals to the New World in 1492, Portugal crossed the Atlantic eight years later, its southbound fleet veering off course and stumbling into the eastern horn of Brazil, probably the very location Portugal's King Manuel I would have chosen if given an accurate map. Pope Alexander VI had authorized the Catholic monarchs of Spain and Portugal to convert the unsaved world, and the pope had drawn a line designating the western half of the planet for Spain and the eastern half for Portugal, an attempt to keep the rival Catholic empires from escalating their conflict. The divide was set at the midway point between Portugal's Cape Verde islands off the west coast of northern Africa and the Caribbean islands Christopher Columbus reached. Drawn without knowledge of the southern hemisphere, the demarcation left the eastern horn of Brazil on Portuguese turf.

Portuguese ports opened the slave trade to the western hemisphere. Enslaved indigenous and African people dug mines, picked coffee beans, and chopped sugarcane, their toil filling ships bound for trading posts around the world. With ports in southern Africa and Southeast Asia, Portugal's chain of territories stretched clear across the maps of the day, anchoring a network of shipping routes spanning from the Americas to Imperial China.

The balance of power shifted as the Spaniards pushed westward, inland from the Gulf of Mexico. One day in 1513, an expedition crested a hill and saw an endless sheet of sparkling blue. Charles was thirteen at the time. Like others who heard the news, he may have wondered if perhaps the East Indies were just across this ocean, if not the last one. Four years later, a recently crowned King Charles met a navigator who'd served in Portugal's 1511 conquest of Malacca, a critical port city that sat at the mouth of the strait linking the Indian Ocean and the South China Sea. Ferdinand Magellan had had a falling out with Portugal's King Manuel, who declined his proposal to find a new route to India by going south of the Americas. So Magellan took the proposal across the border, to the young monarch eager for a route to the Spice Islands that bypassed Portuguese waters.

A successful expedition could bring Magellan riches and power: conquistadors were promised as much as 5 percent of profits on goods shipped back from their conquests. In the Americas, Hernán Cortés named himself governor of the territory he claimed on behalf of Spain, immediately amassing a fortune from the copious silver mined by native laborers. Funded by the state and blessed by the Church, conquistadors had free rein to take over blank spots on European maps however they saw fit, a system that benefited the most ruthless opportunists.

Magellan commanded a crew of about 260 men across five ships—the *Trinidad*, the *Victoria*, the *Santiago*, the *San Antonio*, and the *Concepción*. Among them were Enrique de Malacca, a Malay slave Magellan had bought during the 1511 conquest, and Antonio Pigafetta, an Italian scholar who chronicled the trip in a journal as Magellan's assistant. The ships were stocked for a journey of unknown length, with barrels of anchovies, jars of wine, sacks of flour, and crates of figs, rice, olive oil, dried fish, salt pork, garlic, and cheese. Perils were expected. The cargo holds carried 1,000 lances, 60 crossbows, 58 long-barreled handguns, 7 small cannons, 3 big cannons, 200 shields, 100 sets of chest armor and helmets, 160 pounds of gunpowder, and one and a half tons of lead for making bullets.

But conquering is not all brute force. For trading and gifting, Magellan brought beads, mirrors, glassware, satin, half a ton of ivory, ten tons of copper, twenty pounds of saffron, 2,000 brass bracelets, 4,800 knives, and 20,000 bells in three varieties. For promoting the crown and the cross, eighty Spanish flags and extravagant religious ornaments, symbols of the all-powerful god the Spaniards were introducing.

One item in the bunch was a wooden figure of a child Jesus, carved by a Flemish artist and cloaked in velvet. The doll wasn't yet called Santo Niño. When the ships set sail, he was merely a chip in a pile, a polished hunk of bribery and propaganda.

PEOPLE DEPART THEIR HOMELANDS for many reasons, carrying hope or dread: conquest, work, schooling, shelter, adventure, escape, love, war, famine, slavery, repression, recession, hyperinflation, or just hazy visions of an upgrade in opportunity. The formula varies for everybody, calibrated always to the shifting dynamics of the global chessboard, the laws and technologies and catastrophes that dictate the social order of any civilization. The urge, from necessity or ambition, to pack up, decamp, and build elsewhere traces back to the furthest reaches of human history, hardwired into the most primal corners of our psyches, an instinct perhaps not far removed from that of the butterflies and salmon that set off on near-lifelong journeys to procreate, or the birds and whales that cross the globe for richer feeding grounds.

A hundred thousand or so years ago, according to the latest archaeological evidence I've seen, our earliest ancestors migrated north through Africa, eventually into the Arabian Peninsula, along the Indian Ocean into Southeast Asia, around the Mediterranean Sea into Europe, across desert and tundra into Siberia, and ultimately over the Bering Strait to the Americas. Some scientists have hypothesized that early migration patterns coincided with climate cycles that at certain periods opened new corridors of lush vegetation to follow and at other points turned once-fertile land dry and cold. "Migratory currents flow along certain well defined geographical channels," German British geographer E. G. Ravenstein wrote in his 1885 study of human migration. "They are like mighty rivers, which flow along slowly at the outset, and after depositing most of the human beings whom they hold in suspension, sweep along more impetuously, until they enter one of the great . . . reservoirs."

Movement begat acclimatization and genetic diversity. Based on their geographic location over the course of many generations, people came to develop slight variances in skin color, establishing the hereditary distinctions that would come to define the social construct we now know as "race." These early migrations across the globe, and the ones that followed in the coming millennia, shaped the world as we know it, as languages blended, agricultural techniques evolved, metalwork skills spread, trade routes materialized, and communities morphed into states and then empires, in Mesopotamia, Egypt, China, and elsewhere. The Bantus of western Africa traveled southward and eastward on the continent. Polynesian mariners worked their way down the coast of the Americas. The Celts migrated across Europe. Germanic and Sarmatian tribes journeyed into the western Roman Empire. Nomads from central Asia traversed the Silk Road. Moors trekked to the Iberian peninsula and Bedouins into North Africa. Jewish migrants, expelled from France in the twelfth century, England in the fourteenth, and Spain in the fifteenth, resettled in eastern Europe and along the Mediterranean coast. From one angle, the history of modern humanity boils down to a series of borders drawn and borders crossed, cultures cultivated and cultures erased, homes fled and homes desired.

Only transportation technology restricted the bounds of migration. The epic distance that Moses and his people walked covers barely a centimeter on the basketball-size globe that sits on my desk, a four-hour drive on California highways. Genghis Khan's horseback army controlled what, to most Eurasians at the time, seemed to be the entirety of society, until people began crossing oceans.

Three decades after Christopher Columbus crossed the Atlantic, Magellan crossed the Pacific, the first known expedition to do so. The trip from Spain, around the southern horn of the Americas, and across the largest ocean on the planet, took two years. Two of the expedition's five ships didn't make it far enough west to reach the Far East. Mutinous officers were marooned or killed along the way. Magellan lied to his crew about how much food was left, and they had to resort to eating animal hide ripped from furniture and drinking water that had putrefied yellow. The expedition would have been doomed if not for a run of good fortune. The weather was uncharacteristically benign—thus the name Magellan bestowed upon the body of water, Mar Pacífico, the peaceful sea. And just when things were looking bleakest, the island now called Guam came into view, and it so happened that the natives were friendly. The conquistadors traded for rice and fresh water and went on their way, not knowing how much longer it would be until they reached land again.

These days you can buy a plane ticket from Madrid to Manila, with a stop in Hong Kong, for half the price of my mom's monthly rent, departing and arriving within a span of seventeen hours, just enough time for a couple of movies, a nap, some reading if you feel like it. We've conquered earthly distance, stretched our collective arms around the planet. We can move faster, safer, and cozier but never again into unknown civilization, at least until we cross our next ocean, the black void between here and whatever extraterrestrial life might exist.

When I started this book, there were approximately 8,000 to 20,000 airplanes flying at any given second, carrying people and their things with sanitized ease, climate-controlled vacuum-sealed chambers hurtling through the troposphere, slicing undisturbed through ice and wind, guided by navigational computers that link the whole aviation industry into a single, standardized network. Passengers filed through covered mechanical gangways and onto moving walkways that transported them past food courts and jewelry stores in airy terminals that could be confused for malls. Luggage tumbled into sight from out of nowhere, sliding down a metal chute in the ceiling, delivered on a silver carousel.

If you've picked up a bag at the San Francisco International Airport sometime in the last three decades, there's a chance my uncle Spanky hauled it. He is seventy-two now, the supervisor on his crew of baggage handlers. The younger guys he works with don't believe him when he tells them his age. Still strong and slim, with a ponytail under his cowboy hat, thick mustache over a constant smile, tired eyes behind wraparound sunglasses, Spanky lifts and loads, lifts and loads the overstuffed suitcases, the boxes of fruit, the jangling golf bags, smooth and brisk, knowing just how to grab, just where to hold, to avoid fumbling, to minimize strain. He doesn't respect the supervisors who don't haul alongside their crew. His back might lock up once in a while, but his spirit is spry, the quips coming fast and corny, the joy shining bright as ever when he greets you. The most accurate way I can describe my uncle Spanky is that he carries himself the same way he eats: savoring, patient, purposeful, his plate piled the highest, the last to leave the table.

Three decades ago, his own flight rolled to a stop on the tarmac where he now spends his days. He lifted his own suitcase from the conveyer belt on which he now drops the bags of others.

Only occasionally does he think about the paths not taken, the visions that flash to the front of his mind, tempting him with regret. Every immigrant leaves behind a life. Before he was a baggage handler, before he crossed the ocean, my uncle Spanky was a motherfuckin' rock star.

THE BAND WAS CALLED VST & Company. The S stood for Spanky, who wrote and produced songs and played guitar; the V and T for Vic and Tito, the lead singers. Alongside the half-dozen or so men who made up the "& Company"—drummers, guitarists, keyboardists, and backup vocalists—Spanky, Vic, and Tito rose to stardom in the 1970s, their shiny, sleeveless, sequined vests sparking under the disco balls of sold-out shows. Adoring mobs pursued them into restaurants and hotel lobbies. Bar owners covered their tabs and kept the beers flowing long past closing time. At one gig, teenage students at a Catholic girls' school erupted into such a frenzy that the nuns began splashing them with holy water "to drive away the hysteria that had possessed them," recalled Spanky's brother and bandmate, Male Rigor. They were as big as it gets in the Philippines, A-list celebrities who'd earned themselves a rarefied path to the country's upper-crust comforts.

With a style that blended high-octane disco with traditional Filipino love songs, VST was part of a cultural renaissance that coalesced in those years as balm for the anxieties of martial law under the Ferdinand Marcos dictatorship. The relentlessly upbeat music, dubbed "Manila Sound," washed the country in escapist pleasure, fueling sweaty house parties that pushed on until the curfew lifted at dawn and revelers could stumble home without getting jailed or shot. It was music that sizzled with optimism and innocence—hearts won and kisses promised, caring arms and grooving bodies, fantasies unveiled as reality. The title of the band's debut single, "Awitin Mo at Isasayaw Ko," which immediately went gold, seemed to embody the band's mission statement: "Sing your song and I will dance." Spanky would always say that his favorite part of being a rock star was that moment onstage when he made eye contact with someone in the crowd who was just lost in the melody, swinging to the beat, euphoric.

It's not an exaggeration to say that Spanky was one of the most famous people in the country. He played in celebrity basketball tournaments and performed in a daily sketch comedy show. A magazine listed him as one of the sexiest men in the Philippines—alongside six movie stars, two basketball stars, and somebody called "Jo Anne's boyfriend."

He and his bandmates received invitations from Marcos himself to Malacañang Palace, to entertain dignitaries and cronies lining long banquet tables.

One night in those years, when Spanky was driving home through a winding jungle road, he came across a military checkpoint. When the soldier asked for his license, Spanky smelled the rum on his breath. The soldier's shirt was unbuttoned halfway and the pistol in his hand hung over the open window. His words slurred when he asked Spanky where he was coming from, where he was going. Spanky tensed, hoping the encounter would end with nothing worse than a bribe. And then, as the soldier shined his flashlight on the identification card—

"Oy! Spanky!" the soldier exclaimed, giddy, waving him through. "Spanky Rigor! Ohhh, it's late! Get home safe!"

Those were the years when Spanky thought he would never leave the Islands.

MORE THAN FIVE MILLENNIA before Santo Niño's journey from Spain, the first people to lay eyes on the archipelago sprinkled at the edge of the Pacific were seafaring pioneers and traders riding balangays, plank-wood longboats with bamboo outriggers that kept the ride smooth at top speed over bumpy open sea, allowing them to venture farther out from the coast of continental Asia than anyone before them. No single crew claimed the entire chain of 7,641 or so islands stretching more than a thousand miles along the South China Sea. The two largest islands anchor the poles of the archipelago, with smaller ones clustered in the middle, like bone shards. Some evidence suggests humans were already living on the archipelago by the time the seafaring pioneers arrived: their ancestors had crossed a land bridge before it melted at the end of the last ice age, some 12,000 years ago, when there was no archipelago but a contiguous mass at the tail of the continental peninsula. Those early inhabitants had the place to themselves for thousands of years until wooden boats were sturdy enough to bring others.

Settlers arrived from every side except the oceanic east, forming communities on the lowland coasts and along the rivers and lakes of the highlands. The archipelago bred a collection of clans as fragmented as its land. With shorelines and jungle-thick mountains as borders, hundreds of self-governed villages sprouted, each barangay—named after the balangay by which the settlers had migrated across the sea—united by kinship and ruled by its own datu. A barangay operated as an extended family, a unit of a few hundred people at most, sharing labor and goods, deciding justice through the judgments of elders who counseled the datu, subsisting by mastering their pocket of terrain—coastal fisherfolk, jungle hunters, mountain diggers, lakeside farmers. By 1000 BCE, a trade network flourished across the archipelago, which was home to at least 120 languages.

On Luzon, which is shaped like a plantain and stretches north toward China, the Ifugao tribe of the Cordilleras highlands built spectacular rice terraces that would stand for more than three thousand years. In the central Visayan Islands, locals developed techniques to accommodate their fervor for hygiene, cleaning clothes with citrus, polishing teeth with corn husks, twisting cotton into swabs for ears, bathing daily in the river and anointing themselves with sesame oil. On the southern island of Mindanao, squat and jagged and linked by a string of islets to the massive neighboring island of Borneo, artisans crafted intricate gold jewelry and jars that archaeologists would dig up nearly a thousand years later.

The early settlers developed an intimate understanding of the forces that guided the land, wisdom passed on across villages and over generations. They shared the jungle with dwendes, mercurial dwarfs who are generally friendly but occasionally cause mischief, dropping pebbles on you, things like that. It's best to stay on their good side, so if you do anything that might bother them, like throwing something out the window or peeing on a banana grove (their preferred habitat), you immediately excuse yourself by saying "Tabi apo." Anger a dwende and you find out the next morning when you wake up bald. Those who suffered harsher ills, mysterious fevers or crippling misfortune, might have been cursed by entities even more powerful—engkantos, fairies of a godly realm tasked with guarding the forests and resentful of human intrusion. They live in big trees, inside the tangled, viny trunks of baletes or up on the outstretched branches of acacias, and while they can see us, we can't see them, so we're constantly bumping into them, knocking over their children, crowding our sweaty bodies beneath the shade of their homes. A healer summons the disgruntled engkanto, hears its complaint, begs its mercy, and prescribes to the patient a treatment plan of food offerings and herbal brews.

While empires sprawled across the continents, the archipelago's barangay system held steady, adapting to the times. In the early eleventh century, with trade routes expanding and ship technology advancing, the barangay of Butuan, on Mindanao's northwest coast, became the first on the Islands to engage in diplomatic relations with Imperial China, sending two envoys to Beijing to arrange formal trade rights. Positioned along the shipping route between the Persian Gulf and China, a short hop from Borneo's ports, Butuan boomed, and soon so did Maynila, on the western bay of Luzon, and Cebu, in the center point of the Visayas.

Magellan himself may have heard about the archipelago during Portugal's conquest of Malacca. Local traders had visited the Islands, and by then migration streamed both ways across the South China Sea. Hundreds or more who had been born on the archipelago, mostly Tagalog from Luzon, had moved to the Malay peninsula, opening shops and forming communities along the waterfront. While the exact birthplace of Magellan's slave Enrique is unknown, one theory is that he shared a bloodline with migrants from the archipelago. It's plausible that Magellan purchased him because he intended to return to the region and would need a translator and cultural guide.

The archipelago was a regular stop in the eastern marketplace. Traders bound for the Islands brought porcelain, tin, and silk from China; steel blades and brass from Borneo; precious stones from Burma. In exchange, they found honey and beeswax from the jungle highlands and gold from the mines of the Visayas and Mindanao. Just inland of Butuan, at the edge of Lake Lanao on the highlands overlooking Mindanao's northern coast, the barangay of Dansalan flourished and became a hub of commerce, streaming with Malay and Arab goods, languages, and traditions. The local tribe, the Maranao, my ancestors on my great-great-grandmother Emilia Bato Bato's side, stood at the center of a swirling convergence of cultures.

The dwendes and engkantos lived on through the waves of new arrivals and ideas. Buddhism trickled in from the north, Hinduism from the west. Islam traveled over the Indian Ocean, through the Strait of Malacca, across Borneo, and into southern Mindanao, where it eventually became the island's dominant religion, blending with indigenous beliefs and ushering in a political system that centralized authority around the faith. Muslim missionaries adopted the customs, learned the language, and married into the families of the communities they preached to, while promoting their own association with powerful kingdoms ruled by noble families who were "deeply influenced" by "religious motives," as historian Cesar Adib Majul writes in *Muslims in the Philippines*. Conversion meant alliance with Asia's dominant sultanates. In the fourteenth century, a Hindu rajah in northern Borneo converted to Islam and established the Sultanate of Brunei, one of the first in Southeast Asia. Less than a century later, an explorer from Jolo landed on the islet string at the southern tip of Mindanao and established the Sultanate of Sulu. A century after that— a few years after the Portuguese conquered Malacca in 1511, imposing

Catholicism—a Muslim missionary fleeing the city ventured onto Mindanao, converted the ruling families of the island's largest tribes, and founded the Sultanate of Maguindanao, uniting the island's barangays into a federation ruled by a sultan and locally governed by datus. It was around then, on March 16, 1521, that Magellan's Spanish fleet landed on a small Visayan island a hundred miles to the north, and began pitching Catholicism.

It FELL to Rajah Humabon to decide what to do with the white men. As datu of Cebu, the largest barangay in the Visayas with around three hundred huts, he was the most powerful chief in the region. He oversaw a land fertile with crops and trade. Antonio Pigafetta, Magellan's assistant, remarked in his journal on the riches the conquistadors encountered when they stepped foot in the Visayas—foods spiced with cinnamon, pepper, and nutmeg; garments of cotton and silk; necklaces, bracelets, and rings decorated with gold pieces "as large as walnuts and eggs." Gold was so plentiful that some islanders had gold ornaments drilled into their teeth.

The datu of a nearby island brought the visitors to Humabon, a respected and pragmatic leader whose body was tattooed in triangular patterns, like those of his soldiers. The Spaniards called the Visayans "pintados," or "painted ones," for the markings on their skin. Humabon immediately demanded a tribute, as he did for all trading ships. Through Enrique, the visitors clarified that they were not traders but rather had come to partner with the islanders by bringing them under the protection and authority of the Spanish crown and Catholic cross.

Rajah Humabon faced the same dilemma that confronted leaders all over Southeast Asia, sub-Saharan Africa, and the Americas—the swaths of civilization previously unknown to Europeans: to resist or to submit? A Muslim trader from Siam had told him about ghostly, fire-spitting forces in steel shells pillaging and massacring villages on lands across the seas. The trader may have been referring to Portugal's conquest of Malacca, but similar stories were playing out in other parts of the globe.

Two years before, Hernán Cortés and his conquistadors, having reached Tenochtitlán, the floating capital of the mighty Mexica Empire, had been invited by the emperor Moctezuma to stay at his palace as guests for several months. Suspicious of the emperor's motives and skeptical of their captain's judgment, the soldiers took advantage of Cortés's brief absence from the city to ambush and kill thousands of Mexicas. Hearing of the massacre, Cortés returned with 1,300 Spanish soldiers and 2,000 warriors from Tlaxcala, a rival state eager to topple the empire. A month later, Moctezuma was killed. In his account, Cortés claimed that Moctezuma's own people had stoned him, a scene immortalized in Spanish paintings and mythology. But in recent years, manuscripts and artworks unearthed by archaeologists have challenged the conquistador's story, providing evidence that it was the Spaniards who assassinated Moctezuma.

While Moctezuma's successor, his brother Cuitláhuac, warred with the Spaniards, across the Atlantic Ocean in the Kongo Kingdom, King Afonso ruled an empire of half a million people stretching inland from the coast; he chose a different path. Afonso's father, Nzinga a Nkuwu, had been invited to Portugal by an explorer who'd sailed up the Congo River and reached the kingdom. He'd returned a Christian, changing his name to João, but had since renounced the religion and returned to his old traditions, perhaps disillusioned by Portugal's repeated violations of an agreement restricting which locals could be sold as slaves. Afonso, who had been born with the name Mvemba a Nzinga before being baptized and educated by Portuguese priests, kept the faith, designating Christianity as the Kongo Kingdom's state religion and attempting to use assimilation as a means of diplomacy. "He urgently tried to acquire European learning, weapons and goods in order to strengthen his rule and fortify it against the destabilizing force of the white arrival," Adam Hochschild writes in *King Leopold's Ghost*. Citing scripture, Afonso appealed to Portugal's King Manuel I to send doctors instead of slavers, writing, "In this kingdom faith is as fragile as glass because of the bad examples of the men who come to teach here. Because the lust of the world and the lure of wealth have turned them away from the truth." The monarch's efforts to slow the kidnapping and enslavement of his people proved in vain, however, and in 1539, ten of his young relatives traveling to Portugal for a religious education were snatched en route and sold into slavery in Brazil.

Rajah Humabon couldn't have known the scope of the European conquest beginning to flood across the globe, but contemplating his options for dealing with these heavily armed visitors, he chose the same path as the Kongo kings. Within a week of meeting Magellan, he converted to Catholicism and recognized Spain as sovereign over his land. We can only speculate on his thinking, but his subsequent actions suggest a scheme in motion.

At baptism, Rajah Humabon took the name Carlos, in honor of Spain's king, and his wife, Hara Amihan, took the name Juana, after the king's mother. Magellan presented them with gifts for the occasion. To the barangay, he gave a statue of the Virgin Mary. To Carlos, an ivory bust of Christ bleeding under a crown of thorns. To Juana, the wooden doll of the child Jesus, decked in velvet.

Carlos issued an edict calling on other chiefs to bow to cross and crown, but the datu of nearby Mactan island, Lapu Lapu, a longtime rival, refused to acquiesce. Twenty days after arriving on Cebu, Magellan led sixty men toward the shore of Mactan. Confident in his armor and the cannons on his ships, he'd declined Carlos's offer of additional troops.

The only known written record of what followed comes from Pigafetta's journal. Using longboats to travel around the rocky outcroppings along the island's perimeter, which blocked their warships from getting closer, Magellan and his men landed three hours before dawn, at low tide. Magellan issued Mactan's villagers a final warning. "The captain did not wish to fight them, but sent a message to the natives to the effect that if they would obey the king of Spain, recognize the Christian king as their sovereign, and pay us our tribute, he would be their friend; but that if they wished otherwise, they should wait to see how our lances wounded," Pigafetta wrote. "They replied that if we had lances they had lances of bamboo and stakes hardened with fire."

Lapu Lapu's army, more than a thousand strong in three divisions, attacked from all angles. The cannons and crossbows of the Spanish were too far from shore to reach the battle. Their armor covered only head and chest. Poison-tipped arrows and iron spears pierced legs and arms. According to legend, it was the kampilan longsword of Lapu Lapu that killed Magellan.

Pigafetta and the few other survivors fled to their longboats, but it only got worse from there for the conquistadors. Back on Cebu, King Carlos organized a banquet, inviting the two ranking officers now in charge of the depleted expedition, along with two dozen of their crew members. It was a trick. Carlos's guards slaughtered all the guests but one: Enrique, the slave from Malacca who'd crossed the Indian Ocean with Magellan before serving on the Spanish-funded trip across the Atlantic and Pacific.

Magellan had vowed in his will to free Enrique in the event of his death, but the commanders who replaced him refused to honor it. One theory is that Carlos turned on the Spanish because Enrique, in an effort to escape servitude, told the datu they were plotting to remove him from power. Pigafetta and the rest retreated and left on a single ship, the *Victoria*—eighteen survivors from an expedition of 260. There's no record of what Enrique did once he had his freedom. He may have returned to his homeland, just across the South China Sea. If he did, he would have been the first person to circumnavigate the globe, completing the loop months before the husk of Magellan's expedition staggered into Spain.

Poor Santo Niño, left behind in a foreign land, symbol of a brief and ineffective bond. What became of him in this period remains a mystery. After the baptism, Queen Juana kept the statue in the royal home, but the trail goes dark after the Spaniards' ignominious departure. Was he stashed away in a storage bin, a forgotten relic of the strange and misfortunate visitors? Or was he prominently displayed, as a trophy of King Carlos's brazen ploy? Did Carlos and Juana abandon their Christian names and faith? We can only wonder. Only the accounts of the conquerors survive.

DESPITE THIS INAUSPICIOUS START in the Pacific, the empire persisted, drawn by the archipelago's potential as a trading hub for goods shipped from ports in the expanding territory of New Spain.

Four months after Magellan's death, the Mexicas surrendered to Cortés and his 20,000 soldiers, most of them recruited from the indigenous empire's rivals. Conquest is an expensive endeavor, and it's tempting to think about how history might have played out had the Spanish gotten locked into a long, costly war with the Mexicas, but what actually defeated the Aztecs were the foreign viruses Cortés's ships had carried. Smallpox and chickenpox wiped out hundreds of thousands of native people, an epidemic so vast and brutal that many who witnessed it believed the Apocalypse was nigh. Around 40 percent of Mexica's population died within a year, including Cuitláhuac. With their resistance to the virus built up over generations of exposure, the Spaniards were left standing amid a vast ghostland. Friars preached to the surviving natives that the invaders' immunity was proof that their deity was superior. Many converted. Tenochtitlán was a mass grave when it fell, four months into the siege. The Spanish tore down the city's largest temple and used the stone blocks to build a church that stands to this day.

The fall of Tenochtitlán allowed Spain to swiftly seize a stretch of territory that bridged the two largest oceans, opening a line of transport that ran from Spain to Asia, unimpeded by rival sovereignties. Control of the archipelago at the edge of the Pacific would complete a chain of expansion spanning halfway across the globe. Lured by the wealth and power promised to those who secured new territory for the empire, conquistadors set sail.

The next few efforts didn't fare much better than the first. Ships crashing, commanders dying, crews imprisoned by Portuguese forces before even reaching the archipelago. On one of those failed attempts, in 1543, an expedition landed on the eastern coast of Mindanao, struggled to find food, and soon left, a voyage unremarkable and unsuccessful except for the fact that its captain christened the archipelago under a single name, Islas Filipinas, after Prince Philip, son of King Charles.

If the Spanish had never conquered the archipelago, the name might have disappeared into the footnotes of history. Perhaps the sultanates would have expanded across the archipelago as they did on the neighboring chain now called Indonesia. Perhaps a collection of sovereign states would have shared the archipelago for many centuries. Or perhaps another empire, the British or Dutch, would have swallowed it up, as happened in most of Southeast Asia. But instead came Miguel López de Legazpi, a Basque conquistador who'd risen to become governor of Mexico City, where he saw firsthand the brutality required to secure a conquest. In 1565, commissioned by the King of Spain to establish a settlement on the Filipinas, Legazpi reached Cebu and promptly had his troops shoot the locals and burn down the village, killing hundreds and sending thousands fleeing into the jungle. "They are all barbarians," Legazpi later wrote to the king.

Sifting through the ashes, debris, and few remaining huts once the air was calm, a Spanish mariner found a small pine box. Inside, unblemished, lay the wooden Jesus doll Magellan had presented to Queen Juana four decades earlier. A miracle. A sacred force blessing the conquest. The Spaniards built a church of bamboo and mangroves on the spot and officially deemed Santo Niño "The Most Esteemed Captain-General of the Spanish Forces in the Philippines."

From his perch behind a church altar, Captain-General Santo Niño ruled an army on the frontlines of a long-running war for the world's souls and resources. In a letter to the king, Legazpi predicted that "if the land is settled and peopled by the Spaniards, we shall be able to get plenty of gold, pearls, and other valuables." The conquistadors, at first, faced no unified foe. They allied with datus who agreed to their terms and, with their collection of forces, attacked barangays that refused to submit, a path of conquest through the Visayas and Luzon. But when the conquistadors ventured south, onto the island of Mindanao, they met a resistance they hadn't encountered elsewhere on the archipelago. While the datus of Mindanao were notorious for political squabbles and intrigue, "against the Spaniards and their other enemies they confederate and unite," Don Pedro de Acuña, the governor-general of the Philippines, wrote in a 1603 letter to the king, explaining why the empire hadn't secured control over the island's Muslim inhabitants.

The Spanish called them Moros, or Moors, a familiar adversary. Over eight centuries, Christian kingdoms had fought to retake the Iberian peninsula from Muslim kingdoms, a victorious effort capped off by the formation of Spain. In the marriage contract unifying the kingdoms of Aragon and Castile in 1469, Ferdinand vows to Isabella that he "will be obliged to wage war on the Moors, enemies of the holy Catholic faith." Through new laws and the damning trials of the Inquisition, Spain expelled, converted, or killed most of the country's Jewish and Muslim residents.

Thus Captain-General Santo Niño led his troops south, over the

Bohol Sea, onto Mindanao's rocky shores to begin a war that would last three centuries.

HISTORY RIPPLES INTO PERPETUITY. Decisions, actions, mistakes, and triumphs of one day shape the days that follow, setting irreversible paths into the future, through countless crossroads and detours. Only in hindsight do the consequences emerge with any clarity, and even then all you have to work with are a mess of fallen dominoes scattered to the horizon, always more beyond sight.

My mom and I have argued about the value of peering back at the road taken. She prefers to cast her gaze ever-forward, keep it moving, dust the past off her like crumbs on a silk dress. History contains traumas, regrets, lost times, better days, and old friends turned distant. During one of our interviews for this book, when she couldn't recall the details of some occasion I asked her about, she grew flustered and suddenly snapped, "I don't think about what happened before, I just think about the next steps."

Perhaps it's the generation a step removed from exodus, but close enough to hear the stories firsthand, who are best positioned to chronicle the migrations that came before us. Every family's road to the present bears signposts that reveal the course of civilization, memories and patterns that hold clues to the questions looming thicker with time. My family's story doesn't show the whole picture but unspools as a single thread within a vast tapestry. Some threads have vanished forever. Every day an unknown stretch of the once-recorded past fades away without notice. We salvage what we can.

I WAS LUCKY to grow up hearing about the inflection points, though I knew little about the forces that caused them. The first of my blood to arrive in America was my grandaunt Caridad, who moved to San Francisco in 1949 after earning a U.S. visa for her service in the Allied forces during World War II. My grandparents' initial attempt to settle in the States in the late 1960s had to be delayed when a few of their children were injured in a car accident in Manila; my grandmother Rizalina finally joined her sister-in-law Caridad in 1978, as the Marcos regime battered the Philippines by shuttering the free press, jailing dissidents, and crushing the economy under the weight of crony monopoly. To help her mother through the bumpy landing, my mom's eldest sister, Ging, followed Rizalina across the ocean three years later, in 1981, bringing Jed, who was one at the time, the first in our Filipino lineage to grow up away from the Islands, ending a generational streak tracing back to the Spanish colonial years. They all lived in Caridad's house in the Fillmore District of San Francisco, a city named by Spanish colonizers in 1776. Rizalina slept on the couch, Ging and Jed in the spare bedroom. The surrounding blocks bristled with weedy vacant lots, and some of the streetlights were broken. Caridad warned them to watch out for thieves if they were coming home after dark.

Ging delivered phone books for a few months—carrying the plastic-wrapped directories across slanted sidewalks while baby Jed watched from the backseat of her car—before getting hired to teach kindergarten at a private school. The white principal said he had a good feeling about her because "Filipinos are hard workers and honest." With their combined incomes, Rizalina and Ging moved into a two-bedroom walk-up in the Richmond District, west down Geary Boulevard, where the fog drops lower and thicker.

As the oldest of her siblings, Ging felt a duty to support her mother's dream of laying a foundation for our barangay in the United States. Not only that, but she had the surest entryway across the border. Spanky was a U.S. citizen, born in Manhattan while his father was studying at Columbia University for two years. When Spanky was growing up, back in the Philippines, his neighborhood friends teased him about his foreign birth certificate. They called him "the Americano" and joked that his origin story was a ruse to cover the secret that his parents had found him in a garbage can, taken pity, and adopted him. They bullied him about his nice American toys, his radio, his vinyl records.

Spanky's dad was in the military, his mom a secretary for political and military officials, and they bounced around army bases for several years before landing in a suburban subdivision in Manila's Little Baguio neighborhood. He gained a love for music early on, watching his parents dance to Spanish songs on the radio. His record collection grew. He learned to play the guitar. As a teenager, he and his friends formed a band, performing unpaid sets at proms and parties. After college, he got a sales job in an office he found dreary, so he quit and found a job as a record producer at a Manila studio, where he soon met the people who would define the path his life would take. Ging was a singer in a group called The Ambivalent Crowd while in college studying to become a teacher, and the two began dating after catching glances through the recording booth window. Brothers Vic and Tito Sotto sang love ballads, liked Spanky's ear for music, and proposed that they start a band together, recruiting an ensemble that included three of Spanky's brothers. When Ging and Spanky married in 1977, VST & Company was two years old and "still figuring out our sound," as Spanky puts it. But in 1979, a year after Rizalina began our clan's migration to the United States, VST blew up in the Philippines, their debut single topping charts and filling radio airways. When Ging's U.S. visa was approved in 1980, she was a preschool principal and Spanky was touring the country. When Ging and Jed left for San Francisco in 1981, Spanky was under contract to star in movies and host television shows.

Ging wasn't planning to make California her permanent home. "It wasn't really for me to stay forever," she told me years later. "I just wanted to see how it feels like to live here." She and Spanky took it a month at a time, evaluating their options, exchanging twenty-page letters between visits. In the summers, Ging and Jed returned to the Philippines, spending weeks in the Quezon City compound where our moms grew up. He remembers the place bustling on his first few visits, when most of our family still lived there, served by a staff of maids and drivers. The barangay had been among our world's ruling class back then.

In those years, our grandfather Manuel and our uncles Joey, Paul, Marlon, and Bobby lived in the main house. Joey, the eldest, was studying to become a nurse, and on the afternoons when he tinkered with the engine of his car, Jed sat at his feet, playing with tools. The three younger brothers, Paul, Marlon, and Bobby, would be gone for weeks at a time with Manuel, hunting in the mountains of Luzon for treasure buried by fleeing Japanese soldiers. They lived in a cave, building wooden chairs, tables, and beds, partially shielded from the torrential rains by tarpaulins. Their days were spent digging into the dirt, chasing tips and clues. They'd return to Scout Reyes eager to recharge with lazy days around the patio table, empty San Miguel bottles lined up along the golden-green grass like soldiers in formation. Jed sat on their laps trying to understand the dirty jokes they told in Tagalog, or played tag with his cousins Mico and Roscoe, the sons of Auntie Mae and Auntie Lyn, who lived in a cinder-block bungalow on one end of the compound.

Jed and his parents lived in a one-bedroom cottage on the other side of the main house. Ging still considered it her primary home. She and Spanky had moved in when they got married, and the place still housed keepsakes and photo albums. In the evenings, Jed and his parents played pusoy dos in the living room, slapping cards on the bamboo coffee table as golden rays streamed through the open windows, the street outside quiet except for the birds. Ging and Spanky fell into old rhythms like no time had passed, bantering in Tagalog, quick puns and dry asides that left them both laughing so hard they had to put their cards down.

Jed remembers living like a prince in those summers. The maids cooked breakfast before he woke, usually eggs sunny-side up with rice and ketchup, and they fed him well all day. He bathed in the backyard when the warm rain fell, and when the tropical sun dried the earth, he played basketball on the paved court Manuel had constructed. He knew that his dad was very successful in the Philippines. During his summers in Scout Reyes, he sometimes accompanied his father as a driver shuttled them to television studios, movie sets, and record company offices where packs of important-looking people parted when they saw Spanky, greeting him with respect, handing him papers, offering to grab him coffee, an endless stream of people committed to ensuring his comfort.

Jed cried every time he had to leave the house on Scout Reyes, even though he was the sort of kid who rarely cried. Year after year, the dreaded morning would come and he'd fall apart, bawling inconsolably and looking so kawawa that some of the maids had to turn away. Maids, drivers, aunties, uncles, cousins, and grandpa would line up outside the house waving as the car rolled away, making the whole exit hella dramatic, Jed sitting there staring out the window sobbing and waving back, his parents trying to soothe him.

SPANKY ENJOYED LIFE in the Philippines. He still talks about those final years on the Islands with a sparkle in his eye. At a family Christmas party in 2019, he and Bobby reminisced over the "good old days." Bobby had a wife and two small kids by then, and keeping his family afloat was a feat in which he took great pride after three decades of setbacks and triumphs in the States. He and his wife were hosting our party that year, in a house they had just bought in Rio Vista, an old farming town sprouting new subdivisions along the Sacramento River delta. His hair flowing like a '90s sitcom star, he and Spanky regaled each other with stories from the VST days, when Bobby, in his late teens, worked as their roadie, carrying their equipment, drinking with them till sunrise, traveling with them on buses through dark jungles and flying with them on sputtering prop planes. In celebrity basketball tournaments, which were televised in the hoops-loving Philippines, Bobby was starting power forward on VST's team, a six-foot-two brick on springs, snagging rebounds over taller opponents, dunking with two hands when he got the rock down low. Spanky was a sweet-shooting point guard with sick handles that Jed would one day match.

So essential was Bobby to the team that when a televised celebrity game happened to align with one of the digging stretches, Spanky and his bandmates had no choice but to track him down, though they didn't know exactly where he was and had no way to contact him. They traveled hours up the mountains of southern Luzon, zigging and zagging past remote villages and stopping to ask for directions until someone pointed them toward the campsite, deep in the jungle, where Bobby, Paul, Marlon, and Manuel were treasure-hunting. The next day, Bobby led the team to victory.

During typhoon alerts, Manuel and the boys hunkered down at Scout Reyes, huddled around a table in Spanky's living room, drinking beer and watching the rain. One night, they waylaid a vendor selling balut, bought his entire supply on the spot, and invited him to wait out the storm with them. All night, they slurped through duck eggs and tore through cases of beer, part of a "lifetime supply" that a cash-strapped music venue had offered in lieu of pay for a show.

Their favorite stories were about a bumbling self-declared handyman who'd regularly hung out with the crew at Scout Reyes. "Dude, he didn't have a tool belt so he just hung his tools in his waistband and belt loops!" Bobby said, tears already forming in his squinting eyes, suppressing his inevitable bust-up just long enough to add, "Looks like the real McCoy!" The guy would fix Spanky's roof, and the next time it leaked, as it always did, he'd say—Spanky is a maestro with punch lines, building intensity then slowing into a deadpan—"Sir, if it doesn't rain, it's not gonna leak." That one had them bent over in hysterics, trying not to spill their beers.

They fell into the common lingo of their shared past. Lambanog, an exceedingly strong coconut liquor, was "kisser of the earth." You'd be drinking it all night thinking you were fine, then stand up to go to the bathroom and *boom!* next thing you knew, you were facedown in the dirt—or "planting rice" (throwing up). Take too long to down a shot from the single glass they all shared—dunking it in a bucket of water with each pass "for sanitation purposes," Bobby noted—and somebody was sure to whine, "I'm thirsty!"

Whenever I heard Spanky and Bobby talk about those years, I'd envision them as Island versions of Jed and me. We have our own good old days, which are not so old, of planting rice and kissing earth, him running point while I prowled the paint. Our good old days gleamed with a certainty theirs lacked. We were settled in for the long haul, with established careers and steady trajectories, trekking forward with the reasonable belief that our toil and our feats were a rising pile that we could build on for the rest of our lives. This is never assured, of course. History is littered with the wreckage of seemingly stable bubbles suddenly burst by unforeseen events. But whereas Jed and I only had to fear the unexpected, Spanky and Bobby saw their futures twisting into indecipherable contortions with a slow burn, like a strip of bark atop a bonfire.

During their good old days, the Scout Reyes compound was emptying out. In 1985, Auntie Mae moved to San Francisco. In 1986, Auntie Lyn moved to Melbourne, Australia, where she lived for two years, before making her way to San Francisco. Uncle Joey left for Brisbane, Australia, in 1987, among a wave of Filipino nurses who found work there. Uncle Marlon went to Japan on a tourist visa in 1988 and started working construction gigs. By the time Jed returned for the summer in 1987 and

1988, traveling alone so that his mom could pick up a temp job while school was out, only Bobby, Paul, and Manuel remained at the compound with Spanky, and they were rarely around. Manuel had invested in a business salvaging and restoring sunken ships, and he was often away at sea. Nobody was ever sure where Paul was. As for Bobby, he'd enrolled at the University of Perpetual Help in Manila, where his hours were eaten up by class and basketball practice. Jed went to every home game those summers, leaping from his seat in the front row when Uncle Bobby dunked on fools, shouting "Brick! Brick!" whenever the opposing team put up a shot, to the confusion of the titos and manongs around him in the bleachers, who muttered to one another, "Ano ito, 'brick-brick'?"

Some days, Jed felt like he had the cavernous compound all to himself. He imagined he was an explorer venturing through ancient ruins in an uncharted jungle. Faded yellow photographs of unfamiliar faces in elaborate wooden frames decorated unused bedrooms. Decades' worth of accumulated valuables lined shelves and walls—ceramic vases without flowers, golden trinkets said to carry spiritual powers. To Jed, the old house exuded an aura of permanence, a shrine for all who came before him and all who would come after. Upon each return to the United States, he found himself pining for its tranquil embrace.

In the States, life felt shaky, cramped, rushed, an endless series of complications, adjustments, and sacrifices. At the dinner table, the adults talked of job applications, used car ads, loved ones awaiting green cards—ambitions, next steps, always more to do to reach the bright future that lay before them. There were no maids to cook for them, no drivers to ferry the kids to school. Everybody seemed to be toiling all the time.

A few weeks after Jed returned from his eighth visit to Scout Reyes, Ging told him the exciting news: Spanky would be joining them permanently in San Francisco.

———

TODAY, SANTO NIÑO stands behind bulletproof glass high above the altar inside the Basilica Minore del Santo Niño de Cebu, a star amid saintly icons, gold columns, marble walls, and ceiling frescos. Every year, more than a million people gather in Cebu for a festival in Santo Niño's honor, commemorating the first baptism on the Islands, the moment the conversion began. Following a morning mass in the packed square outside the weathered white cathedral, the worshippers carry Santo Niño on a daylong parade through the city, ending at the waterfront for a fireworks show.

You can find replicas of the Santo Niño de Cebu in the homes of most every Catholic Filipino family, including mine. In the history we memorialize, Santo Niño is the ultimate protagonist, the immortalized founding father of our mythology. Is there much of a point in imagining what would have happened if the not-yet Captain-General had never made it across the oceans—if Magellan's expedition had sunk en route, never to be known? The alternate events and figures punctuating the timeline might be better or worse than the ones in ours, the possibilities endless, and tempting.

As our history had it, Santo Niño's arrival was a critical link in the chain of events that turned us Catholic, Western, and colonized, and when you follow the dominoes through the centuries, you'll see this is the trail that leads to our exodus.

ON A HOT, STICKY Manila morning in the summer of 1988, Spanky sat at an airport bar wearing all white. White fedora, white linen jacket, white linen pants, white silk shirt, white leather shoes. He downed a shot of vodka, then another. The bartender recognized him and gave him an extra pour.

Earlier, at Scout Reyes, he had said his goodbyes to the maids, to his longtime bodyguard, to Bobby and his brothers. He brought a suitcase and two big boxes. He hadn't yet told his bandmates that he wasn't coming back.

When the plane reached cruising altitude, the pilots invited him into the cockpit. The head flight attendant brought him free brandy from first class, even though he was flying in coach. He slept through most of the sixteen-hour trip.

"I was happy," Spanky told me, recalling the flight. "At the same time, apprehensive. I really didn't know what to expect. I didn't have any plans actually. . . . You're leaving the life you led, but then you will finally be coming home to a family."

Ging was pregnant with their second child. Over everything loomed the question of where their children would be better off. They weren't sure how to measure better off. Better schools, better civil institutions, better opportunities to pursue whatever success desired—the vision was as abstract as the ambition was clear. The couple had not so much decided America was that place as they had cast their hopes in the stories they'd heard for decades.

Our family's American barangay was falling into place. Only my mother and a few siblings had yet to follow, everybody drawn to the exceptional nation like moths barreling into blinding fluorescence.

OUR STORIES GUIDE and protect us. Without their lessons, warnings, and triumphs to root us to the past, we float aimlessly, taken by whatever opportunistic forces are quickest to grab, mold, and exploit.

The Visayans who first encountered the Spaniards recorded their history orally. Songs and chants passed down over thousands of years memorialized heroes and villains, storms and battles, creation tales of woman and man emerging from coconut husks or bamboo shoots. Conquest erased these stories, and replaced them with the stories of the colonizers.

In the early years of the occupation, Spanish friars in the Philippines included in their letters back home reports of Santo Niño's whereabouts during the four-decade interregnum between the Magellan and Legazpi expeditions. The figure had occupied a place of reverence during this period of uncertainty, the friars said. The islanders had danced around the young white Jesus, praying to Santo Niño for Spain's return.

CHAPTER 3

CONVERSION

In her adolescent fantasies, my mom strolled down tree-lined promenades in old European cities, dined at sidewalk cafés with menus she could barely comprehend, posed in front of steel and stone monuments familiar from textbooks and films. At nineteen, she had never stepped foot off the Philippine archipelago and was eager to see beyond it.

Paris was the very center of the universe to her mind, the bedrock of modern civilization, the kinetic core of high culture. The city confirmed her sense of European supremacy. And why wouldn't it? In retrospect, supremacy can feel inevitable, destined, merited, rather than the result of converging, often arbitrary, sometimes accidental events and conditions. My mother was born into an epoch of European predominance. If she had been born in another time and place, her admiration would have channeled elsewhere—to the technological ingenuity of the Mesopotamians, the architectural splendor of the Egyptians, the astrological acuity of the Mayans, the scholastic rigor of the Malians, the postal efficiency of the Mongols, the artistic innovation of the Navajo, the cosmopolitan vibrancy of the Ottomans, the intricate craftsmanship of the Mughal, the engineering ambition of the Timurid, the fertile literature of the Qing, the sophisticated couture of the Mindanao Moros, on and on into the bleak infinity of forgotten antiquities.

If she'd been born in Athens during the time of Homer, she would have considered what we now call western Europe a frozen hellscape infested with barbaric cannibals who drank blood from human skulls. If she'd been born in Rome during the time of Julius Caesar, she would have trusted his judgment that the northern tribes, who wore "no clothing but skin," were "ignorant and uncivilized" and "do not know what compulsion or discipline is," as he wrote in his chronicle of the Gallic Wars.

Born in Cairo in the fourteenth century, she would have pitied those pale continental slobs for the apocalyptic plague they'd unleashed onto the known world with their filth. If she'd been born in Samarkand during the fifteenth century, she might have found it quaint how the feeble kingdoms of western Europe poked around an endless sea, in hope of stumbling into a southern or western portal to Asia, home to the spices, fabrics, and metals that made the known world go round. They were isolated out there at the edge of the universe, blocked off from the inland trade routes controlled by the powers of the Eurasian continent. Necessity pushed them farther and farther into the void, and with their sturdy ships, they encountered lands and seas they didn't know about. They built ports and fleets. Maritime prowess transformed the Spanish, Portuguese, British, Dutch, and French into formidable players in the Eurasian economy.

The most powerful continental empire of that moment, Imperial China, made a brief attempt at naval enterprise but ultimately figured its resources were better spent on securing the dominance they already had: the Chinese built the Great Wall, focused their forces inland, and practiced a policy of proud isolationism. The Ottomans of central Asia, socially fragmented but stationed at the center of a flourishing

Mediterranean web of culture and commerce, were more worried about keeping their diverse federation together than expanding it across oceans. That left the so-called New World to the monarchs of western Europe.

With steel and gunpowder bought off the Eurasian trade market, they claimed land they had never before seen as their own and massacred people they knew nothing about. When the natives in the Americas died off from Old World diseases, European settlers imported slaves from Africa to work the suddenly empty territories now in their possession. With unpaid labor cultivating huge volumes of sugarcane, tobacco, and cotton, profits were high. The European kingdoms jostled for control of untapped riches, and the competition sharpened them, spurring invention and initiative. As Spain declined, France and Britain rose. When the development of steam power triggered the Industrial Revolution, the kingdoms of western Europe were well placed to take advantage. Machines processed the materials gathered by slaves and transported by ships. Plentiful coal deposits and dense woodlands fueled an economic acceleration that furnished military might and commercial hegemony. The rulers of China, complacent in their stable and ancient dominion, satisfied with their time-tested systems of agriculture and aquifers, were late to the age of engines. And thus the Europeans swept across the newly globalized earth in a blaze of conquest.

BEFORE WE WERE CONQUERED, my ancestors had been royalty.

My family's blood on my grandfather's side traces to the Maranao tribe from the northern highlands of Mindanao, the southernmost island of the Philippine archipelago. The Maranao, a name stemming from the Iranun word for "people of the lake," nurtured a rich valley of towering coconut palms, dense banana groves, pungent durian fields, drooping mango trees, and roaming carabao in the tropical forest along the waters of Lake Lanao, which blessed them with plentiful fish. The mountains to the east shielded them from typhoons and were filled with gold. The lakeside barangay of Dansalan became one of the most prosperous in the archipelago, and the Maranao became one of the two dominant tribes of Mindanao.

The other clan, the Tausug, who inhabited the island's southern coast, were masters of the sea: fisherfolk, sailors, and pirates who made their living in the waters north of Borneo and the island chain now called Indonesia. The clans occasionally clashed but mostly kept an amicable truce as trading partners.

As the story goes, Shariff Kabunsuan, the Muslim missionary who fled Malacca after the 1511 Portuguese conquest, landed in Mindanao and visited both tribes. Whether inspired by his evangelism or the opportunity to ally with the powerful sultanate of neighboring Borneo, the Maranao and Tausug datus converted to Islam, forming the Sultanate of Maguindanao and appointing Kabunsuan as inaugural sultan. As part of the power-sharing agreement, a woman from each ruling family bore Kabunsuan's children.

The Maranao matriarch was named Bae Angintabo, and it is through her that my family traces our Mindanao lineage. Before his death, Sultan Kabunsuan named her son as successor, and for two more generations Maranaos sat on the throne, which I imagine the Tausug found unfair. To keep the peace, the families agreed to alternate rule by generation thereafter. The next sultan was Tausug, and when he died, his younger brother replaced him, and when the younger brother died, the Maranao expected the seat to return to the north. But that younger brother had a son, Muhammad Kudarat, who believed it was only right that he ascend to sultan.

He informed the Maranao datus of his intentions at a feast the Tausug held in or around 1616, on the southern coastal barangay of Noling, in honor of the northern tribe's founding. Indignant, the Maranao left the party, returned north, and split from Maguindanao, founding the Sultanate of Lanao, a confederation of four states, each ruled by a sultan.

The Spanish invasion was already underway, though it might not have seemed like much of a threat to the Mindanao datus at the time. While the Spanish had managed to conquer most of the Visayas and Luzon, including the short-lived Sultanate of Maynila, by the early seventeenth century they still hadn't made it past the shores of Mindanao. They staged their attacks from the island's northern coast, just below the highlands that rose to Lake Lanao. The Maranao stood on the front lines of the invasion, repelling the conquistadors, who returned again and again in ever greater force until they made it up the mountain.

In 1639, seventy Spanish soldiers and around five hundred Visayan allies reached Lake Lanao. The Maranao datus convened to discuss whether to submit to the colonizers. In one of the most celebrated moments of Mindanao history, Sultan Kudarat raced across the island to meet with them, two decades after their bitter encounter at the Noling festival. Whether time, diplomacy, or desperation had healed old fractures, we can only speculate. In a candle-lit hut on Dansalan, Kudarat rallied them with a speech that might have been lost to time had a Spanish ambassador not been present to transcribe it. "Do you realize what subjection would reduce you to? A toilsome slavery under the Spaniards! Turn your eyes to the subject nations and look at the misery to which such glorious nations have been reduced," Kudarat said. "Do not let their sweet words deceive you; their promises facilitate their deceits, which little by little enable them to control everything."

The Maranao drove the Spaniards off the highlands. From then on, the tribes of Mindanao fought as one against the invaders, the Maranao raiding forts in the Visayas while the Tausug repelled advances along the Sulu Sea.

With gold mines and ports ensuring a steady supply of weapons and armor, the Moros of Mindanao resisted occupation for nearly three centuries, a series of wars, treaties, and clashes that came to be known in Tagalog as the Sagupaang Kastila-Moro. But with each new incursion, the empire gained a deeper foothold on the island, establishing forts and settlements along the northern coast. Just down the mountain from Lake Lanao stood the growing Catholic outpost of Iligan. By the middle of the nineteenth century, with the empire in decline and desperate to ward off sultanate alliances with the encroaching British and Dutch, Spanish forces were surging forward once more, storming the beaches of southern Mindanao, bombarding the islets across the Sulu Sea, marching up the northern mountains.

THE IMPERIAL ORDER has not been good to the Philippines. The name itself honors the conquest, the submission. The Islands had no collective identity until the Spaniards came along, corralling them under cross and crown by force of sword. From there, the name stuck and the bond held, a package deal pursued by imperial powers. As the world consolidated into colonizers and colonized, Filipinos fell squarely among the wretched of the earth, as Frantz Fanon deemed those subject to the whims of distant empires, labor and land for the taking.

Our people shared Spain's paternal attentions with colonial siblings across the globe. Less than a decade after Legazpi burned down Cebu, Francisco de Toledo destroyed the last remaining city of the Inca Empire. As the Mindanao Moros escalated their attacks on occupying forces, Spain signed a treaty with Portugal for the rights to land along the Gulf of Guinea in western Africa, turning the territory into a slave trading hub. By the start of the nineteenth century, Spain controlled more than five million square miles of land, the first global superpower.

No shame in acquiescing to that, flowing with the tides that swept up so much of the world, carrying a salty scent of inevitability. By the Darwinian logic of colonial selection, it's the collaborators who survive and thrive. So it went in the Philippines, where Spanish friars carried out mandatory resettlement programs on behalf of the king. The idea was that it would be easier to tax, convert, and extract labor from the native Indios if the scattered remote villages were consolidated into towns. For cooperation, friars offered datus lofty civil titles and sometimes built homes for the displaced barangays, or agreed to compromises that allowed them to live in rural areas just outside town limits, though no farther than the reach of the church bells, abajo de las campañas. Those who resisted were moved violently or killed. Thus was born a colonial mentality that would live on through the ages, guiding us like gospel. The lesson of the colonized is that life is better as colonist.

My great-great-grandmother Princess Emilia Bato Bato grew up hearing her elders recount tales about her distant cousin Muhammad Kudarat and the three centuries of battles her people had fought against the Spanish invaders, who torched crops and villages with each retreat. Though I can only estimate the year of her birth, Emilia was likely old enough to remember when the Spaniards returned to Lake Lanao in 1891 with 1,200 troops, and her elders probably told war stories about the Maranao pushing the colonizers out of Dansalan and back to Iligan once more. She may have been in her teens when the Spaniards roared back up the mountain four years later with 3,000 soldiers, bearing more firepower, seized the Maranao's Fort Marawi, and conquered the barangay in a battle that left four datus and 150 others dead.

Emilia's father, one of Lanao's four sultans, signed the peace treaty, pledging loyalty to the crown and agreeing to the construction of churches and monasteries on Maranao land. Perhaps weary from a generations-old conflict, perhaps simply outgunned, perhaps sensing the futility of fighting to defeat one empire only to face another right behind it, sultans and datus across Mindanao surrendered their sovereignty to Spain, one after another through the nineteenth century. Not all did. Some retreated into the island's mountainous interior to continue a resistance that lives on today.

A growing number of Catholics settled in northern Mindanao. When Emilia was a young woman she would walk down to the market along the shore, where Christians and Muslims mingled amid boisterous traders and the scents of fresh fish and durian. Maranao Muslims stood out in their bright outfits. The men wore colorful printed jackets with gold buttons, handkerchiefs tied around their heads, malong skirts over dark trousers, curved daggers at their hips. The women wore longer malongs that wrapped around their bodies and over their shoulders like gowns, handwoven tapestries of vibrant geometric patterns bursting with reds, purples, and yellows.

Emilia, though, cloaked herself only in brown. She had converted to Catholicism at some point in early adulthood, becoming so utterly devoted to her new faith that she dressed in the fashion of monks. I don't know why she converted, nor how her Muslim sultanate family reacted when she told them. If at some point she explained her reasons to her grandchildren, my grandfather's generation, they didn't recall it in stories about her. Maybe the arriving missionaries swayed her with their sermons on sacrifice and salvation. Maybe it was all just a political maneuver by a princess attuned to the shifting order of power on her island.

I don't know if she converted before she met Juan Fernandez, a Spanish soldier in the Civil Guard occupying the territory, or if she converted because of him. They married and raised their children in a large wooden house perched on stilts for the rainy days when the lake rose and flooded the land. Tucked amid tropical jungle in a remote pocket of the lakefront, the house was said to be rippling with dwendes and engkantos. It was there, in the depth of the forest, that the sick and cursed found the pious woman in brown. An expert in remedies and rituals honed over many generations, Emilia was a midwife, a fortune-teller, and a healer who expelled evil spirits from bodies with medicinal plants and mystical customs, island knowledge applied in a room decorated with crosses, saintly icons, and a Santo Niño. Old beliefs folded into the new faith—like everything else, the spirits of the jungle must have come from the Lord God, who probably created them on the fifth or sixth day, after the stars but before the birds.

THE SPANISH DIDN'T LAST long on Mindanao. Not four years after the empire took Dansalan, it withered away, clashing with the United States, which defeated Spain and took over its colony in the Pacific. Emilia and Juan stayed in Dansalan, trading one occupier for another. The Americans built schools and the couple's children learned English. Those children had children and raised them, too, beside the lake.

The family held high standing in Dansalan. While Emilia treated patients at the house by the lake, Juan ran a sugar plantation on their land and developed a nearly mythical reputation as a relentless and skilled hunter. With a double-barreled Winchester rifle his father had given him before he left Spain, Juan would disappear alone into the jungle for days, then return with a wild boar over his shoulder and tales of peril. Years later, his grandchildren would remember sitting around him, chewing on chunks of sugarcane, leaning forward in delirious anticipation as he described staring into the beast's red eyes, which glowed like embers in the darkness.

Emilia and Juan's eldest daughter, Luisa, inherited her mother's sureness of conscience and her father's joyous intensity. At seventeen, she married a young traveler from Luzon, Jose Concepcion, who'd set off south in search of fortune and adventure on gold-soaked, barely colonized Mindanao. Born into privileged circumstances, Jose might have been yearning to forge a path that his family hadn't already carved out for him. His grandfather had founded the town of Concepcion in central Luzon, and his relatives included judges and bank presidents. His ancestors were of Spanish, Arab, Chinese, and indigenous blood, fused together in the centuries after Legazpi's conquest, generations climbing the ranks of the Spanish colonial system.

Jose found good-paying work as a postmaster on an American military outpost in Dansalan. Luisa got a job at the local treasurer's office. She designed the house they would build, large and light-filled on the slopes overlooking the water, among neighbors who were mostly Catholic. The couple had seven children. They revered their mother, a jovial and resolute woman who took the edge off their stern, disciplinarian father. Three of those children would have an outsize influence on my life: The second-oldest daughter, Caridad, inherited Luisa's impenetrable will; the middle son, Manuel, her stubborn righteousness; the youngest son, Tomas, her creative spirit.

They studied curricula designed by Americans and worshipped at churches designed by Spaniards. Two generations removed from the age of Moro sultans, the mythology of their ancestral land bent to Western forces, erasing the long history of the Maranao. Once, when Luisa noticed six-year-old Tomas gazing out the window at Lake Lanao, she told him the story of why it was shaped like a slipper: Saint Xavier, in a moment of frustration after not being able to convert the Muslims in the area, threw his sandal on the ground with such might that it imprinted into the land, and water sprang from it.

Each day, Luisa rose at dawn, said her morning prayers, then tended to a sprawling garden so enchanting that people traveled many miles to see it. She cultivated twenty-five varieties of roses, orchids in several colors, and assorted flowers gifted to her by local farmers who admired her work. "Tabi apo," she would say to the dwendes as she stepped onto the dirt. She planted and trimmed with precision and passion, inching up and down the colorful rows, hours and hours bent over and focused, meditative. On the hottest days, she found refuge in the shade of an old acacia tree at the front of the garden. She'd move slowly and carefully toward it, so as not to disturb the engkanto living in the thick canopy, paying respects as she found a seat at the base of the trunk. The powerful forest guardians treated her family well, shielding them from the storms that whipped against the mountains, infusing the soil with abundant life, rewarding Luisa for her service to the land, just as they'd rewarded her ancestors who'd looked after this land for as far back as she knew. From the shade of the tree, she'd watch her flowers dance in the breeze.

One day a group of neighbors approached the house and demanded Luisa cut down the tree. They complained that it was shaped like an ogre smoking a cigar, and it scared them whenever they walked past, especially at night. A satanic omen, they were sure. Luisa refused. The acacia tree brought good fortune, she said. The neighbors dismissed her claims as foolish superstition. An argument ensued. The neighbors said that either Luisa cut down the tree or they'd do it themselves one night while she slept, and while they were at it maybe they'd wipe out her garden, too. Pained and reluctant, apologizing to the deities of the jungle, Luisa cut down the tree.

FIVE GENERATIONS after Emilia converted, Roman Catholicism was in our bone marrow. We wore our devotion with obedient urgency. Scapulars around necks, Santo Niños on altars, Virgin Mary placards on shelves, rosaries hanging from rearview mirrors, memorized prayers before meals, communion on Sundays, confessions whenever possible, three hours of sorrowful reflection on Good Friday. Whatever trouble Emilia may have had reconciling the new Christian teachings with the old truths she held on to, for her descendants the dualism had hardened into a worldview.

In the divine order of the universe I came to understand as a child, I saw no distinction between the realm of immaculate conception and that of the mischievous dwendes. "Our father who art in heaven" carried no more weight than "tabi apo." The devil tried to lure me into sin while white-winged, long-toothed aswang threatened to murder me in my sleep. Job and Noah of the Bible shared a universe with the cursed classmates my mom told me about who woke up bald after disrespecting dwendes. Padre Pio had stigmata on his hands, the sun danced in Fatima, and our ancestors' spirits inhabited the moths that flew inside our homes. The parables ran along parallel threads without conflict. When my elders couldn't find something, they prayed to St. Anthony, patron saint of recovering lost items. When they realized that the sweet plums growing in the yard had turned sour, they concluded that they'd failed to say "pwera usog" upon first tasting the fruit, leaving the tree vulnerable to the spite of a jealous neighbor.

I can never know if Emilia held on to the old ways as a secret act of resistance, a winking acknowledgment to her descendants of an artifice she adopted to protect us, or if she simply blended ingredients to concoct a gospel that reflected her accumulated wisdom, like an alchemist adding elements to a formula. The course was set long before me. With each generation's survival came affirmation of the beliefs that guided decisions and conjured fortune—tools that instilled a sense of control to people at the mercy of the terms set by their oppressors. From that arsenal honed over three centuries of colonization, we developed survival tactics.

ONE MORNING IN 1979, my mother came to the breakfast table with a speech rehearsed for her father: she planned to tell him that she wanted to drop out of dental school to become a flight attendant. She was nervous. Her father was a stubborn and ambitious man, an attorney renowned in

Manila for his righteousness, fighting on behalf of poor tenants and under-paid workers, so cemented to his principles that he refused to pay bribes. She had to maneuver delicately, she knew, plead her case with airtight reasoning and calculated rhetoric.

Money had gotten tight in the household, the economy choked by seven years of corruption under Marcos's martial law, and her parents didn't have enough to pay her tuition that semester. But that was not so much the reason she wanted to drop out of dental school as a sign from God that she should chase the future she desired, rather than burden her parents with enabling her to continue on a path that only mildly inter-ested her. In any case, the mention of money would only provoke her father's pride. "We will find a way to make it work," he'd surely say.

Her parents were faithful to the expectations of the Philippine elite. English was studied in class and practiced at home. Daughters and sons lived with their parents until marriage, and didn't work a job until they graduated from a respected university. In Manila, Manuel and Rizalina set their sights on the next stage of the family's upward climb—to the empire, where there were no bribes to pay and opportunity came to those who worked diligently. In 1978, a year before that fateful breakfast, Rizalina had gone to San Francisco in another attempt to build a settle-ment for our clan in the United States. She arrived on a six-month tour-ist visa, overstayed, and couldn't return to the Philippines until she figured out a way to make the U.S. our home. In the meantime, Manuel held down the compound.

How my mother wished her mother were there! Where Manuel blazed forward with crackling persistence, Rizalina flowed with grace-ful intensity. Twice a day, at the strike of three, she'd kneel to say a prayer in memoriam of the hour of Christ's death—a commitment so permanent that her body often woke for the early morning session with-out an alarm clock. She ate yogurt daily after reading about a hundred-year-old woman who gave it credit for her long life. She wore gold rings, gold bracelets, and a gold crucifix, leopard-print blouses and silk scarves, her eyes soft behind gold-rimmed glasses. She was open-minded, an eager listener.

Over pandesal with eggs and longganisa, my mother asked her father a question. Would he rather be a mediocre doctor who was unhappy with his job, or a great artist, like his younger brother Tomas Concepcion, who lived in Rome? Manuel did not hesitate in responding. Passion was of urgency, in the finite time we're given.

"Well," my mother launched her announcement, "I want to be a flight attendant, and be the best flight attendant in the world!"

After a beat of inscrutable silence, her father responded as she'd expected: "A glorified waitress," he said in his stern baritone. He hadn't raised her to spend her days serving others. That was for families of lower standing, the women working as domestics in Bahrain and Jordan, the men driving executives down Hong Kong streets and scrubbing the decks of cargo ships, a mercenary labor force for the world's privileged class. There was dignity in that work, he believed, but not for the Concepcions. He told her he'd have an answer by the following morning.

My mom was the most obedient of the eight Concepcion siblings, the goody-goody who didn't drink or date. She wasn't sure she had the nerve to take the job without her father's approval. She steeled herself, thought about the promenades and cafés.

But she'd underestimated her father. The next morning, he gave her his blessing. Seeing her surprise, he said, "Oh, Lucy, a rolling stone gathers no moss." She'd never heard that phrase before and assumed it had something to do with the famous band.

MY MOM MOVED to Cebu, where she shared a rented room with another young Philippine Airlines flight attendant in the creaky wooden house of an elderly Chinese woman who liked to cook for them and hear about their travels. The two young women shared a bunk bed on the second floor, where the heat from the roof was so stifling that they left the windows open to let the breeze in. At night, they'd hear the idling engines from the European cars of the suitors picking them up for dates that always left my mom unimpressed. The men were handsome and came from rich families, but she found it distasteful the way they seemed to think that was enough to make her fall in love. With tipsy bluster, they'd go on about the maids they'd hire, the beach house they'd buy on the coast of Luzon, the big shots they were sure to become. How narrow their dreams were! As if everything they could ever want was in the Philippines. As if they assumed she was just waiting for somebody to sweep her up and save her from the fate of being a working woman. Couldn't they tell from the way she carried herself how much she cherished her independence?

She cared for her crisp white uniform blouse, red blazer, and red skirt as if they were a wedding gown, and she never let her black leather handbag touch the ground. When the airline sent a car to take her and her roommate to the airport, they strutted out the door as if a red carpet lay beneath their heels and the wheels of their luggage. At the terminal, they whisked past the lines with the flash of a badge, all eyes on them with their long glossy hair and impeccable posture. Pilots tipped their caps and flirted shamelessly, leaving my mother at once flattered and turned off.

The reality was less impressive than the mystique. While senior attendants snagged the longer trips to exotic cities in Europe and mainland Asia, where they spent their layovers sightseeing, my mom and other junior colleagues clocked their hours on a relentless succession of quick round-trips to Laoag City, Cagayan de Oro, and the other dully familiar cities dotting the archipelago. From high in the sky, the islands looked rugged and plain, endless jungles and yellow-brown fields by day, an invisible dark mass indistinguishable from the sea at night but for some modest speckles of luminescence that marked the existence of civilization down below. At cruising altitude, the more than seven thousand islands in the archipelago all somehow looked the same.

Impatient to see places she'd never seen, my mom kept her eyes open for a path off the islands. In 1984, she landed a job with Saudia airline and moved to Jeddah, into a two-bedroom apartment she shared with another flight attendant on the second floor of a bare-bones complex specially built for the airline's all-woman crews. By then, 130,000 Filipino citizens were living and working in Saudi Arabia, and about a million more had jobs in other foreign lands. As the Philippine economy had continued to shrink through the 1970s, Marcos had signed labor agreements with other countries, establishing a national philosophy that would outlive him. From 1979 to 2009, some 30 million people left the Islands to work overseas. At first, most landed in the Middle East, where soaring oil prices created a growing class of wealthy families in need of nannies, drivers, and maids. In the 1980s and 1990s, they went to Malaysia, Taiwan, Italy, Australia, Canada, and the United States, sending money back home to the husbands and wives who held down the household, and to the children they rarely saw. This flood of remittances became an essential pillar of the Philippine economy, a multibillion-dollar sector making up a third of the nation's export revenue. The workers were revered for their sacrifice. The government encouraged others to follow their example. "Bagong bayani," or "new heroes," they were collectively nicknamed. December, which many of them spent away from family, was christened "Month of Overseas Filipinos." By the mid-2000s, it was a goal of official policy to send off at least a million new heroes each year.

Some worked in nursing or IT, but the overwhelming majority—upward of 80 percent—were domestics, laborers, and deckhands. If service is our people's specialty, it's a superpower honed over centuries. Like all heroes, we didn't choose our superpower, but rather it fell upon us, thanks to a series of ill-fated circumstances.

OUR ORIGIN STORY as a people of service begins at the dawn of the Spanish conquest, when Catholic friars and government bureaucrats went about resetting class hierarchies to their own liking. The bureaucrats taxed the native Indios, as the Spanish called them, and forced them into unpaid public works projects building ships, serving in the military, and preparing food. The friars made the Indios donate crops, which they resold for profit, and charged fees for hearing confession, dispensing communion, and performing other sacraments required for entry into heaven. Friars and bureaucrats made Indios work on their personal estates, framed as a sort of compulsory duty to church and empire. "Extracting the most profit out of the colony turned into a fierce albeit unofficial competition between two rival spheres," writes historian Luis Francia in *A History of the Philippines: From Indios Bravos to Filipinos.* "The population was being asked to believe that their subjugation was really their liberation."

The colonizers trained us with single-minded rigor to devote ourselves to their well-being. Thanks to the archipelago, the Spaniards became very rich, especially in Manila, as they'd altered its name, where they built stone walls to protect the city's center from native revolt and rival invasion. Manila was the linchpin of Spain's global empire. Starting in 1565, almost as soon as Legazpi claimed the archipelago for Madrid, the Manila Galleons set sail on an annual round-trip voyage from Acapulco, Mexico, the sole cargo ship on an exclusive trade route that Spain preserved for 250 years. The journey was a grueling six months each way, but immensely rewarding. From Mexico, the galleon carried tomatoes, avocados, maize, cacao, and silver, along with royal decrees. The return trip brought silk, spices, porcelain, and ivory.

The archipelago served as a meeting point for Spanish and Chinese merchants, a place for processing products and negotiating prices. Indio artisans would carve ivory from Asian elephants into intricate statues of the Virgin Mary or crucified Jesus that would end up on the altars of Spanish buyers in Mexico or Europe. But few goods originating on the Islands themselves made it onto the galleon. The Spaniards had little use for the Philippines beyond the labor of natives and the deep-water harbor Manila provided, and therefore made no effort to keep up the production that had sustained the islanders in the centuries before the conquest. By the mid-1800s, trade contracts for Philippine goods amounted to $5 million, less than one-fifth the worth of products from colonial cousin Cuba, even though the Philippines' population was four times larger. "Precisely because the galleon trade was profitable, the Spanish colonists paid scant attention to developing either the agricultural or manufacturing industry," Francia writes.

Forced resettlement programs left longtime farms abandoned. Schools taught scripture but offered no vocational training. Indios lay at the bottom of a three-class hierarchy, below Spanish elite and immigrant Chinese merchants. The Spaniards were so afraid that the Chinese would take control of the colony that they kept cannons trained on the district of Manila where most of the Chinese immigrants lived, then passed a law restricting the number of Chinese immigrants living on the archipelago to three thousand. The Indios of the colony posed no such threat. Sporadic rebellions in Luzon and the Visayas were quickly suppressed or cordoned off in the mountains, though the war with the Moros in unconquered Mindanao raged on.

For some colonized Indios, the only path upward was outward, away from the only land they'd ever known. They signed on to work on the galleon, loading barrels and crates at the dock, serving food and scrubbing decks on the open sea, surviving on meager allotments of mealy rice and dirty water long enough to see the New World peeking over the horizon. Some Indios jumped ship in Acapulco, settling there or making their way farther inland, as far east as New Orleans by 1850, the first known Filipino immigrants to reach the United States of America.

MY MOM DISMISSED the clichés and stereotypes associated with her nationality. Her father's pride coursing through her, she considered herself of equal or higher status to the pilots who flirted with her and the passengers she served in first class, chismising about them with her colleagues when they did something she deemed "low class," like the man who cut his toenails with a steak knife or the man with such foul body odor that the passenger beside him requested a new seat.

My mom made friends with Pinay coworkers, and they'd cram into one of their apartments on nights off, trading stories and advice, imagining the adventures they'd have with the free flights that came as a perk of the job. Four of them planned a group trip to Frankfurt, where one of them had a sister. "We were so excited," my mom told me years later. "Girlfriends! First time for all of us to Europe."

Two months into her new job, while working first class on an evening flight from Jeddah to Riyadh, she met a twenty-three-year-old Lebanese businessman with a thick mustache, a gregarious manner, and the confidence of one who believed anything could be his if he sweated hard enough for it. On his way off the plane, he told my mom that he would give her a call and introduce himself as "the guy in the blue suit." He didn't ask for her contact information, and she wouldn't have given it. Though she'd enjoyed their brief interaction, she wasn't going to hand her number to some random dude in first class who'd probably flirted through half the cabin crews from Istanbul to Mumbai.

A day or two later, the phone in her apartment rang, waking her from a nap. Annoyed, she lifted the receiver and hung it up, to stop the ringing. She did the same when it rang again, but when it rang a third time, she brought the phone to her ear and asked who was calling. It was the guy in the blue suit—and years later, whenever she told the story, she'd reenact the look of surprise on her face.

My mom's a romantic, and she couldn't help herself: she found his extended pursuit flattering. Remarking that he'd be back in Jeddah later that week, he invited her for coffee, and she accepted, without mentioning that she didn't drink coffee.

"How did you know where to call?"

"I used my little finger," he said playfully. Whenever my mother told the story, she'd never leave out that line. He meant that he used his pinkie to dial an acquaintance at the airline for a way to contact a certain attendant on his flight. It's a bit uncomfortable to think about now—that my entire existence was made possible by some guy at Saudia HQ who had no compunctions about helping a brother out by giving him a pretty flight attendant's name, flight schedule, and home phone number. Maybe they would have met on another flight. My dad's a persistent dude, and maybe he would have flown the same route over and over until their paths crossed again.

On the phone, they fell into conversation, as if they'd known each other for some time. My mom sensed that my dad carried a generosity of spirit that matched her own, and his sureness impressed her. She mentioned the plan for a weeklong vacation in Frankfurt. He asked her if she wanted to spend the week with him instead. They could go to Paris, where he had an apartment.

Off the phone, she pleaded her case to her friends: "It's *Paris!*"

Flying in, she gazed out the window, looking for any sign of the Eiffel Tower. My dad met her at the airport, lifted her suitcase into the hatchback trunk of a rented Autobianchi Abarth, and drove her through the city, past chiseled limestone and elegantly carved brass, arches and columns everywhere, cobblestone squares drenched in orange light, slim-fitting leather and precariously perched hats, baguettes peeking out from open backpacks, the sophisticated indulgences of people who'd rather be nowhere else. My mom took it all in with unbridled glee.

"Oh my God, woooowwww," she said as stared up at the Romano-Byzantine white domes of the Sacré-Cœur basilica, turning in her seat to watch it pass as the car rolled down the Montmartre hill. When Notre-Dame came into view, my mom gripped my dad's hand in her excitement, nearly bursting out of her seat. She gawked at the mannequins behind shop windows on the Champs-Élysées, rattling off the brands she recognized with sarcastically haughty inflection. At Yves Saint Laurent, she tried out perfumes, settling on Rive Gauche. My dad bought her a case, and for years it was the only perfume she used, its blue, black, and silver tin bottle a fixture on her dresser.

"Paris was my dream," she told me years later.

BY THE TIME I entered the world, my family had ridden the tides of history, maintaining our standing, adapting as needed, eventually transforming into urbanized, Anglicized capitalists. We assimilated, acquiescing in erasures of self in exchange for acceptance and opportunity from the colonists. We stuck together, pooling resources to pull up the weakest even at the expense of the strongest. We honored the deities that kept us afloat, fearful that the slightest slip could spell our doom.

Close calls were evidence that the invisible forces were on our side. Take, for instance, that night in Jeddah in late 1984 when my life almost ended, years before it began.

My mom and dad had been dating for months by then, trading visits. My mom liked my dad but had not given over her heart. She told him she enjoyed their conversations and wanted to keep spending time with him but thought of him as a brother. Her career was advancing quickly and she felt no urgency to settle into a serious relationship. She'd worked on secret flights transporting Palestinian soldiers to covert training camps in Saudi Arabia, and on the crew that served the royal family on a plane outfitted with gold faucets, marble countertops, and handsy bodyguards. Her friends teased that she was bound to marry a prince.

Below a hazy pink sky one evening, my mom and dad sat in his car, parked by the Red Sea along the Jeddah Corniche, reading the Bible together. They'd just come from a Christian service in the home of one of my dad's acquaintances. My mom had been heartened to learn that my dad shared her religious devotion. He was such a committed Catholic that he used his political connections in Saudi Arabia to smuggle in Bibles for friends and undercover priests, packing dozens into suitcases that didn't get checked at customs because he arranged a police escort— the same powers he used to get around the country's prohibition on alcohol, which he didn't smuggle but served at house parties. My mom could relate: she'd snuck Christian rock cassettes into the country.

In the car by the beach, they reflected on the sermon and readings at the service, bonded by the thrill of their righteous lawbreaking. As the sun set and the light dimmed, my mom slid the Bible into a pocket on the door. Their conversation continued into the night.

Suddenly headlights pulled up behind them. Two police officers approached the car. Unmarried women weren't permitted to be in public with men they weren't related to. The cop on the driver's side knocked on the window. He spoke to my dad in Arabic, his voice stern and accusatory. My dad's tone was polite and assured, calm and friendly, shoulders shrugging, hands gesticulating. The exchange went on for ten minutes that felt much longer. Sitting silent and anxious, my mom had no idea what they were saying.

Eventually, the voices relaxed, slowed, then traded goodbyes. Once the police car drove off, my dad's tone turned frantic. "They were going to arrest and deport you," he remembers saying in a shaky voice. "I told them we had plans to get engaged." He name-dropped the sheikh he worked with. The officers let them off with a warning. My mom and dad sat in the car for a few minutes, close to tears, panic slowly receding.

That night, my mom would tell me, was the night she was struck with the flickering realization that she was in love with my dad. On the strength of their shared faith, the Lord had bestowed them with a miracle, blessing their bond, a sign from the heavens. All part of God's plan.

They swirled into an intense romance. Months later, they were in Las Vegas, a two-night stop on an eight-day American vacation ending in San Francisco, where my mom planned to introduce my dad to her mother and Ging. My dad was standing at the hotel room window when he spotted the Little White Wedding Chapel. He asked my mom if she wanted to get married. My mom thought it was a joke at first. My dad cheekily noted that the chapel was a historic American institution. Frank Sinatra and Mia Farrow, among others, had married there. My mom put on a white dress with a light blue stripe at the waist, my dad a navy blue suit. They marched up the aisle and traded vows in the afternoon light shining through pink stained-glass windows. The church ceremony, big and festive and sanctioned by God, would come in the near future, the newlyweds agreed. For now, they celebrated by going to Disneyland.

They made decisions one day at a time and kept long-term plans fluid. My mom remained in Jeddah, my dad in Riyadh. My dad didn't think they should move in together until he told his parents about the marriage, and he wasn't ready to do that just yet. His family, a prominent clan of judges, doctors, and executives in Beirut, had expressed their disapproval of the wide-eyed Filipino flight attendant from a distant nation known to them primarily for supplying the world's servant class. My dad preferred not to expose my mom to their coldness. And so little changed in the early months and years after their nuptials. They visited each other with the same frequency and took vacations together to cities my mom had longed to see. Two years passed like this. In 1987, my dad started an energy company, basing its office in Paris, where he would live full-time, but a few of his siblings also lived there, and he still hadn't told his family about the marriage, so to keep the secret safe, my mom couldn't join him in her favorite city in the world.

With my dad no longer living in Saudi Arabia, she concluded that it didn't make sense for her to stay in the country while she awaited their eventual reunion. She was twenty-eight, healthy—*praise the Lord*—and in no rush to figure out her next move. What my dad couldn't offer in proximity, he sought to make up for in financial security. He'd send her three thousand dollars every month, so she could take it easy for a while, spend time with family, and not have to work until she wanted to. He'd buy her a condominium in Manila. He'd arrange for regular visits. My mom accepted the temporary reality. She quit her Saudia job and moved into the sleek high-rise overlooking the Marikina River. She didn't plan to spend much time there, intending to fill her calendar with international travels. In September 1988, she bought a ticket to San Francisco to visit her mother and eldest sister.

She arrived with a tourist visa and a Louis Vuitton suitcase, intending a two-month visit. But a few weeks into her stay she realized she was pregnant, with me. She took it in stride. Awed at the elegance of God's grand design, she felt a serendipitous joy that she could bear her first child under the care of her mother and eldest sister, who was also pregnant, ahead by three months. My mom decided she'd extend her stay in the United States through the first few months of my life, at least until she thought I was old enough to handle a long plane ride without much fuss.

Five years later, we were still in California. Each time my mom's visa expiration date neared, we'd hop on a plane to Paris, to visit my dad, or to Manila, to visit family, before returning to the States with a fresh visa. Each year that passed, my mom was less certain we'd end up in Paris.

FOR MOST OF HUMAN HISTORY, nobody comprehended the world's full geographical scope. Europeans were first to that knowledge, as far as I know, enabling them to define it in their image over the half millennium since. The maps in my school textbooks and on news report backdrops placed Europe at the center. I learned that China is in the Far East and Iran in the Middle East, and that the country I was born in was named after an Italian explorer because a German mapmaker decided so. I took it for granted that English, French, or Spanish is an official language in more than half of the world's two hundred or so countries.

There is great honor in conquest. Statues, ballads, holidays, museums, names of airports and cities preserve the memory of conquerors, upholding the glories of their heroism, justifying the empires they helped build. It is the empires, rich in resources and ego, that keep the records, and their stories trickled into my mind not through any particular source but through the very framework of the world I was born into. The feats of empires ring through time, for becoming an empire means accruing the labor to build, cultivate, and expand, nourishing a beast that grows hungrier as it gains strength.

While the ancient tales of the Egyptians, Persians, Macedonians, Hans, Romans, Mayans, Mongols, Ottomans, Incas, and Aztecs filled my textbooks and TV shows, I heard far less about the cultures they swallowed—for what value is there in understanding the plight of the people whose decisions and desires barely register on the Richter scale of recorded history? To be conquered is to shrink from existence.

From there, it's merely a matter of which empire you fall into. Over the years, I've entertained the fantasy of how French-me would have turned out. Along that parallel thread, my mind spins accents developed, mythologies inhaled, moments of indignant shock upon discovering, probably during a semester abroad in New England, the particulars of U.S. health care costs and gun laws. Would French-me have been condescendingly amused by the absurdities of the foreign empire, or apoplectic? Envious of my Stateside cousins, or pitying?

I shrink in the face of the hypothetical, because playing out the alternate scenarios requires detaching my identity from any semblance of nationhood and the culture it infuses—elements so deeply ingrained that the parallel versions of me can ring true only if I no longer recognize myself. I am no less a product of my country than the grapes that grow in Napa Valley, then are crushed and left to ferment, defined by every rainfall and heatwave. I'm an '89 California mixed brown, full-bodied from fast-food drive-throughs and football hitting drills, with a hint of post-riot Westside hip-hop fury and the slightest trace of Saturday morning cartoon sloth, emerging out of innocence into the noxious ashes of fallen towers, plucked from the vine amid an economic drought unprecedented in the decades of Pax Americana. The slightest shift in the wind changes the whole formula.

CHAPTER 4

GENESIS

Upon landing in San Francisco in 1978, Rizalina had a simple plan: save up to buy a house big enough to serve as our eventual family headquarters. She had no illusions about the math. The savings and experience she'd accumulated on the Islands meant little in the States. The pesos in her checking account didn't go far, thanks to the exchange rate, and though she'd been a senior accountant at the Philippines Central Bank, the best-paying job she could find was as a bookkeeper at a law firm. To make extra money, she babysat for her boss. She had faith that the numbers would work out in the end, with U.S. dollars to her name and U.S. opportunities to propel her. Whatever troubles America might bring couldn't be worse than what she'd left. A decade into her mission, in 1988, with her employment stable and half of her children in the United States, she began scouring housing listings.

My mom and Auntie Ging, both pregnant at the time, offered to split the down payment three ways, but still nothing on the peninsula fell within their budget. Only Auntie Ging had enough credit history in the States to get approved for a mortgage, and the maximum loan the banks offered was $200,000, barely half the price of three- and four-bedroom houses even on the city's periphery. Fortunately, Ging knew a realtor in the Bay Area, an old family friend from the Islands who'd settled in the States some years earlier. He said he knew just the place: Vallejo, an industrial suburb on wobbly legs thirty miles northeast of San Francisco. He himself lived there, as part of a blossoming Filipino community that made up a fifth of Vallejo's population.

With Ging at the wheel of her recently purchased Toyota Corolla, which she'd nicknamed Blue Angel, the three women crossed the Bay Bridge, over the glistening sheet of San Francisco Bay. The congestion of the big city gave way to strip malls, smokestacks, and the rolling green hills that as a kid I thought looked like the legs of a sleeping giant. They crossed the Carquinez Bridge at the mouth of San Pablo Bay, then exited the highway where it overlooked the orca pools and blue-roofed wildlife enclosures of Marine World Africa USA, at the northern edge of Vallejo, and wended their way to the Cimarron Hills subdivision, a maze of sloping bungalows and weedy sidewalks below a patchwork horizon of evergreens, oaks, and palm trees.

They met the realtor in front of a white house with a green roof. The street number was a harmonious 100—no 9s or 6s, with the jagged eccentricities that invited bad luck. Rizalina had already rejected houses numbered 36 and 270, because the sums of their digits were unlucky; already compromising on location, she couldn't afford to skimp on the numbers. Still, the place wasn't exactly what my grandmother had pictured. She'd imagined a four-bedroom house to loom larger. Instead of lush grass there was a lawn of white stones, which the realtor pointed out was a plus because you don't have to worry about watering it, and nine towering evergreens shaped like Marge Simpson's hair—another plus for the modicum of privacy it offered, on top of the minty sweet aroma that greeted you as soon as you got out of the car. Most of the neighbors in the vicinity were Black, but more and more Filipinos were moving into the subdivision, the realtor noted, including, just across the street, a family with two boys around Jed's age.

The interior wasn't glamorous but it was functional. In the front of the house, expanding out from the foyer, the previous owners had built on a den-type area, as good as a fifth bedroom. The kitchen was open, with a long wooden countertop that bridged to the living room, well-suited for a family that made a habit of gathering around the rice cooker for late-night talks over microwaved LO, as my family called leftovers. Beyond the sliding patio door, the backyard had a raised concrete patio bordered by dandelion-heavy grass and a motley band of trees drooping with cherries, pears, oranges, apples, plums, and lemons. The sky was clear blue and the air cool. On the hills in the distance, the windows of mansions sparkled.

The women inspected the property, opening cabinets and closets, testing sinks, peeking out windows, their bottom lips puckered in approval. Our first house in America was a quarter the size of the Scout Reyes compound, with narrow hallways and windows barred with iron, but it was indisputably American, with a two-car garage, an afternoon ice cream truck, and a view of Marine World's summer fireworks. And although Ging was concerned about the distance from San Francisco, where she and Rizalina worked, she recognized that there was little chance they'd find enough space closer to the city, and with more kin on the way, there wasn't time to waste. She signed the deed in her name. "I was just doing this for the family's sake," she remembers. "My mind is like, I gotta do this, I gotta work as much as I can because I need to make the payments."

Our barangay was in the process of a long, complicated, multistage move that left us fractured across the ocean. My uncle Bobby, the youngest of the siblings, had petitioned for a green card, deciding to forgo a professional basketball career in the Philippines to start fresh in California, a place he'd heard about in songs and seen in movies. My uncle

Marlon, who returned to Scout Reyes after being unable to extend his visa in Japan, and my uncle Paul, who couldn't seem to hold down a job, had started organizing the paperwork they needed for American visas. The plan was that once all eight children had exited the Philippines, my grandpa Manuel would join the family in the States. The Vallejo house would serve as a base camp for the new arrivals as they found their feet, looked for work, saved money, and learned the ways of the new land before setting off to secure a home of their own. The down payment was less an investment in property than in country. The signing of a deed formalized our exodus.

Five months later, I was born, the newest member of a household bustling with our growing colony. Eleven people packed into the five rooms. In the master bedroom, Rizalina, Auntie Lyn, and my one-year-old cousin Christian slept on the double bed, and his brother Roscoe, six, slept on the floor. Uncle Bobby stayed in the bedroom closest to the living room. In the corner bedroom by the garage, Auntie Ging, Uncle Spanky, and my infant cousin Lauren shared the bed while Jed took the floor, though he sometimes conked out on the living room couch because the washer and dryer, just outside the bedroom door, rumbled loudly. My mom and I slept on a mattress in the room by the entranceway, a set of white accordion dividers offering some minimal privacy. Room designations were largely temporary, though, as the cycle of family in and out of the house regularly refreshed the status quo.

Thanks to the migrating generation, we were no longer on the outside looking in. My American birthright was a gift I'd done nothing to earn.

LEGEND HAS IT that the people of the Philippines will be freed from oppression when Bernardo Carpio, a Tagalog giant from central Luzon, escapes from his shackles. Carpio was a datu who resisted Spanish occupation. He is so old that his birth name has been lost to time. Locals named him after the medieval Spanish folk hero Bernardo del Carpio, but I doubt he'd approve of the moniker. According to one version of the lore, the Tagalog Carpio is so powerful that the Spaniards have to hire an engkanto to trap him between two boulders in the San Mateo Mountains. The giant's efforts to escape cause earthquakes. One hundred years after his capture, Carpio breaks the chain holding one of his arms. A hundred years later, he frees his other arm. A hundred years after that, he gets his left foot out. By the final decade of the nineteenth century, the struggling masses eagerly anticipate his return, a savior to upend the colonial order.

While the legend has many versions, this is the one popularized by José Rizal, who was already the most famous Filipino person in the world when he recounted the tale of the "King of the Indios" in his 1891 novel *El Filibusterismo*. In the book, a calesa driver asks his passenger: "Do you know, Señor, if the right foot is free by now?"

To Rizal, Carpio represented something the Philippines lacked: a hero people all over the archipelago could rally behind, a symbol rooted in precolonial history to lead a collective fight against a common oppressor. Disjointed by language and geography, the Islands shared little more than "a common misfortune and a common abasement," he wrote in an 1891 essay. The archipelago had only become a single entity under Spain, and only because of Spain did it share a language, Spanish, and (mostly) a religion, Catholicism. The Philippine identity existed entirely in relation to the motherland.

There was no shortage of local displeasure with the colonizer. Indios, forced off their ancestral land, had toiled for generations under farm owners, with few opportunities for advancement and no end of their subjugation in sight. Mestizos, both working and upper class, denounced the colonial government's tax policies and heavy-handed police force. Even some clergy were turning on the empire, disillusioned by patronage systems that favored the military at their expense and outraged at the government crackdown on priests suspected of supporting subversive causes. Rizal's 1887 novel *Noli Me Tángere*, a narrative catalogue of indignities and injustices wrought by colonial authorities, quickly drew the ire of the Spanish government, which banned the book in the Philippines, making it all the more popular as it spread through underground channels.

But Rizal didn't think shared antipathy was enough to forge bonds that wouldn't break when a deal was on the table. Before the Philippine people could form an army of resistance and a government of their own, Rizal posited that they needed the fortification of a shared mythology, a "national spirit," without which "only family or tribal feelings existed." Americans had their Plymouth Rock, a symbol that justified their pioneering spirit. The French had their Enlightenment philosophers, whose ideas inspired armed movements against oppressive monarchies. The Mexicans had their collective memory of the great empire their ancestors had achieved—a painting from that period shows a feathered Aztec crown alongside the red Phrygian cap associated with French revolutionaries. The Haitians had their roots in a collective dispossession and kidnapping from a distant home, and their overwhelming numbers—450,000 slaves working to enrich 40,000 white colonists on a horseshoe peninsula the size of Mindanao.

Decades had passed since the revolutions in those places. In the Philippines, rebellions were sporadic and mostly confined to provincial sects led by messianic figures. There were no golden years to harken back to, no shared origin stories, no evidence to prove these seven thousand islands would be better off as a singular entity under self-rule.

In the Philippines, power flowed from the east. From Acapulco came the annual galleon bearing money and directives. Manila, with its wide boulevards and plazas, was designed to resemble Mexico City, which was designed to resemble the capital cities of western Europe. Because

Madrid was so far from Manila, colonial policies were set by officials in Mexico City until Spain lost the territory in 1821 via revolution. To lure more Spaniards to the Philippines so that they wouldn't be so outnumbered by natives, the empire offered land grants and tax exemptions to Spanish-blooded people born in Spain (peninsulares) or New Spain (criollos), establishing the landholding aristocracy that exists in the Philippines to this day.

There were no laws banning marriage between people of different races, and over the centuries, Spanish, Malay, Chinese, and Japanese lineages wove together to form the basis for the race we now know as Filipinos. Below full-blooded Spaniards and above native Indios, mestizos were free to rise and fall within this yawning middle-ground in the colonial class hierarchy, never writing the laws that governed them but never fully restricted from a chance at comfort. As colonial liberation movements erupted around the world in the nineteenth century, the affluent mestizo descendants of those peninsulares and criollos grew increasingly frustrated that they had no say in choosing the rules that dictated their lives. Rizal learned this the hard way: believing the colonial authorities were open to suggestions, he once wrote a letter to the government explaining that the Dominican friars who owned land in his hometown were charging rents so high that locals were impoverished even as harvests increased. The Dominicans responded by evicting everybody, with help from colonial troops who burned their houses to the ground. Rizal's family had to leave town and settle elsewhere.

While short of being aristocrats, his family had enough money to send him to the country's top schools, then to Europe to continue his studies. It was on those travels during his college years that he adopted the Enlightenment ideals at the heart of his ideology. He worked on *Noli* while enrolled at the University of Paris, earning degrees in medicine, philosophy, and literature. He found a publisher in Berlin and wrote the book in Spanish, which was spoken by mestizos but not taught in colonial schools for Indios. The majority of Filipino people Rizal hoped to reach couldn't read his work.

At that point, the Philippine resistance to Spain wasn't being orchestrated in the archipelago but from Barcelona, where the city's long opposition to Madrid made it a haven for Filipino political exiles. Rizal and these exiles were part of a cohort of worldly, wealthy, college-educated mestizos who dubbed themselves the Ilustrados, Spanish for "enlightened ones." They broadcast their reports of Spanish abuses and their calls for policy changes in *La Solidaridad*, a broadsheet published in Barcelona. One of the paper's guiding voices, journalist Marcelo del Pilar, whose family owned rice and sugar plantations, had been exiled from the Philippines for publishing the first Tagalog language newspaper. Del Pilar translated Rizal's *Noli* into Tagalog a year after its release.

Rizal seemed to recognize the futility of leading a resistance from a distance. He returned to Manila in 1892 to launch a new civic organization, La Liga Filipina, aimed at uniting "the whole Archipelago into one compact, vigorous, and homogenous body," in part by providing legal, banking, and educational services unavailable through the colonial government. The inaugural meeting that June took place at a house in Manila's Tondo District, a dense slum whose narrow alleys were, in the words of historian Teodoro Agoncillo, "as crooked as the [Spanish] administration and as dirty as the conscience of Spanish officialdom." A slight man with a lisp and sharp features, whose signature outfit was a black suit, a white shirt, and a bowler hat perched over hair slicked to the side in a dramatic wave, Rizal presented the organization's purpose and bylaws to an audience of around twenty men, some of whom would go on to earn prominent placement in Philippine history books.

One attendee was Andres Bonifacio, who revered Rizal so greatly he sometimes copied out passages from *Noli*. Bonifacio lived in Tondo and had never been to Europe. His mother worked as a supervisor at a cigarette factory. His father was a tailor who also served in the district government. Though his family owned no land and he lived near people who were truly impoverished, Bonifacio had started reading at a young age in a country where 80 percent of the population was illiterate. He had attended private school and studied foreign languages. But as the oldest of six children, he had had to drop out of school in his early teens to earn money for the household. He worked as a messenger, a rattan broker, and a warehouse watchman. Talented with his hands and artistically minded, he carved wooden canes and crafted paper fans that he sold in the street. In his free time, he continued to read. He read legal texts, French novels, biographies of U.S. presidents, and the Filipino literature emerging in that period.

With independence movements cascading across the globe, the long-running imperial order was in precarious, tantalizing flux. The Americans had toppled the first domino, the French following close behind, then the Haitians, the Serbs, and soon Spain's colonies up and down the New World were unraveling the empire Madrid had maintained for three centuries. By the second half of the nineteenth century, Spain's global holdings had been whittled down to the far-flung islands of Cuba, Puerto Rico, Guam, Marianas, and the Philippines.

By the time Bonifacio reached his twenties, subversive writings had begun to circulate through the archipelago. Marcelo del Pilar published *Dasalan at Tocsohan*, a mock prayer book with satirical litanies such as a rendering of the Ten Commandments that decreed "Thou shalt not die without having sufficient funds for a funeral." *El Progreso de Filipinas*, written by lawyer Gregorio Sancianco, detailed the racist tax system that exempted Spaniards, the corrupt economy that funneled riches to a small group of landowners without incentivizing technological development, and the backward education system that prioritized the memorization of prayers at the expense of all other knowledge. Led by Rizal, the Ilustrados called not for independence but for equal rights as a province of Spain, legislative representation in Madrid, and deeper assimilation into the motherland.

But Rizal's pursuit of incremental reform was plenty subversive enough to get him in trouble. Three days after La Liga Filipina's founding, colonial authorities arrested him and banished him to Dapitan, in the northeast corner of Mindanao. He lay low there, opening a school, running a medical clinic, cultivating coffee and cacao he learned to grow from manuals about American agriculture. La Liga Filipina's inaugural meeting would be its last.

Into the void stepped Andres Bonifacio, who moved with more urgency than the Ilustrados he admired. With the voices of the colonial resistance mostly sequestered in Spain or exiled elsewhere, he founded his own group, the Katipunan, for the purpose of orchestrating an armed rebellion.

THE SPANISH EMPIRE was vulnerable, clashing with rivals all over the world and in deepening debt, having lost its lucrative American territories. To raise revenues, colonial authorities planted the cash crops of the day. As the Industrial Revolution drove up the price of commodities, tobacco and sugar plantations supplanted rice fields on the Islands, creating a growing demand for workers, who were paid meagerly and treated harshly. Some peasants formed rebel groups, others joined Catholic-based sects led by charismatic preachers who combined indigenous traditions with biblical teachings. By 1895, Spain was struggling to contain a revolution in Cuba. Rival powers circled like vultures.

Bonifacio traveled to rural villages, gaining support from rebels, sect leaders, tenant farmers who'd lost land to Spanish claims, and Catholics who considered the colonial government a common enemy after the governor executed three friars on false charges of organizing a military insurrection. At clandestine Katipunan meetings deep in the San Mateo

Mountains, in the cave where Bernardo Carpio was said to be held, the revolutionaries spoke in code, wore masks, and signed oaths with blood pricked from their arms. Initiation rites included a series of questions about the condition of the Philippines in the past, present, and future, to which a member answered that Filipino people were happy before colonization, then brainwashed by the friars, but would eventually overthrow the unjust Spanish rule. One of the group's passwords was "Rizal."

Four years after meeting his hero, Andres Bonifacio sent an emissary to visit José Rizal on Mindanao, requesting his help raising money from Filipino aristocrats to fund a revolt. Rizal thought it was still too soon for an uprising and declined to support it. Instead, he sought to get himself in better graces with the government so that he could one day return to Manila. He volunteered to serve as a doctor for the Spanish army fighting revolutionaries in Cuba, where a yellow fever outbreak hampered the colonial forces.

Bonifacio pushed on with his plan anyway. Katipunan stole guns from Spanish arsenals, sharpened bolos, and crafted spears. The Ilustrados Bonifacio couldn't persuade with rhetoric, he coerced with fear: he leaked to police fake Katipunan membership rolls listing the names of rivals who deemed him too extreme. After a friar tipped off colonial authorities that the Katipunan were printing and distributing revolutionary pamphlets, loyalist vigilantes lynched Indios, soldiers suffocated hundreds of prisoners in Manila by blocking the cell's ventilation shaft with a rug, and the government arrested and executed thirteen Filipinos of prominent local standing. On August 29, 1896, Bonifacio declared war on Spain and launched the rebellion.

A week later, Rizal boarded a ship for Spain, a stopover en route to Cuba. When the ship docked in Barcelona, authorities arrested him on charges of plotting rebellion. Imprisoned in Manila, he denied any involvement in an uprising he called "absurd and savage." Under threat of torture, fifteen witnesses falsely identified him as the mastermind.

Authorities cited as further evidence the Katipunan's use of "Rizal" as a password. His trial lasted less than a day, and he was executed by firing squad in a park near the waterfront. His death birthed the mythic hero he'd been unable to conjure in life, a founding martyr for Philippine nationhood.

More than a century later, that park is named after Rizal. Bronze statues freeze in time his final moment: his face in anguish, his bowler hat neatly at his feet, his back to the soldiers, who wear sombreros and point their rifles. You can tell the bullets have just pierced him from the way his shoulders are bowed back, his arms are half raised, and his head tilts upward, eyes to the sky. His body is mid-motion, poised to fall, though in that frozen moment you can't tell which way. What happens next is perhaps the most famous episode in Philippines history. Rizal had requested that he stand facing the firing squad so that he wouldn't die with his face in the dirt when the barrage toppled him over, but the authorities denied him because policy dictated that traitors be shot in the back. As Rizal falls, though, he twists his body and lands face up anyway, a final act of resistance that would come to symbolize his people's boundless hope for a better day.

VICTORY OVER SPAIN seemed imminent, even though Supremo Andres Bonifacio was a poor military strategist. Madrid's finances and firepower were stretched thin, simultaneously defending a Caribbean island an ocean away and a Pacific archipelago more than twice as distant. Filipino soldiers in the colonial army deserted, refusing to take up arms against their own people. Skilled rebel commanders across Luzon raided forts, defeated Spanish forces, and took control of provinces, while Bonifacio led failed attacks around the capital.

As chief of the Katipunan, Bonifacio expected that once the fighting was done and the new government in place he would naturally step in as president of the republic. But the war was dimming his star, especially in contrast to the rising commanders freeing towns from colonial rule. After a string of victories along the southern coast of Manila Bay, one of those young military heroes, Emilio Aguinaldo, named himself Generalissimo of the revolutionary forces and established a provisional ruling council for the new nation, declaring in a manifesto his intentions to create a government like "that of the United States," and adopting the motto of the French Revolution, "liberty, equality, and fraternity." In December 1896, with a delegation that included his brothers and his wife, Bonifacio traveled to Aguinaldo's hometown, Cavite, to discuss the delicate matter of command hierarchy.

In the Philippines, politics is a family matter. Bonifacio's wife, Gregoria de Jesus, had met him through her cousin, who was an early and trusted member of the Katipunan. When she was eighteen, Gregoria pledged into the revolutionary group, and after the Catholic Church wedding to please their parents, she and Andres married in a Katipunan ceremony. When colonial authorities inspected homes, Gregoria gathered Katipunan documents, hiding them under her seat while she drove a horse-drawn cart around town for as many hours as inspections persisted. After the couple's home burned down under mysterious circumstances, they went into hiding, operating under assumed names, finding shelter with any relatives willing to accept the risk. In her memoir, Gregoria recalled being "treated like an apparition, for, sad to say, from every house where I tried to get a little rest, I was driven away as if the people therein were mortally frightened."

Gregoria's father, an ex-colonial town governor from southern Luzon appointed to head the Katipunan's Cavite chapter, had informed Bonifacio of Aguinaldo's ploy, urging the Supremo to visit. Aguinaldo had been town governor of Cavite when Bonifacio recruited him into the Katipunan years earlier. Like him, Aguinaldo had quit school early to work, but his work entailed his aristocratic family's various businesses; he ran a farm and a sugar mill with his mother and a cattle-and-salt-dealing enterprise with his brothers. He knew his ancestral land well, and in battle his guerrilla army attacked Spanish forces at bridges, lured them into dense mangrove jungles pocked by deep ravines and swamps, funneled them into rice paddies that swallowed their boots, and killed them with bolos, wooden posts, and homemade rifles fashioned from water pipes and iron hoops. Widely admired for his military feats and trusted by his fellow Filipino gentry, Emilio Aguinaldo was well positioned to nudge out Andres Bonifacio.

The December 1896 convention in Cavite didn't go well for the Supremo from Tondo. Outnumbered on Aguinaldo's turf, he lost the vote to determine the revolution's leader. His faction deemed the results invalid, and Bonifacio stormed out, announcing his intention to maintain his own parallel government. Aguinaldo ordered his arrest, and that April, Bonifacio, his two brothers, and Gregoria were captured in a shootout that killed one of the brothers. Bonifacio and his other brother were found guilty of sedition in a makeshift trial and executed in a forest clearing. Gregoria was spared, at least in part due to the sexist assumption that she was merely a dutiful wife innocently following the men around her.

Like other Katipunan, she continued to serve the revolution, impelled by the desire "to see unfurled the flag of an independent Philippines," she wrote. She deciphered coded messages for commanders, learned to ride a horse and shoot a rifle, and marched with soldiers into battle, drinking "dirty water from mud-holes or the sap of vines which, though bitter, tasted delicious because of my intense thirst." She married a Katipunan commander who oversaw the northern lines, and they went on to have eight children.

Many of her kin, marked as enemies to both the Spanish crown and the Aguinaldo regime, fled the violent intrigue of southern Luzon, changing their names and moving to other islands. One of Gregoria's relatives reemerged in the Visayan province of Leyte under a new identity, and he built a new life while Aguinaldo's revolution played out. He chose the surname Tianco, got married, and had a son named Jose Tianco, my great-grandfather on Rizalina's side, a child born onto a land that was up for the taking.

ENTER AMERICA.

The sprawling nation of forty-six states, several western territories, and a mostly agrarian economy shared an enemy with Aguinaldo. Seeing an opportunity to access Cuba's lucrative sugar fields, the United States backed that island's rebels in their uprising against Spain, then declared war on the teetering European empire on April 21, 1898. Three days later, Aguinaldo, who'd been in Hong Kong planning his attack against Spanish forces in Manila, met with an American diplomat in Singapore to discuss an arms deal and a potential partnership. Thus was born a bond between the Islands and the States that lasts to this day.

The terms of the relationship were unclear at the start. Aguinaldo, who recounted his version of events in his memoir years later, envisioned the United States playing a similar role to that of France during the American Revolution, the same role the U.S. was taking up in Cuba at that very moment: wealthy benefactor to a foreign liberation movement aimed at weakening a common adversary. But the U.S. government took a different posture.

First, the state department rejected the initial deal Aguinaldo made with the American diplomat, for a trove of weapons to be paid on credit due after independence. Instead, on April 30, with Aguinaldo still in Hong Kong, U.S. Navy admiral George Dewey led an armada into Manila Bay and wiped out an underprepared Spanish fleet that expected the American attack farther north. Spain's Pacific military was so slow to react to the U.S. assault that its soldiers stationed in Guam, some 1,500 miles east of the Philippines, weren't aware they were at war with America when Dewey's ships had stopped by en route; the Spanish commander on the small island apologized for not issuing the traditional big-gun salute because they were out of ammo. Informed of the situation by the U.S. naval officers, the Spanish commanders on Guam quickly surrendered, and the island became America's first territory beyond the western hemisphere.

Three weeks later, shortly after the U.S. victory in the Battle of Manila Bay, the American navy escorted Aguinaldo across the South China Sea to Manila, where he met with Dewey aboard the fleet's flagship. In Aguinaldo's telling, the revolutionary expressed his plans for Philippine independence, and the admiral assured him that the United States was "rich in territory and money, and needed no colonies." The partners would fight in tandem, the islanders attacking from inland, the Americans storming the coast. Aguinaldo returned to his base camp in a remote mountain cave in Cavite, with a load of American-made rifles and news of the historic alliance. The United States "promised me all that I have asked for," he recalled telling his people, were "going to aid me in all things," and offered "protection as decisive as it is undoubtedly disinterested . . . considering us as sufficiently civilized and capable of governing for ourselves our unfortunate country." Aguinaldo studied America's constitution and found it claimed no rights to colonies. He might have interpreted the 1823 Monroe Doctrine as an assurance the United States had no interest in territory beyond the western hemisphere.

His right-hand man, Apolinario Mabini, was skeptical. Mabini, who'd been a founding member of Rizal's La Liga, was the brains of the revolution if Aguinaldo was the heart. It was Mabini who wrote the aspiring republic's constitution, establishing the first national legislature in Asia. Aguinaldo promoted no ideology but independence, a single-minded devotion he pursued with fury. Mabini warned Aguinaldo to slow down the independence plans until they were sure they knew America's intentions, but Aguinaldo went ahead with commissioning a national anthem, designing a flag, and writing up a declaration of independence that included a line placing the Philippine Republic "under the protection of the mighty and humane North American nation."

The Generalissimo scheduled the document's signing for June 12, at a ceremony in Malolos, just north of Manila. When Admiral Dewey declined his invitation, Aguinaldo set out to find any prominent American able to attend, eventually tracking down a retired American colonel who happened to be in Manila organizing a cinematograph exhibit. The retired colonel's signature joined ninety-seven Filipino names at the bottom of the declaration.

Aguinaldo's forces defeated Spanish troops across Luzon and the Visayas, and by July controlled most of the archipelago, while the U.S. Navy held the colonial government under siege in the old Spanish fortress, the Intramuros of central Manila. An American general proposed giving the revolutionaries artillery in exchange for control over part of Manila, as a base for U.S. troops and officials. Aguinaldo agreed, but the artillery never arrived. "Look what they are doing!" exclaimed Mateo Noriel Luga, Aguinaldo's highest ranking Visayan commander. "If we're not careful, they will soon be replacing our flags with their own all over the country!"

"They are our allies," Aguinaldo replied in a raised voice. "Always remember that."

Aguinaldo again met with American diplomat E. Spencer Pratt, the consul he'd first met in Singapore. According to the Generalissimo's recollection, Pratt reassured him that Washington supported his cause, saying, "As in Cuba, so in the Philippines. Even more so, if possible. Cuba is at our door, while the Philippines is ten thousand miles away." Aguinaldo requested a written statement of American support for independence. Pratt declined, calling their agreement "a solemn pledge" and adding that "the United States government is a very honorable, very just, and very powerful government."

Three months into the Manila siege, as the Intramuros ran out of food and clean water, Cuban and American forces defeated Spain in the Caribbean. After a single barrage that killed ten American soldiers in Manila—the first overseas U.S. combat deaths—Madrid prepared to negotiate terms for full surrender. Communicating through the British and Belgian consuls, Admiral Dewey and colonial governor Fermín Jáudenes agreed to hold a sham battle, so that Spain could exit honorably. As Jáudenes said to Belgian consul Édouard André, he would submit only "to white people, never to niggers."

Dewey didn't inform Aguinaldo, nor most American officers, about this scripted finale. A small group of captains were to lob some shells into an unoccupied patch of land, intentionally missing Spanish troops and city buildings. But the captains hadn't looped in their soldiers, and one platoon was so competent they corrected their captain's apparent miscalculation on target coordinates and landed several direct hits. Upon seeing Americans storming the city, Filipino soldiers eagerly joined the advance, and though a white flag hung over an Intramuros wall, panicked Spanish soldiers opened fire, and the resulting exchange left forty-nine Spanish and six American soldiers dead. Aguinaldo was barred from attending the surrender ceremony. Thus concluded the Spanish-American War.

On January 23, 1899, Emilio Aguinaldo was inaugurated as first president of the Philippine Republic, Asia's first democracy. Mabini was secretary of foreign affairs and head of the cabinet.

Two weeks later, the terms of Spain's surrender were negotiated in Paris, a location agreed upon by Washington and Madrid. The defeated empire maintained its refusal to engage with Filipinos, a demand the United States accepted, rejecting Aguinaldo's request to participate. White men decided the archipelago's fate. The resulting treaty gave the United States possession of Guam, Puerto Rico, and Cuba for free and the Philippines for $20 million.

American troops remained in Manila. Aguinaldo and Mabini weighed their options: the certain bloodshed of war with a new imperial power, against the prospect of acquiescing in hopes the new rulers would be more benign than the last. Foreign Secretary Mabini advised that the evidence suggested the United States was no more benevolent than any European power, what with all those promises they'd broken in just the past year, not to mention the caste system they imposed on their own citizens. He had seen enough to conclude that America "hates the colored race with a mortal hatred."

PHILIPPINE PRESIDENT EMILIO AGUINALDO, facing imminent war with the United States in 1898: "I have a clear conscience that I have endeavored to avoid it at all costs, using my utmost efforts to preserve friendship with the army of occupation, despite frequent humiliation and many sacrificed rights."

U.S. admiral George Dewey, at a 1902 congressional hearing, claiming the Philippine Declaration of Independence that Aguinaldo and ninety-seven others signed in 1898 came as a surprise to him: "I attached so little importance to this proclamation that I did not even cable its contents to Washington but forwarded it through the mails. I never dreamed that they wanted independence."

The white American soldier who fired the first shot, returning to base after killing two Filipinos who taunted him in the dark—mockingly saying "Alto!" every time he shouted "Halt!"—while he was on patrol: "Line up, fellows, the nigger was in here all through these lines."

Teddy Roosevelt, in a speech in New York City while campaigning for governor in 1898, on America's opportunity to expand its empire across the Pacific: "We are face to face with our destiny. . . . For us is the life of action, of strenuous performance of duty; let us live in the harness, striving mightily; let us rather run the risk of wearing out than rusting out."

U.S. president William McKinley, in a speech in Iowa in 1898, on what America encountered while fulfilling its "duty" to live up to "the trust that civilization puts upon us": "territory that sometimes comes to us when we go to war in a holy cause."

McKinley, in an 1898 proclamation describing the strategy to civilize the new subjects across the Pacific: "one of benevolent assimilation."

McKinley, in an 1899 White House meeting with five Methodist Episcopal clergymen, on why Philippine natives would benefit from U.S. rule: "They were unfit for self-government, and they would soon have anarchy and misrule over there worse than Spain's was."

McKinley, to the clergymen, on the United States' ultimate purpose in the archipelago (which had been mostly Catholic for three centuries by that time): "to educate the Filipinos and uplift and Christianize them, and by God's grace do the very best we could do by them."

McKinley, at a banquet in Boston in 1899, on how "these remote peoples" from "that group of islands" would feel about U.S. actions in the long run: "whose children shall for ages bless the American republic because it emancipated and redeemed their fatherland, and set them in the pathway of the world's best civilization."

U.S. postmaster general Charles Emory Smith, speaking after McKinley at the banquet: "Lincoln emancipated four million beings, McKinley uplifted ten million into new light and freedom."

Writer Rudyard Kipling, in his 1899 poem "The White Man's Burden: The United States and the Philippine Islands," on the distant people white men were obligated to civilize: "new-caught, sullen peoples, half devil and half child."

Teddy Roosevelt, in his letter accepting the Republican Party's nomination for vice president in 1900, on what would happen to Filipinos if Aguinaldo ruled the country: "They would simply be put at the mercy of a syndicate of Chinese half-breeds."

William Howard Taft, the first American governor general of the Philippines, coining a nickname for the island people who, he estimated, would need a century "to develop anything resembling Anglo-Saxon political principles and skills": "Our little brown brothers."

U.S. secretary of state William Day, who objected to annexation of the Philippines over what America had foolishly taken responsibility for: "eight or nine millions of absolutely ignorant and many degraded people."

U.S. senator Benjamin Tillman of South Carolina, on the downside of taking the Philippines as a colony: "the injection into the body politic of the United States . . . [of] that vitiated blood, that debased and ignorant people."

U.S. secretary of war Elihu Root—who went on to win a Nobel Peace Prize, supported annexation of the archipelago, and believed colonized Filipinos should have the same rights as Americans—on why he believed the arrangement should fall short of admittance into the union: "Statehood for Filipinos would add another serious problem to the one we have already. The negroes are a cancer in our body politic, a source of constant difficulty, and we wish to avoid developing another such problem."

U.S. senator Albert Beveridge of Indiana, who supported colonizing the Philippines, on why the United States should commit to long-term sovereignty rather than furnish a path to independence: "What alchemy will change the Oriental quality of their blood, and set the self-governing currents of the American pouring through their Malay veins?"

U.S. senator Henry Cabot Lodge of Massachusetts, at the 1900 Republican convention, asserting that the United States should make "no hypocritical pretense" over its interest in the Philippines: "Greatest of all markets is China. Our trade there is growing by leaps and bounds. Manila, the prize of war, gives us inestimable advantages in developing that trade."

Writer Mark Twain, quoted by the *New York Herald* in 1900, on his conclusion that the United States had gone to the Philippines "to conquer, not to redeem," thus violating a "duty" to "let them deal with their own domestic questions in their own way": "I am opposed to having the eagle put its talons on any other land."

U.S. major general William Rufus Shafter, who was awarded the Medal of Honor for Civil War heroics and oversaw supply lines for forces in the Philippines, speculating on the costs and virtues of the mission: "It may be necessary to kill half of the Filipinos in order that the remaining half of the population may be advanced to a higher plane of life than their present semi-barbarous state affords."

An anonymous U.S. congressman, speaking to a newspaper reporter after visiting the frontlines: "Our soldiers took no prisoners, they kept no records; they simply swept the country, and wherever and whenever they could get ahold of a Filipino they killed him."

A marching song of American soldiers, sometime before or after they set fire to nipa huts in villages they suspected of housing revolutionaries: "Damn, damn, damn, the Filipinos! . . . Civilize them with a Krag!"

Anonymous American soldiers, in letters home from the frontlines: "no cruelty is too severe for these brainless monkeys, who can appreciate no sense of honor, kindness, or justice" . . . "I am in my glory when I can sight some dark skin and pull the trigger" . . . "blow every nigger into heaven" . . . "until the niggers are killed off like the Indians."

"Colored Citizens of Boston," in a statement published in the *Boston Post* in 1899, declaring their "solemn protest against the present unjustified invasion by American soldiers in the Philippine Islands": "While the rights of colored citizens in the South, sacredly guaranteed them by the amendment of the Constitution, are shamefully disregarded; and while the frequent lynching of Negroes who are denied a civilized trial are a reproach to the republican government, the duty of the President and the country is to reform these crying domestic wrongs and not attempt the civilization of alien peoples by powder and shot."

An anonymous Black American soldier in the Philippines, when a white bystander asked, "What are you coons doing here?": "We've come to take up the white man's burden."

So BEGAN THE PROCESS of Americanizing the Philippines.

The archipelago was well-suited for a budding empire's imperial ambitions. Unlike Vietnam, Thailand, and Indonesia, its people inherited no shared precolonial culture to unify them in resistance. Rather, some 350 years under Spanish occupation had furnished a class system topped by European-blooded landowners who admired the West, had much to lose, and were open to compromise.

To secure support and funding for his war against the United States, Aguinaldo courted wealthy families, promising to protect their holdings and offering official positions even to those who had collaborated with Spain. He turned over property owned by the clergy to allies while offering no restitution to farmers whose ancestral land had been taken by the Spanish. He didn't lower the tax rate for poor people, nor the rent for tenant farmers. He enacted no programs to develop agriculture on the vast terrain left vacant by colonial resettlement programs. When railroad workers protested low pay, Aguinaldo broke the strike, and in exchange the railroad company granted his staff free rides and his government a 10 percent share of profits.

Aguinaldo had only enough guns for half of his troops, who fought mostly with bolos and booby traps, quick strikes in the dense jungle before disappearing into the nearest village, blending in among the locals. The Americans countered by clearing out villages in Batangas, Laguna, Cavite, and Tayabas (now called Quezon City), poisoning the wells, killing the livestock, burning the homes, and moving residents into hamlets that operated as detention camps. Rice production across the archipelago dropped by 75 percent over the course of the war. Around 90 percent of carabaos, the backbone of Philippine farmwork, were wiped out. At least 100,000 Philippine civilians in the hamlets died from disease or from malnutrition.

The Generalissimo's military strategy was premised on withstanding an extended stretch of suffering: a guerrilla campaign that gained no ground but generated enough brutal damage for the American public to demand a retreat from this distant island chain President McKinley couldn't locate on a map before 1898.

The masses did not flock to the Generalissimo. Pockets of indigenous tribes maintained their sovereignty. Once, while fleeing American forces in the mountains of northern Luzon, Aguinaldo's division was attacked by a group of Igorot hunters, who threw spears at the trespassers crossing through their land. More peasants flocked to local religious leaders. A few barangays cast their lot with the new colonizers even before the war was done. Residents of San Pablo in southern Luzon presented U.S. troops with a homemade American flag; when Aguinaldo got word, he ordered the mayor's execution.

By 1901, two years into the clash with the United States and five years after the fighting with Spain began, Aguinaldo had come around to the realization that his quest for independence was doomed. His army had shrunk, his supplies dwindled, and he was without two of his top generals. One, Gregorio del Pilar, who'd gained notoriety early in the revolution for stealing Spanish weapons by masquerading as a woman, was killed in battle leading a rear defense that allowed Aguinaldo to escape into the mountains. The other, Antonio Luna, a revered military leader who designed the guerrilla tactics that gave the poorly armed Filipinos a fighting chance, was assassinated in an ambush organized by a revolutionary faction that favored surrendering to American sovereignty.

In February 1901, Aguinaldo sent a courier with a message informing American commanders he was willing to negotiate a peace treaty. The courier was captured by U.S. forces and, facing the prospect of water cure torture, disclosed the Generalissimo's location. Aguinaldo was still awaiting a response from U.S. officials a few days later when one of his top generals showed up at his mountain hideaway with a dozen American prisoners. Before Aguinaldo realized what was happening, the fake prisoners and their turncoat captors gunned down his security forces and cornered him in his cave. The dramatic maneuver so captivated the American public that Thomas Edison made a film about it.

Teddy Roosevelt, elevated to the U.S. presidency after McKinley's

1901 death, declared victory in the Philippine war on July 4, 1902, though some Filipino commanders continued to fight on for another decade. In speeches, Roosevelt called these holdouts "bandits and robbers." In the view of Roosevelt and other American imperialists, the Philippine Islands represented a natural progression in the nation's westward expansion. In speeches about the war, Roosevelt likened Filipinos to the Apaches and Comanches clashing with American soldiers on the Great Plains, a series of battles that had provided combat experience for many of the U.S. troops and officers deployed to the Philippines. But the Filipinos, familiar with colonial occupation and resigned to its inevitability, were easier to pacify. One common attitude held that America was the best option among the gauntlet of empires waiting to pounce, that indefinite war was far more likely than imminent independence. Under France, Vietnamese people labored in rice fields under brutal conditions, and nearly seven hundred suspected dissidents were executed without trial. Under British rule, enforced on the ground by a private shipping company, around a hundred thousand people in India were executed for civil disobedience.

More interested in gaining a reliable ally than a mass of foreigners to permanently rule, the United States offered a different sort of proposal: a full-ride colonial apprenticeship in democracy until the young Philippine government was stable enough to enter the world stage. No timeline was set at first, as the U.S. unrolled its promise of benevolent assimilation: benevolence through investment, imports, and military protection, in exchange for willing assimilation into America's racial caste system— unlike European powers, the United States prohibited marriage between white and nonwhite people in its colonies. The occupation would last forty-four years.

As for Aguinaldo, he returned to Cavite with his wife and son after surrendering. Whenever he was in public, he donned a black tie to mourn his short-lived nation. He advocated for immediate independence, turning his home into a flag-draped monument to the First Philippine Republic, but his militancy fell out of favor with the ascendant class of political operators who preferred a more tempered, cooperative approach. Aguinaldo faded from public life for some years before reemerging in 1935 as a candidate for president in the Philippines' first general election—a final checkpoint for the commonwealth before an independence date set for 1945.

Aguinaldo's opponent, Manuel Quezon, had been his secretary during the war with America. After the war, while Aguinaldo retreated to Cavite, Quezon took his ambitions to the neoclassical halls of the brand-new Philippine Legislature Building in Manila, where he became the commonwealth's longest-serving senator, rising to power on a malleable platform that balanced a demand for independence with a commitment to calculated patience. Simultaneously negotiating with U.S. officials and his fellow legislators, he led a campaign to extend American occupation, then later organized efforts to end it. He held his tongue when Henry Stimson, the American governor of the Philippine territory, informed him in a meeting that he doubted the Islands could handle self-governance anytime soon because of the "Malay tendency to backslide."

Due to a bout of tuberculosis, Quezon was unable to attend the 1934 meeting in Washington, D.C., where two of his most prominent allies reached a deal with the Americans for eventual independence. Fearing he'd get no credit for the historic achievement, Quezon voiced opposition to the agreement, stunning the allies who'd worked with him on shaping the terms. He slightly altered the proposal, with cosmetic changes he later admitted would seem "petty" and "small" one day "when the historian passes on what we have all said and done at this momentous period." He traveled to Washington to get the Americans to sign on to the minor edits, then returned to Manila with the bill that would set the Philippines on track to nationhood.

Months later, in September 1935, Quezon defeated Aguinaldo in a landslide.

I DON'T KNOW who my great-grandfather Jose Tianco voted for, or if he voted. Maybe he begrudged Aguinaldo the role he played in driving his father from Luzon. Maybe he bought into the promise of America, the empire he was born under. Maybe he couldn't bring himself to ride for Quezon because he inherited the revolutionary impulse that had pulled his father into his uncle Bonifacio's Katipunan. Or maybe all these political wranglings seemed irrelevant to the life he was trying to build away from the capital.

In his late teens, Jose Tianco had left the Visayas for a job opportunity in Mindanao. The United States, in its effort to gain allegiance from the ruling class of the southern island, promised military support for local Catholics' ongoing clashes with Muslim rebels, who were continuing their long-running resistance to foreign sovereignty. Jose signed on to the colonial police force in northern Mindanao, where he traded fire with Moros in the jungles around Lake Lanao. He settled down in Dansalan, where he married my great-grandmother, Consorcia Orteza. They had six children. Third eldest was my grandmother Rizalina, who was eight when Quezon was elected, born into a generation indoctrinated in American mythology.

While the Spanish sought to win souls with churches, the Americans sought to win minds with classrooms. During the first five years of U.S. occupation, the number of schools on the archipelago tripled and more than a thousand American teachers showed up to teach in them, lured by higher wages than offered at home. U.S. education officials deemed it impractical to have to train American teachers in so many local dialects, so they set English as the language of instruction. By 1915, more people in the Philippines could read, write, and speak English than any other single language.

On both sides of the ocean, the American mission of benevolent assimilation seemed a more honorable strategy than the blunt brutality the European colonizers employed. The America Rizalina knew built schools, roads, railways, ports, dams, and irrigation facilities. From 1900 to 1920, the Philippine literacy rate rose from 20 percent to 50 percent, the highest in Southeast Asia, and the population doubled, thanks to vaccination programs, sewage systems, and an influx of medical supplies.

American cornflakes, canned milk, refrigerators, gramophones, and automobiles were now available for purchase. American architects designed plazas, hotels, and gabled houses with big lawns. Tourists flocked in. Manila became a tropical paradise for the newly arriving Americans, a waterfront metropolis where everybody spoke English, dollars went a long way, and a host of social clubs—the Elks Club, Army Navy Club, Manila Club, University Club, Columbia Club, Polo Club—catered to Western appetites for golf, polo, tennis, horseback riding, and cabaret. The only Filipinos allowed inside were servers. "Manila is the most thoroughly typical American city I have ever visited outside the United States," Edith Stephens, a newspaper editor visiting from Missouri, wrote in a 1908 *Manila Times* column. "I think every American who can, should visit these islands."

To a population suddenly showered with development after centuries of colonial negligence, the deal might not have felt like a golden handcuff. But the empire's end of the bargain included a growing market for American goods and a cheap source of valuable resources. The United States established a monopoly on Philippine imports and served as a near-exclusive customer for most exports, creating an economic dependency that continues today. Like the Spanish before them, the Americans devoted Philippine farmland to commodity crops—hemp, sugar, and tobacco—that had narrow use domestically but sold in high volume for high prices on the international market. Philippine industry was designed to fill specific American demands: factories sewed buttons onto American-made shirts and cut fibers for American-made hats. American entrepreneurs invested, and Filipino landowners gained further wealth. When World War I hit, few benefited as much as the coconut barons of Zamboanga in western Mindanao, for coconut oil was an essential ingredient in explosives. Rice and corn fields dwindled. The social structure that had held for three centuries under Spain stayed in place with the United States in charge.

Despite all the new classrooms, just one-sixth of students reached fourth grade, and only the most privileged continued studying beyond primary school. The rest dropped out to work. One top U.S. education official, Frank White, who by all accounts seemed to take genuine interest in the well-being of the little brown brothers, changed the curriculum in some rural provinces to focus on "useful occupations" like basketry, embroidery, pottery, and raising chickens, rather than "impractical" subjects like reading, writing, and arithmetic. The number of schools shrank with the years.

As the daughter of a well-paid civil servant, Rizalina was assured a place in the educated class. At her school, a few miles' walk from her home, she learned the story of America as told by America, a version that hardened into common understanding across the archipelago and elsewhere around the world.

The story had some holes. America is an unreliable narrator. Its snapshots of indelible moments and heroic feats tell of an idealistic nation's upward march toward equality, evidence that the order of the world is just. In U.S. history textbooks, the narrative climaxes sometime before the present. For children of today, the dramatic payoff comes with the election of the first Black president in 2008. During my childhood, the civil rights movement stood as evidence that America is a land where good defeats evil. In my mom's day, it was World War II that affirmed American exceptionalism. For my grandmother, the Civil War was the turning point in the great nation's moral arc.

In her classroom in Mindanao, she learned about George Washington's cherry tree (evidence of the Founding Father's honesty) and Paul Revere's midnight ride (evidence of the nation's collective spirit) but not about Crazy Horse's resistance to the American invaders (evidence of the genocide) or the 1882 Chinese Exclusion Act (evidence of who isn't welcome in the land of the free). She learned about Ellis Island's gateway to the United States in New York City but not Angel Island's detention center in San Francisco. She learned what children in America were learning. The teachers used regular American textbooks at first, though by the time Rizalina began her schooling, the material had been tailored to accommodate cultural differences: sample sentences for grammar lessons replaced "Mary" with "Maria" and removed references to snow, which pupils had never seen.

Her classmates were nearly all mestizo, the children of Dansalan's professional set. One boy in her class, Manuel Concepcion, was particularly impressive. Studious and quick-witted, he swiftly defeated peers in playground arguments and constantly charmed teachers with his earnest enthusiasm for whatever task was at hand. While Rizalina, no less studious, scored the highest grades in math, Manuel pulled away from the pack in language arts. For one assignment, he recited the Gettysburg Address with such passion and fidelity that Rizalina wondered how Lincoln's rendition could have been any better.

He lived near her, in a house overlooking Lake Lanao, and she often walked home with him, his younger brother Tomas, and his older sister Caridad down the neat dirt paths winding through jungle, which resonated with the chirping of birds and crickets hidden among leaves that rustled in the mountain breeze. Rizalina and Manuel developed a close friendship that in adolescence blossomed into much more. As history would have it, the descendants of revolutionaries and sultans fell in love inside a school with a U.S. flag flying out front.

BY THE TIME our barangay settled in the United States half a century later, the empire was corroding, though that might not have been clear to us amid the rising stock markets and Cold War victory. The shuttered factories, the Vietnam War atrocities, the blight devastating disinvested communities revealed widening cracks in the nation's foundation. Maybe we should have seen even back then, as we booked our flights and packed our possessions, that the ideals we so admired, of inclusion and equality, weren't guiding principles but one side in a long-running battle for America's soul. But reality doesn't always slice through mythology.

We put our heads down and worked, eager to prove we belonged. Uncle Spanky was sitting in a Filipino friend's car one afternoon when he noticed a stray job application form crumpled by his feet. It was for work loading airplane kitchens at San Francisco International Airport. "And then I said, 'What the heck, okay, I'll fill it up,' and then I sent it and forgot all about it," Spanky recalled. "I didn't think much about it until I get a letter telling me to report for my physical. I go, whoa, they got it."

Steady work had become harder to find in Vallejo. By then, fewer than 10,000 people had jobs at the Mare Island Navy Shipyard, a fifth as many as during World War II, when Filipino immigrants and Black people from the South flocked to the base for work building submarines. Unemployment in the area was rising quickly, from 5 percent in 1990 to 9 percent in 1993; in 1996, the shipyards closed. From 1995 to 1997, the median price of a house in Vallejo dropped from $140,000 to $119,000. Unwittingly, our family had stepped into the country just as crime was hitting record highs in cities across the country, the crack cocaine epidemic was peaking, the driving force of the economy was shifting decisively from manufacturing to the financial sector, and wealth inequality was widening to levels not seen since the end of the nineteenth century. Over the three decades following the 1965 immigration bill, the United States had lowered tax rates for wealthy people, cut funding from social services, and increased spending on police, prisons, and military—a formula designed to maintain the order in place since the nation's founding. In the Vallejo hills, the mansions sparkled like daytime stars; the lowland bungalows nestled anonymously in a maze of streets.

Less than a year after my family bought the house, burglars broke in, ransacking the place and stealing the big-screen television. Abandoned cars began to litter the surrounding blocks. A park nearby served as a gathering spot for the Crestside Crips, who kicked back on the benches and slides in their blue ball caps, blue Starter Jackets, blue Air Jordan IIIs, IVs, and Vs. Vallejo's per capita murder rate was among the highest in the nation, and every so often the nightly news showed yellow-taped crime scenes at intersections and parking lots Spanky and Ging drove past on the regular.

"It was scary," Auntie Ging told me years later. "Your neighbors don't have jobs. You're really worried about how your life would be."

The American bargain required hard work and savvy, a navigational understanding that couldn't come fast enough. To survive the landing, my elders clung to their ancient wisdom. We needed every edge we could get. Mirrors faced entryways and beds never intersected with doorways, to keep the feng shui on point. If we bit our tongue or coughed from something caught in our throat, it meant somebody was thinking about us, and to find out who, someone around us had to randomly pick a number, which corresponded to the first letter of the culprit's first name, sparking a flurry of guesses and analysis. On New Year's Eve, we pulled open drawers to purge malevolent forces, and at the stroke of midnight my cousins and I jumped up and down to trigger a growth spurt.

The elders' understanding of their new country developed through a prism of pragmatism as well. They quickly accumulated shorthand. Chinese people were insular and distrustful of other immigrants. Neighborhoods with lots of Black people were dangerous. White people only liked us if we were jolly. Mexican people didn't bother us as long as we didn't bother them. The harder you worked, the more money you made.

Gathered round the kitchen counter, the elders traded notes, compared experiences, concocted. Rizalina described the tax breaks people qualified for if they owned a business. My mom recounted the bus routes she used to take me to the library, as she didn't have a driver's license. Ging and Spanky lectured on regional traffic patterns.

To beat rush hour traffic, they were on the road no later than five thirty a.m. Though Spanky had recently purchased an old custard-yellow Nissan, which Ging nicknamed Buttercup, the household's San Francisco commuters—Spanky, Ging, Jed, Rizalina, and baby Lauren—all piled into Blue Angel, to preserve gas. Ging sipped a Coke for the caffeine boost, rolled down the window for the enlivening slap of cool air, and lit a cigarette if she still couldn't dispel the pull of drowsiness. Rizalina recited the rosary under her breath, rolling the pearl beads between her angular fingers, often reaching the final set of Hail Marys around the time Blue Angel reached Emeryville, where the traffic thickened to a painful crawl.

But this too was a grand American tradition to join, the daily commute a confirmation that our family's choices aligned with the wisdom of American convention, its formula for success. We were a droplet in a mighty river that powered the world's dominant economy. If there were any doubts on those long mornings, inching up the queue for the right to chip in to the public coffer, they tended to dissolve once Blue Angel accelerated past the Bay Bridge toll booth and the traffic cleared, the pace a smooth 55 miles per hour over the water, past Treasure Island, with the mesmerizing San Francisco skyline drawing closer, an undulating checkerboard of wood-framed Victorians flanked by gleaming glassy towers that loomed like canyon walls as the highway entered the city.

Ging dropped off Rizalina downtown, then headed south on the highway to the airport to drop off Spanky, then turned back north to the Visitacion Valley neighborhood, where she dropped Lauren off at a babysitter's house ten blocks from Our Lady of the Visitacion, the Catholic elementary school where she and Jed would spend their day. Next to it loomed the Geneva Towers housing projects along a stretch of lumber yards, recycling centers, and boxy stucco houses. On a good day, if she timed everything right, Ging reached Visitacion Valley in under two hours, leaving her and Jed a full forty-five minutes to nap in the car.

No matter how meticulous she was, Auntie Ging couldn't plan for everything, of course. One foggy and drizzly afternoon in October 1989, she had a stomachache worse than any she'd ever experienced. As soon as school got out, she was eager to get home, but a series of inconveniences converged against her. Jed's soccer practice ran long. Traffic was backed up because of the World Series game at nearby Candlestick Park. The stomachache persisted; Ging had to go to the bathroom. Spanky suggested they make a pit stop at his friend Jun's apartment in South San Francisco.

Just as they were about to leave the apartment, the ground started shaking—a growling, violent rumble that sent everybody under the dining table, knocked frames off walls, and toppled the glass cabinet in a burst of terrifying chimes as ceramic plates and champagne glasses crashed in the flickering light.

Nobody in the apartment was injured in the earthquake. With the power out and the phones dead, neighbors gathered outside, as sirens and car alarms filled the air. Somebody said that part of the Bay Bridge had collapsed.

"You know, if we didn't go to Jun's house, we could have been there," Spanky said to Ging.

The drive home was slow and silent, past sunken pavement and collapsed structures barely visible in the shadows, a long looping trek through the city, over the Golden Gate Bridge, and around San Pablo Bay. After five hours on the road, Blue Angel reached the lights of Vallejo, which wasn't damaged by the quake. A blessing in disguise to be so far from San Francisco.

"I think the Lord was with us, you know," Auntie Ging told me years later. "He knew how to lead us away from the Bay Bridge. It was divine intervention. We would have gone through the bridge if I didn't have that stomachache. It's rare that I have a stomachache in the afternoon. It's a miraculous thing. After that until now, I never had a stomachache."

Optimism was our most potent survival tactic. From that view, misfortune was just God advising you to take another path, and there were plenty available in America.

In 1992, Rizalina and Auntie Lyn moved to Miami to try to start a balikbayan box business for Filipino people who wanted to send clothes, toys, and food back to the Islands (the Bay Area market was too crowded). Uncle Bobby joined them, finding work as a busboy at a resort. Their short sojourn was punctuated by somebody snatching Auntie Lyn's purse from the front seat of her car while she was pumping gas and her sons were sitting in the back. When the business didn't pan out after a few months, they returned to Vallejo, where Lyn saved money from a teaching job, got an apartment in San Mateo, and bought a hotel gift shop nearby. Rizalina moved in with her and worked the register. Uncle Bobby worked at KFC for a year, then got hired at a framing company run by a Filipino American but was laid off after two years. Following a flier promoting a "business opportunity," he fell into a pyramid-scheme gig selling aloe vera juice, and put $1,500 worth of product on his credit card. "It tasted terrible," Jed recalled. "All I remember is the kitchen being full of these yellow jugs and I'd be thirsty and I wouldn't drink it. I want something other than water but this is all we fuckin' have! It just fuckin' sat there." Aunties and uncles were supportive customers, pretty much his only patrons, and their purchases mitigated Bobby's losses. He soon found work at another framing company, then at a warehouse. With his savings, he bought a black Camaro. When he stepped out of the car in his stringer tank tops and colorful bandannas, people sometimes mistook him for the muscular Oakland A's slugger José Canseco.

Whatever struggles were whispered in Tagalog in the kitchen conversations, I wasn't aware of them. The elders kept us insulated from the troubles. In the evenings, as they returned from work, the living room was a din of laughter, long meals, cable TV movies, and Scrabble and Monopoly contests that trained our skills in English and capitalism. My cousins and I often played hide-and-seek, and as we scurried around the house, tucking into closets and ducking under tables, we internalized lessons not much different from what our immigrant parents were encountering on their forays beyond our walls: understand the landscape, blend in, stay quiet, block out the discomfort, and hunker down for the long haul—victory comes only after a while but defeat can strike at any moment, so take nothing for granted. On summer weekends, we played basketball in the driveway while Uncle Spanky and Uncle Bobby grilled burgers and hot dogs over a charcoal flame on the backyard patio, and when the sky turned purple and our stomachs were full, we roasted marshmallows on wooden skewers as the Marine World fireworks splashed high into the night. To Jed, the bustling house was reminiscent of those tropic summers he often thought about. "It felt like having the Philippines in Vallejo," Jed said. "Like having Scout Reyes in Vallejo."

As I approached kindergarten age, my mom realized we couldn't keep drifting along within a holding pattern of tourist visas. Her son was a U.S. citizen, and our family's barangay in the States was stabilizing. She decided to petition for a green card, and it was approved.

At the time, her motive was merely to give me a childhood encased in the love of our tight-knit family. It would take years for the country's mythology to seep into her mind, but once it did, she held that faith as strongly as any other. "I'm happy that you grew up in the United States," she said to me years later, when I asked her if she wished our lives had played out any differently. "The best country in the whole world."

BEFORE SPANKY SETTLED in the States, back when he was visiting Ging and Jed in San Francisco every December, the country seemed almost a fantasy to him. "It was like going to la-la land," Spanky told me years later. "Going to another dimension, another world . . . Everything I see, wow, beautiful. I couldn't see the dregs of life. I couldn't even see garbage. I couldn't see homelessness. No, all I saw was, wow, what a beautiful place."

Those passing years were marked by moments missed. First words, first steps. One visit, when Spanky woke early, expecting to prepare breakfast for seven-year-old Jed and walk him to school as he had the previous year, he found his son at the kitchen table with two plates of warm Pop-Tarts, ready to leave in fifteen minutes whether or not his father was up. Only then did Spanky hear about the incident several months earlier, when Rizalina had slept through her alarm and gone into a panic when she woke and couldn't find Jed, sprinting to the school in her slippers only to find him calmly sitting on the playground bench with his friends. After that, Ging and Rizalina had given him a key and let him go to school on his own, and Rizalina returned to her job at the accounting firm. By the time Spanky got back to town, Jed was on a first-name basis with the crossing guard.

Spanky didn't think about his move to America as a sacrifice but as a necessity. Once his film and television contracts were up, he would be with his family in the land of opportunity, which he would figure out once he got there.

Now he was here, with a job at the airport, handling the liquor carts for smaller commercial planes, squeezing past bodies in the frantic minutes before the boarding doors opened. He loaded and emptied as many as 180 planes a day. "It was taxing," he said. "It was heavy. I wasn't used to it." Many days, he worked sixteen-hour double shifts. The metal drawers of the carts bit into his fingers and palms. Some nights, his hands were still bloody when he got into his car for the fifty-mile drive home to Vallejo. He rolled his windows down to keep himself alert, chain-smoking Marlboro Reds that calmed his tense mind and strained body. One night, a hand on the wheel, the other hanging out the window, he stared ahead at the red rear-end lights up ahead, eyes blinking furiously in a fight to stay awake, choppy white lines stretching before him on the dark asphalt—

A piercing *HOOONNNKKKK* jolted him upright.

Eyes open again, the road veering away, concrete highway barrier suddenly dead ahead and closing fast, moment of panic, life flashing by, then a swerve to salvation, instinctive, back between the white lines to see his kids grow up, and now he was more awake than he'd ever been in his life.

More than once, Spanky thought about quitting. He thought about going back to the Islands, back to the movie sets, recording studios, adoring mobs, and household servers. "Sometimes while driving I'd think, why am I doing this? I'm not supposed to be doing this, but I'm doing it," he said. "But there was a small voice in the back of my head that said: Oh yeah you can do it. You lazy bum. It's about time you work."

OTHER BANDMATES left the Islands. Spanky's close friend Jun had been the drummer before moving to South San Francisco. Spanky's brother Roger, a vocalist, raised his kids in Seattle. Celso Llarina, a producer and guitarist, moved to Oslo. But the V and T in VST & Company, brothers Vic and Tito Sotto, stayed in the Philippines.

Vic still stars in movies and hosts television shows. Tito went into politics. First, vice mayor of Quezon City under President Corazon "Cory" Aquino, then senator under President Fidel Ramos, rising to senate majority leader under President Benigno "Noynoy" Aquino III, then senate president under President Rodrigo Duterte. His children, nieces, and nephews are actors, singers, local politicians. They live in luxury, and their family wealth grows.

THE FIRST TIME I asked my uncle Spanky if he ever regretted coming here was at our family Christmas party in 2016. "No," he said. He gestured at all my cousins and aunties and uncles, the whole clan gathered, eating and drinking and laughing on the couch, around the dining table, leaning against counters in the kitchen, filling every space. How else would he be here with all this family?

In moments of doubt, he thought of his children, who he believed would find more happiness in the United States, away from the constraints of the Philippines, where the rich lived in walled compounds and the poor in aluminum shacks, where his friends had thought he was a fool for not carrying a gun, where he had to pay bribes at the post office and airport. "Whereas here in the States? At least they leave you alone, to do your thing to the best of your ability," he said. "I don't know if I'd be able to give to them what they have now if it were in the Philippines."

The evidence lay before him. Here we all were still standing, still breaking bread as we had for three decades. No matter who hosted the Christmas gathering, its rhythms barely shifted over the years, as if we hadn't been attending a series of annual parties but a single continuous function broken by year-long intermissions. The flamboyant greetings each time the door swung open, the elders explaining the contents of the dishes as if we nieces and nephews had never tasted them before, the rice cooker steaming endlessly to keep up with demand, the drawn-out good-byes that stretched so long you might've thought the world was ending to-morrow, the path to the door packed with people in coats, clutching bags, conversing as if the party was just starting.

It was Auntie Mae who hosted that year, in her house overlooking the Bay in Marin County, north of San Francisco. My mom and I had driven up together in the afternoon, a honey-glazed ham and her famous buko salad in the trunk, but she'd run out of energy by sundown and headed home shortly after the gifts were opened. Her siblings, too, had called it a night just as my cousins and I were congregating in the kitchen for a third helping of food and a second wind of chatter. I remembered how our elders had once huddled in the kitchen in the waning hours of the festivities, their jubilance dissipating as they discussed family mat-ters in hushed Tagalog while we kids sat on the living room floor break-ing in our new toys. In those days we had to sing a song for the adults before we could open our gifts, but one year, without explanation, they stopped asking us to. Then envelopes of cash and gift cards replaced the wrapped boxes under the tree. Then we were giving gifts ourselves, modest at first but more impressive with each year. Reusable water bot-tles. Books. Designer backpacks. Warriors tickets.

We were far from wealthy but we were doing well, with college de-grees and stable careers. And before we could really understand what was happening, it was our hushed voices in the kitchen, assessing the state of affairs. But what to do with the knowledge that your comfort has come at the expense of your elders'?

It was for us, all their generation had done. They'd never expected it would be easy, but it turned out even harder than they imagined. The bills added up. Gas for the daily zigzags across the Bay. Tolls rising to six dollars per pass. Tuition for their children's Catholic elementary school. Mortgage. Food. Money lent to loved ones in need.

Ging and Spanky didn't have any savings in those early years. Their credit cards multiplied, and their debts rose. A few times, they had to borrow money from a priest at their church. A sense of precariousness hung over everything they were building.

"We weren't thinking of the misery," my auntie Ging told me one recent September afternoon, over salt-and-pepper shrimp in an empty Chinese restaurant in the south of the city, her voice rising and falling with her usual singsong enthusiasm. "We just didn't delve on it. We had to just . . . what do you call it? Trudging? Keep on trudging?"

I asked her if she ever considered going back to the Philippines.

"When I'm in church," she said, "just sitting by myself and meditating or thinking and relaxing and trying to smell the roses—it's like I seemed to be blocking my mind of all the challenges. I blocked it whenever we're faced with it. And then when I'm in church by myself that's when it hits me, and I feel so sorry for myself. I feel sorry for Lauren, I feel sorry for Jed." She paused, folded her hands, eyes off to the side, brows wrinkled. Like all her sisters, she'd inherited their mother's resolve and generosity. Nothing came before your duty to take care of your people.

"I wouldn't think of just giving up just like that. Our family is, *when the tough gets going the going gets tough.* We fall but we stand up quickly. It's in our blood to be proud. Proud of the way we carry ourselves, show ourselves to other people. Grandma"—my grandmother Rizalina—"taught us not to show how depressed you look. You have to save face. Show that you're pretending you're happy. Keep your hardships to yourself. We don't talk about it amongst each other. It's like a silent language. Be quiet. Keep our bad, stinky selves to ourselves and don't display it. Even Jed learned it. And Lauren. We learned how to keep to ourselves. Nobody else would know how miserable I would feel sometimes—when I don't care what happens to the house, I don't care what happens to my credit. Spanky, most of the time he would always put in a word or two. 'We can go back to the Philippines, Ging. If you want to go back, let's go back.'"

But they stayed, unconvinced any other place offered as bright a future for their children, leading our barangay through our American landing. Ging kept an eye on real estate listings. In 1994, she spotted a $700-a-month basement studio apartment in Visitacion Valley, near her school and not far from the airport, with just enough space for a small table, a twin-size bed, a fold-out futon, and a rolling clothes-rack. With fuel costs saved and commutes truncated, it was worth the price. On Sunday nights, Ging, Spanky, Jed, and Lauren would head out over the bridge, car filled with a week's worth of clothes and groceries, and on Friday evenings, they'd return to Vallejo for shortened weekends of backyard grilling, driveway hoops, and late-night movies in the crowded living room.

Two decades later, when I asked Uncle Spanky about those early years in the Vallejo house, he replied with a face of theatrical joy: "Wow," he said, "it's paradise."

CHAPTER 5

YOUNG COLONIST

By the time I began my life in the States, Jed was nine years deep in his learning process.

At his first school, in San Francisco's Richmond District, his classroom was mostly filled with white kids who lived in the city's picturesque neighborhoods and had enough pocket money to buy comic books. He'd hide his envy behind a mask of awe as he gazed at the *X-Men* and *Incredible Hulk* panels from over his friends' shoulders, pushing himself to read faster so that he finished the page before they turned it.

At his second school, in Visitacion Valley—where his mom taught and had him transferred to midway through third grade, to streamline the commute after the move to Vallejo—the kids around him were mostly Black, Mexican, and Filipino, along with a few Chinese, and they lived in parts of the city he'd known nothing about. Most of the kids who weren't Black were, like him, children of immigrants. He sometimes overheard them translating conversations between their parents and teachers. When his basketball coach picked up Jed's teammates from home for games at other schools, Jed rode along and got his first look at the Double Rock housing projects up the hill and the Potrero Hill projects farther north. He was struck by how closed-off the buildings were, with their own walkways and playgrounds, inward facing and isolated from the rest of the city.

He had been unhappy to move to Vallejo, so much so that his parents had gone to the trouble of surprising him with a pile of Christmas gifts in the empty living room the first time he entered the house. But he soon made new friends, starting with the Viado brothers, who lived across the street—stout, swaggering Vince and charming, quick-witted Clarence. Riding their bikes around the subdivision, the brothers taught Jed the invisible boundaries of the neighborhood, the Country Club Crest, the Triple C, and showed him shortcuts through the maze of streets. They pointed out which not to cross because an older teenage crew, the Crestside Crips, stopped and questioned anyone who traveled through their territory, demanding deference and extracting tolls. Eroded from a three-decades-long economic backslide and excluded from the development transforming other parts of the region, Vallejo simmered with the angst of the abandoned. "You had to scrap and shit," Jed recalls. "Fuckin' butterfly knives and Mace and shit."

One day when he was nine, during his first summer away from the Scout Reyes compound, he was playing baseball in the street with Vince and Clarence when they noticed a group of teenage boys walking up the road toward them. Jed and Clarence made their way to the curb, clearing a respectful path, but Vince, gripping the metal bat, didn't move. The leader of the crew, Jamal, stepped right up to his face.

"Yo kid, gimme that bat."

Vince stood there, quiet and still, hard eyes staring at the ground.

"Gimme that bat, kid."

Vince stayed silent, shook his head, and—

POP!

An uppercut slammed Vince's jaw. He stumbled and dropped the bat, but he didn't fall. Without saying another word, the crew walked off, leaving the bat. After that, Jamal would cordially nod at Vince whenever he saw him, as if he'd passed a test.

Jed came to see that the neighborhood presented a stark option: be predator or be prey. To keep from getting punked, he and his boys operated with vigilance. They lifted weights in the Viados' garage, joined by a handful of neighborhood friends, mostly Filipino, a few of them Black. When the group rode their bikes to the supermarket by the highway to buy candy and baseball cards, somebody always made sure to bring a butterfly knife, because the fastest route cut through the heart of Crestside Crips territory. The boys dubbed themselves HPP, for Hannigan Pinoy Posse, after the street that connected them. Some of them got custom-made hats with the initials stitched on the front.

Jed's parents had planned to enroll him at St. Patrick's, a Catholic high school in San Francisco, but he scored too low on the admission test. Rather than apply elsewhere or attend a public school in the city, Jed informed his parents he wanted to go to Vallejo High School, where his neighborhood friends went, a painless commute from the house if he got a ride from Vince, plus they'd save thousands of dollars in tuition.

Suddenly free to dress as he pleased after eight years in Catholic school uniforms, Jed was struck by the startling realization that his mishmash bargain-bin wardrobe was unsuited to the daily rigors of public school display. He didn't have a pair of Air Jordans to his name, though he did have immaculately white FILAs to build from. To make those kicks pop extra hard for his first day, he chose black, too-baggy Anchor Blue jeans his mom got at Target. He rummaged through the dozen or so tops in his closet—printed Ts (too casual), Sunday button-ups (too formal), colorful jerseys (too eye-catching). Nothing looked quite right.

He waited until Uncle Bobby, the coolest person he knew, left for work, then slipped into his bedroom, where he found what he was looking for. The white shirt, plain but for the horse-mounted polo player above the heart, paired so sublimely with the Filas that Jed didn't mind that the shirttail hung down to his thighs, the sleeves past his elbows.

Pulling up to Vallejo High with Vince and Clarence, Jed swelled with confidence. Among the group gathered in the parking lot were the familiar, friendly faces of the Hannigan Pinoy Posse. Jed's haircut was fresh, close-cut sides that faded up to a stringy tussle on top, his rattail in the back not yet at his shoulders. His immaculately white Filas threatened to blind any eyes that glanced upon them directly. And his Polo shirt, of course, his Polo shirt was—

"—big as hell, fool, out here lookin' like yo skinny ass shrunk in the wash, this *Honey, I Shrunk the Kids*–looking motherfucker over here."

Everybody busted up. Heads tilted back in tittering glee, arms pulled close as if to keep quivering innards from spilling out. He didn't know the kid who said it, nor the one who went after his too-baggy jeans next. Nobody mentioned his Filas or his haircut.

Jed found it mystifying that for all the money his parents had in the Philippines, in America they couldn't afford the brands in magazine ads and music videos. The rough exchange rate from peso to dollar existed in his mind as a scale weighing Scout Reyes comforts against Vallejo scarcity. The custom-made white crocodile loafers his dad once purchased in the Philippines cost half the price of any of the rubber Nikes and Reeboks Jed coveted in the States. The math was disheartening and disorienting.

When he wore a Larry Johnson Hornets jersey and Above the Rim basketball shorts that he believed to be an impeccable match, a classmate observed that the teal of his jersey was a vastly different shade from the teal of his shorts, drawing cackles from witnesses. One dude was laughing a little too hard. The next morning, standing by the lockers with Vince and Clarence, Jed mugged at the dude "like I was gonna do something." The dude and a friend with him mugged back in response.

"Man, he doesn't know who I am, man," Jed seethed. "Who the fuck is this guy? I'm from Hannigan, get the fuck outta here."

"You know who they are, right?" Vince said.

"Hell naw. Do they know who fuckin' I am?"

"No," Vince deadpanned, "but those guys will fuckin' work you, dude."

Vince calmly explained that the dude he was mugging taught karate at a dojo and the friend with him was a member of one of the gangs at the school. Vince had to pull some diplomacy to calm everyone.

Vallejo High was largely a collection of amiable factions split up by race: Filipino crews, Black crews, Mexican crews, Samoan crews. Jed's homies didn't let him get away with unfounded arrogance, a liability that could disrupt the peace and get them all in trouble. To cut him down, they played a game called "BB Blister" but didn't tell him the rules, which were that anybody who says a word that starts with the letter B gets punched—a game that had originated with the Crestside Crips, who associated the forbidden letter with the rival Bloods. As soon as he said, "but how do you pla—," Jed took a slug to the stomach. The lesson was clear: keep your ears open and your mouth closed. Learn the ways before you get exposed.

Observing Vince and Clarence with newfound urgency, he came to see that he'd misread their recipes for social success. Clarence seemed to be born with good taste, a skilled dancer, rapper, and graffiti artist, a trendsetter in dress and hairstyles, but when Clarence shaved his head after several of his friends copied his long bangs and blow-dried wave, Jed realized that what was worth emulating wasn't his wardrobe or hobbies but his confidence to reinvent. And it wasn't Vince's beefy physique, hot temper, or unwillingness to back down that scored him respect, so much as his ability to resolve conflict without violence, like the time he defused a confrontation with one of the biggest dudes at school by springing into Karate Kid stance, complete with movie sound effects, which cracked up his adversary. "That dude Vince crazy," people would say with a chuckle.

Looking back years later, Jed realized he had learned more in the hallways than the classrooms. He had a lot of good times in high school, at least partly because he and his classmates were able to do whatever they wanted. He got the sense that his teachers showed up every morning resigned to abandoning order. He almost never had homework because students were usually just given class time to complete their worksheets and essays. In ninth grade he was assigned books and math lessons that he'd studied in seventh grade at Catholic school. It wasn't hard to maintain close to a B average.

LAUREN AND I would wake early on Saturdays to watch Looney Tunes, bundled together on the couch with pillows and a blanket. By nine or ten o'clock, we'd get intentionally loud, hoping our childish yelps would stir Jed from his slumber. We'd progress to lightly knocking on his bedroom door—he'd gotten his own room once Auntie Lyn moved to San Mateo— then we'd crack the door and peek in, orange morning light streaming through white linen curtains, window bars casting a pinstripe shadow over the clothes blanketing the floor and Jed, sprawled across the bed, arms and legs splayed beyond the reach of the comforter. By eleven, we'd be crumpling up pieces of paper and lobbing them at his bed like grenades. Eventually, he'd throw on a basketball jersey and go toss some LO in the microwave.

Being around Jed felt like getting answers to a test I'd be taking in a few years. He was the coolest person I knew. By the years of my earliest memories he was collecting Air Jordans, listening to Bone Thugs-n-Harmony, and beating the final boss in Donkey Kong on Super Nintendo. He was fluent in the latest slang, sharp with wordplay, and never missed an opportunity to clown you for some act of foolishness, like wearing your shirt inside out or whining about the outcome of a board game. He was generous and empathetic, almost to a fault; at social gatherings, he'd unfailingly start a conversation with anyone he saw off by themselves looking all kawawa. Once, when he was shooting hoops at the park, he invited a kid sitting alone on a bench to join him, and ended up playing for hours, long after he wanted to go home, because he couldn't bring himself to end the kid's good time.

When evening came, he'd take a long shower, retreat to his bedroom, and emerge looking fresh, in pristine Jordans and starched jeans, ball cap cocked back at just the right angle. No matter what was on TV, Lauren and I would watch as he perfected his fit in the mirror by the front door, tongue tucked under his top lip in concentration, head bobbing like a boxer, checking all the angles, adjusting sleeves, laces, cuffs. We'd usually be asleep by the time he returned.

I WAS the spoiled one in our clan. As the youngest, I was never short on love or attention, and I carried myself like a child prince whose coming sovereignty everybody feared. While the monthly wire transfers from my dad were far from opulent, they were enough to cover necessities and a steady supply of new toys, which my mom showered me with in hopes of compensating for his absence. Her concerns were mitigated as well by the abundance of older influences in our American barangay.

When I was six my mom and I moved into a Victorian apartment building in a posh San Francisco neighborhood. We didn't shy from our international sensibilities. She enrolled me in a Catholic school with a French name, Notre Dame de Victoire. In the mornings, she'd wake me with a song she'd crafted from a handful of French words—"Bonjour, Bonjour, mon amour petit . . ." She pronounced my name in the French style, with the T silent: *Ahl-bear.* That's what my uncles, aunties, and cousins call me to this day.

Our Francophile eccentricities gave Jed plenty of ammunition with which to clown my arrogant ass. His playful taunts, often delivered in a spot-on French accent, were much needed to dull my burgeoning sense of entitlement. In the global dichotomy between those who serve and those who are served, I was sure where I stood. I could see that where others had to struggle, I didn't. To me it was no mystery why. I attributed my comfort to a higher power. "Count your blessings," I often heard my mom say. "Praise the Lord." I gave thanks in my prayers that the higher power was just.

I'd first picked up a vague sense of my imperial privilege when I was five and my mom and I were briefly living in the Philippines while she prepared to settle us permanently in the United States, shipping the bulk of her possessions and selling her condominium. She enrolled me in a private school for kindergarten and hired a driver, Tony, and a housekeeper, Josephine, both trusted relatives of maids who had helped to raise her in Scout Reyes. Their presence felt so steady and ordinary to me that, in my youthful simplicity, I thought of them not as employees but as just two more members of the familial network supporting us, like the uncles and aunties who drove and cooked in the States.

Our move didn't bother me, because we were always on the move. Different as they were, Vallejo, Paris, and Manila each kept me encased in my bubble of comfort. No matter where I was, I had my trove of toys, as much food as I could eat, and a devil on my shoulder reminding me that the very design of the universe bent to my needs.

In the Philippines, the hierarchy was stark and clear, too visible to miss. Only the wealthiest countries can afford to sweep their poorest residents mostly out of sight. In the mornings, Tony and my mom shuttled me to school through grinding traffic, and from the backseat of our air-conditioned car I'd look out the tinted windows and see girls and boys my age selling fruits and sodas at stoplights. Their faces were moist with sweat, their slippered feet blackened from exhaust. Along the road, rows of aluminum-and-cinder-block slums stretched farther than I could see. I'd shrink in my seat from what I now recognize as shame. I desperately hoped that the window tint was dark enough to keep them from seeing me. I wondered what they thought about kids like me, what explanation they'd been given for the distance between us. Then the light would turn green and we'd be off.

The girls and boys selling fruit and sodas didn't look like the girls and boys in my class, who were mostly white-skinned, the children of diplomats, executives, and bankers. Our school offered instruction in English, French, German, and Dutch. I don't remember hearing any Tagalog spoken on campus. Whatever future our parents and teachers imagined for us, it lay elsewhere.

Before we returned to the United States in 1995, my mom took me to my grandmother's coconut farm, which had been in her family since the end of World War II. Now that our family's exodus from the Islands was underway, Rizalina considered selling the land. My mom wasn't sure I'd have another chance to see it.

Sprouting coconut trees and dense banana groves in the northern Mindanao highlands, the farm's land was fertile, but it turned a meager profit, barely enough to justify the energy and expense. Though farmland covered nearly half of the country, the agriculture sector had deteriorated. The Philippine government pursued industrial ambitions, developing urban centers and luring Western businesses, funneling the country's workforce to factories, food service, call centers, and cruise ships. On the farms, subsidies dwindled and infrastructure crumbled. Irrigation was lacking. Narrow, ragged roads limited the transport of goods and livestock. Market prices hovered, low and stagnant. Rather than revamp its struggling farms, the government turned elsewhere for goods. An archipelago with an ancient history of cultivating rice became the world's top importer of the grain.

Rizalina entrusted daily care of the land to her head farmer, Felix, whose family lived in a nipa hut beside the banana trees and handled much of the labor, with a few hired hands enlisted for the most backbreaking tasks, like hauling lumber or clearing trees felled by a storm. It was a forty-minute walk down the mountain to the nearest road, and many more miles to the nearest school, so Felix's four children were raised as apprentices, taught to master the practical art of cultivating fruit and raising chickens, roosters, pigs, and carabao.

In the evenings when she was around, Rizalina sat with the children in their hut, teaching them to read. The brightest among the four was the second oldest boy, whom she nicknamed Sargento because he said he wanted to be a police officer when he grew up and because of the serious manner with which he worked the land. Rizalina vowed to pay to send him away to high school once he was old enough.

On my visit, nine-year-old Sargento guided me around the fields with the sureness of a veteran farmhand. He climbed onto the carabao and steered the animal with gentle tugs of the harness while I sat behind him. He picked up roosters without hesitation, gripping their scrappy wings closed so I could pet them. He climbed the towering coconut trees, arms looped around the trunk, feet gripping the scaly bark, ascending the palm forty feet up within seconds, twisting off the coconuts like lightbulbs, chuckling as he watched them crash to the ground with a hollow thud. With a machete, he'd slice off the top so I could drink the juice and eat the fruit. Though I tried to impress him with my courage, the sight of a giant spider on a banana tree trunk sent me sprinting away in fear.

A photo of Sargento and me sitting atop a carabao was printed and framed weeks later, once my mom and I were back in San Francisco, settling into our new apartment in Nob Hill. It sat on a side table, where it blended into the decor over time.

Many years later, when I'd see the photo of us young boys on that big beast, I'd wonder what became of Sargento.

THE AMERICAN DREAM is premised on humble beginnings, the more humble the better, to showcase the potency of American opportunity. Testimonials to it usually affirm that those at the bottom need only work a little harder, wait a little longer, and trust in a process that ensures we'll all get what we deserve. From the athletes on his walls to the movies he watched to the historical figures he learned about in school, all around Jed were stories of upswing. Yet there he stood, at the inflection point of a downturn. More than a decade into his American life, he was further from comfort than he'd been on the day he was born, a chunky mestizo baby in Manila's finest hospital. Our family had not arrived as humble beginners but proud ones knocked backward, staggered but regaining balance, suddenly aware of how much ground there was to make up. We hadn't fled war or catastrophe. We had simply moved to America.

The summer after his freshman year, when he was fifteen, Jed got a job at the Burger King at the edge of the subdivision and began saving for his first pair of Jordans. He handled the fryer, wrapped Whoppers, worked the register, and served drive-through orders. Sometimes his boys came in, asking for free sodas, sarcastically soliciting his menu recommendations like they were at a five-star restaurant, which Jed appreciated because it meant they weren't off having fun without him, cruising around somewhere, pagers buzzing. He walked the half-mile home, BK-logo hat usually still on when he stepped through the door, carrying a sack of chicken nuggets and fries with ranch and barbecue dipping sauces. If Lauren and I were around, we'd help him eat the leftovers.

He worked through the summer and into the next school year, instead of playing football and basketball. Basketball was his best sport. He'd been the star of his middle school team, a playmaking point guard with handles and a jump shot, so talented that when he'd arrive for games, the crowd in the gym would erupt in cheers. In football, where he'd been the backup tight end his sophomore year, he seemed poised to move up because the starter, a kid named CC Sabathia, had decided to focus on baseball. Sabathia would go on to be selected in the first round of the Major League Baseball draft, signing a $1.3 million contract with the Cleveland Indians, and another kid in Jed's high school class, Brandon Armstrong, would get a scholarship to Pepperdine University, then go on to play in the NBA for three years. At the time, Jed felt that the choices he was making were essential. But looking back two decades later, he has his doubts. "I could've focused more on sports, life, social things," he said. "But I guess you needed money for those."

We'd heard about what it was like growing up in the Philippines, where the children of the well-off worked only once they'd finished their schooling, moved out of the big ancestral home only once they'd gotten married, and had careers waiting for them at the threshold of adulthood. Jed often thought about his summers among the maids and drivers, the television studios where everybody greeted his dad with glowing respect.

Landing in the States, we'd stepped into a history we hadn't fully prepared for and didn't understand at first. Our elders arrived full of faith, ready to make sacrifices so that the next generation could march on, with the assurance of birthright and a familial infrastructure already in place. But that didn't keep us from crashing into American reality, as the post-1965 wave of non-European immigrants threatened a long-established caste system, inducing fears of a coming white minority.

Many evenings, Jed and his friends stood in front of the Vallejo house, staring up at the stars, drinking 40s, smoking blunts, bullshitting. Sometimes, they crashed cotillions, waltzing into a decked-out gymnasium like they were best of friends with the eighteen-year-old celebrant. They'd tear up the dance floor, eat their way through the buffet, and occasionally steal the purses lying unattended on seats. Once, a rumble broke out in the parking lot between Filipino and Samoan gangs, and Jed and the Viados got caught in the mix and had to swing their way out.

Sometimes, when Jed was in charge of looking after his sister, she'd accompany him on his excursions. Seven-year-old Lauren was in the backseat when Jed met his boys in front of some kid's house one night to settle an apparent dispute. Hearing R&B humming behind the garage door, the boys banged on the wooden planks like warriors ready for battle. The door rolled up to reveal a handful of couples startled out of a slow dance. "They look up and they see these dark figures watching over them," Jed recalled years later. "They really looked nonintimidating. They weren't any threat to anybody." No fists were thrown, but Jed was shaken up when he got back to the car, where Lauren was pretending to sleep. "Why are we doing this?" Jed remembers thinking. "This is kinda fucked up, man."

His elders spoke of corruption and civil strife in the old country; they had migrated in pursuit of a place with institutions they could depend on, a civic infrastructure and social safety net that would support their efforts to pull their families to comfort. But this wasn't the country Jed and his friends knew. Their families and many other immigrants had landed in cities battered by the fiscal crises and service cuts of the preceding decades, reeling from the dwindling number of middle-class jobs. They arrived to find neighbors who distrusted the very corporate and public institutions that were supposed to embody what made America great. The view from the ground was different from the view from above, or from outside.

All over the United States, second-generation immigrants were coming of age in places excluded from the country's promises of prosperity. Dante Basco, the Filipino American actor best known for his role as Rufio in *Hook*, explained his inspiration for that performance in a Gizmodo interview by recounting his childhood years in Paramount,

California: "What I was bringing to the character, especially at that time in my life, I grew up in a gang neighborhood. Gangsters were around, drugs and everything. It was a tough time to grow up. It was cool, but it was a tougher neighborhood. And to a degree, the Lost Boys are a little gang. So I think I had a bit of that coming into it."

In his songs, Jonah Deocampo, the Filipino American rapper known by the stage name Bambu, describes his South Los Angeles neighborhood as a place that made him "ready for war," schools where he'd "never seen a single college adviser," and police officers who "treat you like a criminal, pat you down at your school, arrest you over a quota over racist-ass rules."

Joe Ide, the Japanese American noir novelist, grew up in Watts in the years after the 1965 riots, which were sparked when a police officer shot and killed a Black motorist he'd pulled over. Most of Ide's friends were Black, and so were most of the characters in his books. Asked in an interview with NPR how he managed to write such vivid dialogue, Ide said, "The vernacular was my first language. I had to learn to talk like this!" He lived with his grandparents, and though his grandfather didn't speak English and collected Samurai swords, Ide felt little connection to his ancestral culture. "I wanted to be Black, but I knew I wasn't," he told the *New York Times.* "I always felt something of an outsider. I wasn't Black. I wasn't white. I was way far from being Japanese. So I was a lot on the fringe. And I was a watcher. I would listen to people. Listen to the way they talk and imagine what was going on in their heads."

Born in the United States, the children of the wave didn't have to rely on American mythology to understand their country. Black Americans had detailed these truths for centuries, and in the early '90s the messages reached Jed and his childhood friends through the music they listened to.

Hip-hop had replaced shipbuilding as Vallejo's claim to fame, and the city that produced the most submarines during World War II now produced the most Bay Area rap superstars per capita, voices that chronicled their city's plight, depicting scenes that Jed and his friends saw around them. "I'm from the V-A-double-L-E-J-O, where selling narcotics is all I know," rapped Mac Dre, the high-energy godfather of the local rap scene, in his song "Valley Joe." In "Practice Looking Hard," which boomed from bass-heavy trunk speakers at stoplights across the Bay when Jed was fourteen, E-40 paints a portrait of a distressed people with no choice but to toughen up: "A J-O-B in 93 consists of paper rarely," he raps. "And then ya wonder why I'm stubborn, forever lookin' hard, I been scarred."

By fifteen, Jed was sharp enough to recognize that he was falling behind his peers at Sacred Heart and St. Ignatius, where the kids were steered toward Berkley, UCLA, Stanford, the Ivy Leagues. He bombed the SAT on his first try, with a score so low it left him stunned and convinced he wasn't ready for college. He applied to only one school, San Francisco State University, because he figured he might as well, but he considered it a moon shot. On his second crack at the SAT, after months of studying, he got a decent score.

Still, Vallejo's success stories, as Jed knew them, came through sports and entertainment. His high school's notable alumni included E-40 and Sly Stone. He never forgot the day he and his boys were sitting around a small bench press in the Viados' garage, the radio tuned to KMEL 106.1, and a new song came on, a hard beat with high-pitched West Coast synths.

"Yo, y'all know this is that kid that punched Vince?" one of the boys said.

Everybody laughed and clowned Vince, bobbing their heads to the sound of Jamal, now known as Mac Mall, dropping lines about streets they'd been to and gangs they'd encountered. Mac Mall's 1993 debut album, *Illegal Business?*, sold more than 200,000 copies. The first track opens with the raspy voice of an old man asking his companions if they remember a kid from the neighborhood—"What's his name?"—because apparently the kid was rapping now. "I thought the little motherfucka was robbing shit," the raspy voice says, "sellin' dope or something like that, like the rest of them little Crestside motherfuckas. But, naw, he done got his shit together . . ."

Jed's rap skills were modest on his best days, and he'd already abandoned the prerequisites to a professional basketball career. He wasn't sure of his path forward in the States. He didn't know if his grades were good enough to get him into a four-year college, and even if they were, he didn't want to anchor his family with the price tag. He figured he could go to a community college for two years, but he didn't even know what he wanted to study. With little confidence any of that would work out, he crafted a backup plan.

His family name, after all, was still well-known in the Philippines. He was handsome, charming, funny, skilled at imitations and improvisation. He danced with a smooth lean and could hold a tune well enough. He could weave conversations out of thin air, and everybody seemed to like him. Jed's backup plan was to go back to the Islands and become a megastar.

Sure, he wasn't fluent in Tagalog, and he peppered his language with slang few outside the Bay would understand. That didn't dent his prospects as a megastar. It would make for an endearing story: Jed Rigor, the truest of balikbayans, coming home to the Philippines for good, at just the moment when academics and politicians were calling for an end to the exodus, pleading for people to stay and build on the Islands. He would be the poster boy for return, bearing tales of peril and disappointment in the so-called land of the free, blazing a trail for others of his generation. "Leaders of the new school!" he'd dub the cohort. He couldn't tell if going back would make him a hero or a failure.

IN 1852, after California became part of America with the end of the Mexican-American War, Vallejo became the state's capital. The city's founder and namesake, Mariano Vallejo, was still alive at the time, a forty-five-year-old rancher and state legislator who had grown up in California, risen through the ranks of the Mexican military in the 1830s and 1840s, and navigated the tides of annexation with his wealth intact.

Vallejo's ancestors had been among the first Spanish settlers to arrive in the Americas; one was said to have been a captain under Hernán Cortés. By the time he was born, in 1807, Vallejo's family had been in New Spain for nearly a dozen generations, old-money landowners with haciendas in Alta California, a vast frontier territory where the colonizers battled with indigenous tribes. Vallejo was a teenager working as personal secretary to the governor of Alta California when Mexico won independence from Spain. Within a few years, he was a military officer and a member of the regional legislature. At twenty-two, he led a division of the Mexican army into battle against Miwok warriors who'd been raiding the Mission San José in the East Bay. His firsthand experience reinforced his nation's policy in making him see his primary adversaries as the natives who threatened the civilization his ancestors had helped to build.

Dozens of indigenous tribes controlled the sprawling grasslands in the continent's center, clashing with Mexico on one side and the United States on the other. The young countries were kindred spirits—former colonies who'd freed themselves from European monarchy while designing legal systems that rewarded those with European lineage. Hoping to push native people out of Texas, the Mexican government permitted Americans to buy land and settle in the province, but the Americans rushed in so quickly that by 1829 English speakers outnumbered Spanish speakers in Texas, spurring President Vicente Guerrero to enact a series of laws aimed at quelling the influx. He abolished slavery, raised tariffs on American goods, and levied property taxes. When American settlers ignored the directives and kept flowing in, Guerrero barred American immigration altogether.

Vallejo was two thousand miles from the trouble in Texas and even further from the political turmoil in Mexico's capital, where over a four-year stretch of coups and exiles, eight presidents cycled through the office and Guerrero was executed. Around the time American settlers in Texas revolted and split from Mexico, Vallejo was a lieutenant in the Monterey Company leading strikes against indigenous tribes along the coast. Two years later, as commandant general of Alta California, in defiance of Mexican law, he opened the border to American immigrants, fellow Christians offering to build on untouched land, as he saw it. In letters to government ministers, he expressed frustration that the authorities in Mexico City weren't doing more to help develop his region, and he suggested they send farmers to cultivate crops and artisans to balance out the cultural influence of the Americans he was allowing in.

He stepped down from the position after three years, in 1841, and instead took on the role of civic benefactor, lending money to the government and feeding soldiers. The government repaid him with land, adding to his sprawling personal claim across the North Bay. He and his wife, Francisca Benicia Carrillo de Vallejo, lived on their 250,000-acre ranch in Sonoma, where her mother had been one of the area's first winemakers. Vallejo remained in the military, serving as colonel of the local cavalry.

One day in 1844, word of a possible revolt reached the governor's office. The intel had come from John Sutter, a Swiss immigrant who had arrived in Alta California in 1839, been granted Mexican citizenship after a year, then bought 49,000 acres near where the American River (as he named it) met the Sacramento River. The fort he erected came to house the first European settlement in California's Central Valley. When Sutter learned from a confidant that Britain secretly pledged to support a band of California-born rebels plotting a war of independence, he informed the governor, who agreed to let Sutter form a militia to help fight them.

Vallejo didn't like the idea of empowering foreigners to battle fellow Californios. He expressed his disapproval by disbanding his Sonoma cavalry. He carried his allegiance to Mexico loosely, and then not at all. When the United States invaded Mexico in 1846, after Mexico refused to sell Alta California, Vallejo chose to side with America. Perhaps thinking the nation's victory was inevitable, perhaps simply preferring Washington, D.C.'s light-handed policies, he lobbied his fellow Californios to accept the new government—a calculated risk that "cost a great deal" and left him "half dead," he wrote to a friend in 1846, listing the livestock that had been stolen from two of his homes while he was away politicking during the early months of the war.

Five months into the war, a U.S. captain wrote Vallejo a letter sending "hearty thanks" for "your assistance to the government of the United States in the recent emergency, and to your associates whose ready obedience to your call has done much towards allaying natural prejudices and unfriendly suspicions among the various classes comprising the society of California."

America won the war, then annexed California as the thirty-first state in 1850. Vallejo served on the state's constitutional convention and was elected to the state senate, which initially convened in San Jose. Vallejo proposed a stretch of his North Bay waterfront land as the state's permanent capital city. He founded the city in 1851, naming it after himself. His pitch was strong: From the city's hills, you could look far across the state and on a clear day see the Pacific, giving the location great symbolic value. Also, it was logistically convenient, a ferry ride across the Bay to the busy ports of San Francisco and a fifty-mile trail inland to the gold-speckled rivers of the Central Valley, where prospectors arrived from every direction—white Americans with Black slaves from the South, free Black Americans hoping the West was less oppressive than the North, European immigrants weathering frontier trails in covered wagons, Chinese immigrants at sea for months.

The nugget that sparked the rush had been found at John Sutter's lumber mill on January 24, 1848, about a week before Mexico signed the peace treaty that granted the United States sovereignty to land stretching to the California coast. At the confluence of two rivers well-suited for gold-panning, Sutter's settlement hastily evolved into a mining and trading hub, with slapdash wooden structures and gridded streets. Soon prospectors overran the settlement, trampling Sutter's crops and pillaging his livestock. Hoping to bring order to the area and benefit from the sudden commerce, Sutter's son founded a town he called Sacramento, after the river. By 1852, Sacramento had developed to such an extent that it boasted a courthouse. No capitol building ever materialized in Vallejo, however, and by 1855, the state government permanently relocated to Sacramento.

The boomtime economy overflowed with speculators who'd come to California to strike it rich, and not just in ore. Though the peace treaty signed by the United States and Mexico in 1848 included provisions protecting the property of Mexican landowners in California, the chaos of the postwar transition spurred opportunistic Americans to file legal challenges to the land rights, sometimes drafting fraudulent papers that judges couldn't distinguish from valid deeds. In 1862, the U.S. Supreme Court ruled that Mariano Vallejo couldn't prove ownership of around 80,000 acres of his ranch. Similar rulings followed, costing Vallejo more property. By the final years of his life, Mariano Vallejo had land rights to less than 300 acres and was paying rent to stay in his house. By all accounts, he died in 1890 carrying deep regret for his role in ushering the Americans into California.

ONCE AMERICA EXPANDED its borders, it began to close them to most of the world.

Up to 1965, most immigrants to America came from Europe. From 1840 to 1879, 6.3 million people—nearly ten times as many as in the preceding forty years—migrated to the United States, gaining permanent residency status upon landing; three-quarters of them were from Germany (after a failed revolution) or Ireland (after the potato famine). From 1900 to 1939, 18 million people arrived, the majority fleeing impoverished rural Italy and eastern Europe. The waves of new arrivals washed across America from coast to coast, dramatically altering the demographic makeup, the cultural flavor, the civic institutions of thousands of cities and towns.

While people from nearly every continent trickled into the United States in its early decades, the first non-Europeans to land annually by the thousands, according to U.S. Census records, came from China in the 1850s, as the discovery of gold in California spawned cities along the Pacific. By the 1870s, the Chinese were America's fifth largest immigrant group. Though they still made up less than 5 percent of new arrivals, the backlash against them was swift. White Americans burned down Chinatowns all over the West, lynching seventeen Chinese immigrants in Los Angeles and twenty-eight in Rock Springs, Wyoming. In Oregon, after thirty-four Chinese gold miners were killed, mutilated, and thrown into the Snake River, the three white defendants who faced trial were acquitted by an all-white jury. In Vallejo, a mob torched a Chinese-owned store, killing a five-year-old girl.

In 1882, thirty-three years after taking possession of California and the western territories, Congress passed a law barring immigration from China, the first immigration restriction based on race or nationality in the country's history. To process the new arrivals in the wake of the policy, the government built its largest Pacific immigration station, on Angel Island just off San Francisco. Across the continent at Ellis Island, on the Atlantic coast, where the immigrants were mostly European, fewer than 20 percent of arrivals were detained and all but 2 percent admitted, establishing the site as a symbol of America's open arms. At Angel Island, the gateway for Asian immigrants, around 60 percent of arrivals were detained and around a fifth denied entry, establishing the site as a landmark in the country's history of exclusion.

PEOPLE FROM THE PHILIPPINES, though, got special treatment.

In state department parlance, the little brown brothers had been "pacified" by the time World War I came, providing a stable and loyal territory on which the U.S. Air Force and Navy built some of their largest bases. Many Filipino children grew up learning to speak English in an American-run school system, college students could obtain U.S.-funded grants to study in the States, and migrant workers could cross the ocean and find jobs in the sugarcane plantations of Hawaii, the canneries of Alaska, or the fruit fields of California. With fewer Japanese and Chinese laborers to hire, the American agriculture industry sent recruiters to Manila and the surrounding provinces to sign up new pickers. Specialized travel agencies, called "drummers," sprang up across the Philippines, offering to organize transportation for those who wanted to make the journey to the United States. In hopes of winning potential customers, the drummers traveled to rural reaches of the country, promoting a shining vision of America.

Roberto Vallangca, a student from Ilocos in northern Luzon, booked his ticket in July 1927, a month after his twentieth birthday. He embodied his family's best hope for upward mobility. His father had been a farmer, his eldest brother joined in the work once he was old enough to ride a carabao, and though the margins were slim for the long hours the two toiled, they saved enough to put Roberto through primary school and into a prestigious high school near the coast. But during Roberto's third year of high school, his father died, and the farm could no longer yield enough fruit to pay for his classes. "The only remedy, it seemed, was to come to the United States to further my education," Roberto later wrote in *Pinoy: The First Wave,* his oral history compiling accounts of Filipino immigrants. His family sold their land and carabao to pay for his fare on the *President Jefferson.*

Roberto boarded the steamship in Manila with five dollars in his pocket and a rattan suitcase filled with clothes he deemed insufficient for a job hunt in the States. On a stopover in Hong Kong, he spent the five dollars on his first suit. Though he lacked work experience, he spoke English fluently, unlike the many migrants too poor to have had even a few years in a classroom. He had no reason to doubt his choice. Mailboxes back on the Islands filled with previous immigrants' money from American jobs and tales of American promise in Seattle, San Francisco, Los Angeles, and elsewhere. "Excited and inspired by the sights of the port cities, they wrote home of the grandeur and beauty of America and of the seemingly limitless opportunities available in big cities," Roberto wrote. "They built up their hopes and those of their loved ones in the Philippines, not knowing of the prejudice, the intolerance, and the hardships they would encounter."

As ROBERTO and other Filipino people freely entered the States to go to school or to work fields and canneries in the early decades of the twentieth century, nativist policies continued to block out other groups, in a racist backlash to the influx of new arrivals in the preceding decades. This anti-immigrant ideology was pervasive. In a 1905 speech before the National Congress of Mothers, President Theodore Roosevelt called on white women to produce more children in order to avoid "race suicide" brought about by the growing number of nonwhite U.S. residents. In 1917, three decades after the United States banned immigrants from China, Congress passed a law preventing the admittance of virtually all migrants from countries in the "Asiatic Barred Zone"; this exempted the Philippines because it was a U.S. colony. Seven years later, in May 1924, Congress passed a law that limited the number of new residents from any country to 2 percent of whatever its immigration population had been in the United States in 1890, effectively shutting the door to anyone outside northern and western Europe. Public support for the restrictions overpowered concerns for the diplomatic consequences. In Japan, protesters took to the streets, consumers boycotted American goods, and the government unsuccessfully appealed for the United States to reverse the policy. Meanwhile, imprisoned in Germany at the time, Adolf Hitler expressed admiration for the "one state" that presented a model for his own country, writing in his autobiography: "The American Union categorically refuses the immigration of physically unhealthy elements and simply excludes the immigration of certain races."

Pseudoscientific claims of white racial supremacy propped up immigration laws designed to preserve a certain vision of what America was supposed to be. "The brown man, the yellow man, or the black man who is an American citizen seeks the opportunities of this country with a handicap," Congressman Clarence Lea of California testified on the floor of the House of Representatives in 1924. "It detracts from the harmony, unity, and solidarity of our citizenship." Grant Hudson, a Congress member from Michigan, argued that the "huge masses of non-American-minded individuals" posed a threat to "the maintenance of our historic republican institutions."

Dismissing the advanced civilizations that existed in the Americas before Christopher Columbus disembarked, Congress member Ira Hersey of Maine declared that "the New World was settled by the white race." America, he continued, "was, God-intended, I believe, to be the home of a great people. English speaking—a white race with great ideals, the Christian religion, one race, one country, and one destiny. . . . The African, the Orientals, the Mongolians, and all the yellow races of Europe, Asia and Africa, should never have been allowed to people this great land."

Many white Americans shared that view. Most tolerated exclusionary policies. All benefited from a caste system that elevated light skin and European ancestry. Some believed in it so strongly they burned crosses on lawns and committed human rights atrocities. In the early decades of the twentieth century, amid the surge in racist violence following the political gains Black people made after Emancipation, active branches of the Ku Klux Klan littered the northern counties of the Bay Area. The *Petaluma Argus* covered an April 4, 1923, gathering of the Napa chapter: "More than 1,000 hooded figures of the Ku Klux Klan gathered somewhere in the hills of Napa County, participated in a strange ceremony round a fitfully flickering fire, silently and swiftly gathered their robes about them and disappeared into the night, as mysteriously as they appeared." Six months later, a front-page article of the Santa Rosa *Press Democrat* described an "awe inspiring" ritual, witnessed by three hundred cars' worth of spectators in Sonoma County: "Two hundred hooded klansmen, seeming phantoms in the pale moonlight of the evening, participated in the initiatory ceremony. Prior to the exercises, only one or two of the masked klansmen, attired completely in white, were seen on the grounds. As if from nowhere, the 200 robe-clad figures marched from behind a small hill, . . . ghost-like figures walked across the field while the figure of a klansman on horseback was silhouetted against the sky. A short time before the initiatory ceremony started, a huge cross, approximately 20 feet in height and situated in back of the American flag, was lighted, its rays shining on the line of hooded klansmen who walked to the small knoll." The chapter's founder was a publicist who had represented the local government and, before that, made his riches in Atlanta as a scam artist. The newspaper reported that sixteen of the new initiates lived in Vallejo, worked on the Mare Island naval base, and wore military uniforms beneath their robes. Three weeks later, a Sonoma Klan ceremony drew two thousand people, according to the paper, and "traffic congestion at the exit gate for a time resembled the worst congestions of the old Cotati speedway days."

ROBERTO KNEW ONE PERSON in America, his cousin Seriaco, who worked on a farm in Santa Clara County. Seriaco met him at the dock in San Francisco, and they took a bus along a dusty highway that snaked through the coastal mountains before settling into a fertile stretch of green fields. Roberto picked apples and grapes for two months, living at a labor camp, planning his next move, which he hoped wouldn't involve the sort of physical grind his father and brother had tried to spare him.

He made his way to San Jose, a bigger city where the jobs weren't on farms. With his earnings, he booked a room at a cheap hotel and purchased newspapers daily for the job listings. Answering an ad for a "houseboy," he was so eager to make a good impression that he showed up at the address in his Hong Kong suit at six a.m., only to find a grumpy woman in a nightgown who asked him to come back in two hours. When he returned, the woman said she was hesitant to hire an applicant with no experience in domestic work. "I'm willing to learn and I'll do anything," Roberto told her, as he recounted in his book. Just as she was about to send him away, her son, who had a crew cut and "looked like a college boy and a football player," overheard their conversation and said, "Give him a chance, mother."

His first task was to vacuum the living room. He'd never seen a vacuum cleaner before but didn't let on. Grabbing it out of the closet, he carried it on his shoulder, as he had carried large baskets and tools in the

Philippines, and upon putting it down on the living room carpet, he stared at it, trying to figure out how to operate the contraption.

"Go on, take the cord and plug it into that socket there," the woman said, before stepping away to feed the dog. Finally out of his boss's sight, Roberto sprang into action, prodding and poking the buttons and switches, turning over the machine in search of clues on how to work the thing, to no avail. In his frantic inspection, he noticed he'd accidentally pulled the plug from the socket, and when he put it back in, "suddenly, the vacuum motor roared and the machine started toward me," he wrote. "I jumped up with fright and ran to the door. I almost ran into the lady who was watching me from the door."

"Roberto," he recalled her saying, "you are really ignorant—what am I going to do with you?" Yet she didn't fire him on his first day. Instead, she taught him how to use the machine. He was heartened by the thought that Americans were as kind as he'd heard.

He enrolled in a high school nearby, taking classes at night and working during the day, and for a brief moment Roberto's plan continued without disruption. Then the economy collapsed in 1929, fewer families could afford houseboys, and the growing ranks of unemployed people jostled for a shrinking number of jobs.

Over the next few years, Roberto bounced around the Bay Area, chasing rumors of work at restaurants, hotels, and farms. He went to school when he could afford it, sometimes going more than a year without classes. It would take him nine years, across five high schools, before he accumulated enough credits to graduate. When he couldn't afford food, he went to the Chinatown gambling houses, which were open twenty-four hours and offered complimentary meals and coffee.

One spring day in 1932, he and Seriaco boarded a streetcar on Market Street in San Francisco, hoping to find work at the Ferry Building on the waterfront. As Roberto walked down the aisle looking for a seat, a white man behind him kicked him in the calf and said, "Come on, you savages—get out of my way." Roberto didn't understand the man's aggression and wanted to ask him, "What have I done?" but he was already storming past him on his way to a seat in the middle of the car. Roberto stood in the aisle, his mind still replaying the curious incident, until the next stop, when a seat opened up near the front. As Roberto stepped that way, a sharply dressed white man in the adjacent seat placed his newspaper on the seat and said, "I do not want a monkey to sit beside me."

Flushed with embarrassment, Roberto looked around at the other faces in the cab. "Some smiled and laughed," he wrote. "Some said nothing but continued to look at me." He got off at the next stop with tears in his eyes, wondering "what I had done to make these people hate me." He and Seriaco walked the rest of the way.

"This is your first time to experience this, cousin?" Seriaco said to him. "As long as you are here in America, you'll have more and even worse experiences. Just forget it, you cannot do anything about it, cousin."

Roberto hadn't been completely ignorant of the country's racism. He'd barely been in the States a few months the first time young white men in a car hurled obscenities at him. He'd seen establishments with signs stating, "Dogs and Filipinos not allowed." But his assumption that this hatred was isolated to a small minority of ignorant people gradually eroded as he began to see its extent, and the way it was sanctioned by laws, institutions, and social norms.

Police frisked and interrogated patrons at Filipino barbershops, arresting some without cause, and busted into rooms at the hotels housing mostly Filipino immigrants, beating them and destroying their possessions. Servers ignored Filipino customers, even at restaurants without any visible segregation orders—the first time this happened to Roberto, at a half-empty coffee shop on Geary Street, he waited half an hour before realizing why nobody was taking his order.

Before long, immigrants like Roberto discovered that their adopted land was a minefield where the simple acts of living could trigger an explosion of white resistance. Conventional notions of white American masculinity, staking claim to white women, added to the volatility—as Pinoys of the 1930s discovered on their nights out at dance halls. Few Pinays had immigrated to the States, so the women Filipino men most often interacted with were the white "dime-a-dance girls" who charged ten cents per song. Sometimes the women went home with them. Sometimes they fell in love. With those possibilities in mind, young Pinoys wore their hard-earned suits to the halls, loose suits with big ties that swung like pendulums during the jitterbug and flapped like wings during the Lindy Hop. The band onstage rarely played a song longer than two or three minutes. When the music stopped, a whistle blew to indicate that the dime girls were back on the market for the next song. The men outnumbered the women and jostled for attention. You could spot the Pinoys who'd done well at the sicoy-sicoy games at the gambling house that day because they'd dance with the same girl all night.

Anacleto Gorospe, a Pinoy immigrant who arrived in Chicago in 1924, remembered catching angry glances from white men who "resented the Filipino boys dancing with the white girls," as he recounted in Roberto's oral history. There were beatings and shootings. Police rarely investigated. Eventually Pinoys banded together on their nights out. To show that they were not to be messed with, they'd occasionally have someone from the group walk alone down the sidewalk while the others lay in wait. Predictably—they'd learned the ways of America—the bait would draw a gang of ill-intentioned white men, who'd walk right into the ambush. "The Italians always showed up," recalled Conrado Ocampo, a Pinoy immigrant who lived in Chicago before becoming the first Filipino person to graduate from the University of Iowa's dental college. "We would come out with baseball bats and make them crawl on the ground."

Usually, though, there was no pack of Pinoys waiting in the shadows to ward off an attack. In January 1930, white locals in Watsonville rioted after hearing word that a young Filipino lettuce grower, Perfecto Bandalan, was engaged to a white teenager. A white mob dragged Filipino men from their worker camps, beat them, threw them off the Pajaro River bridge, and fired gunshots at their homes. One shot struck twenty-two-year-old Fermin Tobera in the heart while he was hiding in a closet with eleven others.

"I understood it to be a racial issue, because everywhere I went I saw white men attacking Filipinos," wrote Carlos Bulosan, whose seminal book *America Is in the Heart* chronicled his years as a laborer in Depression-era California. "Why was America so kind and yet so cruel?"

THE FOUNDING FATHERS had two races in mind when they created America.

By 1850, the only racial classifications on the U.S. Census were "white," "black," and "mulatto." In 1860, "Indian" was added, the first official count of the Native population. In the decades after the Civil War, the arrival of darker-skinned people from so many places left officials scrambling to keep up. In 1870, "Chinese" appeared on the census; in 1890, "Japanese." Then "Filipino," "Korean," and "Hindu" entered the mix in 1920, and "Mexican" in 1930. Since then, another nine classifications have been added, but the designations remain so imprecise that people of Arab descent officially counted as white in the 2020 census.

To get around these arbitrary categories and leave a bit more clarity on the record, I like to make use of the "other" designation, which provides a text box for specificity. On the 2020 census, I chose "Asian—Filipino"—simple enough, but rather than "white" to account for my Lebanese side, I clicked "other" and typed in "Lebanese Arab." On the question of whether I'm "Hispanic," I answered that I am, though not from any of the Latin American countries listed but from "other," and I wrote in "Philippines."

I like to imagine some sensible census official up the chain noticing my clarification with sudden panic, then hitting a big red button and shouting, "Stop the count! Stop the count! We've got it all wrong!" before marching to Capitol Hill with an armful of thick binders for an impassioned plea to make the census a more accurate snapshot of the populace.

A more representative accounting begins with distinguishing the lanes of American experience: those considered white Americans from birth, those whose ancestors were Native, those whose ancestors were enslaved, and those who arrived more recently.

PEOPLE DESCENDED from the Philippines seem to have a knack for blending into their environment. Part of it might be our penchant for optimism, the sum of our religious faith and the laid-back vibes of island culture. Part of it might be an instinct forged through centuries of colonial submission, when surviving and succeeding meant surrendering to the flow of history as the empires saw it. Our peoples' adaptability has been an indispensable asset, burnishing our reputation around the world as unfailingly warm and polite people, always smiling, glad to serve, not just because it was required of us but because it was in our very nature. David Draper, a white Vietnam war veteran who was stationed in the Philippines and has visited many times since, told me that he was struck by how generous and welcoming locals were, even amid the wooden shacks and dirt floors of poor villages: "I don't know whether Filipinos have a depression gene or not," he said. "Everybody's happy."

And who can be happier than the blessed Pinoys and Pinays on American soil? Our joy is perhaps most noticeable in our wholehearted

embrace of the new land, evident from our relative lack of interest in promoting our nationality: for the fourth-largest diaspora in the United
States, the Filipino presence is relatively light on the cultural stage—
with fewer visible flags, restaurants, fictional characters, and mainstream
symbols than our numbers might suggest. Many of our last names sound
Latinx, some of our faces look East Asian or Central American, and our
kitchens are often stocked with goods from Chinese supermarkets. We
seem to mix easily into the melting pot, just as we desired, often slipping
through without leaving the distinct flavor of any specific origin.

Though I'm half-Lebanese, I grew up feeling full Filipino American—
I knew only my mom's side, the Concepcion branch of my family tree.
But I wasn't sure what that meant here. My understanding of my heritage was limited and literal, just the relatives I knew and a range of disparate artifacts and photographs filled with meaning beyond my grasp.
The Philippines was as indecipherable to me as the United States was to
my mother, yet my ties to that country defined the contours of my
American experience—my skin color, the cities we settled in, the customs and perspectives my mom's generation brought into our households. In my grade school years, I had no sense of how my ethnicity
framed me in the eyes of others, nor had I even realized that such frames
existed.

Looking back to the time in my life before I really knew what racism
was, I can remember two incidents of injustice that in the moment felt
merely arbitrary and confounding. Both occurred in third grade. A few
weeks into the school year, the teacher, who was white, picked out the
students she deemed most advanced at math and assigned them to work
on their own in the hallway, moving forward in the workbook without
the rest of the class slowing them down. I wasn't one of the students she
picked, and I remember feeling hurt and resentful. The previous year I'd
been among the first to learn the multiplication tables, and when the
report cards came in I was the only one in my class to get straight 1's (the

school's version of A's). Three of the kids selected were white, the fourth Chinese American. The slight nagged at me for weeks. Then, one day, the teacher went on medical leave and a substitute took over for the rest of the year. I saw an opening. When math period began on the sub's first day, I sauntered out of the classroom with the other advanced math students. Nobody said anything, and I spent the rest of that school year's math classes in the hallway.

The second incident happened one morning just before Christmas break. I entered the stately stone building and greeted a white classmate standing by the staircase in front of an intricate construction-paper diorama of a winter wonderland: a log cabin beneath a sky coated with what appeared to be baby powder for snow. I started laughing when I noticed that somebody had drawn a smiley face in the powder. My friend asked what I was laughing at and I stuck my arm out and pointed at it. Just then, I heard one of the nuns shouting the principal's name from down the hall. "I got them! I got them!" she said, advancing on us so swiftly that I can only conclude she'd been staking out the crime scene. She accused me of defacing not only this artwork but a series of them—apparently administrators had been investigating a spate of hallway vandalism for some time. I pleaded innocence. My classmate stayed silent, paralyzed by the chiding we were taking. "But I didn't do it," I kept saying, as the nun and the principal went on about respecting property and how I should take school more seriously. "I was just pointing at it." They didn't believe me. I was bewildered. I was a goody-goody kid to a T. Always did my work on time, never disrupted class, not an ounce of trouble. Why didn't they believe me? It dawned on me that I was being done wrong and there was nothing I could do about it. This memory is the first time I can remember feeling outrage. I could sense that something was off but had no idea what or why. I stayed at the school for another ten months, never really feeling comfortable there again, often faking illness so I could stay home. The following October, we moved to

San Mateo, where my mom enrolled me at the Catholic school where Auntie Lyn taught.

Years later, when I was more conscious of race and how it shaped the way people thought about other people, I came to see those incidents with a fresh clarity. I didn't know for sure if my brown skin had anything to do with what happened, but I had a framework for understanding the mechanics of the world around me, explanations for realities that seemed senseless.

THE ELDERS TAUGHT my cousins and me to pinch our noses every day so that our noses would end up narrow like white people's, and not flat like our genes intended. If one of us was lying down on the floor, our elders warned the rest of us not to step over that cousin because doing so would stunt their growth, and the Concepcions had long taken pride in being tall for our race, a blessing we credited to the Spanish blood in our mestizo veins. Unlike our Mexican and Chinese classmates, we didn't speak our parents' native language at home because our parents said Tagalog was useless in America and it was English we needed to master. They taught us only the Tagalog words we needed to survive: "tabi apo" to keep the dwendes from cursing us when we stepped outside, "pwera usog" to ward off hexes from jealous observers when something good happened to us, and "pwera gaba" to block the evil spirits from turning their wrath on us when we heard about somebody's hardship—though I eventually picked up an intermediate understanding of Tagalog from years of eavesdropping on my mom's late-night phone calls with her sisters.

We embraced the Western traditions our American colonizers traced their roots to. My mom decorated our apartment with a High Renaissance aesthetic—ceramics shaped like cherubs, high-backed dark wooden chairs with shiny white seat cushions, couch cushions and teacups with floral motifs. Shelves held small statues of Jesus, Mary, and saints with brown hair and fair skin. A *Last Supper* print hung on a wall.

For my mom, assimilation into white America was neither ideological stance nor endorsement of all that it represented, but something closer to pragmatic instinct. She hummed along indifferently to the national anthem before sporting events, finding the whole spectacle of flags and soldiers an exercise in false idolatry. To pass the test to become a citizen, she studied the textbook summary of U.S. history, hitting the main points, memorizing the amendments and presidents, learning about the generals of the Civil War and the leaders of the civil rights movement. Names, dates, and events etched into a past disconnected from her own—apparitions from a time before she or anyone she knew had stepped foot here. In her mind, America meant the opportunities it presented us, nothing more.

As she understood the situation, most of the people who occupied the spaces we wanted to occupy and controlled the gates to those spaces were white. From third grade to seventh grade, as we followed the trail of affordable housing south to San Mateo, then east to Sacramento, I attended five Catholic, private, and public schools, and every principal and all but two of my teachers were white. Nearly all our local newscasters were white, and all but one of the anchors I watched on SportsCenter were white. The coaches of my favorite athletes were white and the record executives who signed my favorite artists were white. Every pope and U.S. president, white. We had come here to succeed like white people, so who better to guide us?

One way this manifested was in my family's reflexive acceptance of racist stereotypes born in the West. When we gathered at Caridad's house in the Fillmore every Christmas, aunties would pray aloud that their cars wouldn't get broken into. Sometimes they'd be telling a story, and when they got around to describing a person in the story—"He was this tall guy, crossing the street"—they'd note the race in whispered

Tagalog—"itim"—and then go on talking in a regular voice. It was a sign of their discomfort with the subject. To their eyes, race was a mere data point in the calculus of America. Their understanding was tactical. One Christmas, when I wore basketball shorts and a Terrell Owens jersey to our family gathering, one of my aunties whispered to my mom, in disappointment, "He's dressed like an itim."

MY MOM AND I learned parallel stories of America. Her earliest understanding filtered through histories written by white people in positions of authority, broadcast across the ocean in textbook tales of a democracy founded upon Christian values, the reassuring rhetoric of presidential speeches and John Wayne movies, newscasts on internal conflicts that nudged America to a better place, snippets of Martin Luther King, Jr.'s words about seeing the mountaintop and the moral arc of the universe bending toward justice. The understanding hardened with time, packed together by her migrant ambition to learn the rules and climb the ranks.

It only occurred to me years later that while my mom was raising me to blend in among white people, I was a kid who wanted to be Black. I didn't think of it that way at the time. I was simply picking up cues from the influences in front of me.

Sitting on the couch most weeknight evenings, I thought Kenan Thompson and Kel Mitchell were the funniest cast members on Nickelodeon's *All That*, my favorite TV show. I sang along with Tevin Campbell's catchy choruses in *A Goofy Movie*. I venerated Michael Jordan after watching him defeat the Monstars in the movie *Space Jam* and win the first three NBA championships I ever saw. With my cousin Chris, I listened to "Crossroads" by Bone Thugs-n-Harmony, dancing on the carpet to the rappers' rapid-fire verses about their dead loved ones, each of us taking an earbud from Chris's CD player so our parents didn't hear the song's curse words. With Lauren, I memorized the lyrics to "Take Me There," the Blackstreet, Mya, and Mase song from the *Rugrats Movie* soundtrack, as we swayed in our seatbelts in the backseat of Blue Angel.

The summer after second grade, I went to football camp hosted by 49ers fullback William Floyd, and the next year, one hosted by Denver Broncos linebacker John Mobley, accelerating a budding obsession with sports that my mom was grateful for, as she considered it a traditional component of American boyhood. From our games of catch, she learned to throw a football in a spiral and snag a baseball with a mitt, and from the games we watched on television, she developed fierce loyalty to the teams that represented our region, praying for God to bless Jerry Rice and Barry Bonds.

On the patio in Vallejo, Jed and I would mimic the eccentricities of particular basketball players' free-throw routines like a game of charades: Jason Kidd blowing a kiss, Alonzo Mourning tapping his wristband to his face, Jerry Stackhouse squatting to his heels. When Roscoe was redecorating his room, he offered me his Grant Hill and Ken Griffey, Jr., posters, which became the first posters I ever had. When my cousin Mitch moved to California from the Philippines in 1999 at age sixteen, we'd listen to her favorite singer, Aaliyah, in her bedroom while she told me about the classes she was taking at community college, and when her brother, Mico, arrived in 2001, the day before his twenty-first birthday, he advised me to start listening to Tupac instead of Nelly and that other "soft shit" in my CD case.

The contours of American reality unfurled for me in songs, shows, and sports books—culture seeped faster into my childhood brain than classroom knowledge. The stories I heard were set amid unjust odds, neglectful institutions, and repressive forces. I learned about Huey Newton from a Tupac song—"two shots in the dark, now Huey's dead"—before I ever heard his name mentioned in school. I read, in the paperback on my nightstand, that Josh Gibson might've been better than Babe

Ruth, and I watched, from the DVD spinning in our living room, the crew-cutted cop kill Radio Raheem. Like many second-generation immigrants, I learned about our country from Black people.

I didn't know yet about Parchman Farm prison, or Black Wall Street, or the Tuskegee syphilis experiment, or the massacres of the post-Reconstruction era, or the CIA supplying the crack cocaine trade, but I was learning the language necessary to understand the magnitude of that history. From those stories in childhood—warning marks etched on the road by travelers long before us—I picked up on the fact that my family and our fellow immigrants weren't new arrivals merely to a nation but to a long-standing system of racial oppression, suspended somewhere between those who conquered the land by blood and those whose blood built the empire. We had come by choice but in peace, with neither the privileges of whiteness nor the weight of Blackness. Where did that leave us?

EARLY FILIPINO IMMIGRANTS who assumed they would encounter a blank slate upon arrival were surprised to discover that a place had already been set for them in America's race-based caste system.

In the late 1920s, when Anacleto Gorospe entered a St. Louis railroad station restaurant with signs designating white and Black sections, he refused the manager's demands that he sit on the Black side. "I was neither Black nor white and had the right to choose the room I ate in," he recalled in Roberto's oral history. He left when police threatened to arrest him. "It seems that even if a guy is as wise as Jesus Christ, if he is not white, he can't measure up," Gorospe concluded.

The United States legitimized its racial caste system by codifying it into the law with a brute simplicity that failed to account for the arbitrary bounds of ethnicity and skin color. As more immigrants arrived in the States, lawmakers had to increasingly specify who exactly could claim the constitutional rights granted to "free white persons." People from Germany, Ireland, Italy, Poland, and Russia faced xenophobic discrimination in the States, but under the law their whiteness superseded their particular ancestry—they were not prohibited from marrying or going to school with white people, and they were eligible to become American citizens after two years.

The Founding Fathers didn't define "free white person." Takao Ozawa, who emigrated from Japan in the 1890s, went to college in Hawaii, then ran a business, applied for naturalized U.S. citizenship in 1915 as a "free white person"—at the time only "free white persons" and "persons of African descent" could become citizens without being born in the nation. Arguing his case before the U.S. Supreme Court, Ozawa pointed out that the law couldn't deny him the rights of whiteness on the basis of his skin color. "The Japanese are of lighter color than other East Asiatics, not rarely showing the transparent pink tint which whites assume as their own privilege," he stated. "In the typical Japanese city of Kyoto, those not exposed to the heat of summer are particularly white-skinned. They are whiter than the average Italian, Spaniard or Portuguese."

But the Supreme Court rejected Ozawa's petition for citizenship in 1922 because American whiteness is not a measure of color but of ancestry, and Ozawa was "clearly of a race which is not Caucasian," Justice George Sutherland wrote in the unanimous decision. "The conclusion that the words 'white person' means a Caucasian is not to establish a sharp line of demarcation between those who are entitled and those who are not entitled to naturalization, but rather a zone of more or less debatable ground."

The next year, Bhagat Singh Thind's application for whiteness reached the high court. He had left India in 1913 after graduating from college, served as a sergeant in the U.S. military during World War I, then applied for U.S. citizenship as a "white person" in 1918.

His argument centered not on skin color but on lineage: he identified as Caucasian. He presented to the court ethnographic studies and scientific research claiming that his "high caste" ancestry in northwest India traced to the "Aryan race." His blood, he argued, was as Caucasian as that of white Americans because his ancestors had similarly resisted marriage to other races. "The high-caste Hindu regards the aboriginal Indian Mongoloid in the same manner as the American regards the Negro," Thind's lawyers stated.

But the court opted to avoid the messy genealogical task of untangling who is technically Caucasian. No matter what Thind claimed about his "purity of Aryan blood," he wasn't Caucasian according to the "common understanding," Sutherland wrote in the 1923 unanimous decision. The word "Caucasian" wasn't meant to be applied literally but symbolically, the court explained, because laws are written in language "not of scientific origin" but "in the common speech, for common understanding, by unscientific men." In other words, whiteness was whatever white people said it was.

As a result of the rulings, non-European immigrants who had already gained citizenship suddenly had it stripped away. Among them was Vaishno Das Bagai, an Indian immigrant who arrived in San Francisco in 1915, got married, had three kids, and opened up a general store on Fillmore Street. With his citizenship rescinded in 1925, he lost his business and his passport. Three years later, at the age of thirty-seven, he killed himself. His suicide note was published, at his request, in the *San Francisco Examiner*: "What have I made of myself and my children?" he wrote. "We cannot exercise our rights. . . . Humility and insults, who is responsible for all this? Myself and American government. . . . Obstacles this way, blockades that way, and the bridges burnt behind."

American lawmakers justified their prejudices with claims that only white people were capable of fully integrating into civilized society. For immigrants offended by this premise, what better way to prove it wrong than to adopt whatever traits this civilized society valued? How could anyone claim supremacy over someone who spoke like them, dressed like them, and championed their ideals? Assimilation offered the most visible path to privileges reserved for white Americans.

In pursuing the rights of whiteness, Ozawa and Thind didn't challenge the constitutionality of race-based laws but sought to exempt themselves from the excluded races. Proximity to American whiteness requires distance from the castes deemed inferior. In a court brief explaining why Japanese immigrant Takuji Yamashita was denied the right of a "free white person" to buy land in Washington, the state attorney general acknowledged that "the Japanese are quite as capable as the Italians, the Armenians, or the Slavs of acquiring our culture and sharing our national ideals." The "trouble," he said, was their "marked physical characteristics." With this "racial uniform," he concluded, "they will probably never be assimilated." As evidence that anyone who didn't look European could never fit into American society, the attorney general cited "the Negro, the Indian and the Chinaman."

The laws gave little ground on the question of whiteness, but in 1933, Salvador Roldan, a Filipino immigrant from northern Ilocos, didn't have to be white to marry Marjorie Rogers, a white British woman he met on a tennis court in Pasadena, California. Though "Filipino" had been listed on the census for a decade, California's miscegenation law hadn't been updated since it was written in 1880 to cover "negros," "mulattos," and "Mongolians."

In Los Angeles County, where Roldan lived, clerks for years had sought clarification on whether people from the Philippines should be designated as "Mongolians." The county's legal counsel said they weren't, but the attorney general said they were. Four local judges split on the issue. The clerk's office switched its policy back and forth, without definitive guidance. When Roldan was denied a marriage license, he sued the county, arguing that his union was legal because he wasn't "Mongolian." California's appeals court agreed. The judge's reasoning was consistent with the Supreme Court's past ruling on how to define "Caucasian":

"Mongolian" was commonly understood to mean people with Chinese ancestry and didn't include "Malay" people from the Philippines. According to the laws on the books, Roldan was free to wed his Anglo fiancée.

A week later, California's state legislature passed a bill adding "Malays" to the list of races barred from marrying white people.

STILL, THEY STAYED.

Despite what he saw and experienced, Carlos Bulosan kept his faith in the country, writing that America's democratic ideals had instilled in him "a feeling of hope for the future instead of bitter defeat." American racism, he and many others believed, was not a pillar of the country's collective value system but a stain its people would ultimately wash away.

That optimism made more bearable the practical reality that no decent alternative seemed to exist. Those who made it into the country could consider themselves fortunate. In 1934, as part of an agreement to grant the Philippines independence by 1945, the U.S. Congress set quotas for Filipino immigrants: no more than fifty were to be allowed into the States each year. The promise of nationhood did little to alter the prospects of most people on the Islands. Pinoys living in the United States read letters from loved ones who remained impoverished and were now stuck without an exit ramp to try their luck across the ocean.

Grateful for their admittance, many Filipino immigrants thought it best to lie low and keep the faith in America's slow march toward equality. When Jose Sarmiento arrived in San Francisco in 1926, he found that "getting a job was always a problem" because employers preferred to hire white people, he recalled in Roberto's oral history. "So what could we do? We had to take work from any place willing to hire us so we could eat." For fifteen years, he washed bottles at a drugstore alongside two other Pinoy immigrants. One of them had a law degree. Sarmiento found it distasteful when overqualified immigrants complained about the racist hiring practices that blocked them from higher-paid jobs. "They think they are too good to do menial labor," he said. "But I don't think doing any kind of work to get ahead is a disgrace."

He went to night school to get his high school diploma and picked up gigs cooking for white families. One of his bosses was San Francisco's police commissioner. One day, officers detained him on the street, brought him to the police station, and questioned him about the disappearance of a girl in Los Angeles, four hundred miles away. When he denied knowing anything about this, they beat him. He didn't tell them he worked for their boss, and when he saw the police commissioner the next day, he didn't mention the incident. "I just kept it to myself," he said. His standing in the country was too fragile for him to introduce unnecessary complications. "I'm very proud to be an American," he said. "I don't want to be anything else!"

The benefits of living in a wealthy democracy included a widening social safety net, ushered in by President Franklin Roosevelt's New Deal, a massive government spending program that established retirement pensions for all citizens and funded 8.5 million jobs on public works projects. One of those jobs went to Roberto Vallangca, who was hired to paint murals and posters as part of the Federal Art Project. He had developed his artistic talents as a child, using bamboo sticks to sketch on banana leaves because his parents couldn't afford paper and pencil. In his teenage years, people around his hometown commissioned him to paint portraits of loved ones who'd just died, to keep their image alive at a time before widespread access to photography. With his New Deal salary, he enrolled at San Francisco's Heald College to study architectural engineering.

This education came at an ideal time for Roberto. The United States soon entered World War II, and when he was drafted into the armed services, he qualified for a job that kept him in an office helping design ships and submarines. He was assigned to the Mare Island Naval Shipyard, a sprawling base in Vallejo that employed nearly fifty thousand people and had its own hospital, fire station, and recreational sports leagues. Wartime urgency had opened up thousands of government-wage jobs at the base, and people from around the country poured into the city—Black families from the South, white families from the Midwest, Mexican families from California's farming hubs, Filipino military families fleeing the Islands, which had come under Japanese occupation. From this foundation of wartime arrivals, Vallejo would eventually reach the distinction, by some measures, of being the most racially diverse city in America; today, the city officially commemorates Juneteenth, Cinco de Mayo, and Philippine Independence Day.

Those without the privileges of whiteness are left to jostle for jobs and standing, perpetually at risk of getting knocked back down the line. The spinning wheel of world events could at any time land with the arrow identifying you as a threat to America. The Trump administration imprisoned Latinx families for immigration violations, the Bush administration imprisoned people of Arab descent for suspected affiliations with terrorist groups, and decades before that, Franklin Roosevelt's administration imprisoned Japanese communities for fear they harbored spies.

This wartime removal of the Japanese from the picture left jobs, land, and customers up for grabs. In Yakima Valley, Washington, farms that had relied on Japanese employees hired Mexican guest workers who'd been granted visas under a U.S. program aimed at filling labor shortages. In Honolulu, Hawaii, one of the few places where Japanese people weren't expelled, locals boycotted Japanese-owned stores, bringing a surge of new customers to a barbershop and laundromat owned by a Pinay immigrant, Apolinaria Gusman Oclaray. "I took over all the Japanese business," she recalled in the oral history. "They were considered the enemy."

Sometimes white locals attacked Filipino people, confusing them for Japanese, just as decades later white people would attack Sikhs they thought were Muslim. In a country founded with two races in mind, the shades in between get muddled, with designations and definitions shifting based on how the white majority sees it. The caste system is rooted to its poles, the foundational divide between those whose labor fueled America's rise and those who reaped the benefits. Three centuries of bloody negotiation preceded Roberto's arrival in the United States, setting the terms for his social contract: best-case scenario, you get treated as if you're white; worst-case scenario, you get treated as if you're Black.

At the naval bases during World War II, white supervisors would fire Black workers just before they reached permanent status, then rehire them the following week, ensuring they stayed at the rookie pay scale, even after a decade on the job. Black workers were most often assigned to the most dangerous task, loading munitions in and out of ships. Around ten p.m. on July 17, 1944, in the Port Chicago Naval Magazine, about twenty minutes southeast of Vallejo, as a group of workers hauled live bombs into the SS *E. A. Bryan,* a cargo vessel, a load exploded, combusting with the ship's fuel, leveling the pier into wooden shards, wounding 390 workers, and killing 320, more than 200 of them Black. Afterward, dozens of Black workers protested, refusing to load munitions unless the danger was equally distributed among races. Fifty of them were convicted of mutiny in a military court by seven white naval officers. They were imprisoned until the end of the war and weren't granted clemency until 1999.

THE WAR WORKED OUT well for Roberto Vallangca. During his off-hours, he took classes at a chiropractor college, earning his certification before Japan surrendered. For his military service, he was granted American citizenship. The navy transferred him to San Francisco, and there he met my grandaunt Caridad Concepcion, who'd arrived in the city after the war for a job in the U.S. Army's Veterans Administration. They got married and bought a house in the Fillmore District, settling down just in time for America's coronation as a global superpower.

IN THE YEARS after the war, Vallejo transformed from a sleepy outpost into a bona fide American suburb. From 1950 to 1970, its population rose from around 26,000 to 70,000. "City of Opportunity," read the welcome sign on Interstate 80, as the highway curved into a final stretch of rolling green hills and moderate summers before dipping into the Central Valley.

Blocked from buying property in white neighborhoods, most of Vallejo's Black population lived on the north side, the city's farthest point from the marina. To house the influx of workers during the war years, the government built the city's largest housing project, Chabot Terrace, locally and ironically nicknamed "the country club." With their wages suppressed, many Black shipyard workers ended up in the development's low-lying mobile homes. As more Black families arrived, their housing choices were limited to north Vallejo, which became one of America's many "abandoned and identifiable no-man's-lands that came into being when the least-paid people were forced to pay the highest rents for the most dilapidated housing owned by absentee landlords trying to wring the most money out of a place nobody cared about," as Isabel Wilkerson described the formation of Black communities in the North and West in her book about the Great Migration, *The Warmth of Other Suns.*

One opportunistic white developer in Vallejo built a subdivision near the highway targeted at Black customers. By the time my family arrived in the neighborhood, that subdivision, and the ones that sprouted up around it, had become a hub for Filipino people.

With their homeland's history so tightly intertwined with America's, immigrants from the Philippines had a head start on many other new arrivals. They were fluent in the language, had grown up consuming American culture, and found communities already in place when the wave carried them in. A Pinoy manager, Tony Magsanay, took over the gas station next to Vallejo City Hall in the 1960s, and in 1973, a Pinoy candidate, Larry Asera, was elected to city council. In 1975, a Pinay cheerleading captain, Lisa Hullana, won homecoming queen at Hogan High School, and in the 1980s, a Pinoy biology teacher, Mike Santos, coached its football team. Filipino restaurants, grocery stores, churches, salons, political groups, gangs, and festivals sprouted. In 1960, less than 3 percent of Vallejo's population classified on the census as Asian or Pacific Islander; by 1990, Filipino people made up a fifth of the city's population, and by 2010, around a quarter—only Daly City, in the South Bay, has a higher share. In 2017, Vallejo became one of the first American cities to elect a Filipino mayor, Bob Sampayan, a retired police officer.

Memories of the old country's flaws shaped how migrants experienced their new land. Bribes, war, poverty, coups—stories passed down from the elders reminded the children of how fortunate they were to be born in America. In the decades before my family arrived, the children of Black people who left the South during the Great Migration heard stories of their own, carrying similar lessons, though the horrors they recounted were bloodier than anything my family had left. And yet often those children did not see what they had to be so grateful for or impressed by in the place where their families had arrived. "The discontent of the young people unsettled the migrant parents who had fled the violence of the South," Wilkerson wrote. "The parents had come from the Old Country, had been happy to have made it out alive and make a few dollars an hour. *What did they know of the frustration of the young people who had grown up in the mirage of equality but a whole different reality . . . with promises that seemed to have turned to dust?*"

Some of those children found purpose in pushing the country toward the vision their parents had believed in. Huey Newton, founder of the Black Panther Party in 1966 and "perhaps the most militant of the disillusioned offspring of the Great Migration," in Wilkerson's words, was a baby when his sharecropper parents arrived in Oakland after a mob tried to lynch his father for talking back to his white bosses in Monroe, Louisiana. Cesar Chavez, who organized the first successful union of farmworkers in California, was born in Yuma, Arizona, in 1927, three decades after his parents migrated from Mexico. Yuri Kochiyama, a civil rights activist who helped secure reparations for interned Japanese families, was born in San Pedro, California, in 1921, and in 1942 witnessed her father die of illness one day after he was released from FBI detention after allegations that he was a spy were found to be baseless.

For those in the second generation, there was no old country to refract a glimmering sheen upon America.

JED KEPT his megastar backup plan to himself. As the crossroads of high school graduation approached, his doubts about staying ran up against evidence that his parents' investment might be paying off.

Halfway through his junior year, they surprised him with a green two-door Geo Metro hatchback they'd been saving up for. Jed took such pride in the vehicle that he resisted his mother's efforts to christen it with a name, as she had for the other cars in the family.

"Jed where did you park Green Lightning?" Auntie Ging would say.

"Geo Metro, Mom," Jed would correct. "I found a spot down the street."

No longer dependent on tagging along wherever his friends were going, Jed expanded his social circle. He started getting invited to cotillions instead of crashing them. He got a girlfriend and spent most of his senior year with her, at the movies or the mall, or studying in her bedroom.

Who knows what would have happened had Jed not gotten into the one college he applied to? He was more surprised by the acceptance than his mother was. Anticipating the possibility, she had saved up a modest college fund over the years. A few thousand dollars in loans, painlessly obtained on an hour-long visit to the bank, covered the rest of the tuition at San Francisco State University.

The new possibilities excited Jed and served as a target for his un-tapped energy. Two months into his first semester of college, he got a job at Macy's, racking and folding clothes. "Just a lowly Christmas hire," he said. But his bosses liked him, saw that he was good with people, and switched him to selling suits, where he made a commission. Soon he as-cended to the shoe department, where the money was better. On his days off, he worked shifts behind the register of Auntie Lyn's gift shop. Though he was starting to make enough money to get his own place, Jed stayed in the Visitacion Valley studio with his parents and sister, sleep-ing on a cot, and chipped in on rent.

VHS tapes of class lectures played on the TV while his parents and sister sat at the dining table an arm's reach behind him, reading or eat-ing or folding clothes. Jed studied long hours, determined to keep pace with his classmates, who were mostly white, East Asian, or Filipino. He hadn't put much thought into career options beyond megastar, though, and by the second semester of his sophomore year, in spring 2000, he still hadn't decided on a major. His closest friends at school were apply-ing for nursing, one of the most competitive programs at the university. They told him nurses could make forty-five dollars an hour in Califor-nia, with good benefits and flexible schedules. Some were following in the footsteps of older relatives in the profession.

For decades, Filipino immigrants and their children had pursued nursing as a path to upward mobility. Nurses from the Philippines filled shortages in hospitals around the world, most frequently in the U.S., the UK, and other Western nations. Our uncle Joey had been among the thousands of Filipino nurses who found work in Australia. In California, a fifth of nurses are of Filipino descent. The prevalence of Filipino nurses helps explain statistics showing that people from the Philippines have been among the most financially successful diasporas in the United States, with a median annual income of $80,000, second highest among immigrant groups. Nursing offered Jed a chance to be on the right side of the data.

And if the job didn't suit him, he could always try something else. "If I get a degree in nursing I could do whatever the fuck I want," he remembers thinking. "Be an astronaut. Enter the NFL draft. Because if I fail, I could do this." Having survived his first two years of college with Bs and Cs, he didn't expect to get in.

When Jed read out the acceptance letter, his mom and dad cheered like he'd won the Super Bowl. Jed was sure he'd been admitted only because few men applied and administrators were trying to reduce the gender imbalance in the nursing industry.

Regardless, nursing school infused Jed with a clear sense of purpose. His notes, scribbled in neat blue ink, transcribed nearly every word his professors uttered. He quizzed himself with index cards. After class he went to work, in the evening he studied. If the studio was too loud with TV or chatter, he'd bunker in the bathroom with the door closed, sitting on the toilet seat with earplugs in, or he'd study in the garage, amid the laundry lines and the vibrations of the washing machine and the ticking of the car as it cooled down, or in the school's 24-hour library.

To his surprise, he failed his first exam; he thought he'd been prepared.

He sat in his car and cried. Then he stewed for days, sprinting the hill outside the studio over and over, the cold air burning with each breath, until his self-pity dissolved into rage. "I was mad at myself," he said. "Mad at Vallejo for not preparing me." He needed more time than his classmates to do the readings. He struggled to distinguish critical information from trivial digression in lectures. He knew no mnemonic techniques for memorizing facts. He'd gotten by on sheer effort and charm in his early semesters, but now he faced the exacting standards of a profession where competence can mean the difference between a person living and dying. Here was an opportunity to improve his standing, and he was squandering it.

"I was like, Fuck this. Fuck this, dude. This isn't how I'm gonna end my shit," he said. "You ain't gonna get the best of me, man."

THERE WAS NO MAGIC to Jed's turnaround. Realizing his tactics had been all wrong, he turned to those around him for assistance. He began meeting with professors after class. He joined study groups and observed what his classmates were doing differently. He improved his note-taking techniques so that he was only writing down the important details. He asked questions when he wasn't sure he understood a concept. Gradually, the answers came easier.

By his second year of nursing school, Jed had enough of a handle on his academics that his weekends were usually free. He allowed himself the indulgence of exploring San Francisco. To that point, he'd only experienced the city through the narrow dimensions of his childhood—the toy stores in the Richmond District, the dim sum restaurants in Chinatown, the residential blocks of Visitacion Valley and the Fillmore.

On his weekend expeditions into the dot-com boomtown, he let off steam in the neon glow of warehouse raves, dancing with his college friends, euphoria washing over them. After predawn burritos, he'd catch the bus home as the sky's midnight blue brightened into a hazy indigo. With his parents and sister back in Vallejo until Sunday night, the studio would be empty and dark, the curtains drawn. He'd kick off his shoes, crash on the couch, and sleep cozy and happy till early afternoon.

When Jed passed the nursing board exam, he parted ways with his backup plan without ceremony. For the first time he could remember, the road ahead looked inviting. "I worked so hard to get this," he said. "I wanna see where it's gonna take me."

He got a job at a big hospital in San Francisco, working the night shift. The first few weeks were shaky. The neighbor next door to the studio had recently started a band and they practiced several afternoons a week, to Jed's immense frustration. He decided it was time to move out. He picked a studio apartment twenty miles south of the city, in Burlingame, a shoreside suburb with sleepy streets and a low-slung downtown lined with boutiques. It was cheaper out there, and though the studio wasn't any bigger than the one he'd left, "it felt like a mansion" now that the space was all his. With the money he saved, Jed splurged on designer jeans, street art figurines, and multiday music festivals. He got a new car, a silver hatchback Toyota Matrix with four-wheel drive for snowboarding trips to Tahoe. He paired his big-screen TV with surround-sound speakers. He traveled with friends to Spain, Italy, and the Philippines. He ate indulgently, always ordering another round of food and drink to keep the party going, always offering to cover the bill. So comfortable was he with his financial status that he even wore the Air Jordans that as a teen he'd kept untouched in their original boxes as investments.

It was around this time that Jed gave me his durag. He'd had it since he was sixteen, when he braided his hair into cornrows. Even when he wore the durag to sleep, his straight hair kept slipping out. His boys clowned his look relentlessly, so he dropped the style after a few weeks, but he'd held on to the durag for occasions when it complemented an outfit. He couldn't remember the last time he'd worn it.

When he looked at pictures of himself from high school, he jokingly dubbed his past self "Vallejo Jed." San Francisco Jed had bangs, wore tighter pants, and listened to rock and techno. I felt blindsided by his swift transformation. I wasn't sure how to address the impression that my beloved older cousin, whom I trusted, revered, and emulated, appeared to be siding with the colonizers. I handled this distressing matter as he would have done to me: I clowned his ass. I asked him how he could move around in those pants and how many bottles of gel he needed to keep his hair spiky. I expressed disappointment when he was unfamiliar with an up-and-coming hip-hop artist. When I hit a shot over him on the basketball court, I trash-talked his declining skills, how soft he'd gotten.

JED WAS MY BASELINE for what it meant to be Filipino American, a walking catalogue of the cultural traits I identified with. His influence guided me well. Any new classroom I dropped into, I found the same bonds linking me to classmates I knew little about. In fourth grade, many of the boys in my class loved professional wrestling as much as Jed and I did and were impressed that I could raise my eyebrow like The Rock, and roll my eyes back like the Undertaker. During a lunchtime basketball game on my first day of fifth grade, I stole the ball from a respected classmate, and he responded by befriending me and picking me first the next day. In sixth grade, I won the favor of the seventh and eighth graders at our lunch table when I joined them in reciting Snoop Dogg's verse in "Lay Low."

This common ground helped me find my bearings among the unfamiliar faces I hoped to win over. My immersion in the central currents of American culture turned out to be a valuable investment: my hours watching television every day and my efforts to replicate the feats of my heroes granted me currency for social advancement in turn-of-the-millennium Northern California.

Just as my interests brought me closer to classmates who liked basketball and hip-hop, my vague awareness of my ethnicity pulled me into the orbit of any Filipino kid I encountered. Somehow, across the varying demographic arrangements at all my schools, there were always at least a few Filipino students in my circle. We formed friendships almost instinctively, as if by better understanding one another we could forge a clear vision of Filipino identity from the disjointed remnants our parents had left us, which we had cobbled into a genuine but superficial pride. We bragged about our people's cuisine, describing flavors so delightfully intense in sour sinigang, salty bagoong, and tangy dinuguan that you need a spoonful of rice to balance out the taste. We dropped stray bits of Tagalog into our conversations, like "sayang" for throwing away food, "naks naman" for fly outfits, and "ang galing" for impressive shots on the basketball court. We showed our white friends the traditional wooden barrelman on our living room shelves, erupting in laughter when they removed the barrel and the wooden figure's enormous dick sprang up like a jack-in-the-box.

When anyone called us "Asian," we corrected them with "Pacific Islander." We couldn't have articulated the colonial dynamic that distinguished Filipino culture from the rest of the so-called East, but we felt certain we were somehow distinct. The canonical characters of American culture who most resembled many of us were ethnically ambiguous brown people like Aladdin (Arabic), Benny "The Jet" Rodriguez (Mexican), and The Rock (part Samoan). Many of us were mestizos of some sort, and none of us were pure Malay, but we couldn't have traced the genealogy beyond our parents being from the Philippines. We lacked a unifying theory of Filipino culture that identified the shared parameters of our common ground. If challenged, we cited standardized tests that gave "Filipino" its own bubble on the portion asking us to mark our race—affirmative evidence that we weren't quite Asian.

IN THIS PARCHED STATE, I had my first experience seeing multiple Filipino people on a screen, in a 2000 movie called *The Debut*, written and directed by Gene Cajayon, a Filipino Vietnamese immigrant who grew up in Southern California. Dante Basco stars as Ben Mercado, the American-raised child of immigrants from the Philippines. From the opening shot panning the photos on his bedroom wall over a rock music score, the first thing we learn about seventeen-year-old Ben is that all his friends seem to be white. When they come over to his house, he is embarrassed by the vinegary smells wafting from the kitchen and the crude barrelman on the shelf. He doesn't understand Tagalog and isn't looking forward to his sister's debut, her eighteenth-birthday cotillion, which happens to fall on the same night as a highly anticipated keg party. His ambitions to go to art school clash with the demands of his strict father, a postal worker who left a singing career in the Philippines to raise his children in the United States with the expectation that his son would become a doctor.

Our protagonist's predicament would have been straightforward had he merely been detached from his parents' culture—who among us?—but Cajayon delves into the entanglements of our diaspora by showing how Ben's aspirations for whiteness alienate him from his Filipino peers. His parents chastise him for not participating in the preparations for the cotillion, and his grandfather expresses disappointment that he doesn't speak Tagalog or know traditional etiquette, but they don't seem to have a problem with his general association with white culture. His mother warmly welcomes his white friends when they visit, offering them food and asking why he doesn't bring them around more. At the cotillion, the elders line-dance to country and western songs. An auntie gossips about a woman who "thinks she's so great, just because she married a white guy." If anything, in elevating whiteness, Ben has taken after his elders.

He is ill-equipped for the social dynamics unfolding at his sister's birthday party. After the meal, while the elders chat in Tagalog at the tables and the children go outside to hang out in the parking lot, Ben sits idly on the gymnasium steps. Though white American culture fused into the customs of immigrants raised in the postwar Philippines, for their children growing up in the States, Black culture is central. After the elders leave the dance floor, a DJ takes the stage to play R&B, and the children form a *Soul Train* line. Ben barely sways to the music, visibly uncomfortable. Later, in one of the few scenes without Ben, his cousins and his sister's friends put on a break-dancing show. Out in the parking lot, near the basketball court, one of Ben's cousins discloses his theory that Muggsy Bogues, the five-foot-three Black NBA star, is actually Filipino, "even if he doesn't know it," because Filipino hoopers are known for packing serious skills into their diminutive frames—and on top of that, look at his flat nose.

This all checked out, to my eyes. This was the second-generation culture I inherited from Jed. Cajayon validated unspoken observations I couldn't yet arrange into meaning, laying out a template for Filipino American identity, giving shape to a label that had been amorphous to me. Affiliating with Black culture was, apparently, just part of being Filipino American. Ben had rejected his Filipino identity not just by failing to learn the island traditions of his parents but by dismissing the new-world rituals of his cousins. His sister calls him out for thinking he's "better than all of us" because, among other things, "you hang out with white boys." She tells him, "Wake up, little brother, 'cause you know what, you're just as brown as the rest of us." There is no ambiguity in the lesson Ben's arc is supposed to teach.

Watching the film for the first time as a kid, however, I was less sure what to make of Ben's archrival, Gusto, played by Dante's brother Darion Basco. Ben and Gusto were close when they were little kids because their parents are friends, but the boys drifted apart in their early teens. From the moment Gusto appears on screen, greeting Ben coldly, it's clear the two boys will collide before the end credits roll. In contrast to Ben's earnest bashfulness, Gusto maintains a hard exterior. He shows up to the cotillion in a loose jacket and baggy jeans. Unlike Ben's luscious

Hollywood coif, Gusto's hair is cut into a close fade, with a part in the front, as popularized by the rapper Nas. About the only thing the boys seem to have in common is basketball prowess—but lest we viewers make too much of this common ground, Cajayon takes the opportunity to accentuate the gap between them: When the boys remove their button-downs to play, we see that Gusto's undershirt is a ribbed tank top and Ben's is a crewneck. More than once in the film, Gusto punctuates his sentences with the N-word.

Given the choice between the movie's protagonist and antagonist, I related more to Gusto. He dressed like I did, his hair looked like mine, and he used similar slang. Like Gusto, I plugged the N-word into my vocabulary, a shameful period that lasted from age fourteen to seventeen. I thought it sounded cool, the way it carried a casual warmth and rebellion. I used the word freely, if not frequently, with my Mexican, Indian, Arab, and Filipino friends. I can't say I was too young or ignorant to know better. Though we brown kids dropped the N-word when we were together, we were careful to never say it in front of Black kids, because we didn't want to offend, or white kids, because we didn't want them to feel comfortable saying it themselves. These rules allowed us to tell ourselves that we were using the word responsibly, as if it were an intoxicant. We weren't frivolously throwing it around. We weren't trolling or employing it ironically. We didn't savor it, or feel any particular thrill or glee when it crossed our lips. We didn't say the word any louder than any other word when rapping along to lyrics. We said it because we believed that the closer we could get to being Black, the higher our social status would be; under that paradigm, the N-word was a trophy of proximity.

I sympathized with Gusto and felt it unjust that he had to be the bad guy and lose to Ben in the end. Their fated conflict turns out to be over a girl, Gusto's ex-girlfriend, Annabelle, whose affections they pursue throughout the cotillion. Annabelle, played by Joy Bisco, embodies an idealized middle ground between the boys, balancing the various cultures around her without elevating any above her own. Unlike Ben and Gusto, she speaks Tagalog. Early in the night, she performs in the traditional Tinikling dance, banging the bamboo poles that set the rhythm, then later, when the lights are dimmed and the DJ is at the turntables, she leads her hip-hop dance crew into choreographed battle against another group at the party. She is equally at ease in the diametrical worlds of her old flame Gusto and her new crush Ben.

Annabelle serves as Ben's guide on his journey toward embracing his culture. After Gusto calls Ben a "white boy," a "sellout," a "fuckin' coconut"—brown on the outside, white on the inside—Ben confides in Annabelle that he fears Gusto is right. She says Gusto has no room to talk: he used to braid his hair into cornrows. "You think that's bad?" Ben counters. "I used to sleep with a clothespin on my nose to make it more pointed." Annabelle tells Ben she thinks his flat nose is cute, and they kiss for the first time.

When I first saw the movie, I pictured Ben and Gusto on opposite ends of a spectrum of Filipino American identity: the boy trying too hard to be white versus the boy trying too hard to be Black—both fleeing their ancestral culture in pursuit of opposite visions of American identity. The wide gap between them reflects the Filipino capacity to assimilate, our centuries-old strategy of slipping on whatever skin suits our goals. Without the gravitational pull of a core identity, we can drift waywardly. I assumed the movie was simply telling me that enlightenment lay in Annabelle's middle ground. But my simplistic conclusion misunderstood Gusto.

He is not an archetype, as Ben is, but a caricature. He carries himself like he's doing an impression of Nino Brown in the final act of *New Jack City*, an artificial and stilted imitation that never quite convinces you he is as tough as he acts. In *The Debut*'s climactic scene, Gusto and Ben get into a fistfight in a dim hallway, and when the elders rush in to break it up, they discover the gun in Gusto's jacket pocket—a big scandal for all at the party to see. His sin is not merely that he has a gun, but that he carries one even though he doesn't need to. We know his family is well-off. Nothing in the movie suggests he deals drugs, robs people, or otherwise commits felonies that require a weapon. The gun is just part of his look. He shows it off like a prop.

What is at the root of Gusto's interior troubles? The only hints the movie provides point to his stepfather, a white man who married his mother after Gusto's biological father died. Though the math isn't spelled out, we learn that around the time his mother remarried, Gusto started running with a barkada that went around beating up anyone who looked at them wrong. During dinner at the cotillion, Gusto turns away from the table, cringing from embarrassment as his stepfather shows off a few Tagalog phrases and brazenly corrects a Filipino man in a discussion about Malay genealogy. After the gun is discovered, Gusto tries to attack his stepfather for calling him a hoodlum.

It's not hard to interpret Gusto's antics as a desperate attempt to rebel against his proximity to whiteness—if he wanted to get away from that affiliation, what better costume than the superpredator thug that white Americans like his stepfather seem to fear most? Yet in trying to resist whiteness, Gusto has adopted the colonizer's gaze: he does not represent Blackness but the white view of it. We don't see him break dancing with the cousins, or talking revolutionary politics with the guys standing around the open engine of a souped-up Honda, or referencing any of the Black artists or athletes behind the sounds and moves at the cotillion. What Gusto appropriates isn't culture but stereotypes rooted in generations of someone else's suffering. In doing so, he perpetuates tropes used to oppress: he embodies the fallacy of defining Blackness as criminal. I wasn't much different when I called Jed soft for wearing tighter pants and listening to techno music.

Gusto's sin, and mine, was the stubborn front. If the defining trait of

Filipino people is our ability to blend in, Cajayon lays out the rules of engagement. When Gusto calls one of Ben's cousins the N-word during the basketball game, the cousin responds by pointedly calling Gusto "Pinoy!"—as if to remind him that his ancestors weren't slaves. Gusto serves as a cautionary tale on the folly of abusing our superpower.

What a luxury it is to adopt aspects of Black culture without having to carry the weight of being Black. By the time my family arrived in the States, Black people had resisted white supremacy for three centuries, achieving the gains that enabled us to get jobs, buy homes, and eventually vote. History shows that whatever rights and opportunities Black people have in America marks the bare minimum for what we lighter-skinned browns get. The pieces of Black culture I fused into my own identity emerged from a collective experience I wasn't part of and could lay no claim to. What could I give in exchange for all I had gotten? All I could say for certain was that any offering began with an honest accounting of what I had gotten and where it had come from. Clarifying those lines exposes what lies at the core, what collective experiences I'm actually a part of.

Ben's grand realization—the inflection point at which he begins to embrace his heritage—comes when he leaves the cotillion briefly to go to the keg party. He accidentally spills a drink on an inebriated white girl who calls him a "chink." His immediate reaction is not anger or sadness but stunned confusion. All he says, quietly, in response is, "I'm not Chinese." The indignity of being mislabeled is just as revelatory to Ben as the hurt of the slur. This made sense to me in ways that crystalized in my mind over the next few years. A beefy white kid was picking on one of my friends in the locker room before eighth-grade PE class. I pushed the white kid, and the two of us stood chest to chest, trading juvenile insults of the "Fuck you" and "You're a little bitch" variety. Then the white kid escalated things. "You piece of Filipino dog shit," he hissed. I was taken aback. Out of reflex, to defend the honor of my people, because the white kid had crossed a line, I swung. But not with all my might. Not with a jab to the nose or an uppercut to the jaw but an open-handed slap across his temple. My anger had surprisingly dissipated. I felt a hint of appreciation for this white boy. Even in the heat of our standoff, he had acknowledged that I was Filipino.

CHAPTER 6

ALLIES

My mom didn't know how to drive when we settled in the States in 1995.

She picked our first San Francisco apartment, a six-hundred-square-foot studio in an elegantly aging building with a steel scissors-gate elevator and creaky floorboards, because it was a quarter mile from the school she enrolled me in. But within a year in the asphalt landscape of downtown, she decided that my childhood should mean more space to run around in.

Her assimilation required her to break free from old tethers and develop new habits. She observed that a smooth transition into American life and all its conveniences required access to an automobile. So even though she was nervous, she learned to drive, got her license, and bought a light blue Dodge Neon, which she named Neon.

With our new mobility, we moved to an apartment complex tucked amid tall trees in the city's southwest quadrant, near a lake and on a road named after the racist conservationist John Muir. The one-bedroom, first-floor unit had a patio and a walk-in closet big enough for my mom to fit her bed and a small nightstand, and the building's features included tennis courts, a swimming pool, and dozens of kids my age who played tackle football on the sloping lawn along the quiet road. Uncle Bobby, who enrolled at San Francisco City College to attain the American degree he needed for higher-paid jobs, moved in with us, sleeping on the bunk in my room, paying tuition with shifts as a server at Outback Steakhouse.

The commute downtown to my school took about half an hour. My mom took the leisurely route, following the sky-blue "Scenic Drive" signs, which had red arrows on a white gull's wing directing us up the foggy coast and along Golden Gate Park before funneling us through residential roads lined with Victorians and stop signs, and eventually into the honking jostle of the commercial core. Her hands gripped the steering wheel at the recommended ten- and two-o'clock points, and her seat was pulled forward to put her back into a ninety-degree angle with her legs. She abstained from music while driving, wary it would relax or excite her into carelessness. Instead, she set the radio to a Catholic AM station, which in the mornings featured solemn prayers and hymns and in the afternoons sermons and talk shows. She avoided the freeway, which was too fast and perilous for her taste—she'd enlist Uncle Bobby to drive if we ever had to go somewhere outside the city. But there was no getting around the crowded confines of downtown San Francisco, so my mom steeled her nerves and eyed every car around her as a potential threat: you don't know who is in these cars or how they drive, she'd say. She preferred the sunset views and refreshing predictability of the road along the coast.

She noticed, within a month, that the stoplights along Ocean Beach were set to a timer, and if she cruised at exactly thirty-five miles per hour she could catch a series of greens without touching the brake pedal. She pointed out the cars going too fast. "See!" she'd say when Neon passed one coming out of a dead stop at the intersection. She was proud to have figured out the trick. It reaffirmed her belief that the universe contained a constellation of puzzles, big and small, offering paths for advancement to those who solved them. She kept her eyes open for clues. She conceded that much still lay beyond her sight.

The Bible was her primary source of revelation, but as the universe had aged a couple of millennia since its publication, it had nothing to say about stoplights, school districts, or presidential elections. Those modern mysteries she had to figure out for herself. In church, she listened closely to the homilies of the priests, whom she trusted as experts in the field of applying biblical verses to everyday scenarios. In the mornings, she scanned the headlines of the *San Francisco Chronicle*. In the afternoons, she listened to radio deacons and nuns offering advice and commenting on current affairs. On the rare evenings when I wasn't commandeering the TV, she tuned in to *The 700 Club* to hear Pat Robertson listing off all the signs the world was spiraling into doom.

From her sources and deduction, she developed theories about the world. She concluded that global suffering was caused by the prevalence of abortions—God would stop punishing us once we stopped killing unborn children. In her mind, every problem was paired with a precise solution, which circled it weightlessly and invisibly like an electron around its nucleus. You might not be able to see it, but you could glean its existence with the right set of equations. From one of the radio voices, my mom learned of a grand formula designed to counterbalance mankind's constant sinning: if 10 percent of the global population prayed the rosary daily, we'd all be saved. The elegant formula brought her a sense of clarity. The universe made more sense. God was merciful, indeed— so generous that he offered us an out. And a humble ask at that: "Only ten percent!"

Her outlook transcended borders and sociopolitical structures. The Founding Fathers might have cited God in their constitution, but to my mom that was purely cosmetic compared with their policy separating church from state, which she found absurd. How could God be removed from government matters when the Holy Spirit infuses every molecule? Something didn't add up. Then one day, like a gust of wind giving a glimpse behind the curtain, a voice on the radio informed my mom that the Founding Fathers were members of the Freemasons. Initiation into this secret society involved spitting on a crucifix to prove your loyalty to the group above God, she relayed to me with disgust. Not long after, Pat Robertson introduced her to the Illuminati, which in his book he called "a new order for the human race under the domination of Lucifer and his followers." Digging around on our new dial-up internet, she discovered the Bilderberg Meetings, where world leaders convened deep in the woods to perform masked occult ceremonies and debate the fates of the rest of us. In thick paperbacks, she learned that many U.S. presidents had in college become members of the Yale secret society Skull and Bones, which she deemed an entryway to the major league groups.

Her horror grew as she pieced together a conspiracy of monumental scale. My mom was unclear on the operational details, whether these were subsets of a single organization or independently collaborating cabals—that so little information was available seemed to affirm their immense power. But the agenda was clear: a group of the world's wealthiest people were colluding to create a godless global order.

I consumed my mom's insights with hungry curiosity. I shared her suspicion that our surroundings contained cryptic clues to fundamental mysteries. For example, Tupac's unsolved murder. Somewhere online I came across an index of evidence suggesting he was alive and had left us a string of hints about his plans to fake his own death. I printed out the twenty-some-page dossier so that my friends and I could investigate for ourselves the lyrics and videos that foretold his return. "I heard a rumor I died, murdered in cold blood dramatized," Pac raps on "I Ain't Hard 2 Find." "But that was fiction, some coward got the story twisted." Months before his death, he changed his stage name to Makaveli, after the sixteenth-century Italian political philosopher who, the online theory falsely claimed, advocated faking your death to elude your enemies. If you rearrange the letters of Makaveli and the title of the final album he recorded before he died—*The Don Killuminati: The 7 Day Theory*—you can spell: "Ok On Tha 7th U Think I'm Dead Yet Really I'm Alive." (Clearly the Illuminati were somehow involved.)

Because the number seven appears with eerie frequency—declared dead at 4:03 p.m. (4+3), seven days after he was shot, at age twenty-five (2+5), along with similar numerical sightings in his music videos—the theory posited that he'd reappear seven years after his death, on September 13, 2003. We counted down from more than a year out. When the big day came and went, we were stumped. Was he really dead, or had we gotten the math wrong?

For all the conspiracies we saw, we paid scant attention to the ones in plain view.

AS A CHILD I never thought to ask why our family left the Philippines. To me, the answer was intuitive—as obvious as pulling your hand off a hot stove. I knew my mother's homeland to be a place of struggle, its defects manifesting in brownouts, cold baths, roadside slums, bribes at customs, and underwhelming Olympics showings. I knew there had been a dictator named Ferdinand Marcos who killed thousands of people and stole millions of dollars before I was born, and that our family's exodus began during his rule. It all seemed simple enough. Given the chance, of course they left. I assumed anybody would do the same.

Until I began to learn more about the country as an adult, its history existed in my mind as a mostly blank scroll unfurling back through the ages. As a kid I learned of Gandhi, Cesar Chavez, Harriet Tubman, Confucius, Aristotle, Cleopatra, Thomas Edison, Joan of Arc—on and on without a Filipino in sight. I learned of hallowed cities, dynasties, and wars but had barely a footnote of knowledge about the Islands.

America, on the other hand, was master of the universe, police of the world, winner of gold medals, creator of culture consumed across the planet. America defeated the Nazis, organized the United Nations, landed on the moon, and exported democracy across the globe. In the history I knew, America was protagonist.

WHEN CARIDAD BEGAN her second year of college in Manila in summer 1941, the global order was teetering. The Germans swept through Europe and the Japanese stretched their new empire across Asia. The Americans supplied weapons and fuel to their British allies holding the line but kept their military out of the fight, hesitant to get too involved in the bloody squabbles of distant empires. As a possession of the powerful isolationist nation, the Philippines carried on without disruption, until Japan attacked the U.S. Navy base in Pearl Harbor, Hawaii, and two U.S. Air Force bases in Luzon—a nearly simultaneous bombardment in the early hours of Monday, December 8. There was no school that day because it was a holiday, honoring the Immaculate Conception, but Caridad was in class the next morning.

She was enrolled at Philippine Normal College, an institution established in the early years of American colonial rule, and the students around her were kids from well-off mestizo families like hers, the soon-to-be leaders of a generation expected to shape the archipelago's first chapter when it began life as an independent nation a little more than four years hence. The Concepcion barangay was at the center of the action, poised to expand its power beyond the highlands of northern Mindanao. At the tail end of the Great Depression, with their four eldest children attending college in Manila, Luisa and Jose had moved the entire family to the capital, where an influx of American dollars spawned opportunities unattainable elsewhere on the Islands. But now everything was uncertain. Caridad's professor announced that the United States had declared war on Japan, and classes were canceled.

Young and hungry for purpose, the students recalibrated the paths they'd prepared for, the jobs lined up, the sweethearts to wed, the exams, parties, movies, and vacations penciled into calendars that might as well be ripped up and burned as kindling because time had been rendered obsolete, flattened into a dichotomy of before and after.

"The male students started throwing their books in the air," Caridad wrote years later. "Was it jubilation that school was closing? Or was it because they were enthusiastic about helping Uncle Sam fight the enemy?"

Within five months, the American colony fell to Japan.

THE SAMURAI SWORD inches above Caridad's head threatened all that was to come. The soldier's accusation was a death sentence: American spy.

Nearly every day, Japanese soldiers had brought a group of American POWs into the café where Caridad worked, outside a detention camp in rural Luzon, to feed them rice cakes and coffee during breaks from digging roads. One day, a soldier had overheard the prisoners telling Caridad their names while she was taking their orders.

As the sword hung above her, Caridad's mind flashed with stories she'd heard of atrocities committed by the Imperial Army, the Filipino men and women detained or killed for failing to bow in the presence of Japanese officers, tortured for listening to American radio broadcasts, publicly beheaded for collaborating with the underground resistance plotting to upend the occupation.

The soldier's suspicion was damning in itself, even if he couldn't prove it. Truth matters less than the beliefs of those who hold the swords. Caridad's chances of convincing him of her innocence were bleak in any case, but all the more so because she was, indeed, guilty of being a spy for the Americans.

Caridad spoke fluent English, had studied U.S. history and literature in school, and listened to American songs on the radio. She believed in the democratic principles of the U.S. Constitution and admired the nation's humble beginnings, as a former European territory toppling its colonial oppressor before blooming into an empire strong enough to defeat Spain and generous enough to promise the Philippines independence by 1945. Japan's imperial expansion interrupted that plan. Caridad had been stunned and dismayed by how swiftly the tides had turned. The Imperial Japanese Army had taken over much of Asia, driven General Douglas MacArthur and his American forces off the archipelago, and captured the 76,000 U.S. and Philippine troops left behind.

If the sword had sliced her skull that day, Caridad would not have made it across the ocean after the war, the first of our barangay to migrate to the States, nor would she have set up the landing point for the rest to follow. Her fate was one of countless breaks to swing our way, unnerving reminders that before a moment hardens into the past, it exists in the suspended fragility of the present.

Caridad kept cool. She had imagined this moment, prepared for it as keenly as she studied for exams or brushed her loose curls before dances. For centuries her ancestors had dealt with colonizers, studied their desires and prejudices, and learned survival tactics they passed on through generations.

Caridad could tell from the soldier's accent that he had learned his English in Great Britain, probably in London, which would peg him as a member of his nation's privileged class, probably reared to internalize a sense of racial superiority over the darker-skinned people who stood as pawns on the global chessboard. An arm of the empire, he was empowered by the might at his back, carrying out duties aimed at elevating his people to their rightful place in the global order, securing a seat at a table long reserved for people of European descent. She was a humble café server, earning a paycheck in a poor country unmoored by war. In English deliberately broken and heavily accented with the blunted twang of the provincial natives, she uttered short, harried, declarative bursts that rose in pitch with each word, her tone conveying the shame of a servant ignorant of her misstep. She said she was not a spy; she had merely asked the Americans for their names so she could submit an itemized bill to the Japanese commandant who usually covered the tab.

After a few seconds of contemplation, without another word, the soldier lowered his sword, turned on a boot heel, and ordered all the prisoners out of the café. Break time was over.

The prisoners and soldiers had been coming to the café for weeks, and not once had the commandant paid for their coffee.

WHEN THE OCCUPATION BEGAN, Caridad was restless and frightened. The swift retreat of American forces from the archipelago brought about the prospect that the next chapter of the story of the Philippines would not be one of independence but of yet another overlord. New languages to learn, new customs to adopt, new economies to bolster, new plans to script.

Some in the Philippines welcomed the possibility: Better to be ruled by an Asian empire than a Western one, their reasoning went. Japan, after all, was a fellow Pacific archipelago, with barely more landmass than the Philippines and, until recently, barely more say in world events. Far less geographically splintered than the Philippines, over centuries the nation had developed a unified culture that it protected fiercely in the face of regular threats. Larger powers that had tried to swallow Japan, sending armadas flush with soldiers and weapons, had all met the same fate. Mongols, then Chinese, then Russians would arrange blockades, lob artillery, and hold the islands under siege, drawing closer to victory, only to get wiped out themselves by storms that always seemed to come right when things were looking bleakest for Japan. While the scattered land-masses of the Philippine archipelago had made it exceptionally vulnerable to dividing and conquering, the turbulent waters surrounding Japan's mountainous, rocky coastline provided the perfect defense for a nation that wanted no part of the outside world.

In the mid-nineteenth century, Japan's leaders recognized that their intense isolationism had frozen the country in antiquity, the lack of new technologies and ideas keeping it stuck in a stagnant feudal economy controlled by a ruling class of shoguns. Within a generation, the nation reinvented itself, retaining the militaristic pride of its Samurai tradition while stepping into the wider world of global affairs with ambitions of empire building—a transformation known as the Meiji Restoration, which consolidated the political system under an emperor, industrial-ized the means of production, and enacted mandatory military con-scription. By the end of the century, Japan was duking it out with China's Qing Dynasty for control of the Korean peninsula, and winning.

In 1904, after failed negotiations over the rights to Manchuria and Korea, Japan attacked czarist Russia. To many observers around the world, this seemed foolish. Russia was one of the world's foremost em-pires, an old and wealthy kingdom fifty times the size of Japan, with a practically infinite pool of people and materials to resource its renowned army. Since the dawn of the globalized age, no Asian military had beaten a European one. Japan defeated Russia in eighteen months. The victory marked the birth of a new global power. When World War I broke out, Japan sided with the Allied forces, and when the Treaty of Versailles was negotiated in 1919, Japan was the only non-European country in the room. Japanese leaders proposed language in the agreement calling for an end to discrimination against immigrants in the participating coun-tries: "equal and just treatment in every respect making no distinction, either in law or in fact, on account of their race or nationality." France, Italy, and Greece backed the proposal. Australia, Great Britain, and the United States voted against it, and the provision didn't make it into the treaty. Five years later, the U.S. passed a law banning immigration from Japan.

Japan's relationship with the Allies deteriorated from there. By summer 1942, French, British, Dutch, and U.S. territories across Southeast Asia had fallen under Japanese sovereignty. "Our fight is not with you but with America," read fliers dropped across the Philippines from Japanese planes.

To some in the Philippines, Japan's ascent was, above all, evidence that disproved claims of European supremacy. Here was a modestly sized Asian archipelago winning major wars not with overwhelming force but with tactical prowess. Here was a model for collective upward mobility in the global hierarchy. Maybe Japan offered just what the Philippines needed: an emphasis on order, discipline, and unified strength to purge the toxins of decades immersed in the tenets of American individualism and centuries wrapped in the tentacles of Spanish corruption. Or maybe Japan's appeal was as simple as it was to Emilio Aguinaldo: "It was only the Americans who betrayed me."

Under Japanese occupation, however, it was hard to distinguish those who were on board ideologically from those who were just trying to avoid trouble. Early in the occupation, Josefa Escoda, president of the Federation of Women's Clubs, had contacted Japanese military leaders with the idea of opening cafés outside detention camps, to serve coffee and rice cakes to Japanese soldiers and American prisoners out on work detail. Faced with a scarcity of goods and a large population of POWs, Japanese military leaders also agreed to grant Escoda and her team passes to enter the detention camps to sell fruits and vegetables, as a de facto commissary for the prisoners. Caridad had volunteered to join the all-woman staff.

From rumors circulating among students in Manila, Caridad suspected that Escoda supported the Americans, but only after she was hired did Escoda reveal the true nature of their mission: compiling a list of POWs to pass on to U.S. military officials and smuggling into the camps letters, medicines, and reports on the status of the war. They operated as a branch of the underground resistance intelligence operation called the Live or Die Unit.

If there was ever any chance of Caridad accepting Japanese rule, it dissolved within weeks of the occupation's start. Japan did its brand no favors in the Philippines. Caridad had already learned in school about the Japanese soldiers who raped and massacred villagers in China, and when the Imperial Army landed in the Philippines, the occupiers confirmed her reasons for distrust, forcing tens of thousands of prisoners on a torturous march across Luzon that ended with thousands of Filipinos dead. While she was not ignorant of America's crimes against humanity, she considered them historical artifacts of an ever-evolving nation.

So she put on her long white dress and a wide-brimmed straw hat and slipped letters and contraband into straw baskets piled high with mangos, guavas, jackfruit, bananas, eggplant, and okra. To the Japanese guards, she was the face of the unfortunates impoverished and stunted by Western rule, making a living in one of the few ways available to her, and they let her through the barbed-wire gate with barely a glance. She handed the Japanese commanders the choicest pieces of fruit at the top of the pile, then made her way to the prisoners gathered under the high afternoon sun. Before long, she was a familiar face to the Filipino and American prisoners—the face of the good fight, a sign that the bonds uniting the allies were durable enough to burrow a supply channel right through enemy lines in broad daylight. The prisoners picked through the produce with concentration, as if they were very particular about firmness and color. Bottles of penicillin, letters from home, notes of support from locals, and bundles of fresh clothing slipped into sleeves, pockets, and waistbands. One of the prisoners whispered to Caridad the names of the newest arrivals. Walking back home with quick strides, she recited the names in her head over and over, to memorize them. She wrote them down as soon as she was safely behind a closed door, then rolled up the strips of paper, hiding them in the hollow of her bamboo bedpost.

One day, out of nowhere, the guard on duty at the gate demanded to sift through her basket.

"I had to think fast," Caridad later wrote of that encounter. The first thing her eyes fell upon were the soldier's geta, elegant wooden sandals elevated on blocks.

"Kirei!" Caridad exclaimed, pointing to his feet, using the Japanese word for "beautiful." In English, she asked him where she could get such lovely sandals because, gesturing down at her own feet, as he could see, her woven sandals were frayed. The guard, flattered, explained that geta were common in Japan, then let her in without searching the basket.

Before the next visit, Caridad and her comrades informed the commandant that the guards had been so rough with their searches that they were spoiling the fruit. "We complained so furiously," Caridad wrote, "that the guards were ordered not to search us, and not to touch the fruit and the vegetables."

ASCENDING THE RANKS of the resistance movement, Caridad developed a reputation. In the roster the U.S. military kept of underground allies in the Philippines, a single note is listed beside her name: "slick chick."

As third lieutenant of the Live or Die Unit, Caridad had as one of her many tasks delivering the list of POWs to another member of the underground, who then conveyed it to Allied military commanders in Hong Kong. From the rural detention camp, she boarded a train to Manila with the papers bundled inside her bayong, a bag woven from pandan leaves.

America purchased, pacified, and retained the Philippines for operations like this—for locals to take up the cause of the big brother who schooled and governed them. For the purposes of the war, that cause was unimpeachable: defeat the Axis powers to preserve the freedoms of capitalist democracy. But behind that sharp point lay a vast constellation of motives. One of the reasons the United States was so hesitant to grant the Philippines independence was to retain a military and cultural foothold to prevent Japan's expansion across Asia. Japan's rise threatened Americans in a way the European powers did not.

The fear Japan instilled in many white Americans was infamously articulated in a popular 1920 book called *The Rising Tide of Color Against White World-Supremacy*, by Lothrop Stoddard, who built a career warning of an imminent global uprising against the "Nordic race." A *New York Times* editorial endorsed Stoddard's book, which "evokes a new peril, that of an eventual submersion beneath vast waves of yellow men, brown men, black men, and red men, whom the Nordics have hitherto dominated." In a speech before a large crowd in Alabama the following year, U.S. president Warren Harding recommended that people "take the time to read and ponder" the book, because Americans "must realize that our race problem here in the United States is only a phase of a race issue that the whole world confronts."

Black Americans interpreted the book through a different lens. A headline in the *Baltimore Afro-American* sounded a note of optimism in Stoddard's premise: "The New Book by a White Author Shows Rising Tide of Color Against Oppression; Latest Statistics Show Twice as Many Colored People in the World as White."

Yet if Japan threatened the dominance of global white supremacy, it hardly offered oppressed nonwhite people an appealing alternative. In one of history's searing ironies, the most powerful non-European empire of the Industrial Age—the great nonwhite hope that left the Nordics trembling in their cotton coats—partnered with Adolf Hitler, whose Third Reich Germany aimed to establish a master race of "Aryan" whites. Even before the genocidal horrors of the Holocaust were exposed to the wider public, the Führer promoted a platform so violently racist that it cast the United States as a heroic defender of the free world. In the face of such clear and present evil, the choice was irrefutable. So by the time war came, the Philippines was a critical outpost not only for American products and soldiers but for its ideals, and it was filled with allies plotting on the ground against their common enemies.

With the papers in her bayong, Caridad watched the countryside pass out the window, until suddenly the brakes squealed and the train slowed to a stop. A group of Kempeitai, Japanese military police, boarded the car in front of hers, for a random search. The train was crowded with a mix of Filipino civilians and Japanese soldiers, who typically rode public transportation because guerrilla fighters were unlikely to attack it.

As the soldiers made their way down the aisle, searching and questioning every Filipino passenger, Caridad glanced around the car for any means of escape. She noticed, in a nearby seat, one of the guards from the detention camp she had just left, a young private with an unkempt uniform and his hat askew. She had interacted with him so often that she knew his name, Hagiwara. They had never exchanged more than a few words of small talk, but he always treated her more respectfully than his colleagues did. With the officers approaching and no other option coming to mind, she turned to the familiar face, pulled the bundle from her bayong, and handed it to him.

"Hagiwara-san, you keep," she said. "Kempeitai coming."

Hagiwara took the bundle of papers and placed it under his hat. His flat expression gave no indication of his intention. "I wonder what went through his mind at that moment," she later wrote. "Would he give my bundle to the Military Police? Was he a soldier who fought on orders but truly did not believe in war? I never found out."

As the Kempeitai searched Caridad's bag, Hagiwara sat still and silent. They finished going through the train and left without incident. At the station in Manila, Hagiwara returned the papers to Caridad. They parted ways and never saw each other again.

IN A KITCHEN DRAWER of the Concepcion household in Manila were tokens of the family's allegiance, smuggled in through American submarines: a 1941 *Life* magazine with General Douglas MacArthur on the cover and a box of chocolates bearing MacArthur's famous message to the Philippine people, "I shall return."

For more than two years, Caridad had maintained her cover even as the Japanese military closed in. One night, Japanese officers showed up at the Women's Club headquarters and questioned Caridad and her comrades. One was imprisoned and tortured for several months, then released. "She never talked about it and we never asked her to discuss the ordeal," Caridad wrote. Not long after that, Josefina Escoda and her husband attempted to flee to Australia on a submarine, possibly because they got word that their cover had been blown, but they were caught before they reached the coast and never heard from again. "No others were questioned by the Military Police since their capture, and so they must have died with their lips sealed," Caridad wrote. "Somebody up there was taking care of me—I always got out of these situations and was never arrested."

And then one day, Caridad was walking home from the Women's Club headquarters in Manila with a bundle of secret papers when her eleven-year-old brother, Tomas, came running up the road toward her. Nearly out of breath, he said that Kempeitai officers were waiting for her at their home. Knowing his sister was due to arrive that afternoon, he'd slipped out the back door when he saw them approaching and raced down the road he assumed she would take.

Caridad detoured to a friend's house to drop off the documents before making her way home. There she found three officers in the living room, talking to her mother, Luisa. In front of the officers was a Filipino man, on his knees, crying. His name was Pedring, and he was a fellow member of the Live or Die Unit.

"Do you know this man?" one of the officers asked in English.

Pedring interjected, saying to Caridad in Visayan, which the soldiers didn't understand, "I did not tell them anything."

She told him not to worry. What else could she say? But she wondered what they knew. Had they spoken to the commandant who never paid for coffee at the café? Or the young private who hid the list of POW names?

She told the officers she knew the man as a neighbor. The officer asked her where she was on a certain date in 1944.

That day, she said, she remembered well because she was at a funeral for her brother, Boy, who had died from an illness.

The officer asked why, if she was truly loyal to the occupiers, she had not reported any underground activities to the Japanese.

Caridad couldn't help but respond with a trace of sarcasm. "Why is the mighty Imperial Army so worried about small-time guerrillas?"

Her answer was met with silence. The soldiers seemed to be contemplating whether her intransigence was evidence of outraged innocence or nervous guilt. If the soldiers searched the house and caught sight of the *Life* magazine or the MacArthur chocolate in the drawer, the whole family could be implicated as traitors.

But they didn't search the house. They marched out with Pedring; Caridad never heard from him again. Maybe they had made up their mind before she said a single word, thanks to the intervention of Luisa. While Caridad had been making her way home, she had greeted the officers politely and showed them the beautiful gifts her son Manuel had sent the family from Tokyo, where he was enrolled at the Imperial Japanese Army Academy, as a naval officer in training: a sensu fan, papier-mâché okiagari-koboshi dolls, brocade omamori amulets.

AND HOW WAS IT that the same family that had a daughter active in the resistance to the occupation also had a son studying at the occupier's military academy?

The recruitment of top Filipino high school students like Manuel had been part of the empire's effort to form bonds with its newest territory. At first, Luisa believed that no good could come of the invitation. If Manuel accepted, he would be on the wrong side of the war, forever marked as an Axis collaborator. The family's commitment to the American way was so strong that Jose had permitted Caridad to join the resistance even as he barred her from going on dates without a chaperone.

Declining the offer, though, risked drawing scrutiny about the family's allegiances and would likely cost them any chance of favor in the event of a Japanese victory. The invitation had precluded the possibility of the family simply lying low through the war, without having to publicly take a side.

Faced with this difficult decision, Luisa consulted with a priest, who advised that she was looking at it all wrong. Rather than avoid choosing sides, why not plant a foot in both? "How foresighted our priest was!" Caridad later wrote.

Though he arrived in Tokyo skeptical, Manuel soon embraced his unexpected opportunity. He chose engineering as his field of concentration. His classmates came from all over Asia, an impressive collection of superstar students well equipped to lead the region into a new era free of Western oversight. He developed a taste for the hardline discipline his instructors instilled. He learned to cherish the virtue of moral integrity, the determination to hold tight to principles no matter the forces trying to shake them loose. He would carry these beliefs for the rest of his life. Just as Emilia Bato Bato had converted to Spanish Catholicism and Jose Tianco had signed up to work for the American government, Manuel saw the benefits of what these new colonizers were offering. And if Japan succeeded in its quest to dominate Asia, he would be well positioned to maintain his family's standing, probably even to elevate it.

Of course, Japan did not succeed. By the spring of 1945, Germany had surrendered, and the Allies turned their full attention to the Pacific Theater, where the Americans knocked the Imperial forces back across the ocean and retook the Philippines. In Manila, Caridad celebrated with crowds welcoming the U.S. troops, chanting "Victory, Joe, victory!" General MacArthur's return would be memorialized with bronze statues that froze in time his unit's march through knee-deep waters on the shores of Leyte. In Tokyo, the reality of imminent defeat dawned on Manuel and his fellow officers in training. A Japanese general who fled the Philippines disclosed to Manuel that, sensing the cause was lost, he and other commanders had to leave behind the gold artifacts they'd looted from wealthy homes, burying the booty in the mountain caves of Luzon in hopes of one day coming back to dig up the lost treasures. Manuel etched their statements into memory.

A CONUNDRUM FACED U.S. officials in the spring of 1945, as they weighed their options for reaching a peace agreement as quickly as possible. The war in the Pacific had been brutal. Unlike European enemies, who typically gave up when a battle was lost, Japanese soldiers were known to go down fighting, setting off grenades or slashing with bayonets in their final breaths. The Americans worried about the cost of invading the heavily fortified Japanese mainland, estimating hundreds of thousands of U.S. casualties. From this angle, drastic actions seemed a reasonable, or at least defensible, response to Japan's refusal to surrender unconditionally; in this sense, it was Japan that had backed the United States into a corner.

Or so went the version presented in my high school history textbook. But historians would eventually challenge this conventional wisdom, citing evidence that high-level U.S. officials expected Japan to surrender shortly after Allied victory was declared in Europe. Germany's defeat freed up the Soviet military to pivot eastward, which would stretch Japan's battered forces into fighting on two fronts and risk the possibility of the Soviets laying claim to chunks of Japan's territories in mainland Asia—"This would destroy the foundation of Japan," Japan's prime minister later said. In April, the U.S. Joint Chiefs of Staff submitted an intelligence report predicting, "If at any time the USSR should enter the war, all Japanese will realize that absolute defeat is inevitable." In July, the United States intercepted a telegram Japan's foreign minister sent to its ambassador in Moscow, seeking peace talks with the USSR.

U.S. president Harry Truman didn't take this as good news. Rather, as his chief of staff William Leahy wrote in a cable, Truman was "afraid" Japan would negotiate "peace through Russia," which would give Moscow the upper hand in shaping Asia's postwar future. Complicating matters, Truman had been in the Oval Office for just a few months, after the death of Franklin Roosevelt. As vice president, Truman hadn't been part of Roosevelt's inner circle and wasn't privy to confidential military discussions throughout the war. He knew almost nothing about the U.S. development of the atomic bomb, nor the extent of its destructive power, until stepping into the presidency. Seven of eight five-star generals, including Allied forces commander Dwight Eisenhower, advised against using the weapon, deeming it militarily unnecessary or morally unacceptable. Even the hard-charging MacArthur apparently agreed, later writing in a letter that he had "no doubt" Japan would have "gladly" accepted American terms of surrender as long as they allowed the emperor to remain on the throne.

But Truman, wary of the growing influence of Communism, disdained the prospect of Soviet dominance over the eastern hemisphere. He dismissed ideas to enforce a naval blockade around Japan, or to drop an atom bomb over a large unpopulated forest to demonstrate the weapon's strength without mass killing. Instead, on August 6, America became the first country in world history to unleash nuclear energy in combat, dropping the bomb on Hiroshima without warning. Two days later, the USSR invaded the Japanese territory of Manchuria. A day after that, the United States dropped an atomic bomb on Nagasaki.

"The atomic bomb had nothing to do with the end of the war at all," Major General Curtis LeMay later claimed. "The war would have been over in two weeks without the Russians entering and without the atomic bomb."

"Japan was already defeated," Eisenhower would write in his memoir. "I thought that our country should avoid shocking world opinion by the use of a weapon whose employment was, I thought, no longer mandatory as a measure to save American lives."

"The use of this barbarous weapon at Hiroshima and Nagasaki was of no material assistance in our war against Japan," Truman's chief of staff Leahy would write in his memoir. "In being the first to use it we had adopted an ethical standard common to the barbarians of the Dark Ages."

The people of Hiroshima and Nagasaki became unwitting test subjects in an experiment revealing the gruesome effects of nuclear weaponry. They died from the incinerating blast, from skin-peeling burns, from the excruciating vise of radiation poisoning, and from the cancers festering in their bodies. As if to reinforce the patterns of the global age, as if to clarify whose humanity can be disregarded, the United States marked its ascension to the top of the hierarchy of global powers with an unprecedentedly brutal act against the first non-European colonial empire.

Manuel had no choice but to accept that the good guys had won. When the Americans arrived in Japan to begin the business of cleaning up the mess of war, Manuel's language skills made him a valuable asset, and his being Filipino made him trustworthy despite his Japanese military education. The United States hired him to serve as a translator for the war crime trials of Japanese officials to whom he once bowed. He was paid in American dollars.

He found the postwar climate ripe with opportunities. American soldiers were bouncing around Tokyo in a state of euphoria, on the hunt for souvenirs to take home as trophies. Manuel bought Japanese flags, a black marker, and a bucket of pig's blood. He smeared the blood and wrote Japanese proverbs on the flags, then pitched them as battlefield artifacts discovered near the bodies of dead generals. They sold fast and for high prices. Manuel returned to Manila with thousands of dollars in his suitcase.

U.S. dollars went a long way in the Philippines. Manuel bought an American muscle car, finished college, then enrolled in law school. He showed up to class in nicer suits than his professors.

THE SPOILS GO to the victors but trickle down from the top.

The United States guaranteed citizenship to all Filipino veterans who fought with the Allies, but denied most of them, including the underground guerrillas, the benefits given to American soldiers. The U.S. granted the Philippines independence on July 4, 1946, but the CIA kept a guiding hand on the country's leaders, American investors had the right to own mines and forests, and the American military bases remained on the Islands under a ninety-nine-year lease—an agreement

President Manuel Roxas hoped would "focus American concern and interest in the Philippines in the light of other competing interests for US resources in other parts of the world."

Caridad got a job with the U.S. Army's Transportation Corps at the end of the war, then in 1948 accepted a position at the Veterans Administration office in San Francisco. Months later, sitting behind a desk there, she met Roberto Vallangca, who had moved to the city after spending the war years working at the Mare Island shipyard in Vallejo. They married a few years later and bought a house in the Fillmore District.

CARIDAD'S YOUNGER BROTHER TOMAS was thirteen when the war ended. He didn't get along with his father. Jose whipped him with a leather belt for not being studious or religious enough, though Luisa didn't allow more than three lashes. As Tomas later wrote of himself as a child, he was "always drawing" and already considered himself an artist, "and thus free from any restrictions from every possible prohibition."

Tomas and his father had mostly stopped talking by the time he graduated from high school, though he spoke up long enough to tell his father he wanted to study agriculture or the fine arts. Jose replied, "To occupy yourself with the soil you could have stayed in Mindanao. We already have farmers. And if you'll be a painter you will die of hunger. It is better if you enroll in architecture."

So Tomas enrolled in an architecture program in Manila, but left after one semester. "I wash my hands of you," said his father at that point. Tomas transferred to the University of the Philippines College of Fine Arts, but within a semester there grew bored with the monotonous curriculum, then disillusioned after a professor chastised him for spending too much time sculpting his own projects instead of completing the assigned exercises.

Tomas decided that the guidance he was seeking lay overseas, closer to the cultures that had given rise to the art that inspired him to create. He followed his sister's trail, staying at her place with a U.S. student visa granted to him upon admission to San Francisco State University, where he majored in painting and theater design. After graduating, he departed to Montreal for a master's in fine arts, paying the bills by painting portraits and working at an advertising agency. That period "did not satisfy me as an artist," he later wrote. "I wanted to find out if I had the talent to be great." He decided to go east, to Europe.

RIZALINA'S FATHER, Jose Tianco, a colonial police officer, or "scout," had joined the underground resistance in Mindanao and was rewarded generously for his decades of service for the Americans, first fighting the Moros who rejected U.S. occupation, then the Japanese. U.S. colonial officials granted him a plot of fertile land near Dansalan that belonged to Moros who'd fled or been forced off at some point during the colonial period. Tianco hired a staff of workers to plow the soil, pick the fruit, and look after chickens, pigs, and carabao.

High on the national pride of independence, the Philippines government changed the city's name from Dansalan to Marawi, in honor of Fort Marawi, where the Maranao Moros made their last stand against the Spaniards in 1895, and then changed the country's independence date from July 4, the date set by the Americans, to June 12, the date Aguinaldo declared independence from Spain in 1898. But the anticolonial sentiment had little impact on the policies guiding day-to-day life.

While her father managed the farm in Mindanao, Rizalina moved to Manila to begin college. There, she reunited with Manuel. They wed in 1952, and over the next decade settled into their adult lives. Their white-collar careers, as accountant and attorney, advanced and their family grew. They bought the empty corner lot on a desolate stretch of Quezon City and, using a design drawn up by Manuel's mother, Luisa, built the compound big enough to house their barangay for generations to come. The future of the Philippines looked bright. As Manila drew people from all over the archipelago, the Quezon City suburb bloomed with subdivisions and concrete arteries that filled with cars imported from Detroit. Movie theaters sprang up, with marquees boasting the names of American stars. Diners served hamburgers and hummed with jukeboxes spinning Elvis records.

A young president elected in 1965, Ferdinand Marcos, vowed to fortify the Philippines' social and economic bonds with the United States. Declaring, "We shall make this nation great again," he directed infrastructure projects: the construction of bridges, highways, and skyscrapers. He expanded the military, from 50,000 soldiers to 250,000, with the help of U.S. funding, and in 1966, sent troops to assist American forces fighting in Vietnam. The Philippines were a critical ally in a new war, this one against Communism.

The hardest times seemed to have passed. American money rebuilt a battered nation. American images and words spun a common popular culture for a booming generation of peacetime youth. American politicians managed a stabilized world order, spreading capitalist democracy.

Amid all this, the United States passed the Immigration and Nationality Act of 1965, eliminating the race-based immigration quotas that had blocked out most of the world. The U.S. embassy in Manila approved visas for Manuel and Rizalina in 1967, on the grounds that his sister lived in America. Rizalina's pass to the United States took the form of a paper card registering her as "Philippine #8364." In her photo, her hair is blown up in a modest bouffant that frames a steely gaze, a slight smirk, and dangling pearl earrings. Upon arrival, she and Manuel were each issued a pale green Alien Registration Receipt Card, confirming that they had valid claims to permanent residency in the U.S.

In those hopeful years, the superpower seemed to reckon with the sins of its past, taking steps to begin reversing long-running injustices.

The Civil Rights Act of 1964, the Voting Rights Act of 1965, and the Fair Housing Act of 1968 chipped away at policies that had long upheld white supremacy. The number of Black Congress members reached its highest mark in ninety years. Lyndon Johnson's Great Society initiatives reduced educational, wealth, and health care inequities through government-funded social services. And by many measures, the economy was thriving. Federal minimum wage rose twice in three years. U.S. gross domestic product rates hit a three-year stretch of growth, more robust than any since World War II. The manufacturing sector added 4 million new jobs over the course of the decade. At a moment of great bounty, America opened its doors to us.

MY FORMATIVE UNDERSTANDING of world events had two acts: the ancient history conveyed in the Bible and the modern arc approximated at Disneyland, which opened in Southern California in 1955, four and a half decades before my first visit.

I was ten. My mom and I took a 4:30 a.m. Greyhound bus from Sacramento for the fifteen-hour ride through the Central Valley, past fruit fields, oil rigs, and speed traps, around the Grapevine hills, and into Anaheim. My mom slept or prayed the rosary most of the way, while I reviewed the two-day game plan I'd drawn up on a piece of binder paper, which I kept in my pocket, folded four times over for protection.

We stayed at a discount Anaheim hotel with a free shuttle to the happiest place on earth and took the first shuttle out the next morning, arriving before the gate opened.

At Disneyland, history starts in the castle at the center of the park, homage to the glorious medieval years after the bubonic plague wound down, when fair maidens and knights vanquished mysterious evils while kings and queens conquered the farthest reaches of the known world with the Christian God behind them, the Moors in retreat, the seas parting, the age of European discovery dawning. I skipped this Fantasy-land stage on the timeline and went straight to Adventureland, the part of the park I was most excited to see.

Passing thatched huts with tribal masks at the threshold, I imagined myself an explorer entering the menacing labyrinth of an unfamiliar jungle. It didn't occur to me that I was envisioning myself in the leather boots and beige cotton of a colonial-era European explorer. On the Jungle Cruise ride, the river snaked through sub-Saharan Africa, Southeast Asia, and South America, as the tour guide at the front noted—the colonized world mashed together into a pastiche of drums, dances, spears, and loincloths. Crates decoratively stacked on the riverbank were stamped "Stanleyville," a reference to Henry Morton Stanley, who led a two-hundred-man brigade into the jungles of central Africa in the 1870s, relying on forced native labor to carry his excessive supplies, killing hundreds on his path through what is now the Democratic Republic of Congo, the rubber-rich territory he claimed on behalf of Belgium's King Leopold II.

I didn't know Stanley's name then. I was more familiar with Indiana Jones. I had watched all the movies, and I hummed the theme song under my breath as we whipped past giant snakes, poison darts, and bloodthirsty savages on the Indiana Jones ride, my favorite in Adventureland. Rumbling down the track in a make-believe jeep, I was a professor-explorer in the field gathering ethnographic notes to bring back to a campus filled with white students.

The history of the West moves west, from Athens to Rome to Paris, across the Atlantic and into the Plains. Once independent of Britain, the European settlers in America embarked on an inland conquest that would reach the Pacific within a century, statehoods granted at a ferocious pace. Frontierland stood as a living monument to my country's manifestly destined expansion, with a roller coaster set in a mineshaft, a riverboat circling a lake, and a Wild West shooting range. Wearing a felt cowboy hat with Mickey Mouse ears, I imagined myself on a vast and barren plain, with tall red rocks casting jagged shadows and tumble-weeds rolling past. I didn't know that the Plains hadn't always looked so vacant, that they'd been home to bustling communities until Old World diseases ravaged their inhabitants, long before the colonial settlers began their program of massacres and forced relocation.

I lived my fantasies through the gaze of the colonizers. The Haunted Mansion in New Orleans Square was designed to resemble an antebellum plantation. The Pirates of the Caribbean ride featured no apparent Caribbean natives but rather European outlaws who pillaged the trade ships loaded with the gold that paid for enslaved people. In Critter Country, set in the ambiguously old American South, my favorite ride was Splash Mountain, which had a thrilling downhill finale and a cast of animatronic animals from the 1946 movie *Song of the South*, which is about a Reconstruction-era Black servant telling a white child parables about the virtues of resilience in tough times and never running away—"an insult to American minorities," deemed Harlem congressional representative Adam Clayton Powell, Jr. Disney hasn't shown the film since 1986, but it wasn't until summer 2020 that Disneyland would change the ride's theme, its implications at last too blatant to avoid, unlike the more subtle tributes to oppression scattered around.

The first part of the park we passed through on our way in and the last on our way out was Main Street U.S.A., an idealized vision of early-twentieth-century small-town America, decked out with ice cream parlors, trolley bells, straw hats, and accordion music, a grotesque phantasm straight from the mind of Walt Disney, the racist, sexist, homophobic, antisemitic, union-busting mastermind behind some of the fondest memories of my childhood. Disney based Main Street U.S.A. on his own hometown, Marceline, Missouri, as he remembered it from his childhood, when it was segregated under Jim Crow–era enforcement. "For those of us who remember the carefree time it recreates," he said when the park opened, "Main Street will bring back happy memories."

All around me were the settings for myriad traumas. Thank God I couldn't see any of that, because once you do, you can't unsee it. Pity the child who wanders Disneyland in a haze of despair.

In hindsight, the edifice was delicate. When we rode It's a Small World, I scanned the landscape of animatronic child dolls, looking for the one that represented me amid the alleged cultural diversity on display— twelve minutes of Inuit fisherfolk, Nordic ice skaters, lederhosen-clad Germans, British guards with tall black hats, French cabaret dancers, Spanish flamenco dancers, Scots with bagpipes, Dutch girls with blond pigtails, Italians riding gondolas, Russians in red bonnets, Arabs charming snakes, Indians beside a silhouetted Shiva, Japanese women bowing in kimonos, Chinese acrobats balancing jars, an Egyptian sphinx, sub-Saharan Africans with afros playing drums beside a lion, Mexicans in sombreros dancing around a bigger sombrero, Peruvians in ponchos on a mountain, white Americans sitting on hay bales, and so on. I nearly jumped out of my seat when I noticed the shirtless brown dolls wearing grass skirts and leafy crowns who apparently embodied South Pacific people at large. As if willing it to be true, I pointed out the generic dark-skinned islanders and said to my mom, "There's the Philippines!" On our second time through, I devoted myself to listening closely to the dozens of languages singing, a merry global chorus. No matter how closely I listened, I didn't hear any Tagalog. You can only fit so many cultures in a twelve-minute ride.

WHEN I WAS A CHILD, my awareness of my family's existence before coming to the States was drawn mostly from my mom's recollections. She's a vivid storyteller, recalling details about attires and scents, mimicking voices in dialogue, strolling patiently through the plot, always in present tense, before speeding her pace as the climax nears, pausing at the precipice of the big reveal, then delivering the boom like a sports announcer: "Oh my God! Can you believe?" Photos that hung in our homes came to life in my imagination. The oldest picture in my mom's possession, tinted yellow and slightly faded, shows the eight Concepcion siblings as children, sitting around their parents on the couch and the floor, looking proud and content in the living room of their big house in Quezon City. The image gripped me with wonder—countless decisions and forces, colliding and combusting, by will and by chance, charged a current that flowed from the moment the picture was snapped to the moment I stared at it on the wall.

The Concepcion siblings were born into privilege. They attended the most expensive private schools. They were raised by nannies while their parents worked prestigious jobs. Rizalina managed ledgers at the Philippine Central Bank. Manuel represented wealthy clients in civil lawsuits and poor clients in land disputes. But with eight children to feed, clothe, and educate to the standards of Filipino high society, the household budget stretched tight. Aspiring to a level of wealth that would transcend borders, Manuel decided to start a business, applying his naval engineering background to an enterprise salvaging and reselling materials from ships that had been sunk during the war. With whatever income he had to spare, he invested in bigger boats and heavy machinery capable of fishing out and towing in the massive battleships littering the vast Pacific floor. They existed in his mind like Ahab's white whale. Eventually, he set his law practice aside to focus full-time on the salvage business.

My grandparents were well connected and well positioned to accelerate the family's ascent. Rizalina's best friend, Baby, was the sister of Congressmember Ramon Mitra, minority leader of the Philippines house of representatives. Manuel's old classmates in the Japanese military academy were government ministers and business executives across Asia. The couple developed a plan like the one others of their standing had followed: they would be a transpacific family, shuttling freely across the ocean, with children educated in the States and business interests on the Islands. They would maintain a California base, as well as an ancestral home in Quezon City for occasional visits, to oversee the farm Rizalina's family owned near Iligan and the lakeside land Manuel's family owned in Marawi.

With their passage cleared, Rizalina and Manuel began the family's migration while Luisa and the maids watched over the kids at the Scout Reyes compound. In September 1967, my grandparents moved into the house in the Fillmore with Caridad and her husband, Roberto. A mile or so west, thousands of young people converged on the Haight-Ashbury District, with colorful vans, flowers in their long hair, and messages of peace and love. A mile to the south, in the Castro, men held hands with men in public, and the Missouri Mule offered a haven for gay people to gather freely and safely. A few blocks east, in the Fillmore, the Black Panther Party distributed food and political pamphlets calling for racial equality, and posters bearing the faces of Malcolm X and Stokely Carmichael plastered building walls. A few blocks north, in the Fillmore's music halls, bodies swayed to the Grateful Dead and Jefferson Airplane. To Rizalina and Manuel, these backdrops were no more than confirmation that they had entered a nation pushing forward, driven by the will of its people. At the tail end of a tumultuous decade, America had withstood assassinations, protests, and riots with its institutions intact.

TWO YEARS AFTER they arrived in San Francisco, the plan was going smoothly. Rizalina got a job as a department store bookkeeper. Manuel managed his ship-salvaging business from afar and had his Chrysler transported to California. In order to secure status as permanent residents, they had to live in the United States for five years, but this timeline wasn't a problem. With a staff of maids and drivers to help Luisa tend to the children back in Quezon City, Rizalina and Manuel had the luxury of patience. They had enough wealth to cover the expense of moving ten people thousands of miles. If all went according to plan, they would be permanent residents and their children would all be in San Francisco by the end of 1972.

It almost seemed like destiny. For centuries our barangay had survived a series of conquests, wars, and occupations. Ancestors escaped doom through a delicate formula of savvy and luck. Emilia Bato Bato ducked the Spanish invasion that swarmed Mindanao's resistant Moros. Jose Tianco slipped away from the American bullets that downed Luzon's revolutionaries. Caridad Concepcion avoided the Japanese samurai sword. The tides of history, it seemed, were no match for us. We were a blessed people, with invisible forces—engkantos and dwendes, angels and saints—on our side. And now, finally, we were bound for the promised land. Long colonized, we were set to burst from an ancient cocoon to emerge as colonists.

Manuel returned to Quezon City in 1969 to prepare the passports and visa applications for all the kids. His green card would remain valid as long as he was back in the States within a year. Seeking to catch up on time with his children, he took on the duty of driving the younger ones to school. With his Chrysler in San Francisco, he borrowed a Renault from a friend. My mom and Joey squeezed together into the passenger seat. Lyn, Bobby, Marlon, and Paul piled into the back. They were on the highway, sputtering through the traffic in sporadic bursts, when a truck rear-ended the car with such force that the Renault flew through the air before crashing down into a heap of vehicles. Five-year-old Bobby, seven-year-old Marlon, and fourteen-year-old Lyn were bleeding from their heads when Manuel pulled them from the tangle of smoking steel. Six-year-old Paul was unconscious.

From the hospital, Manuel called his wife, informing her that Paul was in a coma. Rizalina booked the next flight to Manila. Though the thought crossed her mind that leaving the United States might complicate her residency application, that bureaucratic matter felt meaningless, a minor thing to sort out later. Paul's coma lasted four days, and it would be months before he seemed fully recovered. The close call left Rizalina shaken and hesitant to step away. Having been apart from her children for two years, she savored her time back in the Philippines.

THE LAST TIME Rizalina and Manuel were in the States together was Christmastime 1996. My mom hosted that year's party at our Nob Hill apartment, to celebrate the latest branch of our American settlement. Manuel and Rizalina held court through the night, at the center of the festivities that seemed to mark an important new chapter in our barangay's migration, a sign that our exodus was nearing completion.

Only Paul and Marlon remained in the Philippines by then. The family discussed plans to bring them over, but complications kept springing up. Rizalina and Manuel felt guilty for leaving them alone that Christmas, and the following December they were back in Quezon City. For the Christmases that followed, the role of elder statesperson of our California barangay passed to Caridad, who hosted the party in her duplex. The floral couch, vertical blinds, green shag carpet, and wood-paneled walls harkened to the boom years when a couple of college-educated military veterans could buy a decent-size house in the city and quickly settle into the American middle class. Now the duplex was paid off, and Caridad rented out the bottom half at a rent that covered her bills. She decorated the steps to her upstairs unit with pewter and marble elephant figurines, as if to remind visitors of the house's long memory.

THOUGH JUST FORTY-SEVEN SQUARE MILES, San Francisco can feel sprawling for the variety of vibes it packs in. You can be in the heart of North Beach, an old Italian neighborhood brightly lit by big-windowed pizza joints and the red neon signs of beckoning strip clubs, then walk down a single alleyway and end up in the middle of Chinatown, where the smell of steamed dumplings wafts down narrow sidewalks and into dimly lit bars with handwritten menus. The camera shop Harvey Milk owned in the Castro District before becoming the city's first openly gay city official is four blocks from the high school Carlos Santana attended in the Mission District, where mariachi bands march through restaurants. The cherry blossoms in Japantown's central plaza are practically around the corner from where Louis Armstrong and Charlie Parker were rumored to have met for the first time, at a Fillmore District jazz club called Bop City.

Each rush of newcomers found space where they could on the hilly peninsula. Every inch is precious in San Francisco. The city welcomes all, but not everyone can fit. Who stays and who goes depends less on the whims of the free market than the policies set by elected officials. Zoning regulations ensure most structures outside downtown are low-slung, to protect views of the city's plentiful vistas and keep the city from feeling crowded—its population in 2000 was almost exactly what it was in 1950. The laws declare an aim to preserve the "essence of San Francisco." Architecturally speaking, Haight-Ashbury doesn't look much different than it did when young people flocked there for the Summer of Love. Pacific Heights remains flush with legally protected Victorian-era houses, still standing through earthquakes because the neighborhood sits on bedrock, which absorbs the shockwaves better than the sand and landfill below other parts of the city. After the 1989 earthquake damaged the Embarcadero Freeway, which blocked off the waterfront, city officials removed it, and today the old industrial ports just south of the Bay Bridge sizzle with sports bars, a baseball stadium, a basketball arena, and luxury condominiums. When the San Francisco Giants won the World Series in 2012, Jed and I joined thousands of others spilling out of bars into the intersection outside the ballpark, spraying champagne we'd purchased from a Safeway down the street, which had shelves of bubbly ready at the front.

Such a scene would have been unlikely outside the Giants' old baseball stadium, Candlestick Park, which never had any amenities nearby. Shortly after that stadium was built in 1958, on an industrial stretch at the edge of the Bay, the city began constructing public housing projects all around it, on hills overlooking the toxic Hunters Point Shipyard and in the valley between the highways, the places in the city where land was least valuable. The neighborhood contained one of San Francisco's two predominantly Black communities, along with the Fillmore. After ballgames at Candlestick, the spectators would file into the parking lot and head for the highway, taking their money to neighborhoods designed for commerce. Like many cities, San Francisco was built by design.

THE FILLMORE DISTRICT was one of the few places in the city where Caridad and Roberto could buy a house in 1957, before the Fair Housing Act prohibited overt discrimination and before the wave of non-European immigrants broke the largely binary American caste system. Roberto set up his chiropractic practice on the ground floor, and Caridad left her army job for better-paying work as a secretary at a law firm. She recalled being the only brown face among the applicants in the waiting room.

Caridad and Roberto frequented jazz clubs and literary readings, fortunate to catch the tail end of the Fillmore's cultural prime. Duke Ellington, Miles Davis, Dizzy Gillespie, Billie Holiday, Count Basie, and Fletcher Henderson passed through, many at the Bop City club. A patron named Pony Poindexter recalled a session at the venue: "We all settled back to look and listen to some real piano playing. Still, several hours went by and no one moved. It was daybreak. No one moved."

The Fillmore's Black community had grown in the years after World War II. Many new arrivals moved into properties that had belonged to Japanese families sent to internment camps. Maya Angelou, who chronicled her years in the Fillmore in the 1940s in *I Know Why the Caged Bird Sings*, described the "visible revolution" that transformed a neighborhood where the least privileged were left to compete for scarce resources:

> On the surface it appeared to be totally peaceful and almost a refutation of the term "revolution." The Yakamoto Sea Food Market quietly became Sammy's Shoe Shine Parlor and Smoke Shop. Yashigira's Hardware metamorphosed into La Salon de Beauté owned by Miss Clorinda Jackson. The Japanese shops which sold products to Nisei customers were taken over by enterprising Negro businessmen, and in less than a year became permanent homes away from home for the newly arrived Southern Blacks. Where the odors of tempura, raw fish, and *cha* had dominated, the aroma of chitlings, greens and ham hocks now prevailed. . . . The Japanese area became San Francisco's Harlem in a matter of months.

The Harlem Renaissance of the West was short-lived. Bop City closed in 1965. That decade, Caridad and Roberto watched eminent domain policies mow down scores of Black-owned homes and businesses in the blocks around them. The city mostly built low-income housing projects in their place, setting aside a portion of cleared land for new commercial ventures. Displaced property owners were compensated with a check for the value of their land and a certificate that guaranteed them a place at the front of the line to claim a spot in the neighborhood whenever the so-called "urban renewal" project was complete, but this ended up taking two decades; some 96 percent of the certificates would go unused. One large plot, a sixty-square-block stretch once containing

10,000 residents, was cleared to make way for shopping and entertainment venues, but banks and other lenders declined to invest, so the expanse of weedy dirt stayed fenced off and vacant for years.

When America's postwar economy turned, Black communities were hit first and hardest. Facing fiscal crises in the 1970s, federal and local officials slashed funding for social services that helped reduce racial inequities. Public school classrooms became more crowded. Civil servants lost their jobs. People needing homes or mental health treatment spiraled into destitution. Housing projects deteriorated from lack of maintenance. Rates of unemployment, crime, and drug addiction rose nationwide, especially in big cities with high concentrations of residents with low incomes. White people with means fled for the perceived safety of the suburbs, taking their tax dollars with them.

As in many neighborhoods transformed by mid-century "urban renewal" projects, the Fillmore fell on hard times, becoming a notorious hub for the vice trade. By the late '70s, among the most visible local figures of upward mobility were pimps and drug dealers. The area seemed drained of every public service but one: policing. To combat rising crime rates across the country, a broad bipartisan swath of politicians expanded police departments so that officers became the first responders to any disturbance, and the solution to any social problem increasingly became throwing people in prison. More police duties justified the need for more officers. The budgetary cycle born in those years built inertia: cuts to public programs leading to more crime leading to more police spending leading to more cuts to public programs.

With Johnson's "War on Poverty" replaced by Richard Nixon's "War on Drugs," police officers patrolled Black neighborhoods like an occupying force, empowered to act aggressively at the slightest suspicion or infraction. Internal quotas and federal grants incentivized officers to make as many arrests as possible, and within three decades the number of people in U.S. prisons ballooned from fewer than 250,000 to more than 1.5 million. Laws extending prison sentences put even more power in sworn police statements. Laws protecting police behavior allowed officers to kill civilians anytime they feared for their lives.

The tough-on-crime strategy stripped the Fillmore of thousands of breadwinners who spent years behind bars for minor crimes. Somewhere along the line, the neighborhood's name changed. People living in the higher-income part of the district north of Fillmore Street began calling their community Lower Pacific Heights, so that their property values wouldn't be damaged by association. Some around the city started calling the blocks south of Fillmore Street the Western Addition, after the projects that had gone up a few blocks from Caridad's house, as if to redefine a proud neighborhood as one primarily associated with poverty.

JUST AS ROBERTO and his fellow Filipino migrants before the war learned that America's racism had outlived slavery, so too did Caridad's cohort observe that the civil rights movement did little to erode prejudices based on skin color.

Maria Victoria Bunye arrived in the United States in the mid-1960s, on a college grant from the Peace Corps. Before her first semester at Georgetown, she and other grant recipients from around the world attended an orientation at Indiana University in Bloomington. On the last day of the gathering, before heading to the airport, she and another student, Lester—"a gentleman from a former British Colony," she recalled—went to a restaurant for lunch. They sat at the table talking for several minutes. Lester was going to the University of Maryland for a postdoctoral program in physics. Maria had been a teacher in the Philippines and would go on to write two textbooks on Cebuano, one of the main languages on the Islands. She remembered the restaurant being nearly empty. "None of the many waitresses there came to serve us," she said. She didn't realize what was happening until Lester suggested they go elsewhere. "He picked it up right away because he was Black," she said. "His disgust, disappointment, everything."

Later, on a trip to California, she met a Filipino student who showed her an enlarged photograph of an old sign that read "No Filipinos or dogs allowed." That history hadn't been taught in Maria's classrooms in the Philippines. She began to see the country differently, quite surprised by the scope of American hatred.

"Suddenly, everything I learned about racism, segregation, cerebral without experience, came together," she said. "I said to myself: It's true people are discriminated against because of the skin color, and you don't have to be Black."

Jess Teruel Esteva, who went on to become a newspaper publisher, got a visa to the United States in 1945 because his father-in-law was a colonel in the army. After the war, Esteva and his wife began looking to buy a house in San Francisco. One day, his wife saw one she loved and put down a deposit. A day or two later, they got a call informing them that their application had been rejected because another buyer had put in an offer before them. Jess went to the house to retrieve the deposit. Soon after he returned home, the phone rang. It was the real estate agent he'd just seen.

"Are you still interested in the house?" he asked.

Jess said he was.

"I think you can have it."

Jess asked what happened.

The seller had met Jess's wife, who was shorter and darker than her mestizo husband. Upon learning that the fair-skinned man he'd seen was the one trying to buy the house, the seller said to the agent, "Hey, he's not Filipino. Sell him the house."

It was the transcripts of such stories that Caridad and Roberto began collecting into the book *Pinoy: The First Wave*, which was published under Roberto's name in 1977. Caridad would go on to publish two more volumes of oral history, *The Second Wave* and *The Third Wave*. And while the migrants in their pages note the discrimination they encountered and the reality that life in America was harder than they expected, like Carlos Bulosan they remained convinced that America was the best place for them to be and heartily encouraged others to follow in their steps. The book's introduction captures the sentiment, describing immigrants as "those of us who were not fortunate enough to be born American."

ONE NIGHT when I was nine, my mom, Uncle Bobby, and I watched the movie *Mississippi Burning*, which is based on the 1964 lynching of three civil rights workers and introduced me to the Ku Klux Klan. Taking in the harrowing scenes, I was haunted by the fear that armed white supremacists were going around attacking darker-skinned people. After all, I could recite the names and feats of athletes from that period, so it was far from ancient history to me. My mom calmed me with assurances that the coordinated racist violence of the KKK was a relic of the past. That such a drastic improvement could occur within three and a half decades seemed to confirm America's trajectory. Just imagine what the country would look like after three and a half more decades!

I was more familiar with the heroes of American history than the villains, the triumphs more than the tragedies. When I had to pick a historical speech to perform in front of my eighth-grade class, my mom suggested the Gettysburg Address. She had childhood memories of her father spontaneously performing it at the dinner table. He would explain that the speech was a proclamation of righteousness at a moment when America's moral compass spun like a roulette wheel. Framed with the hindsight of knowing how things turned out, I found its words comforting in their measured uncertainty: not even Lincoln could say for sure whether the nation "can long endure," but the future he lays out comes to pass. The "unfinished work" gets completed when the United

States prohibits slavery, and the soldiers who perished in battle "shall not have died in vain." Indeed, the nation "shall have a new birth of freedom," entering a period of mending wounds left by a conflict that nearly ended the American experiment. In the end I was glad to have picked Lincoln's famous speech because it turned out to be very short and gave me an excuse to stand on a chair while I delivered it. My understanding of history at the time entailed little more than a collection of sequential facts, such as that Abraham Lincoln was tall and freed the slaves.

The history classes at my California schools taught that Native Americans were killed by white settlers and the Civil War was caused by the Southern states' insistence on owning slaves. But it was less clear to me how these events connected with one another or with present-day affairs. We didn't dwell on the motives.

Our curriculum was not unique. A high school history textbook for advanced placement students nationwide describes "frequent sexual liaisons" between plantation owners and slaves that were only "sometimes" rape. A passing line refers to Thomas Jefferson's "romantic relationship" with Sally Hemmings. In some states, mostly in the South, students are taught that slavery was a key element of the Civil War but not the central cause.

How to introduce children to the idea that their country was founded by people who believed in white supremacy? U.S. schools typically put off that reveal for as long as possible. In California, Oklahoma, and South Carolina, Harriet Tubman and Frederick Douglass are presented to young students as essential historical figures without any lessons about the institution they resisted. Once slavery enters the syllabus, it fits into the American story as an example of a fight for progress, a social ill ultimately toppled. In Georgia, students are asked to "explain how the significance of slavery grew in American politics, including slave rebellions and the rise of abolitionism."

There is less focus on the wide swath of Americans who supported or were indifferent to slavery, the beliefs they held to justify the possession of human chattel, and the horrific daily experiences that enslaved people endured. History textbooks in Virginia and Washington state avoid holding anyone explicitly responsible for slavery, instead presenting the institution through a passive voice that ignores the agency of those who benefited from it. "African men, women, and children were brought to the Virginia colony and enslaved to work on the plantations," the Virginia textbook states. "Enslaved African Americans were denied basic rights." It was not white plantation owners but "the Virginia colony" that "became dependent on slave labor." Washington students read about the "forced movement of African people as slave labor" and "how the growth of slavery throughout the South created an economic system dominated by large plantation owners." A 2017 analysis of fifteen state standards by the Southern Poverty Law Center found that none "make meaningful connections to the present" or address "how the ideology of white supremacy rose to justify the institution of slavery." Instead, the teaching focuses on feel-good stories that deal with slavery's end, rather than its inception and persistence.

From that angle, white supremacy is a toxic trace, now nearly eradicated, a bug rather than a feature designed into laws and conventions. Racist violence is explained away as the unacceptable hatred of bad apples, rather than as the extremist expression of a wider effort to defend the white dominance that seemed to be slipping away.

The conspiracy attempts to hide a fundamental fact: American injustice is intentional.

AN HONEST ACCOUNTING of U.S. history would address the reality that every advance toward equality came with bloody resistance and high costs. In the years after the end of the Civil War, Black people faced a wave of unchecked terrorism—of the five hundred or so white men indicted for murdering Black people in 1865 and 1866, not one was convicted, according to historian Eric Foner. After Black people exercised their new liberties to vote, own land, and run for office in the late nineteenth century, white supremacists responded with lynchings, riots, and voter suppression campaigns. White authorities used harsh, discriminatory legal codes to imprison Black people for minor infractions, sentencing many to decades of the hard labor once performed by slaves. The earliest police forces in the American colonies were formed in the South to apprehend runaway slaves and suppress slave revolts, and later, local police enforced Jim Crow laws and separate-but-equal policies.

Blocked from accessing white banks, Black people built a financial hub in the Greenwood district of Tulsa, Oklahoma, which was known as "Black Wall Street," until in 1921 a mob of white vigilantes burned it down and killed at least seventy-five residents. Upwardly mobile Black homeowners in the postwar boom years were restricted from buying property by federal loan policies that refused to insure mortgages in mixed-race communities, and went on to accrue less equity because banks reduced appraisal values for properties with Black neighbors. When a Black couple in Cicero, Illinois, managed to purchase a home in a previously all-white neighborhood in 1951, a mob of white people broke into the house, burned their possessions on the lawn, then torched the property.

Black residents could do nothing to stop the government from tearing down their homes to build the structures white communities rejected, such as highways or public housing projects. Black children who integrated white schools faced jeering, spitting crowds of white people. Black protesters calling for equal rights faced beatings for sitting at whites-only lunch counters; dogs, batons, and water hoses for marching in the street; and fire bombs for their bus trips through the South. By 1960, less than 4 percent of police officers were Black, and law enforcement tactics often centered on "preventative patrolling," which amounted to stopping, frisking, and questioning anyone police deemed suspicious for any reason.

It was one of those stops, in August 1965, that sparked the uprising in Watts that lasted a week and concluded with more than five hundred buildings across the city damaged or destroyed and thirty-four people dead, including twenty-three shot by LAPD officers or National Guardsmen. A year later, after a white police officer fatally shot a sixteen-year-old Black boy in San Francisco's Hunters Point neighborhood, protesters took to the streets, smashing store windows and throwing rocks at the mayor. A year after that, Black residents in Detroit protested the police raid of a bar hosting a welcome party for Vietnam veterans, and in the uprising that followed, officers killed thirty-three Black people.

California's governor put together a commission to investigate the causes of the Watts uprising. The panel's conclusion was straightforward: it had stemmed from a lack of economic and educational opportunities for Black people. In a 101-page report released in 1965, the commission recommended "emergency literacy and preschool programs, improved police-community ties, increased low-income housing, more job-training projects, upgraded health-care services, more efficient public transportation, and many more." Few of the recommendations would be implemented.

This moment, in the late 1960s, marked a crossroads in the United States. The postwar boomtime was winding down. The pot was about to shrink. A wave of immigrants was on the way. An undeclared war in Southeast Asia had no end in sight. Black people continued to fill the streets, calling for equality. Four years after the first civil rights bill passed, Martin Luther King, Jr., was assassinated by a white supremacist.

That was the state of America when Manuel and Rizalina returned to Quezon City in 1969. They liked the Catholic and cosmopolitan John F. Kennedy, respected the strong-willed Lyndon Johnson, and tolerated the cynical Richard Nixon, but above all admired the smooth turns of

American democracy. They couldn't say the same about their own country, where Marcos rigged ballots to win reelection, declared martial law, killed dissidents, and ushered in an economic downturn that halted our family's ascent. Rizalina tried to return to the United States less than a year into the dictatorship, in May 1973, but her green card was confiscated at the airport because she'd been away from the country for nearly four years, longer than acceptable for a permanent residency petitioner. A memo from the U.S. embassy in Manila to immigration officials in Washington confirms that her green card was then "destroyed in central office." Paying mortgage and tuition bills took precedence over migration plans. Years passed without any mention of American fantasies.

Then, in 1977, Roberto died from a heart attack, leaving Caridad in the States, alone with their son, Ricardo. Rizalina tried again to rejoin her sister-in-law.

A decade earlier, she had a menu of appealing options. Now every path seemed perilous. Though her tourist visa granted her six months, Rizalina planned to stay indefinitely, hoping that if she waited long enough, the situation would somehow resolve itself. From all I know about my grandma, I imagine she would've been uncomfortable about her illicit mission. America's respect for the rule of law was among the traits my grandparents most admired about the place.

WHEN RIZALINA RETURNED in 1978, the Fillmore looked different than she remembered, with more boarded-up storefronts and broken streetlights. Caridad warned her about the neighborhood's "bad elements." For safety, they commuted to work together. Rizalina got an accounting job at a law firm downtown, not far from the law firm where Caridad worked as a secretary. One evening, on their walk home from the bus stop, a man with a gun robbed them of their purses. They were still catching their breath when the police arrived. It must have been then that the idea flashed in Rizalina's mind. Among the pilfered items, she told the officers, was her green card.

With a police report in hand, she requested a replacement card from the Immigration and Naturalization Service. Weeks later, like magic, a replacement card appeared in the mailbox. The information on it was identical to the original that had been confiscated at the Manila airport, complete with the 1967 issue date. Just like that, it was as if she had never left the United States! America had corralled us into one of its neglected corners, maybe hoping we'd give up and leave, but the joke was on the colonizers: their neglect had led to our legitimacy! What poetic irony!

If only I could confirm the details. The tale has lived on as a fable in our family lore, carrying the lesson that everything happens for a reason, a reminder to trust in God's plan. I first heard it from Auntie Ging, who heard it from Rizalina back when it happened. There's no doubt about the mugging, but Ging couldn't be certain about what followed; the particulars of public policy wasn't the point of the story. My grandmother's immigration file, which I got through a public records request, offered no answers and few clues. Her successful application to become a naturalized citizen in 1987 stated that she had been living in San Francisco since 1967 and included a photocopy of her laminated Resident Alien card. You can tell from the photo that the card had been recently updated: Rizalina is in her fifties, with wavy locks framing a weary face lined with creases. The memo denying her permanent residency in 1973 didn't say she wasn't living in the United States, just that she "was unable to show" that she was. Across the thirty-two pages of documents, there is not a single date or claim indicating when she left the country after her 1967 entry, nothing proving that her visa was ever invalid, nothing suggesting she ever applied a second time. But neither is there anything verifying that she received a replacement visa in 1978. She had slipped through the cracks somehow, perhaps in the manner described in our family fable, perhaps another way. In the end, it might not have mattered. My grandma was right about just having to wait long enough. Less than a decade after she arrived, President Ronald Reagan granted amnesty to undocumented immigrants.

Upon hearing my conclusion that the story of the magical visa was possible but unverified, my mom stepped in to set the record straight. With adamant certainty, she assured me that my grandmother had not broken any laws. "She was very careful about that," my mom said, noting that Grandma had been a meticulous accountant and reminding me of those three a.m. prayer sessions. "We did it the right way."

IN RECENT YEARS, as I reached the age my mom was when she had me, our worldviews had diverged to such a degree that we couldn't seem to talk for more than ten minutes without arguing about basic facets of reality.

We never set out to debate. Usually, my mom would mention something she'd heard recently: that the Democratic Party was brainwashing Black people to have abortions in a plot to keep their population small, or that Nancy Pelosi died years ago and was replaced by a robot. "How interesting, huh?" she'd say. I'd tell her the information was false, and then we'd have a back-and-forth about the credibility of various news sources. Sometimes, I'd be able to prove the information was wrong or misleading. When she texted me memes recounting that Democrats supported slavery and the first Black senators were Republican, I explained that segregationists switched parties in the century after the Civil War, fleeing Franklin Roosevelt's New Deal social programs, then John F. Kennedy's civil rights agenda.

"Whoever writes this stuff is trying to deceive you," I'd say. "Why do you think they keep giving you all this wrong information?"

"I don't know," she'd reply. "Maybe." She'd note that she never accepted anything she read as confirmed fact. She just liked to explore the possibilities. She was curious about how the world worked, but to her mind the information channels I recommended were off limits. She'd begun to mistrust the *New York Times,* the *Washington Post,* the *San Francisco Chronicle,* and other traditional news outlets in the mid-2000s because of all the reporting on the Catholic priest sex abuse scandals. The Freemasons had planted these pedophile infiltrators to sabotage the Church, she hypothesized, and the media was unfairly attacking the institution while missing the real story—probably because the Freemasons were running newsrooms, too. Since then, she'd been on the hunt for reporting she could trust. "It's actually the mainstream media's job to fool the people!" she said. "They've been lying to us all these years." Her own son was no exception.

She found her displeasure echoed on Fox News, the sun of an expanding right-wing media solar system. As new planets materialized in its orbit, my mom ventured further and further out to explore. She subscribed to the Judicial Watch daily newsletter, picked up copies of the *Epoch Times,* caught up on big events with clips from One America News Network, and filled pockets of free time with an assortment of random YouTube channels purporting to reveal truths the mainstream media won't tell you. More and more public voices were making proclamations about left-wing conspiracies. When she heard Trump complaining about the "deep state" shadow government trying to destroy America, my mom was ebullient—here was official recognition of what she'd known all along!

To her eyes, the curtain was lifting. She discovered that her disparate suspicions aligned into a grand, unified conspiracy theory of everything: QAnon combined the clarifying certitude of $E = mc^2$ with the cryptic elegance of the Fibonacci sequence. The theory's originator, known as Q, an anonymous online poster claiming to be a government official, alleged that there was a global cabal of powerful people who worshipped Satan, but it turned out their aim wasn't just to wipe out

Christianity, as my mom had thought, but to protect the child sex trafficking ring they benefited from as abusers and investors. It occurred to her that, given their expertise and agenda, these were surely the same conspirators who framed the Church. "I never knew how evil these people are!!!" she texted me. "Now that I've learned the truth, I want to show my support for my country!"

My mom was enthralled by the collective effort to piece together clues that seemed to be scattered everywhere you looked, from the tail numbers on the presidential airplane to the order of words in Trump's tweets. I was alarmed by how many people seemed to share these baseless beliefs, a community whose growing numbers convinced my mom that she was on the right track. She told me about the "Patriots" and "truth-seekers" she met on Twitter and LinkedIn. Her Twitter feed, which she'd originally signed up for to keep track of my work, morphed into a surreal mash-up of her divided interests: enthusiastic posts about Trump's fight against the deep state, complete with the official QAnon hashtags, alongside tweets promoting my BuzzFeed News reporting into things like police misconduct. "I hope @POTUS & @DOJ would read the investigative criminal justice stories of @AlbertSamaha," she tweeted, punctuating the message with "#TRUMP2020." I'd love to know what her eighty-four other followers thought about her, this passionate MAGA woman with reliably far-right sensibilities except for her inexplicable peddling of a news outlet Trump once called a "failing pile of garbage." Eventually, Twitter suspended her account, for sharing misinformation and on suspicion that she was a bot—the email she received asked her to confirm her personal information. Another sign of the liberal conspiracy, she said. "They are silencing Patriots like me!"

An impenetrable fortress of circular logic encased her beliefs. Any policy that made Trump look bad, she chalked up to reckless exaggerations by biased journalists. When priests, archbishops, and even the pope criticized him, she denounced them as undercover collaborators in the

satanic conspiracy. It wasn't hard for her to wall herself off from anything she didn't want to hear—her sources churned out a steady supply
of propaganda and disinformation for her to use to patch any holes.
When I began to see that our political disputes were constantly spoiling
our interactions, I stopped trying to convince her. I'd correct facts and
explain why I disagreed, but I eased up on the emotion and accepted
that nothing I said could dent her fortress. At least she lived in California, a heavily Democratic state where her vote wouldn't sway presidential elections, I'd tell myself. But my mom didn't let me off so easily. She
took my distaste for Trump personally and felt it her duty to keep her
only child from damnation. As long as I opposed Trump, I was on the
side of the "forces of darkness." I had never heard her defend any politician as vocally, loyally, stubbornly, as she did Trump, a messianic hero
in her mind. "I believe God has given the world this man who could end
the evil of the Luciferian cabal/deep state!" she texted me.

Our debates never reached resolution. About all we could agree on
was that these were important issues and the gap between us was troubling. How could we not talk about it?

"I wanna give back to America for all the blessings," she said. "Imagine if we were in the Philippines now! Oh my gosh! My only regret—do
you want to guess?"

Not a single guess came to mind. My mom's relentless optimism had
rendered me incapable of identifying a possible regret in all these years.

"Give up?" my mom said, through a grin that I could practically hear
over the phone. "I wish I knew politics before."

In the past, she had scoffed at politics as lesser than religion. It hardly
mattered who held elected office, because power was bestowed by the
Most High. In that oblivious Before time, she hadn't yet learned to see
government officials as vectors carrying forward God's will. Just look at
the Bible, filled as it is with mortals acting on behalf of the Holy Spirit.

"But of course I didn't know any better," she said. "That's why I'm sorry that, you know, I'm sorry that my son is so liberal. Only because I was so ignorant about politics before."

"Well, I'm glad," I said, pushing the words out through a soft laugh.

"What? That I made this mistake?" I found it endearing that no matter how many hours we debated the same points over and over, my mom's confusion and pity never waned, as if she woke up each morning convinced that today was the day her son's heathen phase would end. "How can you be on the side of corrupt politicians?"

"They're all corrupt, Mom." I didn't completely believe this, but I knew she did. I could pull her back to shore with this rhetorical lifeline if she grabbed hold and let go of her unconditional reverence for America's worst president to date.

"All politicians are corrupt, okay," she said, raising my hopes. "But Trump was a businessman, not a politician."

"He was a corrupt businessman, and now he's a corrupt politician."

"At least he cares about the American people."

It went on like this, as always, back and forth until we eventually reached a detente, tepidly agreeing that it was healthy to hear out perspectives far from your own. Tempers didn't flare, voices didn't rise, frustration stayed in hibernation. Instead, a strange peace came over me. To my eyes, the world was falling apart—authoritarianism rising, democracy slipping, ignorance spreading, cruelty rewarded. Millions of Americans pledged loyalty to a racist, sexist, ignorant man who enlisted avowed nativists as his advisers. Some of his supporters followed him not because they'd been manipulated but simply because he called Mexicans "criminals" and "rapists," because he deemed developing nations in Africa and the Caribbean "shithole countries," because he declined to denounce neo-Nazi groups sparking deadly clashes—because, as writer Adam Serwer put it in *The Atlantic*, he represented "a promise to restore an idealized past in which America's traditional aristocracy of race was unquestioned." Others, like my mom, followed because he embodied whatever reactionary agenda his propagandists projected onto him.

I had to resist the temptation to succumb to hopelessness, the rising dread that the arc of the universe doesn't bend toward anything good but snaps from the fight to control it. Every year seemed to get wilder, scarier, more chaotic and uncertain than the last. What evidence suggested a turnaround was imminent? What flashes of brightness could I wish upon? What kind of balm in these horrible fucking times could relieve the malaise gripping every inch of my body every second of the day? All this time, I realized, I didn't have to look far. My mom was more hopeful than she'd ever been.

What a benefit our divide turned out to be! The worse things looked to my eyes, the better they looked to hers. For all the bullshit raining down upon the planet, at least my mom was happy. I counted my blessings, just like she taught me.

THERE IS NO easy way to break from paradigms that long defined your worldview.

As a child, I thought there was no greater authority on the fundamental rules of the universe than my mother, who seemed to be in tune with the Divine. Anything I learned filtered through her insights.

Even at sixteen, I followed my mom's teachings like a disciple. I prayed Psalm 91 before football games for protection and wrote a pair of verses onto my cleats. Whenever I suffered even a minor injury, I splashed myself with holy water from Lourdes, France, where an apparition of the Virgin Mary had infused the grotto with divine healing powers. My mom had filled a dozen or so bottles on a trip there in the '80s, when she and my dad were dating. After two decades, our stock was running short, so our 2005 trip to France came just in time.

The night before our flight from Paris to Lourdes, I fell ill with food poisoning. At the airport in the morning, before we even reached the check-in counter, I threw up on a potted plant. I threw up again in the airsickness bag as soon as we got on the plane, prompting a concerned flight attendant to ask, "Is this your first time flying?" I felt miserable, encased in a blurry membrane of fatigue and nausea. "Don't worry," my mom said, "we're almost in Lourdes." There was no better place to be physically incapacitated.

Once at the shrine, a castle-like church with thin spires and stone ramparts, we bounded straight to the grotto, where my mom splashed the holy water onto my forehead, praying out loud for God to heal me. I felt a spirit sinking in, benevolent and purifying. The nausea seemed to fade. My energy began to pick up. My mom filled a bottle with the water. We left the grotto and walked toward the church. I went about five steps, then hopped off the pathway, and hurled a bucketload of watery bile onto the grass, a process I repeated once more before we reached the church.

I lay down in the pew with my eyes closed. My mom rested a hand on my head, dabbing more holy water onto my cheeks and neck every few minutes. The church was silent except for the echoing footsteps of worshippers sliding in and out of pews with their heads bowed. I asked my mom why it wasn't working, the holy water. God has his reasons, she said helplessly, after a contemplative pause. She looked stricken. The water had reportedly cured blindness and paralysis yet seemed no match for a simple bout of food poisoning. Had she been mistaken?

I could only reason that the mysteries of the universe were sometimes too complicated to pin down, that new facts could dent old paradigms without warning, that not even my mother had the answers to everything. This was a revelation to me, opening up realms of possibility and uncertainty. It was like learning, as I did in later years, that the artists of classical Greece had painted their sculptures in vibrant colors, with olive or tan or brown skin, but the pigments faded with time, then got scrubbed off when the artifacts were discovered, and so for many years people associated this bleached whiteness with classical beauty. What other assumptions had I taken for granted?

I thought back to a trip we'd gone on the previous year, with Auntie Ging and Lauren, to spend Christmas 2004 at Granduncle Tomas's villa in an ancient hilltop village in western Italy. The property was hundreds of years old, encased by castle walls, with an iron door big enough to block an elephant. Behind the stone cottage lay a grassy yard that stretched to the turrets of the old city wall, at the edge of a cliff overlooking the countryside. The land had once served as part of the city's military defense, then later housed monks, before ultimately coming into the possession of a prominent family of nobility. By the 1960s, the land belonged to Count Sebastiano Bonmartini, who fell in love with Tomas and bestowed him lifetime rights to the place.

The villa doubled as Tomas's art studio. You couldn't reach an arm out without touching one of his creations. His most recent obsession was Alexander the Great, and the young conqueror's peach-colored face sprawled across canvases leaning against a wall. Bronze sculptures of nude bodies in various contortions loomed on platforms standing around the living room and patio like party guests. Stacks of books leaned precariously like rock formations. A half-full bottle of J&B whiskey stood beside a crowded ashtray, one of at least five in the living room. Seven Belgian shepherds scurried around, barking and panting, somehow never knocking anything over. The whole scene was tinged with a fantastical sheen befitting my granduncle, who for Christmas gave fifteen-year-old me a strip of condoms I don't think he realized were expired.

In the dark of night, the eccentric wonderland twisted into an eerie stillness. The sculptures cast lifelike silhouettes against the dark blue sky. The dogs slept, spread out across the living room like blurry, rustling shadows in the faint moonlight. The two bedrooms were at the far end of the villa, tucked behind an iron door that opened onto the living room. My mom and I shared one room, while Auntie Ging and Lauren joined Granduncle Tomas in the other.

On our second or third night, my mom and I were wide awake from jet lag. We lay facing each other on adjacent twin beds, talking about whatever, when suddenly we heard the shuffling of slippers. The light in our room was on but the hallway beyond our open door was dark. The footsteps continued for longer than seemed necessary to duck into the bathroom or cross the hallway to the living room and kitchen. No lights turned on and there were no sounds but the footsteps. The shuffling got louder and sounded like it was about to pass by our room. Though I knew it was probably Lauren clumsily stumbling around in the darkness, I was too scared to look at the doorway, so I kept my back to it and watched my mom's face while she watched the doorway as the steps grew louder and louder, and then quieter, and then nothing could be heard. My mom's face barely flinched.

"Who was it?" I asked. "Was it Lauren?"

"I don't know," my mom said hesitantly. "I think so, maybe."

What she saw was a girl with long dark hair in a long white nightgown. Lauren had a white nightgown, right? Was she getting a midnight snack or a drink of water? Before we could exchange more than a few words, a thunderous clamor erupted from the living room—it was the dogs, they were barking madly, violently, torrentially, for minutes straight, until, without warning and all at the same time, the barking turned to soaring, symphonic howling, before melting into quivering yelps, horrifying whines that had me bugging the fuck out. My mom's face was as frozen as mine, and in petrified, mystified silence, we waited for whatever was happening to play out, for an explanation to emerge, some hilarious misunderstanding. Then, with the precision of an orchestra, the dogs at once fell silent.

My heart banged furiously against my chest. We waited for Lauren to come shuffling back from the kitchen or wherever. She had a white nightgown, right? She must not have been bothered by the dogs' howling. Maybe she had accidentally passed out on the couch or at the dining table. Lauren's a heavy sleeper.

My mom and I stayed up for another two or three hours, barely slept, and woke up before anyone else, including the dogs. We waited in the living room, eager for answers. Eventually, Lauren shuffled into the living room in a black T-shirt and gray sweatpants, still wiping sleep from her eyes, to find my mom and me staring at her like we'd seen a ghost.

"Did you wear that to sleep?" I blurted out.

"Huh?" said Lauren. "Did I wear what to sleep?"

"That," I gestured. "Did you change when you got up?"

"What? No. What are you talking about?"

Somehow Lauren, Auntie Ging, and Granduncle Tomas had all slept through the tremendous clamor and didn't recall any barking. I felt a little bad having to break the news to my granduncle that his house was haunted, but he shrugged off the unexplained incident. The ghosts, he said, visited often.

When I tell people that story, citing it as the reason I believe in ghosts, I usually skip over the detail that I didn't actually lay eyes on the mysterious girl in white. Secondhand ghost sightings aren't nearly as convincing. To streamline the anecdote, I describe what my mom saw with as much conviction as if I'd observed it myself.

CHAPTER 7

COLLISION SPORT

In June 1999, my mom bought a house for $163,500, a good price for three bedrooms, two bathrooms, and a backyard with a swimming pool in the white part of town.

Sacramento wasn't her first choice. The city was low and sprawling, unsuitable for walking, with hundred-degree summers and freezing winters that encased parked cars in ice. Our closest relatives were at least ninety minutes away by highway, which she still didn't drive. Since we'd settled in the States four years earlier, she'd been on the hunt for property she could afford on the $45,000 yearly allowance from my dad. But she had very specific stipulations for location: it had to be near a high school run by Jesuits, the Catholic order she admired for their commitment to discipline and education. Her first choice for me was St. Ignatius, in San Francisco, but like her mother a decade earlier, she found nothing there in her price range. Next on the list was Bellarmine, in San Jose, but the South Bay was also too expensive. The only other Jesuit high school in Northern California was Sacramento's unambiguously named Jesuit High School, and to her relief, she found an affordable listing within a few miles of the campus. My dad covered the

20 percent down payment. My mom and I moved in a few days after I finished fourth grade. About a year later, my mom and dad divorced.

It was his idea. My mom had been fine with the status quo. Over the years she had accepted the reality that their distance might not be resolved anytime soon and, in fact, embraced the benefits of our circumstances. My dad's financial support gave her the freedom to focus her energy on the task of motherhood. She had no hobbies other than daily Mass, and her primary interests involved researching what schools I should attend and what foods I should eat. She learned to cook Lebanese food so I could stay in touch with that side of my heritage. She traded in her light blue Dodge Neon for a gold Jeep Cherokee—which she named JC, using the brand's initials to honor Jesus Christ—because it had more trunk space for the bags of sports equipment my friends and I loaded in after practices and games. She volunteered as chaperone on field trips, supervised my homework assignments, and was usually the first parent to pull into the school parking lot for afternoon pickup. She was proud of how sharply she'd diverged from her own parents' example. "You know, Albert, it was the maids who took care of us," she'd say on drives home from school. "All these years I've never needed a babysitter for you! You're so lucky!" The only times I ever heard her complain about my dad was when his wire transfers were late. She'd sit on her bed with the phone on speaker, checking her bank account to see if the money had come in, the verdict delivered in a robotic automated voice that became familiar in our household. The money always eventually came.

So when my dad requested a divorce, my mom's immediate concern was ensuring my needs would still be taken care of. She informed me of the developments in a calm tone, neither surprised nor disheartened. Thank God they hadn't married in church, she said. Their Vegas nuptials made it easy to get an annulment, absolving them from sin. A blessing in disguise. She didn't press my dad for much money, though he was a wealthy man. She requested $25,000 in one-time alimony, $45,000 in annual child support until I finished college, and a handshake promise that he'd cover the costs of my education. "My American Dream is the best education I can give to my son," she recalled years later. "Giving him the fishing pole and not just the fish."

Officially independent, my mom needed a career. She hadn't worked full time since her years as a flight attendant. Her last paycheck had come during our early months in San Francisco, after a modeling agent had approached her on the street and arranged a couple of runway gigs—my mom didn't find the work very stimulating and lost interest within a year, preferring to focus her energy on raising me. Now, starting from scratch at thirty-nine, the sudden opportunity to redefine herself excited her. While house-hunting in Sacramento, she'd watched the realtor with keen interest, intrigued by the size of her commission. All over the country there were people trying to sell houses and people trying to buy houses, and you could get a five-figure payday just by bringing them together.

Over her years searching for a home to buy, my mom realized something important about the States. The country's central offering wasn't the American Dream. That was an outdated concept. When James Truslow Adams coined and defined the term in 1931, it may have seemed like the United States was on the way to establishing "a social order in which each man and each woman shall be able to attain to the fullest stature of which they are innately capable, and be recognized by others for what they are, regardless of the fortuitous circumstances of birth or position." In the decades since, the term expanded to include meanings beyond "opportunity for each according to ability or achievement"—it meant children better off than their parents, and the peacetime comforts of a suburban house with a white picket fence, a two-car garage, and a trusted school system. A 2017 Pew Research poll found that most

Americans defined the essential components of the American Dream as "freedom of choice in how to live," "having a good family life," and "retiring comfortably."

But "Dream" is an apt word. In the twenty-first century, income inequality is wider in the United States than in any other developed nation. More than three-quarters of Americans live paycheck to paycheck, and around half of Americans born in the 1980s earn less than their parents did at the same age. If anything is clear about America, it's that opportunities are distributed not according to merit but to caste, ensuring that the wealthy stay wealthy and the poor duke it out for the limited spots on the upward track. Not everyone can be a winner, and the further down you are, the more competition there is. To make riches in the richest nation in the world, you have to access its tricks.

Over her years of looking for a house, my mom noticed that the prices kept getting higher—the average home value rose 23 percent from 1995 to 1999. A thought occurred to her: This is a country that conjures money out of thin air. That's what it does better than anyplace else. All this time, she'd thought that home ownership embodied the American Dream, the final checkpoint marking the culmination of all the hard work. But really, buying a home was not the end of a journey but the beginning, not a symbol of efforts past but a substitute for efforts future. A home didn't embody the American Dream but the American Way: the chance to earn riches without lifting a finger. To "make your money work for you," as my mom put it.

Within two years of my mom buying the house in Sacramento, home values rose 9 percent across the country, even higher in our neighborhood. Decades of data attested to her conclusion that there was no better investment in America than property. Since the census began tracking housing sales data in 1963, annual prices had risen with barely a hiccup, dipping only on three occasions but never falling even 4 percent in a year and always rebounding into upswing within two years. By 2001, my mom had gained around $20,000 on her investment, just like that. She refinanced her $130,000 mortgage for $150,000. With part of the cash influx, she applied for certification as a realtor. For weeks, she buried her head in thick study guides, memorizing regulations, statistics, and trends. She set out to understand the housing market not merely to sell property but because she intended to invest her earnings in American real estate.

THE WHOLE POINT of our moving to Sacramento was so I could attend Jesuit High School, but I didn't in the end. It wasn't because we couldn't afford it. I told my mom I didn't want to go there because it was too preppy. Though I didn't quite realize it at the time, what I meant by "preppy" was "overwhelmingly white," a descriptor that also applied to the Catholic school I attended for fifth grade and the private school I attended for sixth. For seventh grade, my mom had transferred me into a public middle school that offered an advanced program that continued on into high school, called International Baccalaureate, which from her research she concluded was an exceptional educational option, despite its lack of theological curriculum. "You just have to make sure your faith is strong!" she'd said.

Satisfied that I hadn't renounced my faith, my mom let me continue on to the public high school most of my eighth-grade classmates were going to. Just off I-80 in north Sacramento, tucked within a residential enclave of '50s bungalows, Mira Loma High had been built in the airy, sun-bleached minimalism of mid-century California, with open walkways linking big-windowed brick buildings and a sprawling asphalt square framed by enormous oak trees.

Within weeks, I realized how strange a place it was. The hierarchies, cliques, and archetypes I'd come to expect from movies and television were absent, in large part because the campus lacked the sort of centralized culture that defined my understanding of conventional American high school experiences. Instead, the student population was divided into three groups: there were those who went to Mira Loma because it was their designated neighborhood school, and those who commuted in from around the city to attend one of the two advanced programs offered, International Baccalaureate and International Studies. Many of the local students were Black or immigrant Mexican kids who lived in apartment complexes north and east of the school, along a commercial thoroughfare lined with fast-food joints. The International Studies students were mostly white and second-generation Mexican kids who wore Abercrombie & Fitch polos and shell-toed Adidas, drove used cars with souped-up sound systems, and lived in the new subdivisions on the city's flat, autopian outskirts. My International Baccalaureate classes, meanwhile, included the wealthiest students—white and second-generation Indian, Persian, and East Asian kids from canopied neighborhoods with big lawns south and west of campus—along with a diverse assortment of high achievers from working-class families.

My prize for being in this particular program in this particular school in this particular state was access to a curriculum that pushed me to challenge the mythologies I'd taken for granted. Our English teachers used *Gilgamesh* of Mesopotamia, instead of the *Odyssey* of Greece, for our Hero's Journey lesson, and assigned books by Toni Morrison, Maya Angelou, Arundhati Roy, and Chinua Achebe. A junior-year project called Empowerment required us to research and reenact a countercultural movement: competition for first dibs from the list of choices was so fierce that my friend Jack's group showed up to school at four in the morning to snag the Black Panthers and my friend Javie's group scored the Beats around sunrise, while my late-arriving group had to settle for the 1968 Democratic National Convention. For our exam on World War II, our U.S. history teacher had us write an essay arguing whether or not America needed to drop atomic bombs on Japan to end the war, and our History of the Americas teacher prescribed a heavy dose of Howard Zinn. By senior year, Ivy League sweatshirts were common in our classrooms.

The school's composition made it a statistical anomaly in a country where economic well-being tended to correlate with educational achievement. Then and now, Mira Loma regularly boasts the highest SAT scores of any high school in the Sacramento region, even though around half of its students live close enough to the federal poverty line to qualify for subsidized lunch, a rate three times higher than the next nine top-performing schools.

We all brushed shoulders in the hallways before splitting up into the classrooms that kept us on our respective tracks. The imbalance of U.S. education presented itself in microcosm at our school. By the age of fourteen, you sat among the privileged or the neglected. So entrenched were our divides that they caused no tension on campus. Everybody just accepted the state of things and minded their business. At lunch, the IB nerds kicked it under the oak tree by the gym, the IS preps convened around the steps at the edge of the quad, and the local kids sat in and around the cafeteria. The breadth of our diversity empowered us all. There were too many squares around to pick on anyone for being a square, too many kids without money to make fun of anyone for being poor, too many backgrounds represented to make fun of anyone for their ethnicity.

Only when kids from these separate universes converged on the school's sports teams did I ever see that balance threatened. My sophomore year, it was a friend I'll call Tommy who disrupted the peace. Tommy was in my inner circle then, along with Jack and a friend I'll call Chucky. We were all in IB classes together and on the football team, and in the chaos of freshman year friendship-making, that was more than enough to forge a strong bond. Before even our first day of classes, we had together survived "Hell Week," the late-summer tradition of intense conditioning to prepare players for the season. We endured hundred-yard sprints in hundred-degree heat and crashed our bodies in "Bull in the Ring" drills. In class, we partnered on projects and complained about practice, like how one particular coach would shout at you—"Ramirez, get in the other line!"—and go ballistic when you didn't respond—"RAMIREZ! Get in the other line, Ramirez!"—only to realize he'd gotten your name wrong and you had no idea he was talking to you. We spent our weekends playing video games instead of going to parties, driving out to Berkeley to watch Cal football games, and sometimes staying up until sunrise arguing over the ways of our world, like whether Green Bay Packers quarterback Brett Favre was overrated, or whether girls preferred boys who aggressively pursued them or played it cool. None of us drank or rebelled in any conventional way. When I started getting cocky my sophomore year because I made the varsity team and dated a junior-year girl, they were quick to suppress my burgeoning ego with a torrent of mockery. I rarely thought about the fact that I was the only one in our foursome who wasn't white. The only time it crossed my mind was when Tommy would say racist shit.

The objectionable nature of his remarks was usually subtle, leaving him room to deny any personal prejudice. I'd hear it when he said the word "Mexicans," which he occasionally uttered in the sneering tone of a slur. He deliberately mispronounced the word "Arab" as "Ay-rab," mimicking the pronunciation of Americans who seem to relish disrespecting people they fear. He said "Blacks," but with a trace of irony in his voice that made clear he knew better. I couldn't tell whether he believed what he said or whether he was just trying to get a rise out of us. Tommy could be an obnoxious contrarian, a troll more than anything. We got numb to his antics because his discrimination didn't discriminate. He said sexist shit too, as well as ableist shit, homophobic shit, and antisemitic shit, and just about any other offensive shit you can imagine.

The hate he projected never felt threatening, because it was isolated.

Tommy represented a worldview that seemed endangered at our school. My white classmates' political expression took the form of "Free Darfur" shirts, antiwar backpack pins, and trying to get our history teacher to admit he voted for John Kerry in the 2004 election (he thought it improper to disclose his political leanings but hinted that the answer was obvious to anyone paying attention to his lessons). More common were white kids like Chucky, who didn't seem to put much thought into matters of race, or Jack, who displayed his admiration for Black culture on Halloween one year by donning dark sunglasses and a White Sox cap in homage to N.W.A rapper Easy-E (with no blackface).

When we'd call Tommy out, he'd counter that we were soft for being offended, and we'd move on with the familiarity of longtime dance partners. I attributed my friend's hostility to his own deficiencies. He hated on others to distract from his discomfort in social situations. He'd put up a spiky shell that drove people away so that he didn't have to deal with them. He treated his friends the way people usually treat strangers (with chilly suspicion), and he treated strangers the way people usually treat people they don't like (with standoffish antagonism). We liked him because he didn't take himself too seriously, and his disregard for common sense was worthy of television sitcoms. For a lunchtime wager, he once ate an entire portion of wasabi from a supermarket sushi platter, earning him five dollars and a stomachache so bad he had to go home from school early. When he interacted with people he didn't know, his hard shell foiled his attempts at sarcasm. "Do you want tickets to the 6:35 showing?" "No, we just got here early for the midnight one." We'd chuckle in the backdrop as he sorted himself out of mundane misunderstandings.

But he liked to push things. By the middle of sophomore year, I'd gotten angry enough to punch him in the chest on two occasions. After he whipped me in the arm with his belt during a locker-room argument, another friend, tired of Tommy's antics, gathered his clothes on the floor and pissed on them. Another friend, Dre, would chase him around the field after he said something racist at practice. Tommy didn't seem worthy of an ass beating. He was harmless. He was outnumbered. He was just a sad, insecure boy who didn't seem to know any way to draw attention other than to insult. Soon, Dre developed something of a routine that other Black teammates joined. Tommy would provoke them, they'd chase him down, and after a round of halfhearted body blows, it would all be over, everybody laughing. Tommy took the derision with a smirking silence, like he knew he deserved it but enjoyed the game.

Nobody told Mike the routine. Mike was new to our school. He was a local kid, soft-spoken, friendly. His first week at practice in the spring of our sophomore year, Tommy said some racist shit, and Dre's band of merry pranksters took off after him, caught him in the parking lot, and the bit played out as always. Except this time after Dre and the regulars let up, Mike stepped in and clocked Tommy in the cheek with a right hook that knocked him face-first into the asphalt.

Tommy cut down on saying racist shit after that.

IT WASN'T LONG after my mom started showing houses that she realized she was a natural. A buyer's hesitance was no match for her enthusiasm and optimism, which she delivered with an earnest air that strangers couldn't help trusting. She hunted for potential clients wherever we went, from grocery store checkout lines to church parking lots. When she saw someone who looked remotely like her, she'd rush up to them and ask, "Excuse me, are you Filipino?"

She sold nine houses her rookie year, mostly for Asian and Latinx immigrants. By her third year in the game, she was pulling in six figures after closing $12 million worth of deals, earning herself a spot in the Masters Club, a list of high-performing realtors that drew in even more business. She celebrated her ascendancy by upgrading her ride—out with JC and in with a black Mercedes-Benz SUV, which she drove for two years before trading it in for a silver Mercedes sedan. She didn't give names to the Benzes. The brand said all that needed to be said. For me, she bought a '96 Toyota Camry, gifting us both a freedom from each other we'd never had. Feeling stable in her independence and untethered from driving me around, she began socializing outside church for the first time in years. She dated. She went out dancing downtown with friends. Always, she kept an eye out for investment opportunities.

All across the country, houses were selling like never before. In 2003, one million people bought a house in the United States, more than in any previous year. The trend was most pronounced in the West, where from 2001 to 2005 the number of annual home buyers rose from 239,000 to 358,000. The dividends were instant. By early 2004, our home's value had risen enough for my mom to refinance her mortgage for $202,500, and then again later that year for $282,500 at an adjustable interest rate that started at 1.25 percent. She used the cash for a $94,000 down payment on a second property, priced at $466,000, a 2,675-square-foot vacation home perched on 12,000 square feet of mountainside land overlooking a lake. During that period, around a third of all new mortgages were for buyers who already owned at least one other property. Within two years, as average home values rose another 10 percent nationally, she refinanced the vacation property for $492,000, then refinanced our Sacramento house for $300,000 at a 6.99 percent adjustable interest rate. She had more cash in her bank account than ever before. She had more debts, too, but so did countless others. In America, she'd learned, you have to spend money to make money.

When my junior year English teacher assigned us to stage a photograph that used symbolism to capture the essence of our family, I posed my mom and me side by side in front of her Mercedes. She wears a black suit and carries a thick binder of home listings. I'm in my varsity letterman jacket, gripping a football in the crook of an arm. With our free hands, we're both holding flip phones to our ears, looking off in opposite directions. Subtlety wasn't my strength. I intended no irony or criticism in the image, no commentary on the intensity of our assimilation: mother promoting the American Dream, son a cliché all-American teen. I was proud of our success, and I presented our preoccupations as a boast. Nothing in the picture marked our ancestry or alluded to any culture but the American one we so aggressively represented. I defined us by our obsessions. I couldn't have imagined that by the end of the decade my mom would no longer be selling houses and I would no longer be playing football.

In those years I considered football the core of my identity. My Myspace profile picture was an action shot of me running with the ball during a game. My wardrobe consisted of T-shirts and hoodies bearing the names of universities I hoped would offer me athletic scholarships. I worked out alone in the school weight room before class in the morning, and in the off season I spent my afternoons conducting drills out on our dusty field. I avoided alcohol and weed purely for fear of diminishing my performance. I returned from summer football camp at Princeton and told my mom I was no longer interested in the university because I found the coaching staff unimpressive.

When a classmate once asked me what I loved about football, I replied with a soliloquy on the virtues of the game. Eleven players on offense against eleven players on defense, each side with the central goal of pushing the other backward, an aim only attainable through collective strength. All it takes is a single weak point to ruin it for everybody, so you put your body on the line for your teammates because you don't want to let them down. Each play brings unavoidable violence that forges the bond across race, class, and religion, all of you risking pain and punishment for that shared glory of victory, all of you getting knocked down but getting back up because you're all in it together, all of you sacrificing for a common cause, et cetera, et cetera.

I meant what I said, but I should've recognized, even back then, that it wasn't an accurate reflection of the game. In football, the glory and the pain are not, in fact, equally shared. It was easy for me to speak of collective sacrifices because I wasn't the one who had to do most of the sacrificing. Football is unique in that way. Unlike in basketball, soccer, baseball, hockey, and rugby, where everybody in the game handles the ball at some point, in football, there is a clear delineation between those who do and those who don't. Indeed, of the eleven players on offense, five are specifically prohibited from so much as touching the ball once the play begins. Their jobs are simply to protect those who move the ball forward, score the points, and get the glory. Football terminology is a bit disrespectful about this division of labor: the positions tasked with the dirty work of smashing helmets every play are bluntly called "linemen," while those who handle the ball are admiringly dubbed "skill players." While the feats of the skill players are memorialized through statistics, such as yards, catches, and touchdowns, the efforts of the linemen are absent from official records, living on only through the compliments and criticisms of their coaches and teammates. They are the backbone of the team, as they are constantly reminded, performing honorable duties far more essential than the flashy exploits that garner cheers from crowds, highlights on television, and attention from girls. Even the most elusive runners are helpless without strong blockers, and strong blockers can turn even the clumsiest runners into stars.

A culture's pastimes reflect its values. There was a grain of truth in my claims about football's unifying power. This force didn't live on the field, as I assumed, but beyond it. For all America's divides, no common ground is broader than football fandom. Watching the Super Bowl has been the country's largest ritual for half a century. More people tune in than are registered in any single political party. Of the fifty most viewed television broadcasts in any given year during my lifetime, more than half are NFL games. Yet what are we to make of the fact that the game's popularity is exclusively American? While baseball and basketball have gained substantial international followings over the years, American football has stood out as just another marker of American exceptionalism.

It's fitting that the country's most popular sport mirrors the walled inequities of its economic system. The anonymous frontline grunts keep the machine running without the opportunity for greater glory, while the "skilled" running backs and wide receivers are distinguished by their individual merits, breaking tackles and leaping for catches. The hierarchy is cemented in the game's fundamentally rigid setup—player movements are limited by rule, their actions dictated by a precise script—and at the top of the pyramid is the player who handles the ball most: the quarterback, the face of the team, leader by default, burdened with the bulk of decisions but rewarded with outsize praise, an executive who takes blame and credit. As a football player, you're taught to accept this division of labor. Young quarterbacks are groomed to captain the ship just as young linemen are trained to relinquish ego.

Since its formative days, football has reflected America's vision of itself. It was a rough and rugged game, imported from Europe but adjusted to pioneer sensibilities in the late nineteenth century: to enhance scoring possibilities and codify previously unsanctioned brutality, players on offense were allowed to block defenders from the path of ball carriers. This created the constant state of violence we came to know and love, by establishing the expectation that everyone on the field should be crashing into someone on every play. The term "contact sport," which applied to a range of games from wrestling to basketball, didn't seem sufficient for football. "Football is not a contact sport," the legendary coach Vince Lombardi once said, "it's a collision sport."

In football, violence is not incidental, as in soccer, or limited to specific instances of jockeying for the ball, as in hockey, but rather serves its own practical purpose. When you boil it down to its essence, the point of the game is to take your rival's land, marching toward your goal by forcefully driving them backward. The game's language instills this spirit of conquest: the fifty yards you're defending is your team's territory—"the 49ers are all the way back on their own ten-yard line"—and the fifty yards closest to the goal you're trying to reach is your opponent's—"the 49ers are already at the Cowboys' twenty-yard line." Football is a zero-sum game: every yard you gain is a yard they lose.

The sport began to gain widespread popularity in the era of Manifest Destiny. Here was a country of enterprising roughnecks who believed that they deserved claim to whatever they could snatch. You had to keep your head on a swivel, because threats lay hidden across the vast wilderness that covered the bulk of the continent. Americans might not be as refined as their European cousins but they were at least tougher, braving harsh winters in log cabins, wiping out buffalo herds, cloaking themselves in bear skins and beaver pelts, settling disputes with pistol duels, venturing out onto grounds they'd never charted and building from scratch. One reason Americans have always been so resistant to acknowledging the enormity of slavery is that it undermines a central tenet of American mythology: that this is a nation of doers, builders, workers with dirty boots and callused hands; that it was purely persistent enterprise that put this country together, not slave labor. Americans distance themselves from that history with a reverential pride in individualism and physical toughness. "Nothing in this world is worth having or worth doing unless it means effort, pain, difficulty," declared Teddy Roosevelt, who came to embody rugged Americanism even though he was born into a wealthy patrician family. "No kind of life is worth leading if it is always an easy life."

Football was central to instilling this identity. By crashing their bodies in fierce competition, privileged young men could develop the grit they needed to one day run the country. The game was most popular at elite northeastern universities. Yale, Columbia, Princeton, Rutgers, and Harvard organized the first official competitions, revised the rules, and shaped the sport into something resembling the version we see today, though it was much more brutal back then. When a doctor told one Navy player in 1893 that he'd suffered a head injury so severe that he risked death if he ever played football again, the player had a shoemaker craft him a leather helmet so that he could keep playing—an innovative accessory that wouldn't become common for another two decades. After an 1894 Harvard–Yale game left five players hospitalized, the schools banned the sport for two years. Harvard's president deemed football "more brutalizing than prizefighting, cockfighting or bullfighting." At least forty-five college football players died from injuries suffered on the field from 1900 to 1905, the year President Teddy Roosevelt called for rule changes that would ward off calls for prohibition. He was a fan of the game. His son played for Harvard, and many of the men on his Rough Riders were former players. "In life, as in a football game," he once wrote, "the principle to follow is: Hit the line hard; don't foul and don't shirk, but hit the line hard!" Locking arms in a "flying wedge" blocking formation was banned, the forward pass was legalized, and the game opened up from a grinding midfield scrum to a more tactical duel of deception and anticipation. In-game deaths became rare. Playbooks became sophisticated.

While rule changes over the years restricted certain forms of violence, violence would remain central to football, as it's a game based on moving and toppling people by force. It's hard to enjoy playing football without at least a mild taste for the brutality. For some of my teammates, the violence was the appeal. They hollered when we lined up for tackling drills at practice, and before games they hyped themselves up by banging helmets with anyone in sight. One boy was so committed to trading punishment that he'd preemptively pop Vicodin painkillers so that he could throw his body around without worrying about his nervous system slowing him down—instead it was his narcotically blunted motor skills that ended up slowing him down. I was grateful for these teammates because their reckless abandon made them eager executors of the dirty work, leaving the rest of us to opt for the elements of finesse. My thrill was catching the ball and eluding defenders. I didn't avoid contact but I engaged hesitantly and fearfully, aware that the slightest mistake—a head too low or a knee too high—could lead to catastrophic injury. I dreaded tackling drills and hoped I didn't get matched with one of the kids who loved to hit. If I was lucky enough to pair up with Jack, we'd mutually ease up on impact but fall hard enough for it to look good. Otherwise, all I could do was bite down on my mouth guard and trust the laws of motion, which state that you either dispense the bigger blow or get knocked backward, because somebody has to absorb the energy. Daily repetition in this prisoner's dilemma taught me that collisions hurt more when you brace yourself, and that, counterintuitively, the cleanest, surest way to survive without injury is to give yourself over to the sport and try to maximize your impact.

It didn't take long for my body to acclimatize. Bruises and aches began to tingle with the satisfaction of a hard day's work. For the first few weeks of my freshman season, I hovered around the field's periphery, jostling on blocks and reaching for tackles, anxious that violence would find me, but then something slid into place in a game against Colfax High School, on a rainy field in the Placer County woodlands. The upperclassmen had warned us about Colfax, "a bunch of corn-fed white boys" who took football as seriously as anybody in America. The hour-long bus ride took us past the familiar grape farms and orange groves of the valley's rural lowlands, and deep into the pine forest foothills rising toward the Sierra Nevada. To calm my nerves before games, I listened to upbeat jams that got my serotonin flowing, like SWV's "I'm So into You" and Mase's "Welcome Back." "Why you listenin' to that soft shit?" my teammates would tease, bouncing around to the window-rattling bass of E-40 and Keak da Sneak, driving inhibitions away with Thizz Face scowls and the brash, carefree energy of Northern California hyphy music.

Once we were on the field, lined up inches apart, the hulking movie villains I'd imagined dissolved, revealing teenagers like ourselves. Beneath their helmets, their eyes reflected the same anxiety I felt. In the opening minutes of the scariest game of the season, instead of the fear I was accustomed to, I felt a great rush of relief. My relief sprang euphoric with each hit I gave and took. The soggy, muddy grass cushioned my falls and kept their runners off balance, making it easier to knock them over. I felt stronger for surviving collisions with these vaunted boys, all the more for getting the better of the exchanges. I hopped up off the ground with the giddy pride of a kid getting off a roller coaster. I began wishing for the violence to come my way, craving the crisp crunch of a clean pop, newly confident in my aggression. This is the core expectation of football culture, and once it entered my bloodstream, I understood the game with fresh clarity. Even on plays when I had minimal responsibilities, when I knew the ball was nowhere near me, I could find the satisfaction of laying a hit vicious enough to draw *oooh*s from the crowd. I dove at the knees of bigger boys and launched my helmet into the jaws of smaller boys. I no longer resisted the game's nature but flowed with it, one with the laws of motion.

No, the Colfax boys weren't so terrifying. But they were very good at football, and they trounced us 48–7.

OUR TEAM was famously bad. By my freshman season, the varsity team hadn't won a game in two and half years, twenty-six straight losses that established us as the butt of local jokes. "So how much did you lose by this time?" our classmates would tease, implying that it wasn't worth wasting breath asking if we'd won. If there was any trace of bullying at our school, it was the nerds picking on the jocks. Our exploits carried no special virtues in our classmates' eyes, and no special appeal. While our opponents fielded thirty or more players on their varsity rosters, we could barely maintain the mandatory minimum of fifteen. Other teams scheduled their homecoming weekends to align with their game against us, to ensure that their students enjoyed an easy win to kick off the festivities. We developed an expertise in the aesthetics of tissue pomps and papier-mâché.

When our varsity managed to win its first game of 2003, an astounding outcome that made newspaper headlines, we freshman on junior varsity figured we'd arrived just in time for the turnaround. In truth, our pit was too deep for a single win to boost us back to sea level. Kids who prioritize football enroll in schools with superior gridiron traditions, institutions that invest in experienced coaches, lush grass, state-of-the-art equipment. We didn't even have our own stadium and had to play home games at a rival's campus. Football is expensive, and if you aren't good enough to attract corporate sponsors or alumni donations, you'll practice on dried-out fields, drink water from a plastic pipe at the end of a hose, and lift weights on torn leather benches hemorrhaging foam. Cycles of winning and losing gather inertia. As any struggling team knows, Monday's ambitions, fueled by thoughtful game plans and inspiring rhetoric, falter on Friday's proving ground if the laws of motion aren't on your side.

Our varsity lost the rest of its games in 2003, a demoralizing slide that pulled the upperclassmen into a haze of apathy. The starting quarterback got expelled a month into the school year for shooting up a teacher's car with a pellet gun. The top running back and wide receiver were both kicked off the team when they got caught smoking weed on our bus ride home from a pulverizing loss. Our coach saw to it that our next practice was devoted to collective punishment.

Coach Steve Macias was the wiry son of Mexican immigrants, a fortysomething cook at a golf club restaurant who'd mastered the art of motivational speeches. With limited numbers and talent, our aspirations rested on discipline and willpower. Coach Macias spoke stirringly about us taking the field like "a bat out of hell" and committing ourselves with enough passion to "run through a wall." My sophomore year he distilled his vision into a symbol meant to embody the hard-nosed mentality we aspired to: a red metal lunch pail, the kind steelworkers and coal miners bring to work. A team captain would carry the clanking totem onto the field before games, and there it would sit on the sideline to remind us that football wasn't about glory or grace but the perseverance to do your job on every play.

The coach didn't invent this symbol. The lunch pail has been a staple of football motivational tactics for decades, a cliché wrapping the sport in a certain blue-collar spirit. Coaches pepper their praise with industrial-age language. A committed player "clocks in every day," a hard worker has a "motor," a selfless teammate "brings his hard hat." The names of two of the NFL's most storied franchises hark back to the glory years of America's factories—the Green Bay Packers honor the region's meatpacking workers, and the Pittsburgh Steelers use a logo based on a design created by the United States Steel Corporation. Professional football was born a century ago in the midwestern cities where smokestacks sprouted, drawing young men with well-paid union jobs. Chicago, Detroit, Cleveland, Green Bay, Buffalo, Rochester, Canton, Akron, Dayton, Kenosha, Toledo, Racine, Muncie, Rochester, and Decatur fielded the teams in the fledgling National Football League.

Football's evolution mirrored the country's. The wild energy of frontier expansion channeled into industrious efficiency, like the steam powering pistons and conveyor belts. America rose to global supremacy on the might of its manufacturing sector, which supplied the materials necessary to build the most powerful military in history. The twin pillars of factory and battlefield uphold football's foundational virtues.

Linemen fight "in the trenches." Attacking defenders "blitz" the offense. A deep pass is a "bomb." A quarterback is a "field general." A large part of the game's early appeal at elite universities was that it gave young men a taste of war without the deadliest elements. In the postwar boom years, football was evidence Americans retained their grit even through peacetime. Theirs was the nation that built things and won wars.

With power comes leisure and disposable income. By 1954, more than half of U.S. households had a television set. Land of microwavable "TV dinners" and Madison Avenue advertising agencies, America was the first country to place TV at the center of popular culture. The medium arrived in living rooms just in time to show footage of postwar tranquility lapsing into turmoil: atom bomb tests in the desert, uprisings in big cities, assassinations at public gatherings, bleeding American soldiers in distant jungles. Football offered a counterbalance, a reminder of the country's foundational virtues, a national ceremony in a fracturing empire. A growing share of Americans spent their fall weekends watching the game—college on Saturdays, pro on Sundays. The first Super Bowl, in 1967, drew around 25 million viewers, the second around 40 million, and by the end of the next decade the broadcasts tallied more than 70 million, a third of the U.S. population.

If baseball, with its slow pace, few movements, and daily presence, filled the needs of a population accustomed to the background hum of radio, football perfectly served a country pivoting to the television age. Its live-action violence presented stakes more visceral than scripted Hollywood combat, but not as frightening as the footage on the nightly news. Close-up sideline shots of battered faces twisted in agony or bursting in ecstasy provided the purest, safest drama anywhere on screen. Slow-motion replays captured the balletic grace of leaping, spinning, and bounding bodies otherwise lost amid the chaotic action. Even the game's rhythm—a few seconds of intensity followed by half a minute of pause—seemed tailor-made for a television audience, with built-in breaks to slip into the bathroom, grab a beer from the fridge, or hear the announcers thank the corporate sponsors. As networks bid for the rights to broadcast NFL games, the league's annual revenue from television contracts rose from $16 million in 1965 to $162 million in 1978 to $420 million in 1982 to $900 million in 1990. Football became a prized commodity.

As the financial value of America's most popular sport rose, most of the places that first invested in professional football didn't share in the NFL's prosperity. Of the fourteen cities with teams in the NFL's inaugural 1920 season, just four remained in the league when the first Super Bowl aired in 1967; in all, twenty-two cities that fielded teams in the league's first decade are no longer on the pro football map. The league had quickly outgrown its regional roots, expanding first to big northeastern cities like New York, Boston, Philadelphia, and Washington, then West Coast metropolises like San Francisco and Los Angeles, then sprawling sunbaked suburbs like Tampa and Phoenix. But while the vacated Rust Belt cities faded from public consciousness, the imagery of their boom times lived on.

It didn't cross my mind that the lunch pail could just as easily symbolize workers' efforts to make their jobs less grueling. What is a lunch pail but a physical manifestation of break time? To counter their employers' impulse to minimize costs, factory workers formed unions, organized strikes, and collectively bargained for retirement pensions, stricter safety protocols, shorter hours, and higher wages. They met with stiff resistance from management. When Larry Itliong arrived in the United States from the Philippines as a teen in 1929, he found work at a cannery in Alaska that required him to sign what was called a "yellow-dog contract," which barred union membership. The pay was low, the camps were squalid, and the job—gutting and packaging fish in a steamy factory—was grueling. One day, Itliong lost three fingers in an accident, earning him the nickname "Seven Fingers." Outraged by the

conditions, he organized Alaska cannery workers, then spent the following years helping establish unions for longshoremen in Washington state
and grape growers in California, where he led the first big agricultural
strike after World War II. The average salary for a unionized manufacturing worker rose from around $21 a week in 1914 to more than $100 in
the 1950s. At its peak, the industry promised long-term, middle-class
income for around 19 million people, a fifth of the U.S. workforce. By
mid-century, more than a third of U.S. workers were represented by
unions. In 2013, a California school district renamed a middle school
after Itliong and fellow labor leader Philip Vera Cruz. Itliong–Vera Cruz
Middle School was the first school in the country to be named after
Filipino Americans, though I didn't learn about the men until I was an
adult—a shame, because they embodied just the sort of message our
team could've used! Collective bargaining offered a counterweight to
the authority business owners carried under U.S. law, enabling under-
dogs to defeat titans with the strength of their numbers. But my imagination was constrained by the mythologies embedded in the sport.

With an enterprising population, sprawling terrain, and temperate
climate, the United States has always been good at making money, but
the question has always been how to distribute it. When labor was no
longer free, it was cheap and often secured through exploitative contracts that left workers—sharecroppers in the South, miners in Appala-
chia, fish packers in the Pacific Northwest—indebted to employers.
Private enterprise is premised on maximizing profits, and left to its own
devices keeps stretching for more. Employers could legally lock in their
workers during shifts, until 146 people died in the Triangle shirtwaist
factory fire in Manhattan in 1911, leading to state laws establishing
workplace safety requirements. Drug companies could print false claims
on packaging until a tonic for teething babies fatally poisoned some of
them, sparking tighter federal regulations on ingredient labels in 1913.
The federal government set minimum standards for wages and safety, but

the United States stands nearly alone in the world in the power its government grants private companies over their workforces. Unlike more than 90 percent of other countries, the United States doesn't mandate paid sick leave, and of the thirty-seven developed nations represented in the Organisation for Economic Co-operation and Development, the United States is one of three whose minimum wage hasn't risen over the past two decades. States that raise wages, taxes, or benefit requirements risk falling behind in the competition to lure and keep jobs. During the postwar boom years, eighteen states passed laws weakening union protections. We remember those boomtime manufacturing jobs fondly because they paid well, but it was because they paid well that companies sought cheaper alternatives when possible.

As the United States signed international trade deals with allies and rivals in an effort to establish a global marketplace, companies moved factories and supply lines to countries where labor was cheaper. From 1979 to 2014, as Super Bowl viewership rose from 75 million to 112 million, the number of manufacturing jobs in the United States fell from 19 million to 12 million. America increasingly specialized in providing services instead of making things—financial services to grow money, insurance services to protect it, sales services to spend it. Wall Street bankers became "Masters of the Universe" who moved around millions of dollars an hour. By the early 2000s, more than a third of all profits in the U.S. economy were generated by the financial sector. Lower-paid employment without collective bargaining filled the vacuum left by the vanishing industrial sector, and today 30 million people, a fifth of the workforce, are in the retail or hospitality industries, which encompass two-thirds of the country's minimum wage jobs.

By the end of the 1980s, the rate of union membership had dropped to half its mid-century peak. As president, Ronald Reagan captured the spirit of the times, firing 11,345 air traffic controllers on strike for higher wages and promoting an economic theory positing that the wealth accumulated by the business class would "trickle down" to everybody else. The marginal tax rate on the highest earners dropped from 91 percent in 1963 (for income over $200,000, the equivalent of $2.5 million today) to 70 percent through the 1970s, before nosediving under Reagan's administration to 50 percent in 1982, then 28 percent in 1988. Minimum wage fell behind inflation and is now worth 40 percent less than in 1968. By 2007, the richest 1 percent controlled 35 percent of U.S. wealth, an even higher share than during the Gilded Age at the end of the nineteenth century, when the top 2 percent owned 33 percent of the pot. Everybody else takes as much of the leftovers as they can, with the next 20 percent controlling another 35 percent, and the deeper down the line you go, the more desperate the competition for the remaining scraps. Like football, capitalism is a zero-sum game, and the further behind you fall, the harder it is to gain ground.

Such inequalities have sparked revolutions throughout history, but the United States has warded off mass uprising by keeping its standard of living just high enough and keeping its promise of ascent just real enough that its people prefer to make the system work for them rather than overthrow it. The trick works best if the pie keeps getting bigger: if any American can buy stocks that rise or homes that accumulate value. So the politicians and executives who sway laws made it easier for Americans to buy stocks and homes.

By the time my mom became a real estate agent, a person making close to minimum wage could get a mortgage with affordable monthly payments and hardly any money down. The trade-off was fluid interest rates that could rise and fall with the market, meaning those affordable monthly payments could skyrocket at any time. But the market was stable, and if a homeowner needed a jolt of cash, they could draw out a new loan based on their investment's rising value. From 1996 to 2006, ascending home prices increased U.S. household wealth by $6.5 trillion. The whole setup made the United States feel richer than it was. People retired into comfort not because the country diverted more money into pension funds but because companies and unions invested pension funds in a stock market that soared ever-upward. People could buy houses not because their income was higher but because big money loans were more accessible than ever. Lenders didn't have to worry about whether their clients could afford the deal because they often sold the mortgage rights to investment banks that packaged the debt into "securities" that hedge funds, pensions, and speculators around the world could buy shares of, collecting dividends as long as homeowners kept making their monthly payments.

Imaginary money papered over cracks in the foundation. The numbers were there for all to see, but the United States trusted wherever the free market guided it. Capitalist democracy had beaten monarchy, anarchism, fascism, and communism to emerge as the dominant system of the global order, validated by the clearest metric available—survival. Why change course now? America was winning.

Alas, lessons are clearer in defeat than in victory. By that measure, my sophomore season was enlightening. We lost every game, usually by humiliating margins. Opposing coaches would always tell Coach Macias that his Mira Loma Matadors were the toughest bunch of scrappers they'd ever competed against. We'd hop off the ground without even dusting ourselves off, then slam our bodies back into the grinder no matter our deficit. We'd limp off the field bloody and bruised but with the respect of our adversaries. While our opponents rotated in fleets of players, we fielded the same eleven or twelve boys for the entire sixty-minute contest. By the second half of the season, injuries left us with fourteen eligible players, one short of the minimum, so a teammate with a broken arm in a cast agreed to suit up for the remaining games and inconspicuously stand on the sideline to prevent a forfeit. Opposing coaches and players chuckled in admiration when they caught sight of him. Football people love that sort of reckless commitment. At the end of the season, Coach Macias told us that he was proud of us, that our record didn't reflect our determined performance, that we'd exhibited the resiliency necessary for the rigors of life, that we'd lived up to the vision he projected onto the red metal lunch box.

Without realizing it at the time, I internalized the most enduring American lesson of all: hard work and perseverance are never enough.

THIS LESSON WAS NO SECRET. It was enshrined in the U.S. Constitution. Just as the three branches of government were designed so that no single one could abuse its power, checks and balances were written in so that the will of the masses posed no threat to the wealthy white men making the rules. The American founders preserved slavery, counted Black people as three-fifths human for census purposes, limited suffrage to white men who owned property, and established a representative electoral process that ensured the popular vote wouldn't set federal law or choose presidents. Inequality was intentional, for a leisure class needs a labor class, and to gain money, someone else has to lose it. As a role model for future democracies, America paired its ideals with pragmatism: democracy is malleable; shape it to your needs.

Upon gaining independence in 1946, the Philippines replicated the American version of democracy. An executive office, a supreme court, and a two-chambered legislature managed the government. Two major parties competed for votes. The constitution limited presidents to two four-year terms. But while four of the first five U.S. commanders in chief served out their maximum eight years in the White House, the Philippine presidency seemed cursed.

Manuel Roxas, the republic's inaugural office holder, collapsed from a heart attack and died after giving a speech less than two years into his first term. His successor, Elpidio Quirino, suffered from severe stomach ulcers that left him hospitalized in the United States for two months during his fourth year in office, dooming any chance at reelection; he died from a heart attack three years later. Ramon Magsaysay, a beloved populist who once said that "bare feet will always be welcomed in the president's palace," perished in a plane crash a little more than three years into his presidency. The next two, Carlos Garcia and Diosdado Macapagal, managed to make it through four years in office in good health, but lost their reelection campaigns. Twenty years into nationhood, not a single Philippine president had made it to a second term.

Ferdinand Marcos would be the one to break the curse. After defeating Macapagal in 1965, his infrastructure program might have bolstered his popularity enough to earn him reelection fair and square, but he planned to "leave nothing to chance," as the *Philippines Free Press* reported at the time. Newspapers coined a catchphrase to describe Marcos's campaign strategy of violence, intimidation, and bribery: "guns, goons, and gold." He won in a landslide, taking 5 million votes—no previous candidate had gotten even 4 million.

While the young republic had never been short on rumors of corruption, Marcos's brazen election grab damaged his reputation. On the night he delivered his state of the nation address in January 1970, thousands of protesters filled streets across Manila, including outside the U.S. embassy to denounce America's ongoing support for Marcos. Even then, he angled for a way to extend his reign. At the June 1971 national convention to begin the long-planned process of revising the 1935 constitution, Marcos lobbied for a third presidential term, only to find that national sentiment had swung so far against him that delegates were more interested in a proposal to ban his wife, Imelda, from succeeding him in office. The legislative elections that fall removed any ambiguity about how the public felt about its first two-term president: Marcos's party was trounced, losing six of eight senate races. His chief critic, Senator Ninoy Aquino, seemed bound for Malacañang Palace once the 1973 presidential election came around.

But first the country had to get through 1972, which happened to be my mom's final year in primary school.

IT WAS A BAD YEAR for the Concepcion family.

That spring, on a trip to the mall with her friends, my auntie Lyn, seventeen at the time, caught sight of her father out shopping with a woman. "Is that your mother?" one of the friends asked. It wasn't.

When Rizalina confronted him, Manuel confessed. He had a mistress. They had an infant child together. He supported them financially.

For Rizalina, the infidelity was just the start of the betrayal. The household budget had little room to spare even without the obligation to support a second family. The eldest Concepcion sisters were still in college. The three youngest brothers were halfway through primary school, with more than a decade of schooling ahead of them. Rizalina and Manuel agreed to split up their financial affairs, a tangible mark of a rift that never quite mended. Rizalina would take care of the girls, and Manuel was in charge of the boys.

Doing the math, Manuel revealed to Rizalina that he couldn't afford to enroll the boys in the same schools as their sisters. In June, they decided to send ten-year-old Marlon, nine-year-old Paul, and eight-year-old Bobby to live with Rizalina's cousin in Dumaguete City, in the Visayas, where tuition and other expenses were cheaper.

With the Scout Reyes house suddenly unsteady and half empty, my mom, the youngest of the girls, remained enrolled at Maryknoll, a prestigious and expensive all-girls academy in Manila with primary and secondary schools, as well as a college. She was at the kitchen table on the morning of September 23, 1972, eating breakfast with her mother and sisters, when the telephone rang. Rizalina picked it up. It was her best friend, Baby Mitra. Her brother Ramon, the congressmember, had been arrested, along with hundreds of journalists, professors, and other politicians, including Ninoy Aquino. All news outlets except those owned by Marcos allies had been shut down. On a three p.m. broadcast, interrupting a cartoon show, Marcos's press secretary announced to the world that the president had declared martial law, nullifying the constitution. As justification for the crackdown, Marcos claimed that Communist forces were attacking the Philippines.

Within days, Marcos appointed his cronies to head the Central Bank, which soon became his personal treasury. Baby and Rizalina quit in protest.

Seven months later, Rizalina tried to return to the States. At the Manila airport, she presented her conditional U.S. permanent residency visa, but it was denied because she'd been away from the country for more than a year. She would have to begin from scratch: resubmit the forms, wait a few more years. With the dictatorship rocking her household with a host of new problems, Rizalina put aside the visa matter to focus on stabilizing her family's suddenly tenuous place in the Philippines.

My mom's life didn't change dramatically at first. "We were so rich in the beginning," she said. A driver took her to school in the mornings and picked her up in the afternoons, as usual. The house was quieter since her brothers had left for Dumaguete, and her parents rarely interacted. She could go days at a time without thinking about the political turmoil simmering throughout the country. Almost thirteen, she was primarily concerned with making good grades so that her parents wouldn't get mad at her.

That summer, her cousin Earl, seven years older than her, stayed at the Scout Reyes house. His parents lived in Dumaguete—they were the ones looking after Marlon, Paul, and Bobby—but Earl attended a boarding school in New Jersey on a scholarship. His year in the States had left its mark. "Good change," my mom recalled. His English lost most traces of his old accent, and his hair had grown fashionably down to his shoulders. "He was walking and talking like an American," she said. He told her stories about how little his American classmates knew about the Philippines. "Don't you live in trees?" one kid asked him, to which he responded, "Yeah, trees so tall we use elevators." My mom cracked up at that.

Her school wasn't yet on break, so he'd walk around Manila during the day, then they'd hang out at the house in the evenings. One night, she found him sitting on his bed with his head in his hands. "And he was so sad," she recalled, "and his hair was cut up to the ears. 'What happened?' And he said, 'Well, the police saw me, and he said I'm not allowed to have this long hair, and so he cut it.' 'What?!' And then he started to cry. At the time I wasn't so knowledgeable. You find out that there's such a law in your country that you're not supposed to have long hair? Oh my God. It happened to my cousin, and he's a scholar. He just came from the United States as a scholar! This is ridiculous. I was shocked. What a law. I was too young to even react. You're so innocent. You're so naive. I don't know anything about that. All I know is for the first time I find a law under martial law that no guy is supposed to have long hair. And my cousin was really crying. He loved his hair. He'd been back less than a week."

THE DICTATORSHIP LASTED until 1986. Afterward, historians, journalists, and human rights investigators tallied up the damage: 70,000 suspected dissidents arrested, 35,000 tortured, at least 2,500 confirmed executed without trial, and around 700 more disappeared and presumed dead.

A Philippine commission tasked with tracking down the public funds Ferdinand and Imelda Marcos stole for personal use estimated their ill-gotten gains to be at least $5 billion, likely double that—the exact figure difficult to pin down, what with money laundered through the purchase of artwork and U.S. property, and stashed in bank accounts in the United States, the Cayman Islands, Hong Kong, and Switzerland. The latter account alone held $356 million when the regime fell. When Marcos was elected in 1965, the Philippines had the second strongest economy in Asia. By the time he fled into exile two decades later, the country was one of the poorest in the world, so deep in the red that it spent nearly 20 percent of its export revenue just on interest payments for a national debt that had risen from $2 billion in 1972 to $26 billion in 1986. In terms of dictators, Marcos was one of the most successful. He wasn't assassinated. A large chunk of his family's wealth was hidden effectively enough to avoid later efforts by the Philippine government to reclaim billions of dollars unaccounted for. He spent his final years in Hawaii, and after he died, Imelda returned to the Philippines and won a seat in congress. A generation after his dictatorship, his daughter Imee was elected governor of their native Ilocos province, and his son, Bongbong, became a senator. In 2016, Ferdinand was ceremoniously transferred, with military honors, to the national Heroes' Cemetery in Metro Manila.

Yet before he became the wealthiest ruler in the eastern hemisphere, he was on the outside looking in. On the northern tip of Luzon, boxed in between the sea and the Cordilleras mountains, his home province of Ilocos developed in isolation, sprouting unique traditions, as well as the brand of stereotype sometimes levied against those who grow up in rural settings: provincial, crude, stingy. When Marcos headed south to Manila for law school at the University of the Philippines, he probably carried a chip on his shoulder. His family was well-off—his father was a lawyer, his mother a teacher—but didn't have the generational wealth of his most privileged classmates, or the established legacy often required for admission into Manila high society.

Though his father, Mariano Marcos, was elected to congress when Ferdinand was eight years old and though he gained a reputation as a skilled orator, his political career was brief and uneventful. After six years in office, he lost reelection, and then a subsequent bid to regain the seat. Two days after that election, his victorious opponent was shot dead. At twenty-three, Ferdinand was convicted of pulling the trigger and sentenced to death the same year he passed the bar exam. He represented himself in his appeal to the Supreme Court, delivering a performance so impressive that his conviction was reversed, not because there was any new evidence absolving him, but because the judges acknowledged that it would be a shame for such a brilliant young mind to go to waste.

World War II began the following year, and Mariano ended up serving the Japanese military as a publicist during the occupation. In doing so, he may have saved his son's life, for when Ferdinand, a major in the Allied forces, was captured, Japanese officers quickly released him from detention because of Mariano's service. Ferdinand went on to complete an undistinguished tour without further incident. The elder Marcos wasn't as fortunate. Captured by Philippine guerrillas in the final months of the war, he confessed to collaborating. According to an account by the guerrilla commander overseeing the execution, Mariano received the sentence reserved for traitors: he was drawn and quartered via carabaos, and his remains were hung from a tree as a warning to others.

Pursuing a career in politics after the war, Ferdinand compensated for his somewhat unseemly background with a simple solution: he lied about it. He claimed his father had been executed by the Japanese. He claimed his own military record had earned him thirty-three war medals, including the Distinguished Service Cross and the Medal of Honor. Those lies would come to light only later. Running for his father's old congress seat as a charismatic thirty-two-year-old war hero, Marcos quickly made a name for himself as a political prodigy, beginning a streak of electoral victories that lasted until his exile nearly four decades later. After three terms in the house of representatives—he married Imelda during this period—he was elected to the senate in 1959, rose to minority leader a year later, then senate president three years after that. Unlike most of his rivals, Marcos built his base of support away from the capital: he was beloved by fellow Ilocanos, and Imelda came from a prominent family in the Visayas, securing him two loyal voting blocs that carried him to the highest vote total in the national senate election. Not since Manuel Quezon had the Philippine public witnessed such a dominant political force.

Only once Marcos reached the nation's highest office did he finally encounter a challenger of equal talent. Marcos must have seen Ninoy Aquino coming a mile away. There was no question he was familiar with the man. His wife, Imelda, had dated Ninoy before meeting Ferdinand. Ninoy said he broke up with her because, at five-foot-six, she was too tall for him, but the chismis was that he left her because he met a woman from a more prestigious family, Corazon Cojuangco, whose old-money clan owned one of the country's largest sugar plantations.

The Aquinos were as elite as it gets on the Islands. Tracing their lineage back to Spanish colonial aristocracy, they owned a hacienda in Central Luzon. Ninoy's grandfather was a general in Emilio Aguinaldo's revolutionary army, and his father was a senator who served in Quezon's cabinet before the war. Like Marcos's father, Aquino's father collaborated with the Japanese occupiers, but in a more respectable manner, as the puppet government's speaker of the assembly, so he wasn't executed. Where Marcos invented accolades, Aquino accumulated them. At seventeen, he covered the Korean War for the *Manila Times*, earning a Philippine Legion of Honor award for his journalism. At twenty-two, appointed by President Magsaysay as the government's emissary to a Communist rebel group, he negotiated their unconditional surrender, earning him a second Legion of Honor award. A year later, he was elected mayor of Concepcion, the town founded by the ancestors of my great-grandfather

Jose Concepcion, and six years after that, at the age of twenty-nine, he became governor of Tarlac province.

Elected to the senate in 1968, he wasted no time before hammering President Marcos, at first directing his criticism at the expanding military budget. He escalated his attacks in early 1969, railing against the ballooning costs of a national cultural center under construction on the Manila Bay waterfront, a project spearheaded by Imelda Marcos. "A monument to shame," Aquino dubbed it, calling the first lady "a megalomaniac, with a penchant to captivate." The first-term senator's florid speeches made front-page headlines and played a part in turning the public against the administration.

To any neutral observer, a natural cycle in Philippine politics seemed to be playing out. Just like every president before him, Marcos seemed fated for defeat after a single term in Malacañang Palace. But Marcos had used his time in office to solidify his power in a way none of his predecessors had attempted. He had discerned that his true power lay not so much in his ability to persuade voters, but rather in the bonds he forged with his nation's great benefactor.

Perhaps their years on the outside looking in had taught Ferdinand and Imelda the fine art of manipulating those who considered them inferior. American dignitaries got the full Marcos treatment. Tactics included heavy flattery—a staple of Filipino hospitality, turned up to the max—and opulent state dinners, meticulously planned by the first lady, featuring choruses, ballroom dancing, and a forest of floral arrangements. The Marcoses weren't shy about their indulgences. American intelligence officials were aware that a portion of U.S. military and economic aid subsidized Imelda's famous shoe collection, among other personal expenses. Sticky-fingered heads of state were nothing new, and a little bit of graft was a modest price to pay for a dependable ally. The Marcoses won over every U.S. president from Lyndon Johnson, who fawned over the charming Imelda and didn't care much for Ferdinand but still called him his "right arm in Asia," to Ronald Reagan, who developed a close friendship with the aging dictator. The couple boasted sparkling reputations across the ocean. The *New York Times* described Ferdinand as "a debonair, slender but combative man" with "abounding energy," and repeated the false claim that he was the "most decorated Filipino soldier in World War II." *Time* praised his "dynamic, selfless leadership." *Life* said Imelda had Jackie Kennedy's grace and Eleanor Roosevelt's energy.

All the pomp and excess may have given off an impression of frivolity that belied the deadly serious schemes being hatched below the surface. The relationship between Philippine and U.S. leaders had long been defined by deference: little brown brother striving to curry favor from the superpower calling the shots. Undergirding the dynamic was a presumption that whoever held office in Manila was a disposable figurehead, interchangeable with any number of slick-haired candidates, all of whom needed U.S. backing to get anything done. But this paradigm was outdated, and Marcos knew he had far more leverage than the Americans were willing to admit. Communism was spreading like a blaze, and he was an indispensable fire line. Philippine voters might be turning against him, but as long as the White House approved of his command, his grip on power was secure. So, with his term limit nearing and his rivals surging, he made his move.

Declaring martial law was a gamble based on a strategic calculation. Marcos understood something critical but unspoken about U.S. doctrine: for all its talk of democracy, America cared more about capitalism.

By 1972, Marcos had no shortage of evidence. Any rulers who expressed the slightest interest in socialist policies placed a big red target on their back. Any rulers committed to protecting American business interests had a ruthless ally behind them. It was colonialism by another name.

CIA operations removed a democratically elected prime minister in Iran in 1953 (Operation Ajax) and a democratically elected president in Guatemala in 1954 (Operation PBSuccess) to install authoritarian rulers. In Congo (later Zaire) in 1961, the United States backed a Belgian plot to execute Prime Minister Patrice Lumumba, the newly independent nation's first elected leader, replacing him with Mobutu Sese Seko, who established a dictatorship that would last thirty-two years. In 1964, the United States backed military coups that ousted presidents in Brazil and Bolivia, and the following year, the U.S. backed a right-wing military regime in Indonesia that massacred hundreds of thousands of political opponents. In Chile, the U.S. spent $3 million for a propaganda campaign against socialist presidential candidate Salvador Allende; then, after he was elected in 1970, "created the conditions as great as possible," in the words of U.S. secretary of state Henry Kissinger, for the 1973 military coup that led to his death, ushering in the fifteen-year dictatorship of Augusto Pinochet.

The United States justified these interventions by pointing at the Soviets, who were doing the same, intent on spreading their Communist ideology over most of the world if nobody stopped them. Coming off the high of winning the bloodiest war in history—and you could say the same for the Soviets—the U.S. acted with a hubris that came to define the superpower's late-twentieth-century foreign policy. The stalemate in Korea hardened Washington's resolve to keep other dominoes from falling. Next in line was Vietnam, just across the South China Sea from the Philippines, which was home to the two largest American military bases in Asia. The United States couldn't afford to have its little brown brother turn red.

American intelligence officials had been keeping close watch. Communist factions springing up in the Philippines after World War II faced off against CIA operatives on clandestine missions to diminish their numbers and undermine their ability to recruit. The Americans exploited locals' superstitions. Villagers would hear a booming voice from high above claiming to be God and ordering them not to join the Communists—a ploy executed through a speaker system on an airplane. An "evil eye," painted by operatives under cover of night, mysteriously popped up on walls and trees facing the homes of suspected Communists, indicating that they were cursed. When Filipino forces killed Communist rebels, American agents hung the bodies upside down from trees and punctured their necks with two holes, draining the corpse of blood, to fool locals into thinking that the deceased had been killed by an aswang.

In the first decade after World War II, the fight against the Communist forces was led by Ramon Magsaysay, who was minister of defense at the time. His commitment to the cause won over American officials, who handpicked him to become president in 1953. Magsaysay, who defeated incumbent Elpidio Quirino in a landslide with 70 percent of the vote, was genuinely popular but benefited from American dirty tricks. Before one of Quirino's campaign speeches, CIA agents drugged his drink, making him sound incoherent, drawing further attention to public concerns about his health. When a political rival criticized President Magsaysay for conceding too much in deals with the United States, the CIA planted stories that he was an undercover agent for Communist China.

By all measures, the efforts to wipe out Communist revolutionaries were effective. By the time Marcos was in office, armed Communist rebels numbered fewer than 3,000 across the country, down from around 15,000 two decades earlier. But what if there were more? And what if they were turning more violent, too, staging public attacks on civilians and elected officials? As their popularity declined, Ferdinand and Imelda warned U.S. diplomats that the Philippines faced a growing Communist threat, an assertion that contradicted American intelligence. But their

alarm seemed prophetic when, in August 1971, a bomb went off at a political rally in Manila, killing nine people and wounding ninety-five. Over
the next thirteen months, at least fourteen more bombs exploded around
Metro Manila, usually in the middle of the night, rarely injuring anybody
but instilling an aura of fear that carried into the wet, hot, chaotic summer of 1972, as torrential rains brought disastrous flooding across the archipelago and violent demonstrations raged outside the U.S. embassy.

Citing the ongoing bomb threats, Marcos suspended due process
rights, allowing police to detain anyone for any reason—perhaps a trial
balloon to see how his American friends might react to totalitarian tactics. Halfway into the bombing campaign, officers discovered a boat
filled with explosives they claimed belonged to Communists. Then, on
September 22, a convoy carrying Marcos's defense minister was ambushed by gunfire. That night, the president signed Proclamation 1081,
granting himself unlimited authority to combat "ruthless groups of
men . . . waging an armed insurrection and rebellion against the Government of the Republic of the Philippines in order to forcibly seize
political and state power in this country, overthrow the duly constituted
government, and supplant our existing political, social, economic and
legal order with an entirely new one whose form of government, whose
system of laws, whose conceptions of God and religion, whose notion of
individual rights and family relations, and whose political, social, economic, legal and moral precepts are based on Marxist-Leninist-Maoist
teachings and beliefs." The wave of arrests began three hours later.

As it turned out, the bombings, the ambush, the boat, and the violent
street demonstrations were all orchestrated by Marcos himself, or at
least by his security forces, which included a secret death squad nicknamed "the Monkees." It's hard to say how much of this U.S. leaders
knew at the time, but what is clear is that American diplomats had been
aware Marcos was plotting to extend his rule, and intelligence officials

quickly learned that the attack on the convoy was part of a false flag campaign. Years later, my mom would remember Marcos's power grab as her first glimpse at the dirty machinations behind the curtain, her first inkling that hidden conspiracies shaped the realities in sight.

As Marcos had anticipated, the United States did nothing to stop him. To the contrary, American officials seemed quite relieved by the turn of events. "This place is a hopeless mess," Francis Underhill, a diplomat at the U.S. embassy in Manila, told journalist Raymond Bonner. "Power is so dispersed that nothing can be done. Graft and corruption are rife. The streets are unsafe. The Philippines needs a strong man, a man on horseback to get the country organized and going again."

Why leave the fate of the Philippines in the hands of a fickle public when you can have a dictator ensure American interests are protected? Marcos annulled court rulings limiting American investment in Filipino businesses and membership on Filipino company boards. The murder rate in Manila dropped by 90 percent within the first few weeks of martial law. The military seized weapons from the private paramilitaries of wealthy landowners. One U.S. Senate staffer, dispatched to the Philippines to observe the impact of martial law, reported that "a measure of order and discipline has been introduced into Philippine affairs." Annual military aid from the United States rose from around $25 million in the late 1960s to more than $100 million in the early 1980s.

LOOK AT THE ORDER dictatorships brought to the so-called Third World! Misfortunate places, in the minds of most white Americans, suddenly emerged as showcases for American spectacles. What did they know of Zaire, once land of the Kongo Kingdom, before dictator Mobuto Sese Seko hosted the Rumble in the Jungle in 1974? What did they know of the Philippines before Marcos hosted the Thrilla in Manila in 1975? For all Don King's eccentricities, he was too savvy a promoter to fly America's most famous athletes into harm's way, into chaos, into anywhere lacking the institutions to protect the sanctity of a globally televised sporting event. Those were placed safely in the hands of allies.

From the staticky sounds pouring out of the box, American viewers thousands of miles away could hear the crowds in Kinshasa and Manila throwing their voices behind Muhammad Ali, the Louisville Lip, the People's Champ, the Greatest, the Black man banned from boxing for three years because he refused to fight in a war he didn't believe in. "My conscience won't let me go shoot my brother, or some darker people, or some poor, hungry people in the mud, for big, powerful America, and shoot them for what?" he said in 1967. "They never called me nigger. They never lynched me. They never put no dogs on me. They never robbed me of my nationality, or raped and killed my mother and father. Shoot them for what?"

THE CONCEPCION SISTERS threw parties at the Scout Reyes house. With the furniture pushed up against the wall and a bowl of orange juice and vodka on a table, girls and boys stood on opposite ends of the living room, pairing off on the cleared hardwood. A record player sang the Bee Gees, the Beatles, the Beach Boys, Aretha Franklin, Elton John, Earth, Wind & Fire. "We don't listen to Filipino artists, we don't watch Filipino movies," my mom recalled. "That's for our maids and drivers."

There was no VST & Company yet. Spanky Rigor was still a producer, recording the sort of ballads that got sung at the banquets Madame Imelda hosted at the palace. Ging was part of a group that sang them. She and Spanky, both in their midtwenties, had just started dating. Lyn and Mae were in college. All of them still lived at home, as was standard for unmarried children, making the Scout Reyes house a constant den of action, with everybody's friends and suitors passing through.

Thanks to my mother's older sisters, the Concepcion name was well known among the private school set by the time my mom was a teenager. They were beautiful, modest, and fun-loving, educated at Maryknoll, and from a respectable family. The boys who came around the house attended Ateneo or De La Salle, the sons of mayors, senators, and moguls. My mom's closest friend, Rosalinda, was the daughter of a small-town mayor who ran an illegal logging business. Her house had nine bedrooms and an elevator. Her Barbie collection needed two shelves. She rode to school in a limousine. A maid carried her backpack to and from the vehicle.

Rosalinda's family lost the house before she finished college. My mom didn't know the details. Such a swift fall wasn't unusual in those years. No family was immune from the dictator's wrath. No family's power matched his. Marcos had allies to reward, and bank accounts to fill. Eugenio Lopez, a Marcos campaign donor and owner of the nation's largest electric company, was patriarch of one of the families that had run the country for centuries. Marcos wanted the company, so he had Lopez's son charged with plotting to assassinate him. The old oligarch had no choice but to sell the company to the government for $220 million, around half its value.

A nervous energy coursed through Manila high society. Families long accustomed to pulling the strings found their power suddenly hollow—everything they'd built was now at the mercy of the dictator. My mom could sense the anxieties and insecurities in the boys who tried to impress her by showing off the guns they kept in their backpacks, drunkenly firing rounds into the smoggy sapphire sky. She pitied these poor, spoiled boys so desperate for a taste of the power they expected to inherit, boys born to think that anything they wanted lay within reach, yet who couldn't even stay out past midnight.

The drivers pulled up around 11:30 p.m., a procession of luxury cars parked along the compound's exterior wall. "Because if you get caught in the road after curfew they take you to jail," my mom said. "It just became a fact of life. You get used to it."

THOSE WITH THE LEAST to lose took the brunt of Marcos's crony capitalism, which monopolized industries and consolidated wealth among a chosen few. On Negros, the country's fourth biggest island and the heart of the sugar industry, around 2 percent of the island's people owned 98 percent of the sugar fields, where workers made 81 cents a day on average, far below the country's minimum wage. Marcos's strict enforcement of laws apparently didn't extend to labor violations.

Within the first five years of martial law, even as Marcos officially raised the national minimum wage, factory wages dropped by 30 percent while consumer prices tripled. The commodities boom carrying the economy busted with the global oil crisis, shrinking the price of critical Philippine exports like sugar, which fell from 65 cents a pound in 1974 to 8 cents a pound within two years. Two out of three Filipino people lived below the poverty line. Despite hundreds of millions of dollars in economic aid from the United States, the per-capita calorie intake among Filipino people was lower in 1976 than it had been in 1960. A 1979 World Bank study found that "one-third to one-half of the population is too poor to purchase and consume enough food." Around 40 percent of deaths in the country were caused by malnutrition, and around 20 percent of deaths were children between the ages of one and four—a fatality rate nine times that of China and sixteen times that of Japan. By the mid-1970s, around 70 percent of the Philippine population was worse off economically than they were before martial law, and by 1980, 40 percent were classified as "urban poor" by the World Bank, up from 24 percent just five years earlier. Over those years, Marcos spent $3 billion to bail out allies facing ruin.

What could be done? The deteriorating conditions in the Philippines didn't shake the United States from its support for the dictator. Rigged legislative elections filled congress with more Marcos allies. An entire generation of politicians who opposed him were either behind bars or threatened into silence. Too-intrepid journalists and student protesters vanished or were found dead. Speaking out was punishable by torture. Marcos's goons electrocuted people with cattle prods, burned their flesh with cigarettes, forced them to stand naked in front of an air conditioner for hours, and subjected them to the "San Juanico Bridge": suspended by their shoulders on one bed and their feet on another, the victims were beaten when their body fell. The *New York Times* reported on the regime's torture methods as early as 1976.

Many Filipino aristocrats with much to lose simply went along with the new way of doing things, paying the bribes, looking away from injustices, hoping to keep their families afloat. Such a strategy had served my ancestors well since the years of Spanish rule: better to be colonist than colonized, right? But this time our family resisted. After quitting the Central Bank, Rizalina started a shirt-making business with Baby; they sewed made-to-order dresses, blouses, skirts, and trousers in a rented office space, for far less income than their accounting jobs had brought in. Manuel's finances were doing no better. Because of his refusal to pay bribes, he was unable to get the required permits for his ship-salvaging expeditions, and his legal cases languished at the bottom of court dockets.

BEFORE MY MOM'S THIRD YEAR of high school at Maryknoll, her parents transferred her to a less expensive school, St. Theresa's, then laid off their drivers and all but one maid. For the first time in her life, my mom had to take the bus.

One of her old grade school friends attended St. Theresa's, and my mom would see her on the bus in the mornings. The girl didn't come from much money. She lived "deep in the boondocks" in a modest house without even maids. "We were supposed to be in a better position than her family," my mom recalled, and now here she was, taking the same bus to the same school. When the friend asked my mom why she transferred to St. Theresa's, my mom said it was because her brothers had returned from Dumaguete City and attended a boy's school near St. Theresa's—this was true—but she preferred to take the bus rather than squeeze into a crowded car with them. At the time, she couldn't bear to utter the truth. "We didn't have the money anymore. All the people's money goes to Marcos. I felt so sad. I felt so embarrassed."

Memories from those years became sticky reminders of the traumas she hoped to protect me from, affirmations that made her grateful for America, the land that took so many of us in.

DURING MY THIRD YEAR at Mira Loma High, our toil finally seemed to be paying off.

In our dim, cramped locker room, as Mistah F.A.B.'s choppy Oakland drawl thundered from a boom box and the musty scent of countless practices lingered in the air, we all crowded around the newspaper.

> Matadors football appears to be ascending like a Barry Bonds home run. And the team is dispelling the myth that Mira Loma football players are a bunch of soft, bookworm-like preppies who lack talent and are devoid of a mean streak to knock heads. There's now a cult-like campus following for the squad, and players show a gritty gridiron aggression . . .

We'd won the first three games my junior season, our varsity team's longest winning streak in years, earning us a feature in the *Sacramento*

Bee. Students packed the stands, waving signs and bellowing chants. The jerseys we wore to school on game days carried newfound clout. We were the boys behind Mira Loma's stunning turnaround, and we carried ourselves with swagger.

When our beloved Coach Macias was fired after my sophomore season, I was so upset that I cornered our principal between classes to express my displeasure in an urgent speech I'd prepared in my head for days. But the man who replaced him turned out to be uniquely suited for the task. Coach Steve Stephens, a burly white man in his midthirties, had been a PE teacher at our school for a decade, and to his eyes there was no shortage of athletic ability at Mira Loma. The problem, Coach Stephens surmised, was that because so many kids commuted in from distant suburbs, we lacked the community pride and campus culture necessary to draw kids to a losing team. "Because kids come to the school from all over the place, we don't have a neighborhood-type appeal in this area," he told the *Bee.* "But this time the real goal is to really get into all these diverse groups and try to bring them all together and build from that." He knew nearly every kid at our school, having spent his days watching us run laps and do push-ups, and so he was well positioned to identify and recruit talent, tailoring his pitches with the precision of a politician on the campaign trail. Boys on our very good basketball team bought into the idea that they'd develop a hard-nosed physicality that would serve them well on the court. Boys who'd never considered playing sports were intrigued to hear that football didn't require exceptional speed or strength as long as you were tough and willing to hit. A wave of local kids signed up. Our varsity began the year with more than forty players. "All I can tell is that I wouldn't be hanging out with a lot of these guys on campus had it not been for football," one teammate told the newspaper.

The article praised our team's "atypical" composition, noting that our roster included kids "of 16 different nationalities," including two Ukrainian immigrants who knew almost nothing about the sport when they joined. A dozen of our best players were the children of immigrants from Mexico, Jordan, Japan, Cape Verde, and the Philippines. We had white IB kids on our offensive line and Black local kids on our defensive line. Our starting quarterback was a speedy Filipino American boy who liked to drag race his Honda on dark suburban backroads, and his best friend, a starting defensive back, was a roughneck white kid who showed us how to shoot guns on camping trips near Lake Tahoe. We presented a stark contrast to most of the teams we faced, who were homogeneously white or Black.

We were flying high. No way I would've believed that we'd lose our remaining seven games, including our final contest against a team newly headed by Coach Macias. I decided it was my duty to keep us from sliding back into the dark ages the following season. I was team captain, one of three "standout players" mentioned by name in the newspaper article. I continued to dream of playing college football and understood that top programs were more likely to scout for talent on winning teams. But above all, I took it upon myself to pull our team back into glory because I took football way too seriously.

Before games, I delivered speeches about "shocking the world." At halftime, I'd slam my helmet into lockers in expletive-filled tantrums denigrating our efforts. After every loss, I sobbed in the locker room, face buried in my gloved hands, with a teammate or two to share in the anguish. Our poor girlfriends would be waiting in the parking lot an hour after the game's conclusion, asking anyone exiting the locker room, "Are they still in there crying?"

The most shameful episode occurred on the night of our homecoming game. All five "princes" on the homecoming court were on the team, and the plan was that we'd leave the locker room early at halftime, to ride in a procession of convertibles that would carry us and the five "princesses" to a stage where the public address announcer would reveal who was voted "king" and "queen." But we were losing at halftime, and, by my judgment, needed to focus on certain strategic adjustments for any chance at a comeback. I refused to go out for the ceremony. My boy Javie, a fellow "prince" who usually cried with me after games, quickly seconded my proposal. Our teammates didn't want to leave us hanging, so they joined the boycott. The princesses rode to the stage dateless, a curious sight to the confused crowd. A teacher eventually coaxed us to at least show up for the ceremony, so we trudged out to the stage with sour faces. When they announced my name as king, the teacher had to ask me to smile for the photo, and as soon as it was snapped I stormed back toward the field, making clear to all that I found the whole thing frivolous and couldn't wait to get back to the truly important matter of playing football. In the words of Javie's mom, we "looked like assholes." We ended up losing anyway.

Javie took the sport about as seriously as I did. The stakes weighed heavy on us not because our lives depended on what happened on the field but the opposite: our prospects were bright and stable. Javie's parents, immigrants from Mexico, had built a comfortable household in Natomas, a young suburb burgeoning with crisp subdivisions. His mom was a school nurse, his dad a botanist who'd written college textbooks. Worried about his son developing a sense of entitlement from a middle-class upbringing, his dad occasionally took him out to the fields a few hours north where he used to pick fruits as a teenager, to make sure Javie experienced a slice of the toil that went into their family's ascent in America. Javie would say those scorching days covered in itchy peach fuzz were harder than any practice he'd ever had. The lesson sank in. Javie was an exemplary student, transferring into the IB program because the IS classes weren't challenging enough for him. He was president of the Chicano club, prom king, a captain of the football team, and one of a handful of kids whose social life sprawled across the school's three divisions. Like me, he grew accustomed to things working out in his favor if he put in the effort. Winning football games, though, was a gaping exception. No matter how deeply we cared about the enterprise, we couldn't bend the laws of motion.

Not all of our teammates appreciated our intensity. Tommy and Chucky would giggle in the back of the pack during our inspirational speeches and ignore our orders to pick up the effort. Tommy had calmed his public trolling since his sophomore year knockout, but he had the confidence of a senior now and had developed a running mate in Chucky. They played off each other, more brazen when they were together. While Tommy jabbed his racisms quickly, before slipping away, Chucky would just stand there and spew, not with any menace or scowl but in the goofy, jovial tone of a talk-show host. "Look at these beaners," he'd say to Javie and another teammate, Julian, who was also a team captain and the son of Mexican immigrants. There were jokes about deportation and crossing the border and wetbacks.

We tried to let the racist comments roll off us. We knew they reached for racism because they had nothing else to hit us with. We were homecoming and prom royalty, football captains, top of our class, brown-skinned All-American teens who embodied the changing flavor of the country's melting pot. We ran shit. I sensed resentment more than hate in the slurs. Tommy and Chucky had grown up in a climate of anxiety that echoed across schoolyards, campaign speeches, cable news broadcasts, and internet comment sections. They regurgitated tropes and catchphrases. I don't know what was in their heart, but I know they aimed to sting.

One evening at the end of practice, Julian told Chucky that if he said that racist shit one more time he was going to punch him in the face. "I'm not playing," Julian said. Walking to the parking lot, Julian, Javie, and I gamed out the scenarios for what would happen when Chucky inevitably said something racist. If he punched back when Julian hit him, they'd fight. If Tommy jumped in, Javie would take him. And since I was on friendly terms with all parties, I'd make sure it didn't get out of hand.

The next afternoon, the three of us walked to the locker room together, hyped up, anticipating justice. Chucky and Tommy were already there, halfway suited up. We put our stuff down on the bench across from them. Chucky gave a friendly nod.

"Sup guys—"

And *POW*, a right cross to the jaw.

There was no fight, just a stunned silence. Chucky hunched over, grimacing. Tommy wide-eyed, disoriented, afraid he was next. Javie covered his open mouth with a balled fist in the universal sign for "Ohhh shit," but Julian stood calm, rubbing his right wrist. He'd sprained it with the force of the punch, requiring him to wear a splint for the rest of the season.

"What the fuck, man?" Chucky managed. "No more racist shit, bro," Julian replied, and there wasn't, not for the rest of the season. With the nostalgia of our final high school months setting in, Chucky reverted to the happy-go-lucky demeanor he'd had freshman year, his heel turn leaving barely a trace, as if he'd shed a skin. Though he maintained a carefree nihilism at practice, he was sensitive: he cried after tough losses and apologized for mistakes he made on critical plays. After the final game of our senior year—a mud-soaked 21–14 victory over local rival Rio Americano High on a rainy and blustery Saturday afternoon, bringing us to a record 3 wins and 7 losses—Chucky celebrated by breaking into a sprint and diving into the muck chest-first, gliding like a swan for yards. The further he got from the toxic impulses, the more I wondered whether it wasn't so much the fear of violence that shifted his behavior but the realization that the blades he threw cut deeper than he'd assumed. He was just messing around, repeating words he heard from others. But I sometimes wonder how far he might have pushed it if he'd never felt the pain of consequences, whether at some point the mask fuses with flesh.

While Chucky retired from nativist trolling, Tommy's provocations matured into a more elegant strain. Years later, during a long email ex-

change debating issues that included his "problems with Multiculturalism," he wrote to me, "You are the rap blasting, ironic-cloth wearing,
apple cider sipping, socialism spouting, urban living, suburban raised,
expensively-educated, faux-sophisticated, middle-class twat that is the
most homogenous, visible portion of what is largely referred to in the
media as the white 'millennial' children currently living in the US. It
seems you or your family have already assimilated." We lost touch
shortly after that. Our friendship had carried a gamesmanship that, in
the invincible tenor of youth, I enjoyed as much as Tommy did. His
stubborn taunting was a puzzle I believed I could unlock with the right
combination of rhetoric and indifference. Navigating racism felt like just
a normal part of living in America, the dark cost of the First Amendment right to free speech. Kids in stadium bleachers shouted "monkey"
and "wetback" loud enough for us to hear on our march from the locker
room to the field. One classmate, a Muslim girl who wore a hijab, recounted how her family woke up to discover graffiti on their garage door,
"Terrorist" in dripping black paint. I'd seen news reports about white
men murdering people who to their eyes looked vaguely Middle Eastern, including Indian Sikhs, in the days and years after 9/11. Amid those
horrors, Tommy's slurs felt benign, more about provoking than threatening. As football taught, there was virtue in getting used to the hits,
hopping up without showing pain, bringing more force on the next play,
and if the laws of motion were in my favor I could knock my friend back
from whatever it was that fueled his racism. But trade blows long enough
and you start to wonder how many more you're willing to take before
walking away.

THE WORST INJURY I suffered in high school was a sprained knee a
few weeks into my junior season. The first doctor we saw suggested I get
an MRI to make sure nothing was torn, but my mom and I worried that

sort of probing technology emitted electromagnetic frequencies harmful to the body. We got a second opinion from an acupuncturist, who said he'd treat my knee and I could play if it felt strong enough. My mom was a proponent of natural healing techniques. She studied reflexology and treated ailments with remedies like ginger tea and hot salt water. She warned me to avoid the "toxins" in sodas and pharmaceuticals. My faith in this guidance was so strong that when I separated my shoulder at a football camp in Berkeley, I turned down the ibuprofen Javie offered me, for fear of damaging my liver, and gritted my teeth through the searing pain. I can't say whether the acupuncture helped the knee. I managed a few plays in the next game and felt healed after about three weeks. But the injury turned out to be a blessing in disguise, my mom and I soon realized. She hit it off with the acupuncturist, a pleasant white man who had served in Vietnam and treated my teammates free of charge. They got married, and she moved into his house early in my senior year. She planned to renovate and rent out our old house once I went off to college in the summer. With the eventual rental income, she was thinking of investing in gas stations and strip malls, essential outposts for the suburban land rush.

IN AN INTERVIEW with the *Sacramento Bee* a month after graduation, I described my plans to one day play professionally, then in retirement write about my football experiences. Without hesitation, I put myself in the company of all-time greats: "You never read books about LaDainian Tomlinson's or Jerry Rice's high school playing days," I told the reporter. I decided on a college based on which football program would give me the best chance of getting drafted. On the questionnaire for incoming freshman players, I wrote that I chose the University of San Diego "for coaching staff, opportunity to play for a championship team, good academics, and beautiful campus."

A more detailed explanation begins with my first visit, in the summer before twelfth grade, for a football camp where I hoped to impress head coach Jim Harbaugh, a fiery-eyed former NFL quarterback who liked to race his players up dusty hills during summer workouts. For two straight years under Harbaugh, the San Diego Toreros finished at the top of their conference. His NFL ties, charismatic intensity, and staff of experienced assistants drew players good enough to receive competing invitations from bigger, better-funded programs. Though USD didn't offer athletic scholarships for football, it could cover the costs of the $46,000 tuition with academic scholarships and financial aid for qualifying recruits. The team's best player was quarterback Josh Johnson, a standout at Oakland Tech High School overlooked by top college programs because he missed most of his junior season with a leg injury. Harbaugh was so committed to signing Josh that he picked him up in the East Bay, because Josh couldn't afford a flight down, and drove him seven hours on I-5 for a campus visit. Josh said the place looked like "a castle on a hill" when it first came into view. Students slept and studied in off-white Spanish Mission–style buildings, walked along promenades lined with palm trees and fountains, and ate meals on stone benches overlooking the ocean. Several of Josh's younger teammates followed him to San Diego. By the start of my freshman year, Josh was one of the most dominant quarterbacks in the country, a sure bet to be the first USD player selected in the NFL draft. His promise brought scouts, and the chance to catch their attention as they observed our practices with crossed arms and eyes hidden behind sunglasses.

Our team's demographic makeup looked nothing like the rest of the school's. Most of our classmates were white and hailed from Southern California's most affluent counties. Less than 5 percent of the university's 5,500 students were Black, about 1 percent Pacific Islander, but more than a third of our hundred players were Black, and a half dozen were Samoan, Tongan, or Filipino. The perpetual cycle of morning workouts, afternoon film sessions, and evening practices, which took up half my waking hours, ensconced me in the familiar world of locker rooms and playbooks. Asleep before 11:00 p.m. and out the door by 6:15 a.m., I'd drop by my dorm during the day to shower before class and nap before practice, rarely seeing my roommates until the evening. Saturday, when most students went to the beach, was game day. I wore my lifestyle enthusiastically, as an identity, strolling around campus in the Nike sweatsuits and T-shirts given to football players, my limp a badge of honor.

Only on sporadic occasions did I second-guess my commitment, and only fleetingly. It would usually be when I'd return to my dorm, exhausted, to find my roommates giddily playing video games or debating political issues, often with friends from down the hall. I liked these guys, escaped into their realm for a few hours, then reluctantly slipped off to bed while their good times continued. I'd force my eyes closed on the top bunk to the sound of them watching *Entourage* on the other side of the wall.

I was drawn to their discussions about matters I hadn't put much thought into. My singular focus on football had left me with broad swaths of ignorance. I was ill-prepared for my first election as a voter. I believed the country should do more to help poor people—I'd learned that much from Tupac—and had a vague sense it would help if rich people paid more taxes. But the mechanics were lost to me. For the practical matter of who to vote for, I turned to trusted sources. My cousin's girlfriend, a thoughtful law student, volunteered on Hillary Clinton's presidential campaign, so I figured I'd check the box for her. My dormmates, though, had strong opinions. Gibran, a Mexican American theology major from Kansas City, put up a Barack Obama sign in our common room. Steve, a white business major from Orange County, had a Ron Paul sign above his desk, alongside newspaper columns clipped from the *Wall Street Journal*. Gibran advocated for open borders and against Proposition 8, the California ballot proposal banning same-sex marriage rights. Steve argued that an unchecked influx of new immigrants would strain government resources, and that matrimonial law should reflect the biology of reproduction. On those two issues, I sided with Steve. I thought it was unfair that some immigrants had a head start at getting into America because they were right next door, while others had to journey halfway across the world, and I knew the Catholic Church deemed homosexuality a sin. I'd yet to shed the foundational beliefs I'd inherited.

On the question of president, though, Gibran won me over by explaining Obama's plan for universal health care, though my superficial impulses played an equally powerful role once I learned that Obama was the biracial son of a single mother, spent part of his childhood on a Pacific island, played pickup basketball, quoted hip-hop lyrics, and had worked as a community organizer in disinvested Chicago neighborhoods. At the time, my ideology aligned wholly with my mom's. She wasn't yet a citizen, so she didn't pay much attention to the campaigns of candidates she couldn't vote for anyway. She'd had no strong opinion on the 1996 presidential election pitting incumbent Democrat Bill Clinton against Republican challenger Bob Dole—she considered them interchangeable, for the most part, cynical members of a distant political class. Four years later, she supported George W. Bush for the presidency because his opponent Al Gore was pro-choice, but her political apathy was clear from her relaxed demeanor on election night and through the dispute that followed—my mom isn't capable of hiding even the slightest passion. By 2004, after years of rejecting political party affiliations as secular labels, my mom concluded that she could trust Republicans on abortion policy, and therefore could trust them on other issues, too. But she still valued my judgment more than any other, so when I expressed my support for Obama in 2008, she signed on too, and though she wasn't yet a citizen, she persuaded her friends and siblings to vote for him.

Here and there around campus, I saw a few white students wearing

T-shirts that read "NObama." I'd think to myself how ridiculous they looked. I could see promoting an idea or a candidate, branding yourself with a marker of your identity, but what was the pleasure of defining yourself in opposition to a single person? I was in a Tuesday night class when the election returns rolled in. When I got back to my dorm, Gibran was on the couch in front of the TV, hands clasped in joyful serenity. A line from my favorite song, "Changes," popped into my head: "Although it seems heaven-sent, we ain't ready to see a black president," Tupac rapped. I remember thinking that it was a shame he wasn't alive to see how far we'd come in barely a decade.

A COUNTRY that considers itself a meritocracy can justify any inequity. In the final decades of the twentieth century, U.S. policy operated under the premise that a robust social safety net would discourage people from working harder to climb out of poverty. A 2019 study by Yale researchers found that Americans tend to vastly underestimate the consequences of economic oppression: though the median Black family had 5 percent as much wealth as the median white family in 1963, respondents estimated it closer to 50 percent, and though Black wealth in 2016 was 10 percent the size of white wealth, respondents thought it was around 90 percent. "People are willing to assume that things were at least somewhat bad 50 years ago, but they also assume that things have gotten substantially better—and are approaching parity," one of the researchers, Jennifer Richeson, wrote. "The mythology of racial progress exerts a powerful hold on our minds."

On autumn weekends, the scholarship recipients and millionaire celebrities performing extraordinary feats on national television presented parables of upward mobility. Receiver Jerry Rice's strong hands were attributed to a childhood catching bricks for his brick-laying father in the Mississippi Delta. Football coaches journeyed to distant pockets of the country searching for promising talent. High schools, colleges, advertisers, television stations, and entire cities invested millions of dollars in the sport. Wins and losses swayed local economies. There's no hiding a poor blocker or tentative runner when the whistle blows, and a single misstep can leave a teammate vulnerable to injury, so teams came to learn that racist discrimination is a competitive disadvantage.

The sport had been almost exclusively white in its early years, a time when racial segregation was justified by false claims of biological inferiority. Athletic competition offered a platform for disproving that paradigm for white audiences. After boxer Jack Johnson defeated Jim Jeffries in a 1910 match billed as the "Fight of the Century," white people rioted across the country, burning Black neighborhoods, and Congress passed a law banning transport of boxing footage across state lines to keep the masses from seeing a Black man knock down the county's best white prizefighter. Even as Black athletes won Olympic gold medals and heavyweight titles, college and professional sports teams maintained unofficial quotas or prohibitions on Black players.

Sixteen of the inaugural entries into the Pro Football Hall of Fame, in 1963, were white players; the seventeenth was Jim Thorpe, who began playing football at an academy for resettled Natives in the early 1900s, won two Olympic gold medals (pentathlon and decathlon) at the 1912 games in Stockholm, and served as first president of the NFL. Thirty more white players were inducted into the museum over the next five years, before the first Black player, Emlen Tunnell, was inducted in 1967. When a second Black player, Marion Motley, got into the Hall of Fame in 1968, around fifty white players had already made it in. Over the league's first decade, nine Black players had appeared on teams, but by 1944, when Motley joined the navy, there were none. He played on a military football team coached by a man who also happened to coach a professional team in a newly formed league called the All-America Football Conference. Motley's first year in the AAFC, 1946, the NFL also fielded a Black player, though not by choice: the State of California barred the Los Angeles Rams from playing in the publicly owned Los Angeles Coliseum because the NFL's all-white teams violated "separate but equal" laws. With a running style that resembled a rhinoceros, Motley led the Cleveland Browns to AAFC championships his first three years, and when the franchise joined the NFL in 1950, he led that league in rushing yards and won another championship. When the American Football League launched in 1960 as another challenger to the NFL, the upstart drew from a pool filled with plenty of players skilled enough for the pro game but blocked by unspoken racial quotas. The AFL's product so quickly threatened the NFL that the leagues merged within a decade, and the quotas dissolved. A football fan born the same year as the NFL would have entered retirement watching America's most popular sport played mostly by Black athletes.

The lessons trickled across the football world. In 1970, the integrated University of Southern California Trojans walloped the all-white University of Alabama Crimson Tide 42–21. Unverified reports claimed Alabama coach Paul "Bear" Bryant scheduled the game so that his school's boosters could see firsthand the talent they were missing out on by unofficially barring Black players despite federal laws mandating integration—the program was already facing a civil rights lawsuit. USC running back Sam Cunningham dominated the game, rushing for 135 yards and two touchdowns, leading one of Bryant's assistant coaches to quip that "Sam Cunningham did more to integrate Alabama in sixty minutes than Martin Luther King did in twenty years." A *Los Angeles Times* headline declared: "Hatred Shut Out As Alabama Finally Joins the Union." An article in the paper describing the scene at the Birmingham stadium quoted an unidentified man saying: "You know, I sure bet the Bear wished he had two or three of them nigger boys on his team NOW." The following year, a Black player received a football scholarship from Alabama for the first time.

Efforts to integrate football suited white interests, and like most things that suit white interests, the endeavor was well funded. Private high schools cover tuition costs for underprivileged students with exceptional football abilities. Clothing brands like Nike and Adidas sponsor top-tier high school and college programs with equipment and cash. Each year, U.S. colleges grant more athletic scholarships for football than every other sport combined. Hundreds of scouts aren't scouring music recitals for piano prodigies or robotics competitions for engineering prospects. Football offers a path around the systemic headwinds designed to maintain America's caste system. In the zero-sum game of capitalism, Black people have lost the most, "bent at the bottom of a growing pyramid of commerce and industry," as W. E. B. Du Bois wrote in *Black Reconstruction in America*, published in 1937. The sin of slavery has yet to be rectified, nor have the subsequent decades of pillage and lynchings, nor the discriminatory practices that blocked job and housing opportunities during the country's most fruitful economic upswing. Most unions banned Black members for years, ensuring the most desirable jobs went to white people. U.S. policies diverted education funding away from Black communities, suppressed the value of Black-owned homes, and disproportionately imprisoned Black people. But on a football field, meritocracy stands a chance against old prejudices.

For a long while, most of the white football coaches who ran the industry believed that Black people lacked the mental capacity to play quarterback, the most strategically important position, the face of the team. The false assumption of white intellectual superiority persisted longer than the assumption about physical supremacy. The old prejudices shifted to accommodate the undeniable evidence that by the second half of the twentieth century, many of the world's best athletes were Black. The updated mindset was infamously reflected by television commentator Jimmy Snyder, who in 1988 said that Black people were "bred to be the better athlete" from generations of slavery, when "the slave owner would breed his big woman so that he would have a big black kid."

The lie is harder to maintain in the vacuum of athletic measurement. The first Black quarterback inducted into the Pro Football Hall of Fame, Warren Moon, spent six years in the Canadian Football League, winning five consecutive championships, before an NFL team offered him a job in 1984. He was the only Black quarterback in the league that year. Four years later, Doug Williams, who began his professional career in the short-lived United States Football League, became the first Black quarterback to win the Super Bowl. Two years later, Steve McNair, a star high school quarterback in Mississippi, turned down top-tier college programs because they wanted him to switch to running back or defense, and went on to set records at the smaller Alcorn State on his way to a standout NFL career. His first year in the league, 1995, McNair was one of eight Black quarterbacks under NFL contract; when he retired in 2007, there were seventeen. The following year, my former teammate Josh Johnson was selected in the fifth round of the NFL draft. He was still employed in the league thirteen years later, in 2020, when a third of teams opened the season with a Black starting quarterback, the highest mark in league history.

The progress plays out on the nation's center stage, more visible than the advanced classes, executive boards, and bank accounts that tell the truer story of American opportunity. For all the glory it brings, the game leaves no shortage of players with battered bodies and sunken minds. Like boxing before it, football increasingly becomes a sport for those without good options, awarding upward mobility to an exceptional few, at a high cost, for the entertainment of a mostly white audience.

THE FULL COST wasn't as clear in my day, at the dawn of concussion protocols and brain damage studies. I drifted from the game organically.

I spent my summer after freshman year, in 2008, back home in Sacramento, instead of staying with my teammates in San Diego, where upperclassmen organized workouts. I wanted to see old friends I hadn't seen since Christmas break. My mom and the acupuncturist set up a room for me in his two-story house, which had a gym in the garage and a driveway basketball hoop shaded by oak trees. I worked out every day, convinced in the moment that I was honing my physical condition as diligently as my teammates were, but in hindsight the apathy was already creeping in, enough for me to ease up at slight discomfort, because there was nobody urging me to push a little harder. Little by little, I eased up into a carefree summer of bike rides, hookups, and designated driving to house parties. The changes to my body were invisible, though, and I wouldn't be aware anything was amiss until I returned to the football field at the end of summer.

I was no more aware of my mom's suddenly dire financial situation— had not the slightest inkling that the economic crash all over the news had reached our household. When her interest rate rose, she was unable to find renters willing to pay a monthly fee high enough to cover the rising mortgage cost. Her real estate income collapsed with the bursting of the housing bubble. The number of new homes sold each year sank from more than a million in 2006 to a third of that by 2011. Fewer people wanted to purchase depreciating property, and most who'd held on to their homes had no interest in selling for less than they owed. From 2007 to 2009, the average value of a U.S. home dropped from $247,900 to $216,700, the steepest fall since the 1930s. By 2010, median household wealth had been cut in half, the slide even steeper for Latinx households, who lost 86 percent of their wealth, and Black households, who lost more than 98 percent.

By summer 2008, my mom was behind on her mortgage payments for the Sacramento house and the lakeside property, owing around $8,000 on each. In June, she defaulted on her mortgages. Owing a grand total of

$850,000 in loans and interest, she sold the Sacramento house for less than her debt on it and lost the lakeside property to the bank, one of the 6 million foreclosed homes in the United States to be auctioned off in the final three years of the decade. In barely eight months, my mom lost all she'd built over eight years.

That summer, as we stood in the kitchen filling the fridge with groceries, she revealed to me the details she'd hoped to keep me from worrying about. Like so many others, she was past the point of turning it around. She had filed for bankruptcy, she said with tears in her eyes, the first time I'd ever seen my mom cry. I consoled her by saying we could buy all the houses we wanted once I was in the NFL.

But within days of returning to San Diego, the dues from my lackadaisical summer were more than my body could bear. I failed the preseason conditioning test, which required running from one sideline to the other and back in under eighteen seconds, sixteen straight times. My lungs were maxed out by the fourth sprint, leaving me a straggler in the pack, and by the seventh my Achilles had flared up with tendinitis, sending me to the trainer's room. Making matters worse, the new crop of freshman included two talented prospects who played my position, cornerback. They quickly surpassed me on the depth chart. I didn't help my cause by daydreaming during film sessions. With the projector running, the room dark, and sunflower seeds rattling on Formica tables, I scribbled in the margins of my playbook story ideas for the school newspaper. The Saturday games played out with me on the sideline, my jersey dry and without grass stains when I returned to the locker room. Even before the season was over, I knew I wouldn't return for another. Whatever gridiron fantasies might lie on the road ahead, I was certain I wasn't willing to pay the tolls. The realization faded in gradually, as new interests pulled me from my disintegrating plans.

I was most worried about telling Javie. I put off the call, overcome by the thought of letting him down. We were running mates in our football dreams, workout partners kicking up dust on the yellowed Mira Loma field, summer camp confidants trading observations about the boys from other schools, and now college football contemporaries going through the rigors of our chosen paths. Javie played receiver at Occidental College in Los Angeles. On phone calls, we'd trade highlights, gripes, and encouragement. Our rapport steeled me, lifted my spirits. I felt bad about taking that away from him as he played on without me.

He called me the weekend our sophomore seasons ended, a few days before Thanksgiving break. I wasn't sure if I should go ahead and tell him or wait until we were face-to-face in Sacramento. Before I could decide, as our opening pleasantries wound down, he said, haltingly, "Dawg, I quit football."

"Oh shit, yo, I did too!"

Javie started busting up. "Oh my God, dude," he said through cackles. "I was hella nervous about telling you."

He joined a club rugby team instead and shifted the rest of his extracurricular energies toward a university investment fund he and a few other finance majors managed, as well as the themed parties he and his roommates threw in their weathered bungalow. The first one I attended, the spring after we quit football, I was such a novice drinker that I passed out on Javie's bed during the afternoon barbecue, then woke up hours later during the living room dance party so that I could throw up all over his bathroom. Free from my old constraints, I scheduled my classes for the afternoons, stayed up till sunrise, and consumed the available intoxicants. I rearranged my plans toward journalism and spent my newfound spare hours writing articles for the school newspaper. I read more and began to better understand the mechanics shaping the urgent matters I'd long ignored. I could drive around as often as I wanted, staying as long as I needed wherever I was welcome, with friends in Los Angeles or Santa Barbara on weekends, with Jed in Burlingame or Lauren in Oakland for winter break, with a girlfriend I met on summer break who lived in Stockton. I kept a bag of clothes and toiletries in my trunk, and on more than one occasion napped in hotel parking lots when I was too sleepy to drive.

At the end of my sophomore year, May 2009, with my boxed and bagged possessions stuffed in the backseat of my car and an Andre Nick-atina mixtape in the CD player, I made the familiar journey north across the desert, through the valley, and into Sacramento, which had been my home for a decade, for what I didn't know would be the last time. Later that summer, my mom asked the acupuncturist for a divorce, and they parted ways on good terms. She preferred the independence to move and decide as she pleased, without having to worry about someone other than me. She no longer wanted to live in Sacramento, where her business ties had expired anyway. If she was going to start from scratch, she might as well relocate to the only place that made sense: San Diego, where she could be close to me and the ocean. She loved the beach and had been taken with the city's coastal beauty on her visits.

Before the end of summer, she found a cheap in-law unit attached to a big house owned by a retired pilot. A few weekends into the fall semester, I flew up to Sacramento to help her load her clothes and appliances, my old books and toys, a few pieces of furniture, and the rest of our household goods into the back of a U-Haul. I drove the truck south on I-5, and my mom trailed in the silver Mercedes, her first time driving the freeway. She gripped the wheel high and tight as our humbled convoy swept past the orange groves, oil rigs, and speed traps.

CHAPTER 8

MOVING

For as far back as I can trace, my family found blessings through movement. Juan Fernandez left Spain as a young soldier from a modest family, and within a decade on the Islands married a Maranao princess, Emilia, and obtained lakeside farmland. Their oldest daughter, Luisa, went on to wed Jose Concepcion, who left his family's rigid aristocracy in Luzon for the more adventurous climate of Mindanao and rose to postal commissioner of a U.S. Army base. The eldest Tianco, who changed his name and fled Luzon after Andres Bonifacio's execution, rode out the war against America far from the action, in the Visayas, then Mindanao, and his son went on to work for the colonial government and own fruit fields. Rizalina, Manuel, Caridad, and Tomas, all born in Dansalan, decamped to Manila for the schooling that launched them toward professional success. Rizalina and Manuel would have stayed a step ahead of martial law too, had it not been for the car crash that delayed the family's exodus from the Philippines. They knew to move. Their misstep was staying too long.

Ṭomas had first gone to Paris in 1960, after two years of saving from his advertising job in Montreal. His plan was to stay for six months,

immersing himself in the city through the summer and fall and attempting to find out if he could make a living as an artist, knowing that if he
couldn't, his advertising career would be waiting for him across the ocean.
He got a room at a boardinghouse across the street from Saint-Germain-
des-Prés church, which he'd recognized from a Maurice Utrillo painting, and around the corner from Les Deux Magots, where Pablo Picasso
and André Gide were regular customers and where on James Baldwin's
first night in Paris he had dinner with Richard Wright. Tomas sipped
wine at sidewalk cafés, browsed books at the wooden stands along the
Seine, and strolled through museums as slowly as his legs could manage
while he examined paintings and sculptures he'd long studied from afar.
Each day filled him with inspiration and enlightenment. Not once, though,
did he touch a canvas. When it was time to go back, he felt he hadn't given
himself a chance. Six months wasn't enough. He gave notice that he would
not be returning to his job.

Tomas was all in on Paris until winter set in. He took a train to Mar-
seille, where he spent a few days before continuing on to Rome, "guided
by romanticism like a butterfly," he wrote in his memoir. He spent most
days, morning to night, at the Piazza di Spagna, sitting on the steps at
the base of a sixteenth-century church, watching people, painting them,
and selling his work. "It is full of people," he wrote, "but I see few foreigners like me." Tomas wondered if he was the only Filipino in all of
Italy. He had gone farther across the world than any of his Island-born
ancestors. The distance stirred in him not so much homesickness as
pride at the ground he'd covered.

It helped, of course, that the new place reciprocated the embrace.
After a month exploring the city alone, he encountered an old friend, a
musical composer whose portrait he'd painted in Montreal. He joined
the composer's social circle and soon was spending three nights a week
at a popular nightclub whose owner always gave them a table near the
dance floor. The new friends "are curious about me, this dark man from

the East, and they want to know about my life," he wrote. "What can I tell them? I say I am a painter and their interest heightens—my being an artist seems somehow significant to them. They are curious about my exoticness. I am definitely an aberration in this town. While we dine I tell them about myself. My new friends remind me of children excited to hear a fable."

One morning, Tomas sat on the Spanish Steps reading letters from the Philippines and leafing through the *Philippines Herald*. As he recalled, "A short man, plump with a friendly face, unexpectedly turns toward me and says in English: 'You want to make a movie?'" The man took him to a dimly lit apartment, thick with cigarette smoke, to introduce him to a director, Federico Fellini.

"Do you sing?"

"Yes."

"You will sing in my film."

Fellini was so taken by the young brown man's striking appearance— his intense eyes, high cheekbones, and chiseled jaw—that he cast him as an extra in three scenes of *La Dolce Vita*. Only when Tomas arrived on set did he learn that his role "involved more than singing," as he put it. He "had to also dance, dressed in gold leaves, in net-like tights, while wearing a Thai pagoda and a Chinese mask." He suddenly understood why his services were in demand. His other roles in the film were as a pimp and as an American sailor who dances the "boogie woogie" with Magali Noël. Next, for a movie called *Adventures of the Tropics* that was never finished, he was hired to play the son of a native tribal chief on a generic South Pacific island. After that, he played the son of Genghis Khan. The jobs paid well and opened doors to high society and wealthy patrons eager to have their faces immortalized on canvas. His commissions granted him the financial stability to buy an art studio and pursue his own projects, the work that would earn him exhibitions in Paris, London, New York, and Palm Springs and contracts for public statues in

Jerusalem and Los Angeles. Caridad was his publicist and joined him on trips. He gained renown for his bronze sculptures of figures in motion, dancing, sunbathing, throwing a javelin, capturing the "rhythm, movement, and the lyricism of the human body," as he put it. One American art columnist described him as "a modest artist but considered genius."

One day, an art collector introduced Tomas to a potential client, Count Sebastiano Bonmartini, whose family had owned land in the region for six centuries, stretching back to the time of the Medici dynasty. Over hours of portrait sessions, the men became close. Sebastiano invited Tomas to Bonmartini family gatherings in opulent dining rooms and on countryside terraces, and to his castle villa sixty miles north of Rome. A society column chronicling one of the lavish parties listed Tomas among the notable guests and recounted "liveried footmen in tail coats and knee britches," "walls covered with leather," and "60 foot high ceilings, ornately encrusted with gold." The Bonmartini clan's dominion seemed unbroken by time and cemented in place, layers upon layers of shared past, never having to start over from scratch even as borders shifted and flags changed, durable as a bronze bust. I imagine the dream of every immigrant disembarking on new soil was to pave that first layer in the hopes of building something so permanent.

Tomas had stepped into a realm removed from the choppy tides of colonial conquest. History seemed to move slower and stretch further back before dissolving into the forgotten past. Art born on this land lived longer. As he approached forty, a decade into his Roman dolce vita, Tomas eased into an idyllic existence. Now fluent in Italian, he sipped afternoon cappuccinos and capped off meals with limoncello but also cooked pancit and adobo for luminaries who passed through the city, their Ferraris, Maseratis, and Lamborghinis lining the block. Josephine Baker, Silvana Mangano, and King Constantine II of Greece were among the guests at his Sunday dinner parties. A Marlboro Red in one hand, a glass of red wine in the other, Tomas held court with stories about Saint Xavier's slipper forming Lake Lanao, his grandmother Emilia healing patients cursed by engkantos, and his mother Luisa convincing the Japanese soldiers that his sister Caridad supported the occupation. The Islands were an indelible part of him. He visited Manila at least once a year, often for art shows, and spent evenings in his studio writing letters to loved ones there before starting his late-night sculpting sessions.

When Marcos declared martial law, Tomas immediately returned to the Islands. He joined the underground resistance, meeting in secret with Cory Aquino, wife of imprisoned senator Ninoy Aquino. His eldest sister, Mary Concepcion, who lived in Manila, was also a member. Tomas slipped in and out of the country for five years until he learned he'd been targeted for arrest. Back in Rome, as chairman of the Movement for Free Philippines' Italy bureau, he organized the rising number of Filipino workers in the country into a labor union and chastised friends who praised Imelda Marcos for her glamour. He delivered a speech to the UN Commission on Human Rights urging "rich industrialized and developed nations to desist from extending any form of aid and assistance, be they economic or military, to the present morally-bankrupt authoritarian dictatorship form of government in my country." In magazine interviews, he called attention to the oppression of Mindanao's Muslims. His Sunday dinners now hosted union meetings. After the Aquinos were exiled to the States, Tomas met with them, usually over breakfast in New York City, whenever he was in the country for art shows.

Wracked by the anxiety of troubling times with no end in sight, what else could he do but keep working? Commissions for bigger projects came in. He sculpted a bronze statue of Pope John Paul II in Guam, then did Pope Paul VI in Rome, working through the nights to meet deadlines. His art in this period reflected his radical turn. His sculpted figures were no longer in joyful, recreational motion but frozen in toil and yearning. His 1982 exhibit in New York featured twenty-five sculptures of prisoners in various states of entrapment. After Ninoy Aquino was shot dead at the Manila airport in August 1983, Cory chose Tomas to memorialize the leader in bronze.

FOR MORE THAN A DECADE, Ferdinand had been careful to neutralize Ninoy, his greatest threat. Six years after arresting him, the dictator allowed the senator to run for office from his cell but rigged the vote. When Aquino suffered a heart attack in 1980, Marcos released him to seek medical care in the United States, avoiding the backlash that would have resulted from a popular politician dying in federal custody. Marcos's only condition was that Ninoy stay away from the Islands indefinitely. Ninoy led the opposition from Boston, where he was a visiting professor at Harvard, and called on President Reagan to withhold economic aid from Marcos. But Reagan stuck with Marcos through the fraudulent elections of 1981 and the widespread protests that followed. To tip the resistance movement into a critical mass and lead it on the front lines, Ninoy decided to return to Manila. His supporters prepared for his arrival by tying yellow ribbons all over the city. On the flight in, he spoke openly about the possibility of getting killed. As news cameras rolled, he exited the plane, descended the stairs, took a few steps onto the tarmac, then, at the crack of gunfire, fell to the ground bleeding, a martyr dying on international television.

Within hours, the government blamed a Communist assassin, though the accused man had no chance to explain his motives because soldiers killed him on the spot. An investigation years later cast doubt on the official conclusion but wasn't able to prove who was behind the conspiracy. It remains a mystery who orchestrated the plot, though there are no shortage of theories accusing Imelda's kin, high-ranking members of the military, or a cousin of Cory who'd turned against the Aquinos—by the time of the assassination, Ferdinand was severely ill with lupus, so circumstantial evidence might suggest a mastermind seeking to eliminate the competition in the race to succeed the ailing dictator. The most obvious suspect, Ferdinand himself, might be an implausible culprit, based on what we know about his political savvy: surely, he would have predicted that such a brazen and brutal act would galvanize all who opposed him, jeopardizing his reign more than any speech his rival could give. The People Power Revolution rallied behind Cory, elevating her to standard bearer. On the one-year anniversary of Ninoy's death, hundreds of thousands of people marched across Manila, decked in yellow, and gathered at the airport to witness the arrival of Tomas's statue.

When Ferdinand Marcos attempted to claim victory over Cory Aquino in the 1986 election, a sea of protesters filled the streets, election officials walked off the job, and top military officers resigned. Eventually even Reagan advised Marcos he had no choice but to step down. The deposed ruler stashed whatever treasures he could and fled the presidential palace by helicopter, another drop in the exodus. Marcos spent his exile in Hawaii, where he died from lupus in 1989. Without bloody battles or chaotic successions, the Philippine people had toppled a dictator and restored democracy. Tomas celebrated with hundreds of other Filipino expats outside the Philippine embassy in Rome.

THREE DECADES LATER, Tomas was at the embassy mourning Cory Aquino's death. He walked with a cane, shuffling slowly in his white pants, and his hearing was poor, so the old friends and young officials greeting him had to shout their respects. I trailed him with a notebook in hand, trying to stay out of the way while scribbling down every word I could catch. At twenty, I lacked the ear filter of a seasoned reporter and couldn't begin to know which details would be important once it was time to capture the scene in writing. To that point, most of my published stories covered Manny Pacquiao, the rising boxing star from Mindanao who had ignited a surge of cultural pride in me and my Filipino American friends. We'd split the pay-per-view TV bill and watch his fights, decked out in shirts and bandannas bearing the sun and stars of the Philippine flag, shouting "Mabuhay!" when his opponents fell to the canvas. Maybe pride naturally spurs curiosity, or maybe I was just self-conscious about so loudly repping a country I hadn't seen since I was six years old, but it was around the time Pacquiao became world welterweight champion that I began to feel a desire to learn more about the place my elders had left.

The Filipino community weekly newspaper I freelanced for didn't pay, much less cover any expenses, so I made it to Rome with the help of my dad's child support payments and the heavily discounted plane tickets my uncle Spanky could access as an airline employee. My idea was to follow my granduncle around in the days after Cory's death and ask him about his memories of the revolution, something like a profile of an unsung participant. I had primitive notions of Philippine history, could list names and dates of the People Power era but little else before or after. The Marcoses were villains who made the country worse in 1972, the Aquinos were heroes who made the country better in 1986. The revolution was a triumph that filled me with pride for my distant association. My grandparents had resisted the corruption, my granduncle Tomas had joined the effort to topple the regime, and my grandaunt Mary was on the commission tasked with tracking down the money Marcos hid around the world. I imagined tales of narrow escapes and clandestine debates, a thrilling crescendo.

But Tomas couldn't think about that period without shifting his gaze to the frustrating aftermath. At his villa, sipping wine in the afternoon glow, holding forth on Philippine politics, he'd bang his fist on the rusty patio table, though somehow never hard enough to knock the drooping ash from his cigarette. "The corruption remained!" His baritone carried across the yard and over the stone walls as he picked up steam. "Filipinos must no longer be exploited!" Six years after the revolution, Tomas had returned to the Philippines, appointed by newly elected President Fidel Ramos to be a special congressional representative for overseas Filipino workers. They continued to pour out of the country, more each year, finding low-wage service jobs in richer places on terms that often left them vulnerable to abusive employers. Tomas's job was to hear their complaints, lobby for stronger legal protections in foreign countries, and represent their interests in the legislature. He learned that the insurance coverage the Philippine government provided its bagong bayani was so limited that some ended up stranded in war zones because they couldn't afford transportation out. A congressional investigation into his queries revealed that the insurance companies bribed the secretary of labor for government contracts and that the secretary of foreign affairs was complicit. Both resigned. Marcos and his cronies were no longer there to hog the country's spoils, but other aristocratic families jostled to fill the vacuum, maintaining the order in place since the colonial years. Farms deteriorated further, cities got more crowded, and new opportunities rarely trickled down beyond those with fluent English and a college degree.

My granduncle traced the histories my understanding lacked. He introduced me to our sultanic ancestors, explained the roots of the ongoing Moro resistance in Mindanao, and gave me a book about U.S. support for Marcos (Raymond Bonner's *Waltzing with a Dictator*). The subject of his most passionate lecture was the sovereignty of Sabah, a large peninsula on northeast Borneo, just off the tip of the Sulu archipelago. The land—about twice the size of Switzerland and rich in petroleum, copper, zinc, lumber, cacao, and palm—had once belonged to the Sultan of Brunei, who gifted Sabah to his cousin in Mindanao, the Sultan of Sulu, in gratitude for the latter's help in quelling a rebellion in 1703. Generations later, in 1878, the Sultan of Sulu leased Sabah to the British on a ninety-nine-year contract in exchange for the advanced weapons he needed to combat Spanish invaders. Eighty years into the lease, in 1957, Britain granted independence to most of its Southeast

Asia territory, including Sabah, which became part of the newly formed Malaysian Federation. The Philippine government disputed Britain's right to determine Sabah's sovereignty and declared a legal claim to the peninsula, to no avail. The will of the empires won out as usual. Tomas believed the Philippine government should prioritize reclaiming Sabah, through diplomatic means if possible, violence if necessary.

"All that for a strip of land? What difference would it make?"

"Filipinos have to fight for what was stolen."

The catalogue of theft is long and ancient—wealth, land, sovereignty, history, and life lost to colonizers and their allies. Theft fueled the empires, improved the lives of their people, and set the course for the global order that remains in place today. Names, currencies, and borders reflect the desires and compromises of colonizers. The powers of the imperial age remain among the world's richest economies and most influential governments, while the territories they conquered clean up the pollutants, corruptions, and inequalities left behind.

What do the world's colonists owe the colonized people whose suffering paid for their luxuries? Certainly much more than they have been willing to give. Until the debt is paid, the imbalances of the colonial order live on. Tomas believed the first step toward leveling the scales was to reject the terms of the colonizers. Taking back Sabah wasn't about gaining natural resources or serving the will of ambivalent locals but reversing a pattern of passivity and resignation hardened over four centuries. A solid strike against the colonial mentality that infected our minds, to varying degrees.

The Philippine ruling class took after the Americans they admired, conjuring money out of thin air, gobbling up as much as they could, building wealth without lifting fingers. José Rizal had theorized more than a century ago that a collective mythology was necessary to unite the fragmented archipelago into a singular people. Since then, the Islands have accumulated martyred heroes and epic tales, yet the nation's defining ideals reflected only the capitalism and Christianity passed down from coloniz- ers. The aristocracy running the country answered only to the old order that had brought them to power. Tomas often punctuated his stories about political rivals with "They don't care about the workers!"

THERE WAS A TIME in Tomas's life when he'd been eager to battle those corrupt aristocrats. But in his early sixties, when he served in congress, he was at the tail end of those ambitions. In 1995, when his three-year term was up, he returned to Italy. Over the next decade and a half, two Philippine presidents and a supreme court justice would be impeached or arrested on corruption charges. Tomas followed the news, kept in touch with old political friends, and resisted the dwindling urge to jump into the action. By his math, he had spent too many hours of his life in the political arena rather than his art studio.

Though he kept an apartment in Rome, he moved his work to Seba- stiano's villa in Tarquinia, setting up his small table and metal swivel stool near the patio doors that offered a view of sky peeking over the parapets. With hands slick from a dip in the water bucket by his feet, Tomas transformed the soppy gray clay, pushing and pressing with the sides and tips of his fingers, smoothing cheeks, sifting hair, pinching lips. The finished clay pieces were made into molds, then cast into bronze, Tomas's material of choice, a material his Maranao ancestors had once employed. What draws closer to permanence?

The pull of his homeland, the strain of leaving behind troubles for others to deal with, the guilt of attaining a comfort inaccessible to most—it all turned over in Tomas's mind as he shaped the sculpture that would become one of his most acclaimed. *The Prisoner* echoes Mi- chelangelo's marble statues known as the Slaves. Tomas's prisoner is a man leaning backward in anguish, his hands and feet tied behind him, his limbs taut, his face twisted in urgency. The harder the man tries to resist his bindings, it seems, the greater the pain. He fights to escape despite himself. "You know, after all these years I'm still a Filipino citizen," Tomas said during one of our afternoon conversations. "Fifty years I've lived in Italy, and still a Filipino citizen!"

His assistant, Ric, a Filipino overseas worker who lived in a small stone cottage behind the villa, prepared his meals and drove him whenever he had to go out of town, though he rarely left town anymore. With Ric helping him keep steady on his walks around Tarquinia, Tomas shuffled slowly with his cane down the cobblestone streets, the twisting alleys, the sloping town square, past pink and peach buildings with orange-shingled roofs and mahogany doors, greeting white-haired shopkeepers and sun-wrinkled locals reading newspapers at sidewalk tables, tipping his flat cap and booming, "Buongiorno!" His Italian betrayed no trace of his origins. He was so comfortable with the language that he wrote his memoir in Italian. Other than when he was talking to Ric, Tomas rarely had reason to speak Tagalog, especially once his hearing problems made his once-regular phone calls back to the Islands difficult.

His ties to the Philippines were fewer by the year, as loved ones migrated and old friends died. Most of his nephews and nieces lived in the States, where they pursued the stability he'd managed to find by settling farther across the world than anyone else in our barangay. Not everybody could drop into Rome, get plucked off the street into blockbuster films, and live out their dreams in a hilltop villa. A lot of people just want a place to live peacefully, a reasonable job that pays the bills, and opportunities for their children to do the same or more. America's exceptionalism spawned from the promise of being that place for anyone who needed it. Who better to lead the world out of the colonial age than a colony that grew into an empire and welcomed others fleeing tyranny? Who better to reckon with the fruits of oppression than the idealistic democracy whose sins are so brutal and present? Who better to share the wealth than the land that mastered the science of making money? Tomas cheered for America. If there were going to be empires, the world could use one that marched toward worthy ideals.

On the first day of my summer 2009 visit, after we left the Philippine embassy and drove to his villa, Tomas tossed his cap on a shelf and shuffled straight to his work station. Cigarette between his lips, he unbuttoned his shirt, untucked his tank top, and tapped a long pole of ash into the glass tray on his desk. From decades of molding clay, his fingers were slanted at terrifying angles. The tips of his thumbs veered outward, away from the rest of his hand. His other fingers leaned the opposite direction, like lanes curving around the bend of a racetrack.

"I've started a new bronze," he said, pulling the plastic bag off the clay form.

Though the work was not complete, I recognized the face of the forty-fourth president instantly. He'd been working on it for nearly three weeks, he said, and he hoped to send it to Washington, D.C., as a gift to Barack Obama.

After I left Italy, we kept in touch through letters. On yellow-brown parchment that made his messages look like archaeological discoveries, he described the progress on his sculptures and plans for future exhibits in California. "I think I just have too many projects, too many at one time!" he wrote. I told him about my early days in New York City, where I was in journalism school and Javie was interning on Wall Street and we rode out our first humid summer sharing a grimy apartment near Penn Station. When Tomas warned me to "watch your step" while reporting in unfamiliar neighborhoods, he added, apologetically, "I don't mean to be boring." From St. Louis, where I got my first job, I wrote to Tomas about the best barbecue ribs I'd ever tasted, the central boulevard that divided the white and Black halves of the city, and the stretches of vacant, busted-up brick buildings missing walls, like dollhouses. "Study the city carefully," he advised. "Make friends, but choose them well, you will need friends." He sent me photos of his latest clay forms, and I sent him folded-up copies of my newspaper articles, along with breathless testimonies about the lessons I was learning on the job. Often, my missives chronicled my rising frustration about the turn my country had taken in response to Obama's election, the instant backlash and obstructionist opposition party. Worse, I was beginning to feel the effects of my budding ideological divergence with my mother.

The earliest sign of what was to come emerged within weeks of Obama's inauguration, when my mom discovered, from reports on Fox News, that under the president's health care plan, taxpayer money would fund some abortions.

"Is this true?"

"Yes, but—"

My explanations about the wider benefits of universal health coverage couldn't match the weight she placed on the issue she cared about most. Once my mom associated Obama with a tolerance for abortion, he became an enemy to her. By 2010, she was asking me how sure I was that Obama was born in the United States and a Christian, because the people who'd pointed out the abortion policy were raising questions about his legitimacy. The more I pushed back against the false assertions, the more my mom began to suspect that I'd drifted from the course she set. "You're becoming so secular," she'd say.

Living on her own, with me out of the house and many miles away, she had more time to follow world events, watching and reading news on her laptop. She never stayed in any one place for long during this period. After living in the in-law unit in San Diego for a month, she got a job as a home caretaker for a bedridden elderly woman who offered her the use of her house's attic studio, which had an electric stove, a bathroom, and lots of natural light. My mom's plan was to return to real estate whenever possible. Six months later, deciding she'd have a better chance in familiar territory closer to her networks, she moved back north, renting an apartment in Benicia, just east of Vallejo. She found work at a call center in the East Bay, then as a nursing assistant in Walnut Creek. To shorten that commute, she moved to Concord, where her apartment was smaller than the one in Benicia but closer to a grocery store. Her income covered necessities but left no margin for unexpected expenses, like car repairs and parking tickets. She bought a compact silver Hyundai and sold her Mercedes. Three years into her nomadic purgatory, she decided to move in with her brother, my uncle Marlon, who had two spare bedrooms in his house in Vallejo.

The last of his siblings to arrive in the United States, landing in 2001, Marlon worked as a nurse at the county jail, a job as stable as it was stressful. My mom had developed a taste for living alone, the silence and sovereignty of it, but removing rent from her monthly bills opened up prospects that would've been impossible otherwise. She found commission-based jobs selling condominiums in the Oakland hills and newly built homes in Fairfield, staying afloat through lean months, each deal enough to carry her budget for weeks.

I visited every Christmas, and witnessed everybody's gifts becoming more modest, but wasn't around for the family events in between and rarely heard word of the deteriorating financial conditions setting back the elder generation. Aunties and uncles downsized their comforts and revised their expectations. Uncle Bobby defaulted on his condo in Sacramento and moved into a rental in Vallejo. Uncle Spanky and Auntie Ging canceled their plans to retire at sixty-five. My mom and Uncle Marlon exchanged conspiracy theories about liberals backed by an all-powerful cabal of global aristocrats. Only when I moved back to the Bay Area for a job in 2012 did I feel how far the ground had shifted.

The casual weekend hangouts were held in unfamiliar apartments and town houses now. Agreements to split the bill occasionally supplanted our age-old battles to snag the check. Late-night kitchen conversations, once dominated by the question of how to get Uncle Paul to the United States, now included discussions about when to declare bankruptcy, short-sale a house, or pick up a second job. Moving in with Marlon and my mom, I was suddenly right back in the thick of things.

I wasn't planning to stay at the house long, but my $36,000 salary didn't support many options in the area. A Filipino grad school friend and I were searching apartment listings in San Francisco, submitting applications for the few in our price range, meeting landlords and trying to impress them with our advanced degrees, professional credentials, and affable demeanors, just two nonthreatening brown men in H&M slim-fit jeans and oxford button-downs with the sleeves rolled up. But the field was crowded, and months would pass without even a whiff of a lease.

To BEAT the stickiest morning traffic and reach my San Francisco office at a reasonable hour, I was out the door by five thirty with a thermos of coffee and a backpack rustling with notebooks and pens. In the cobalt glow of a highway at dawn, I listened to NPR newscasts but switched to KMEL 106.1 if I felt my eyelids getting too heavy, usually around the time I hit the bottleneck before the Bay Bridge. Our newsroom was near Fisherman's Wharf, in an office building with a terrible parking situation. You could pay fifteen dollars for a spot in the garage for the day or hop-scotch among two-hour-max spots along the road, though you usually had to circle the block a few times before one opened up. I waited out rush hour in the city, working late at the office, reporting in the field, or meeting with friends. I preferred driving through San Francisco at night, when the lights were on and the streets were empty, the cold breeze gusting through open windows, the glassy skyline reflecting brightly in the Bay, the final sight of the peninsula before crossing the bridge.

I followed in the grand family tradition of long, sleepy-eyed commutes. But of course my circumstances were different from those of my elders, cushioned by the soft foundation my family had laid. I had only myself to worry about, no one behind to pull along, and many who'd come before me to prepare breakfast, offer a spare room, manage the family's collective affairs. On my way out of the city, I sometimes stopped by to see Caridad, who was living in the bottom shotgun unit of her duplex now, and renting out the upper floor to tenants. Two months into my stay at Uncle Marlon's, it occurred to me that she had a pull-out futon in her living room, which was about the size of my college dorm room. I asked her if I could stay with her until I found an apartment, and she seemed happy to have the company. The city was no longer our family's center of gravity. Her son, Ricardo, lived in South San Francisco with his wife and kids. My mom, Uncle Marlon, and Uncle Bobby were in Vallejo. Auntie Mae was in Sausalito, north of the Bay Bridge. Auntie Lyn and my cousins Roscoe and Chris were in San Mateo. Jed was in Burlingame, Lauren in Oakland, Mico in Torrance, and Mitch in Long Beach. Auntie Ging and Uncle Spanky were in the city most often, still spending work nights in their Visitacion Valley studio, but they spent their free days at the Vallejo house. Our barangay had sprawled many miles beyond Caridad's original settlement. She had complained to Tomas that "everyone is out of the city," he told me in a letter after learning that I was moving in with her. "Yes, I am happy you are there."

The Fillmore property had served her well. She'd survived the years of vacant lots, and now, in a time of rising rents, the monthly checks she got from her upstairs tenants covered her bills. She spent her days reading the books on her shelf she'd never gotten around to and walking around the city, stopping for lunch at old vinyl-coated diners and Chinese restaurants with big round tables and aquariums along the walls. In the evenings, she danced to swing music at the Tonga Room. She got married in her seventies, to a man she'd known in the war years and unexpectedly encountered at a veterans' hall in the city, but when he died in 2010, she felt alone in the city once more. She was having some problems with her tenants, who against her wishes had nailed up a plywood wall across the living room and subleased the makeshift "bedroom" to a third occupant, in a bit of San Francisco housing rush opportunism. Caridad joked that she hoped the men would think she was bringing in a younger relative to try to intimidate them.

The downstairs unit was a cramped fit for two people, and to get to the bathroom I had to go through Caridad's room, but her hearing was as bad as Tomas's, so there was no risk of waking her in the middle of the night. Now I had a place to park my car and could take the bus around town and stay out till last call with the peace of knowing I didn't have to be alert and moving at five thirty in the morning. It felt like progress.

MY GRANDMA RIZALINA never stopped moving. Over her decades in the United States, she stayed with each of her daughters at various points and spent months at a time in the Philippines, checking on the farm and visiting her son Paul and husband Manuel. She was sorting through files in an office in Mindanao when she died in 2010. The memorial was in a cathedral in Oakland. For the first time in fourteen years, Manuel flew to the States. He stayed at Uncle Marlon's house, in the guest room at the end of the upstairs hallway. For months, he grieved, reminisced, joked, and feasted with his children and grandchildren, until one night, he died in his bed. His body would rest beside Rizalina's in Oakland, together in America at last. I moved into Marlon's guest room weeks later. The following year, shortly after I moved in with Caridad, Tomas died.

With his death, the castle villa property returned to Sebastiano's family, and our family had to figure out what to do with all of Tomas's work and possessions. Though he'd lived in Italy for fifty-three years, he had no blood there. Halfway around the world, dozens of sculptures and scores of paintings—about a hundred pieces in all, by Roscoe's

count—waited for us to decide who got what, determine whether anything should go to a museum, and pack and ship each item back to the
States. A small contingent of uncles, aunties, and cousins with vacation
time available spearheaded the mission to sort through the contents of
the villa. When they returned, we gathered at Caridad's place to page
through the papers and photos they brought back.

Sometimes the universe aligns with divine precision. As Caridad
navigated the legal process of evicting her tenants for violating their
lease, Jed and his girlfriend were looking for a place big enough to move
in together. Caridad's duplex was two blocks from the hospital where he
worked, the upstairs unit had plenty of space, and our grandauntie was
eager to have tenants she could trust. The old tenants left, but just as Jed
was starting to pack, he and his girlfriend broke up. We both recognized
that I was an unwitting beneficiary of his heartbreak: he needed someone to split the rent. Though Caridad had offered the two-bedroom unit
at a below-market family rate of $1,800, Jed's budget had to account for
$80 haircuts, $200 Air Jordans, and annual trips to the Burning Man
festival. The second room was mine.

From the beginning, our cohabitation felt charmed. In the fall, we
hopped bars by the ballpark to watch the Giants win the World Series,
in the winter we hosted a Super Bowl party to watch quarterback Colin
Kaepernick and coach Jim Harbaugh bring the 49ers within five yards
of a title, and in the spring we shouted ourselves hoarse at Oracle Arena
as Steph Curry led the Warriors to playoff victory. Sports had always
been a primary ingredient in the glue bonding us. We'd leaped out of
our upper-deck seats together as Garrison Hearst sprinted for a ninety-
six-yard overtime touchdown, jeered at the pitchers who walked Barry
Bonds rather than risk his smashing the ball into the Bay beyond the
outfield fences, driven from San Diego to Las Vegas to watch Manny
Pacquiao fight Oscar De La Hoya. We'd ridden the thrilling crests of our
fandom, like Pacquiao's string of thunderous knockouts, and weathered

its painful crashes, like the Giants' 2002 World Series Game 6 collapse and the long stretches of the pitiful Warriors at the bottom of the standings, with gallows humor and a stubborn faith that better days would come around. Now that we were both grown, living together in the sliver of our overlapping young adulthoods, our joint emotional investments suddenly rewarded us with an absurd windfall, a state of revelry that seemed to stretch before us indefinitely. We pushed aside our awareness that the blessings could not be permanent, glad not to know how it would all end one day—Manny knocked out cold, Kaep blacklisted, Klay Thompson tearing knee and Achilles. We cherished our good fortune while we had it. How blessed we were that our migrating elders hadn't landed anywhere else.

On the final night of 2012, I wandered the city our barangay had long strived for, taking in its luxuries. I grabbed a burrito down the street from the duplex, dropped by a friend's house in the Lower Haight for beers and joints, surprised Jed on his shift at the hospital to toast juice cups, then made my way through Polk Gulch and across the Marina, past tearful couples arguing outside bars with three-figure cover charges, and finally into Fisherman's Wharf. At a restaurant at the edge of the pier, Uncle Spanky and his band, a quartet of sixtysomething Pinoys who called themselves The Young Once, performed '60s rock covers for three dozen or so titos and titas, who sat at tables swaying enthusiastically, clapping to the beat. From her chair near the front, Auntie Ging sang along.

Spanky and his buddies had been jamming in a garage for years but only recently started doing weddings, birthdays, class reunions, '70s-themed bar nights, New Year's Eve celebrations. Sometimes crowds requested he sing the songs they knew him best for, and though Spanky thought it inappropriate to play VST hits with his new band, he was touched by the apparent demand for his old music. He and a few VST members in the States, including two of his brothers, began organizing reunion shows in Filipino enclaves across the country, drawing audiences bigger than they expected. Between his new band and his old one, Spanky was soon filling his off-days with two or three gigs some months.

Though his crowds were not as big as they once were, and his hips didn't sway as swiftly as they once did, and his pay barely covered the band's expenses, Spanky jammed like the rock star he'd always been, pointing and ad-libbing and tilting his guitar during solos. We drank Coronas during his break, then watched the fireworks over the Bay.

WITH HER POOR HEARING, Grandauntie Caridad rarely noticed our cheering or our cacophonous parties, but from upstairs we could hear the orchestral scores and florid dialogue of old Hollywood movies blaring from her bedroom TV. Jed and I would try to figure out what she was watching. As new inhabitants in her long-standing domain, we didn't want to disrupt the ecosystem she'd built, except to be helpful whenever possible. Taking out the garbage. Moving heavy potted plants. Offering a ride somewhere. One morning, when Jed was about to get into bed after a night shift, he saw a plume of smoke out the window. He raced downstairs in his bare feet, burst out the door, into the yard, and there was the fire, blazing inside a metal bucket, and there was Caridad sitting on a folding chair, burning old bank statements and voided checks. "Oh Jed, there's no need to be alarmed!" She'd done it for years in that very spot, between the trees and the garbage bins. He bought her a paper shredder the next day.

When she died in spring 2013, my cousins, Uncle Bobby, and I carried the casket, and in the eulogy, I told the stories of her close calls during World War II, the determination she carried into her migration, perhaps the reason so many of us were gathered in South San Francisco on that overcast morning.

She had purchased the first piece of property our family ever owned in America and held on to it long enough to pass it on to others. Her daughter-in-law, our auntie Donna, was our new landlord, and with the bottom unit open, my mom moved in, beginning her longest stretch of residency since the housing crash. After I left San Francisco for a job in New York, Lauren stayed in my old room for a while, then got an apartment in East Palo Alto with a friend. Soon, Jed was married and had a baby, and the upstairs unit filled with plush animals and wooden blocks of the sort that had once carpeted the Vallejo house.

Uncle Bobby had two kids, my cousin Mico had a daughter. With the new generation, America officially became the land of our descendants. It wasn't the promised land the elders had envisioned but a broken place locked in a war to fix itself, a country of boom and bust, invention and theft, indulgence and brutality. Holding it all together were imperfect but credible institutions, a standard of living decent enough to keep people from revolting, and a general sense that everyone had a fair chance to vote on the solutions. Better than most alternatives.

When our family gathered in Vallejo for a nephew's baptism in June 2016, our afternoon-long discussion centered on the state of the Philippines. Out on the patio with my uncles, three beers deep, I expressed dismay: Rodrigo Duterte had been elected president a month earlier, and already his war on drugs had killed more than a thousand people. Most of them were poor. Many had committed no crime other than buying or using illegal intoxicants. Some were just in the wrong place at the wrong time. I called the president a tyrant, a new Marcos. To my surprise, my uncles on the patio, my aunties in the living room, and my mom at the kitchen counter all loved Duterte—his fight against corruption, his aggressive foreign policy agenda, his promises to uproot the old order. I couldn't believe it. I decided, in that moment, that it was my responsibility to shift our family back toward righteousness. I dropped statistics on the rising death count and news reports on the human rights groups calling the president a mass murderer. I cited the commandment about not killing, reminded them of the parents and children of the victims, and recounted our bloodline's history of defending the rule of law against authoritarian excess. As if channeling Tomas, I raised my voice, flailed my arms, stood up from my chair. My uncles met my indignation with restraint and calm.

"Albert, you make good points," Uncle Spanky said, "but you don't understand."

"What's there to understand about extrajudicial killing?" I said. "The courts should determine guilt and punishment."

"The courts are corrupt," said Uncle Joey, who was visiting from Australia. "The judges cannot be trusted."

"Then the answer is to fix the courts," I said. "To reform the system, not to go around it."

"Albert," said Uncle Bobby, still calm, still sitting, still swirling the beer in his bottle like he had all the time in the world to hear me out. "You're from America. It's different here."

"You don't understand what it's like in the Philippines," said Uncle Joey. "Duterte is just what the Philippines needs." He went on about the renewed hope he felt for the country, the faith he had in this leader bringing tears to his eyes.

Until that June day, I hadn't thought deeply about my distance from the Philippines. It existed in photos, memories, and boxing matches, so I took for granted an intimacy with the place that had long dissolved. The realization sparked an idea for a story that I began working on, to try to understand what circumstances could drive people to willingly pledge their loyalty to an authoritarian, and I planned my first trip back to the Philippines in twenty-two years.

MY MOM MET ME in Taipei wearing a royal blue blazer-skirt combo and holding a book with Donald Trump's face on it. She always dressed fancy for flying. As we waited at the gate for our connecting flight to Manila, she showed me the other books she had in her purse, including a small hardcover edition of the U.S. Constitution.

Finally a U.S. citizen, she'd voted for the first time in 2016. Her support for Trump caught me off guard. She'd begun the campaign season backing Ted Cruz, for his aggressive Christianity and staunch anti-abortion stance. She found Trump vulgar. "Bastos naman," she'd say of his womanizing and crude remarks. But when he was all that was left on the Republican side, her grudging support quickly hardened into loyalty, a process accelerated by her rising antipathy for Hillary Clinton, who was at the center of apparent scandals filling my mother's email inbox and YouTube recommendations. Bolstered by an expanding far-right media ecosystem supplying disinformation about the candidates, she elevated Trump from a noxious necessity to a decent man who'd made mistakes in the past but found his way, a modern-day Saul.

"Trump is not a perfect man. God chose him to serve His purpose," my mom texted me. "The prophets have said Trump is anointed. God is using him to finally end the evil doings of the cabal which has hurt humanity all these centuries. . . . We are in a war between good & evil."

In that war, she considered silence complicity, so she evangelized, in drawn-out phone calls with loved ones, rote interactions with strangers, and Twitter posts bursting with hashtags. Where I saw a dangerous rise in worldwide authoritarianism, she saw incorruptible saviors strong enough to overturn the corrupted order.

"You will see!" she'd say. "All in God's time."

She was officially with me on the reporting trip as my translator, and unofficially eager to take care of some business while she was on the Islands. She'd brought a thick folder of old cases that her father, Manuel, had never been paid for, in case we had time to try to track down the clients. She had to check in on her brother Paul, to make sure he'd been getting all the money his siblings were sending. And she held on to a faint fantasy of one day buying, renovating, and managing her mother's farm, which her cousins on the Tianco branch of the family were planning to sell.

We packed a dense itinerary into two weeks, more than a dozen big and small cities from the northern tip to the southern edge, for interviews with vendors, farmers, professors, drivers, politicians, cops, writers, business owners, lawyers, dentists, and anyone else we encountered. My mom's eager warmth and talent for phrasing hard questions in a way that sounds totally innocent made her an exceptional translator. When we visited Ilocos Norte, Marcos's home state, I worried she'd let her tongue slip and talk some shit, but she kept her wits, maintained an air of naive curiosity, and had our driver going on about how Marcos was a great leader who took care of his people, why, he'd built the very bridge we were crossing.

So highly revered is Marcos in Ilocos that the region boasts three museums dedicated to his life. His mother's old home, where he was born, is a shrine to the humble rural beginnings of the first Ilocano president. His father's old home, where he grew up, honors his meteoric rise from the top of his law school class to the halls of government. The lakeside mansion constructed during the height of his power, nicknamed "Malacañang of the North," showcases the highlights of his reign, displaying a collection of carefully selected truths. As we wandered through the exhibits, my mom playfully questioned the museum tour guides, feigning ignorance, shooting me wry smiles when they answered with canned lines of propaganda. "How can they believe all this?" she whispered to me.

It was all laughs until we got to the exhibit about Marcos's war medals. The placard on the wall, and the tour guide before us, repeated the lie that Marcos had been the most decorated soldier in the nation's history. There in front of us, two of the World War II medals he'd claimed hung in gold-framed glass casing. My mom was incensed. She took photos, determined to capture evidence of this injustice. She began in-terrogating the guide, attempting to hide her anger beneath a fake sheen of awe.

He really won all these medals? Where did they come from? How do you know he won all these medals? Did they tell you he won these medals?

Her cover was slipping. The museum guide, a skinny college kid working this part-time job for some side money, stuttered something about the "controversy" over the medals, and before the exchange could spin out of control I jumped in with a softball question to change the subject.

My mom was still fuming after we left the museum.

"That is not right!" she said. "How can they spread these lies? Why doesn't anybody correct this? How can they do this? These Marcoses are so shameless!"

Our trip triggered for my mom reminders that seemed to validate our family's decision to settle in the States. She expressed astonishment at the jumbled traffic, pity for the young children selling fruit by the road, sympathy for her old friends who had dreamed of coming to Amer-ica but never made the move. When our cabdriver in Manila told us that a cop had pulled him over earlier and threatened to give him a ticket if he didn't hand over some cash, my mom whispered to me, "See, that's why I left."

In between those moments, we experienced the luxuries the country had to offer. Our dollars went a long way toward waterfront hotels, ex-travagant feasts, and private drivers with tinted vans. We had kin across the archipelago. A college friend of my mom's who now owned a hotel picked us up from the airport in Manila and took us to lunch at one of the restaurants her parents owned. A classmate from dental school hosted us for several nights at her home, an airy concrete compound with a staff of maids and a plant-filled courtyard that led to her dental clinic, tucked behind a solid metal gate on a narrow side street in downtown Makati, the financial center of Metro Manila. I imagined it as a reasonable approximation of our alternate life somewhere in the multiverse.

On the morning of Good Friday, my uncle Carlos picked us up in a chromed-out white Chevy pickup truck that barely fit down the street. Carlos was my grandfather Manuel's son with the woman who wasn't Rizalina. He was on good terms with our side of the family. He remembered Manuel fondly, appreciated that he provided financial support, and had hung out with Uncle Bobby and Uncle Paul when they were in their teens and twenties. He had a wife and a daughter and ran a business selling audio equipment, which was profitable enough for him to afford a vacation condo in the southern Luzon mountains. We barreled down the highway past empty green fields that stretched to the jungle horizon and north to Pampanga, one of the provinces where men dressed as Christ reenact the crucifixion on Good Friday every year. Good Friday was the most sacred day in my home growing up. From noon to three, the hours Jesus hung on the cross, my mom didn't let me watch TV or read anything other than the Bible. Even now, with me off in my adult life, my mom is sure to text just before noon every Good Friday to check that I am properly honoring the moment.

We didn't hit traffic until we reached the outskirts of the town hosting the ceremony, where people and vehicles funneled into the one-lane road from every angle. Among the stream of people was a procession of shirtless men lashing their backs with whips embedded with razors. Their blood splattered onto the white truck as they passed, limping forward at twice our speed. We arrived early enough to find a parking space in the field behind the viewing area. Across the lot stood dozens of tents bearing the logos of Gatorade and Smart Communications, a local wireless provider. Vendors sold food, drink, religious memorabilia, and umbrellas for shade, an instant purchase once we realized we had two hours to kill in the midday tropic sun. Hundreds of us stood in the field, packed against a railing along the dusty path on which a man dressed as Jesus would carry a wooden cross up a hill.

We were out there maybe half an hour when Carlos suddenly reported he'd secured us chairs in the shade, under the VIP tent closer to the hill. My mom cheered the news, beaming as the security guard exchanged nods with Carlos and waved us into the cool, spacious embrace of improved circumstances.

"Wow, first-class treatment naman! You know the security guard?"

"We're brothers!"

"Ano? What do you mean?"

He explained that they were in a sort of club. They threw parties sometimes and helped out other members they encountered, even if they'd never met them before.

"Ah," my mom said knowingly, "like a fraternity, di ba?"

"Kind of," Carlos said. "Have you heard of Masons?"

He lifted his hand to show a brass ring with triangular shapes. My mom nearly gasped but held it together, discreetly shooting me a wide-eyed look to make sure I was aware.

HERE'S WHAT I WROTE when it was time to fill the blank pages that night:

Early in the morning, two other men had gone up on the hill. Their hands and feet were nailed, and the crosses were raised as their faces twisted in pain. Our crucifixion, though, was the 3 p.m. showing, which felt especially meaningful because it was the hour of Jesus's death.

A few minutes before the hour hit, there was our Jesus carrying the cross up the hill, his legs wobbly, his chest heaving. An entourage of worshippers followed behind him. We all took photos.

Many of these Jesuses were repeat performers. I'd heard the story of one of them, who after surviving a 30-foot fall in the 1980s, after having accepted his imminent death in the long seconds before hitting the ground, decided that the only way to properly thank God was to feel nails pierce his hands and feet on every Good Friday that followed. My mother saw this as an extreme act of faith, a recognition of the immense debt of gratitude we all owe. But I saw something else. I saw a man who had run out of options, a man searching for greater meaning in the new life God had gifted him, a poor man with nothing to give but his pain. Only desperation, I concluded, could drive a person so far.

As our Jesus dragged the cross slowly up the dusty incline, I felt a rush of anticipation. What was going through this man's head? Was he dreading the moment to come? Or was he embracing it, cherishing the purpose it instilled in him as hundreds of us watched under the hot sun?

At the top of the hill, he placed the cross on the ground and laid himself on it, arms extended. His entourage formed a circle around him. We craned our necks to see our Jesus amid the crowd of bodies. He was still. His head tilted back against the wood. His chest rose and fell slowly, as if he were breathing himself into serenity. Several men stood right beside the cross. Their task, I assumed, was to hold our Jesus down in case the pain caused his body to flail. The others in the entourage got down flat on their stomachs. A man went around the circle and whipped them on their backs and on the bottoms of their bare feet. Another man went to the head of the cross and knelt down. I took it that he was in charge of putting the nails in. My heart raced. We waited.

A hush fell over the grounds. Every eye was on the hill. Some in the crowd stood on their toes. Small children sat on shoulders. Birds chirped in the distance. A gust of wind rustled the tents. A few people peeked at their watches—about five minutes to 3. We waited some more.

Eventually, the man in charge of the nailing stood and walked to the edge of the hill and looked over the crowd, into the parking lot, gesturing with his hands. A staticky message came over the radio of a security guard standing next to me: They had forgotten to bring the hammer.

The hour of Christ's death was nearing, two minutes and counting, and a hammer still hadn't come. The entourage gave up and raised the cross, no nails or blood or anguish, just a tired man, his wrists tied to the bars, his feet on a ledge. We took more photos, but it felt like a letdown. Jesus hopped off a few minutes later. The crowd began to disperse. Some went up the hill to take photos. One teenager got up on the cross and posed as Christ.

As the man who played Jesus in the ceremony walked down the hill on the dusty path, a group of onlookers argued about what they had just seen.

"He didn't do the nails!" one man said.

"No, no, he did! They hammered it! You just didn't see it," said another. He pointed at the Jesus, about twenty yards away. "Look, on his hands, there's blood!"

But there was no blood.

SOMETIMES YOU CAN'T HELP what you see. All you can do is try to correct the blurs, tints, and delusions once you catch them. For a while, I understood the sacrifices that bolstered me to be in the moving, in the uprooting and starting fresh, the perilous journey and deceptive destination. I measured the cost of an exodus by the damage wrought on the travelers because I was born into a household of travelers. It was as simple as comparing past circumstances to present, no more mysterious than the games asking you to find the differences between two pictures. The cost to those left behind was more abstract. Any misfortune befalling them could be chalked up to the accumulating troubles that triggered the exodus in the first place.

Growing up hearing about my uncle Paul, the last among his siblings left on the Islands, I'd wonder where it all went wrong for him. Theories abound among my aunties and uncles. My mom and others speculate that his fate had been set by the head injury he'd suffered as a young child, which perhaps rewired his brain in some way. My uncle Bobby posits that their childhood years in Dumaguete, away from their sisters and parents, contributed to a sense of alienation that nudged Paul toward recklessness. They were on the wrong side of their household's unintentional inequities, born too late for the prime stretch when the most expensive schools were in reach, the economy was growing, and their parents were an affectionate young couple. But they were old enough to see the tail end of what they missed, and the sudden inflection point.

Next thing they knew, they were scrunched in the dank, stuffed third-class cabin of a ship with their mother, Rizalina. The trip from Manila to Dumaguete took four days and three nights. Years later, Bobby remembered the sweat in the steamy heat, the sputtering roar of the engine, the smell of vinegary adobo passengers packed for the journey wafting with the minty menthol plumes from countless cigarettes. They slept on cots in pitch dark. "It's like sardines of people," Bobby recalled. "You could get fresh air up on the deck, but once you go back at nighttime, people are sleeping and snoring and you have to be careful not to step on them." It was his first time on a boat, and the violent rocking below deck nauseated him. He made it up the stairs just in time to throw up over the railing and into the choppy sea. The brothers were confused why they weren't staying in the first- or second-class cabins above deck. They spent as much time above deck as they could, until a wave knocked Paul's glasses overboard.

They thought they were just visiting their uncle, a judge who lived in a big house without electricity in the rural highlands of Dumaguete, and realized the move was long term only when Rizalina took them to the local school for an admissions test. They didn't yet know Visayan, so they had to speak English with their classmates and teachers, who didn't know Tagalog. Bobby and Paul were best friends in those years. On a dirt court behind the schoolhouse, they learned to dribble and shoot a basketball, within a few years were known as the best players at the school, and soon after were the first among their peers to dunk. Though Bobby and Paul were dominant on the playground together, Bobby was more serious about the game, joining organized teams that traveled around the region for tournaments. Sometimes Paul snuck on the bus with a bottle of gin to share, and after games kids from all the teams would toast cups, share cigarettes and joints, and pass around pipes for smoking shabu, a crystal methamphetamine shipped in from Japan and mainland Asia. Shortly after their uncle died and Bobby, Paul, and Marlon returned to Quezon City to complete high school, Rizalina left for San Francisco. Then their sisters Ging and Mae followed to the States, their sister Lucy left for Saudi Arabia, and their eldest brother Joey and older sister Lyn left for Australia. By the time their uncle Tomas's bronze Ninoy Aquino statue landed in 1984, it was just the three youngest brothers and their father left on the Islands.

When they graduated from high school, Manuel unveiled to them his grand idea to end the family's financial slide. He'd masterminded it over decades, tinkering with the details in his head, holding tight until he needed to dip into this carefully considered insurance plan. Together, father and sons, they would track down and dig up the treasures buried by fleeing Japanese generals at the end of World War II. The sons could go to college after they struck gold. From his knowledge of Japanese military movements and his conversations with old connections, Manuel narrowed the search down to a patch of mountainside in southern

Luzon. And so, as the revolution was unfolding, the three youngest brothers and their father lived in a cave for months at a time.

They set up tarps over their beds to block the heavy jungle rain, ate rice and meat cooked over a bonfire, and spent their days moving thick mud and hard soil with shovels and pickaxes. Three years into the excursion, with still no sign of treasure and his sons growing restive, Manuel decided to cut his losses, and they all moved on with their lives. Bobby got a basketball scholarship, filling his hours with schoolwork and practice. Marlon left for Japan on a tourist visa and found construction work. Paul found odd jobs and spent most of his time out of the house with his friends. With the dictator's bribery tax no longer in the way, Manuel turned his energies back to his ship-salvaging business, venturing deeper and deeper into the ocean for the rusted steel hulks still waiting beneath the water, four decades after the war. Every day without a big score was another blow to his wobbly bank account.

The knockout blow came not from Marcos, but from perhaps the only force more powerful than him in the Philippines. During an expedition at sea, my grandfather pulled in a massive battleship, a huge score, his white whale. On the way back to land, a storm hit and wiped him out. As if by act of God, he lost everything. Shortly after that, sheriff's deputies evicted our family from the big house on Scout Reyes, repossessing it and everything inside.

Bobby graduated from college around then, a decorated basketball all-star. Professional teams recruited him. He wasn't sure what to do. With most of his siblings gone and the family compound stripped away, he had difficulty imagining a long-term future in the Philippines. Manuel and Paul moved into a smaller house, without exterior walls to protect it or maids to care for it. But to Bobby, every year of staying felt like another year of falling behind. In California, there was a house with spare bedrooms and siblings with jobs. He knew he'd make the plunge sooner or later, so he figured he might as well get a head start.

All through the low-paid jobs of his early years in the States, he avoided thinking about the parallel path he'd left behind. He made new friends and fell into the drug scene, picking up his old shabu habit, though he found the meth in the States much rougher than what he'd inhaled on the Islands. He realized he had a problem when he caught himself getting excited about lighting up during the workday.

As far as I know, nobody in the family had any idea about Bobby's recreational activities at the time. Ever fearful of exposing us to his addiction, he was discreet. He never got high at home, stayed out no later than Jed, and seemed to always be on the couch watching movies with us or on the patio grilling meat. He tried to quit cold turkey a few times but kept reverting to his habit. Eventually he decided he needed to pull himself away from the temptations he'd cultivated in Vallejo, so he moved in with my mom and me in San Francisco in the late '90s, pushed through the withdrawals and urges, and got clean while studying for his associate's degree.

He wanted to study engineering. Though he had a degree in business administration, he believed an American degree would carry him further, and he'd that heard engineers made a lot of money. Within weeks at San Francisco City College, he realized he was too far behind in math, and also that he needed to spend all his free hours working in order to pay tuition. The more hours he worked, the higher the numbers rose on his paycheck, and the less interested he was in school. It took him four years to get his associate's degree. He decided he was done with school after that. He was nearly forty.

After my mom and I moved to Sacramento, he joined us, got a job as a server at a retirement home restaurant, then moved into his first solo apartment, feeling like he was once again starting with a blank slate.

When my cousin Mico landed in California in 2001, the day before his twenty-first birthday, he sought advice from Bobby, who had been just a few years older when he made the transition a decade earlier. Like Bobby, Mico had just graduated from college, harboring vague optimism about the American opportunities his migrating kin had benefited from. In childhood, he'd lived in the Scout Reyes compound with his father and younger sister, Mitch, while his mother, my auntie Mae, laid the groundwork in California. Jed's summer visits had given Mico a peek across the ocean. Jed kept making references to *Star Wars*, which Mico hadn't seen, and was astoundingly good at the arcade pop-a-shot basketball game that Mico had only played a few times. "I didn't know how to talk to him," Mico said years later. Wonder and envy tinged his fantasies about America. As a teenager, he noticed that his American cousins seemed to be growing taller and thicker than him, and he thought to himself, "If only I had the protein in the U.S."

Weeks after graduating from college with an aircraft engineering degree, Mico turned down a well-paid job as an airplane mechanic in Singapore and left for California, landing the day before he turned twenty-one because it was the last day he was eligible to obtain a visa through his mother's U.S. residency. His cousins there, he found, were fully enmeshed in the material luxuries of the richest nation. "You guys had everything," he said. "All this cool stuff. Got Jordans. Perfect life." But when he applied for engineering jobs, he heard back from none.

He later realized that he should have seen it coming. When he turned to his elders, it was clear as a Visayan lake: Uncle Spanky, a rock star on the Islands, was a baggage handler in the States, and Uncle Bobby, the college basketball standout, balanced plates of food for white people who could afford to be served. Legends to Mico, they were now grinding to barely pay the bills. "Who am I as a nobody that can't adjust in the United States?" he couldn't help thinking.

Following Uncle Spanky's trail, he got a job loading bags at the Sacramento airport. This was late summer 2001. A few weeks after he started, 9/11 hit, a lot of people stopped flying, and Mico was laid off.

"I hated my first days in the U.S.," he said. "I kinda felt like pretty much I was left behind. Screw America. Who are you guys?"

He might have gone back if Uncle Bobby hadn't given him some perspective. What Mico needed to know was "you can have your hopes, your dreams, but when you reach America, you have to start from the ground floor."

There seemed to be a lot of jobs in logistics with decent wages, handling the movements of commercial America. So Mico loaded trucks for FedEx, manual labor he'd never imagined doing back in the Philippines. When a management position opened up, his engineering degree gave him a leg up on his peers. He got the promotion, parlayed that into a higher-paying job at another company, a fashion brand, and then moved down to Orange County with his wife, settling into a neighborhood with a good school district for their daughter.

All things considered, life worked out fine for those who moved. After several months at the retirement home, Uncle Bobby found a higher-paying job as a loss prevention officer at Sam's Club, and after a few years, he was promoted to manager and bought a condo. Though the foreclosure hurt, he kept moving up at his job, and by 2012, he earned enough to buy a house in Vallejo, this time with a higher down payment than in the pre-crash rush.

Back on the Islands, Uncle Paul continued to drift. His parents caught him stealing money. Like Bobby, he succumbed to the pull of shabu. He had no ambition to leave, or perhaps succumbed because he had been left behind. Manuel and Rizalina funded his stints in rehab and refused to cut their ties to the Islands until Paul joined us across the ocean. After Bobby left, Marlon returned to the Philippines from Japan. When Paul was jailed for several weeks on charges of drug possession,

Marlon brought him lunch and kept him company every day, handing him bowls of rice and meat through the cell bars. Then Marlon's U.S. visa was approved, and he joined us in California. Manuel moved back to Mindanao, into an apartment in coastal Cagayan de Oro with Paul, and got back to practicing law, mostly land dispute cases, representing tenants who couldn't always afford to pay him. On the southern island, Manuel was closer to his ancestral land, the patch of farm his grandparents Emilia and Juan had owned since the Spanish years, as well as the farm Rizalina managed. But no one in our family had been looking after his grandparents' land, and by the time he returned, local Moros had reclaimed the territory. Rizalina's farm, though still in our family's possession, had become more burden than investment. For better or worse, we had placed our stakes five thousand miles away.

Manuel might have spent his final years knowing he would never make it across the ocean. I can't say for sure. He died before I knew to ask him, just as my grandmother died before I had any sense of her journey. After they were gone, the rest of us had to figure out how to care for Paul. Everyone chipped in what they could. First we hired somebody to look after him. I don't know whether his brain chemistry fueled the addiction, or whether his vices triggered the mental health issues that sent him down a dark spiral. I don't know all the details. What I know is that he suffered from a psychosis of some kind, delusions, invisible forces that pulled him into dangerous situations, like walking down the highway with no destination in mind. He was a handful for his caretakers, argumentative and aggressive, a problem unless he was on certain medications, which we sent money for. Then we learned the caretaker was embezzling our remittances. In late-night kitchen conversations, we debated: The caretaker took a lot of weight off our shoulders, maybe she deserved whatever extra she could get. Our verdict was to send Paul elsewhere. My mom's cousin Earl, the one who'd had his hair shorn by soldiers, the one whose parents took in Bobby, Paul, and Marlon in

Dumaguete, ran a bed-and-breakfast where paying guests could live in nipa huts below coconut trees in the jungle highland. Earl agreed to watch over Paul and let him live in one of the huts.

HERE'S WHAT I WROTE about the day my mom and I visited Paul on our trip in spring 2017:

> Uncle Paul was standing on the side of the dirt road, waiting for us, when we pulled in. He held a mug of black coffee and was dressed in a crisp blue button-up shirt and pressed black slacks. He wore nonprescription glasses with a Batman logo on the side. He was clean now. We hadn't seen him in more than twenty years.
>
> My mom greeted him with a long, loud "Hiii Paaauuul!" but Uncle Paul could muster only a soft "Hi." From the decades of shabu and the pills he now took to keep his mind calm, he was a faint echo of whatever he had once been. Sitting in his small hut, beneath a thatched roof covered in spiderwebs, I asked him many questions, just small talk and family gossip, and he answered them with short, simple sentences. It was like talking to a well-behaved but bashful child. Yet below his numb demeanor I sensed a warmth stirring, bits of his old humanity piercing the surface. He asked me only one question that afternoon: He asked me how my father was doing.
>
> So I told him. My father was doing well. For most of my childhood, I saw him about once a year, but once I moved to Brooklyn, I began to see him more frequently. He had business on the East Coast. We ate steak in fancy restaurants, drank whiskey in five-star hotels, and bonded over politics, history, art, and all that other grown shit. His wife, a fellow industrial engineer he'd married some years earlier, occasionally joined us. I was twenty-four when

my dad told me I had four half sisters. We were in cushy leather chairs at the Plaza Hotel, sometime between Christmas and New Year's, and I had no idea my four sisters were an elevator ride away in a suite somewhere high in the building. He said he wasn't ready to tell them yet because they were young, all under twelve at the time. I wasn't hurt or resentful, I counted my blessings, but I did wonder about the parallel lives my siblings were leading, the what ifs.

The only thing that really pained me was that my proximity to his wealth brought reminders of my mom's backslide. Maybe we would have been better off in Paris, or in Beirut, where my dad and his family lived in an elegant compound. But my mom never seemed fazed. Everything happened for a reason, she said, all part of God's plan. She had a resilient spirit. She saw salvation on the horizon no matter what lay in between.

My mom spoke to Paul like she would speak to anyone else, bubbly and inquisitive. She brought up some of their old neighbors on Scout Reyes. She grasped for their names, which Paul recited quickly and surely, as if they were lyrics to a favorite song. Many of those old friends had also fallen into addiction. Nearly all of them were now dead.

"How lucky we are to still be alive," my mom said, and Paul smiled faintly and nodded.

We took him to Jollibee's, where we ate fried chicken and spaghetti. Afterward, we went to a mall and my mom bought him a T-shirt. He picked one that said "Brooklyn" across the front. When I asked him why, he said he liked the design.

Then we dropped him off, said goodbye, and drove away. "Thank God he has a place to stay," she said. "At least he has a home." The next morning, we flew to Iligan City to visit my grandmother's farm.

———

MY UNCLE PEPO didn't want to take us to the farm. It was too dangerous, he said, and he didn't want me kidnapped on my first trip back to the Philippines after all these years.

Uncle Pepo, my mother's cousin, a dentist of modest means, was the farm's de facto manager because he lived closer to it than anyone else in the family. From his home in Iligan City, a bustling industrial town on the northern tip of Mindanao, the farm was less than an hour's drive up the mountains. Yet even Uncle Pepo hadn't been there in years.

In the Philippines, the dangers vary by region. On the northern island of Luzon, Communist insurgents attacked from base camps hidden in the mountains. In the Visayas, a cluster of touristic islands in the center of the country, military forces warded off an attempted terrorist attack by Abu Sayyaf, a jihadist group pledging allegiance to ISIS. In Mindanao, the threat came from the Islamist rebel groups determined to form an independent state for the country's Muslim minorities. In 1989, the Philippine government granted the rebels partial autonomy over a crescent of land along the eastern coast of Mindanao. The region is a hub of militant activity. Communist guerrillas, Muslim separatist rebels, and jihadist terrorist groups have all made base in the area. The fighting got so bad shortly after our visit that President Duterte declared martial law over the entire island of Mindanao. Uncle Pepo and other locals considered the rebel-controlled land off-limits, and the area just outside its border a danger zone. Our farm sat five miles from that border.

In this danger zone, and even farther into the island, the rebels sometimes ambushed military forces on patrol and bombed electricity towers and churches. To raise funds, they kidnapped—and my American-looking ass dripped with dollar signs.

"What they do is they kill the Filipinos to show they're serious, and hold the Westerners for ransom," Uncle Pepo told us.

But my mom, stubborn as cement, thought her cousin had inflated the risk in his mind. She had visited the farm often when she was young. My mom didn't believe the tensions could have gotten so much worse in the years since. And, she asserted, this was our family's land! Were we simply to abandon it now, because of political tensions that had existed for hundreds of years and would maybe exist for hundreds more? She was persuasive. This might be our last chance to see the farm, she told Uncle Pepo. Dollars go a long way, and maybe she could even accrue enough funds to renovate the property.

The land yielded few crops and was barely profitable. My mom's cousins who remained in the Philippines, all busy with professional careers, wanted the farm off their hands. It was only a matter of time before Uncle Pepo found a buyer.

"I should check on the farm anyway," he conceded.

And so, on the tenth day of our two-week journey through the Philippines, we boarded a gray van with tinted windows and headed up the mountain.

"At least it's safer now that Duterte is president," Uncle Pepo said.

My mom nodded knowingly.

The morning we left for the farm, the island was on red alert and traffic clogged the mountain road. Ahead of us, a long line of vehicles snaked toward the military checkpoint, where guards with machine guns peeked into windows and trunks.

Tensions had been thick all over the Philippines in recent days. Government agencies reported terrorism threats. Security guards checked underneath cars at parking garages in Manila. Masked police forces patrolled mall parking lots. The United States issued a travel advisory discouraging people from visiting the country. At a hotel in Cebu, the biggest city in the Visayas, staff called the police to report that ten men from Mindanao were checking in. A SWAT team arrived, only to discover that the men were actually just government workers in town for business.

Worry was running especially high in Iligan City. A local waterfall, normally a big tourist attraction, was closed to the public because it powered the hydroelectric plant that supplied much of Mindanao, making it a conspicuous target for rebel attacks. "SORRY WE ARE ON RED ALERT STATUS," read a big sign at the gate.

We rolled slowly to the checkpoint. Because we were headed south, out of the city and toward rebel-controlled land, the guards on the road took only a passing glance before waving us through. Across the road, the northbound lanes were at a standstill.

The barricades behind us, traffic cleared and our bulky van chugged up the mountain past thickets of coconut trees and banana groves and wooden shacks. Pepo and our driver, his friend Clelan, seemed on edge, sitting stiffly and silently in their seats at the front. My mom's mood was lighter.

"Will I look like too much of a tourist if I wear this hat?" she asked Uncle Pepo in Tagalog, trying on a straw hat she'd bought at a market.

"No, you'll be fine," Uncle Pepo said. "There won't be many people around once we're on the farm."

"Okay, good," my mom said, before adding with a chuckle, "I don't want it to get us kidnapped."

Nobody else laughed.

Fifteen minutes after we left the checkpoint, Uncle Pepo told Clelan to pull over.

"This is where our land begins," he said.

There was no marker indicating that this portion of land was any different from all the other land we had driven past. Just another thicket of coconut palms and banana groves along the highway. A wooden shack sat under the shade of fat leaves. In front, laundry hanging from a rope between two trees formed a makeshift fence.

I felt a rush of excitement, but by the sullen look on Pepo's face, I could tell he felt differently. I'd barely cracked the door when he said, "Stay inside the van." This was not yet the farm, he said. That was still farther up the mountain. This was just the edge of our land. He pointed to the shack, where an old woman sat on the porch and a teenage boy stood beside her, and said, "They're not supposed to be here."

I felt for those squatters. In a country with astounding economic inequality, and with very limited resources for the have-nots, you scratch for everything in reach. And if you find a patch of unoccupied roadside land, with trees bearing fruit you can sell, you jump on it and build a home. Several of my relatives in the Philippines told me that this mindset is more like a guiding principle—an ethos of taking all you can get away with. People might complain about squatter camps popping up near their neighborhood and politicians skimming off the top, but they have little faith that the rules of engagement will ever change—so what else can you do but play along?

The way I began to understand it, these were not acts of deception, but of tacit understanding, an ongoing state of negotiation beneath the surface of Filipino society. I saw it most clearly every time we drove through chaotic streets crowded with buses and cars and motorcycles. Lanes were meaningless, every inch of space an opportunity for advancement. Drivers zigged and zagged, hustling, but when you cut somebody off, you warned them with a quick honk-honk and they acknowledged you with a honk-honk reply that seemed to recognize that it was all part of the game. There was none of the shouting and steering wheel slamming so common in America. There was no pretense of courtesy on these roads, no expectation that anyone would follow the rules.

It is not so much a selfish mindset as a team-first mindset. People look out for themselves and take care of their own. More than anything else, the Philippines is a collection of family units jockeying for power and wealth at every level of the class hierarchy, from the impoverished strivers to the oligarchs. At the top, you see the same last names running for office now that your grandparents saw decades ago. The three top vote-getters of the 2016 presidential election each had politician fathers.

At a dinner at his home, Felipe Antonio Remollo, the mayor of Dumaguete City in the Visayas, whose father and grandfather were also mayors, told me that politics is the "national sport." Indeed, Filipinos follow the game as they would basketball, well-versed in the names of the players, loyal to the dynasties of their region, antagonistic to their rivals. The biggest rivalry is still Aquino versus Marcos. It persists to this day: Cory's son, Noynoy, was president before Duterte, and in 2016 Ferdinand's son, Bongbong, was runner-up for vice president (which in the Philippines is voted on separately from president).

There wasn't much Pepo could do about the squatters. He told them they had to leave and offered advice on where they could move to, but he knew they were unlikely to go. They had a far greater stake in the land than our family did.

We continued up the mountain until we reached another wooden shack, this one bigger than the last. It was a small general store whose tin roof connected to a small cinder-block house in the back. A family of tenant farmers who worked on our land lived here, Pepo said. The plan was to wait for the head tenant farmer, from another family, who would lead us to the heart of the farmland, which lay still farther up the mountain, through dirt roads that cut deeper into the jungle, across land that didn't belong to us—land where a local face was necessary for safe passage.

When we got out of the car, we were greeted by three barefoot women in headscarves. One offered us a tray of Coca-Colas and chips from the store. Another brought us plastic chairs, which she placed in a narrow dirt alley between the store and the house. The third woman was much older, their mother, and she sat, hands folded in her lap, beside the doorway of the home. The day was sunny with a cool breeze to take the edge off the heat, and from the shade of the alley I could see inside the house, which was dark and sparsely furnished.

The women said they had known our family for many years. When their family first began working on the land, they were the only Muslims for miles. Now, perhaps more than half of the families living on this part of the mountain were Muslim. Most, if not all, had sought to escape the tensions roiling farther south, where jobs were limited and young men were joining the rebels not out of ideology but for stable employment.

The head tenant farmer, Felix, arrived a few minutes later. A short fiftysomething man with a weathered face and a firm handshake, he teased us that of all the days to visit, we had visited on a red alert day. We thanked the three women and turned back to the van, where Clelan had waited with the engine running.

A few feet behind the van, two hard-faced young men sat on a motorcycle, watching us. I did a double take and when I looked again, I saw that the young man in the front of the motorcycle was watching not us, but me specifically. He wore a white shirt, black shorts, and a black hat, and when he turned on his engine, he pulled a black scarf over the bottom half of his face. I quickly looked away and got into the van. Felix hopped in next to me.

Uncle Pepo waved to the young men. He said they were there to escort us to the farm. The motorcycle took off and we followed.

The young men made me nervous. I kept thinking about that guy in the white shirt and his intense, deliberate stare. I wondered if it was a look of resentment—at this young American in his bright green polo shirt, eager for a taste of the authentic Philippine jungle experience, fancy phone filled with photos of slums and banana trees, stories of adventure to share with his affluent friends over forty-dollar bottomless mimosa brunches in New York City, so brave to have ventured through exotic dangers, so cultured to have spent such time in the far reaches of an underdeveloped nation.

Insecurity and self-consciousness do a lot to the brain, and that's the excuse I'm using to explain why, as we drove farther up the mountain, I wondered, fleetingly, if these young men on the motorcycle planned to kidnap me. They were strangers to me, after all, leading us through remote roads that twisted deeper into the jungle. This was their land, and people are capable of wild things when they're desperate.

There was poverty all around us. There had been poverty all around us every day of our trip, juxtaposed against the gleaming skyscrapers and crowded malls and pristine beaches and mountain vistas and unending natural beauties that dominate every square mile of the Philippines. Over the course of those two weeks on the Islands, I drew closer and closer to the realization that the 1986 revolution had been a failure. It had not been a revolution to upend the social order, but a revolution to return the gears of power to the oligarchs who had felt cheated and helpless during the Marcos dictatorship.

Even my relatives who had fought for the revolution and worked in the administration that followed acknowledged this. "Everybody was euphoric," said my uncle Joe Tale, who worked as an attorney for Cory's cabinet. Once they had finally defeated Marcos, they seemed to assume that progress was inevitable. But they had no vision for the country beyond ending the dictatorship. "We weren't thinking about the business of government."

This failure explained why, even outside Ilocos, Marcos was not the universally loathed figure I had assumed he would be. Not long before our trip, the dictator's remains had been moved to the Heroes' Cemetery, to lie alongside the bodies of soldiers and dignitaries—a decision approved by the country's supreme court, despite protests. It was in this climate that Bongbong, Ferdinand's son, ran for vice president, falling fewer than 300,000 votes short of victory. He filed papers for a recount, and, at the time of our visit, there seemed a real chance he might win the appeal and become second-in-command to a seventy-one-year-old president with questionable health and threats of assassination against him. At dinner with Mayor Remollo, I had asked, "So we could be pretty close to another Marcos presidency?"

And the mayor replied, "I don't think that would be such a bad thing."

He added that he still believed Marcos had been the nation's greatest president.

"Sure, he had twenty years to do it, but he accomplished far more than anyone else," he said. "In the Philippines, we need a benevolent dictator."

Thirty years of liberal democracy, he pointed out, had not fixed the country's deep-rooted problems. And while I disagreed with his assessment of Marcos, I had seen no reason to think that the progress since 1986 had been anything more than incremental.

There had been promises of spreading resources outside Manila and the handful of other urban centers, bolstering the agricultural sector, developing the strained farmland that covers much of the country. Instead, the farmland continued to deteriorate, lacking irrigation systems and paved roads—which helped explain why a country with so many farmers remained the world's biggest importer of rice.

Uncle Pepo understood this reality well. The conditions of our family farm made it unappealing to potential buyers. There was its proximity to conflict, of course, but perhaps just as troubling, there was no way to get to the crops by car. A narrow dirt path, accessible on foot or motorcycle, was the sole artery to the main road two miles away—an imposing obstacle to anyone hoping to boost the farm's profitability with modern equipment. Building a road was a nonstarter without government support: The path crossed land that did not belong to us. So our farm remained in the past, tilled and picked by hand.

The young man in the white shirt driving the motorcycle turned up the dirt path and stopped at the top of a hill. He hopped off, and his partner accelerated toward the farm. Clelan parked our van on the shoulder and we stepped out, onto the dirt path. The young man walked down the hill. I saw that he was still eyeing me. He walked toward my mother, glancing at me every few steps.

"Is that Albert?" he said to her.

"Yes," she replied.

"I'm Sargento."

SARGENTO HAD WORKED on the farm all his life. By the time he was ten, he had mastered the skill I'd so admired, of shimmying up coconut trees, machete in one hand, bare feet gripping the rough trunk, twenty or thirty feet in the air, knowing just how to drop the fruit so it didn't crack and splatter all over the grass.

He was born into a family of tenant farmers who lived on our land, but our farm didn't make them much money. They worked the field hard, the three oldest brothers plowing and harvesting, their sister tending to the chickens, goats, pigs, and carabao.

His father, Felix, was well-respected in the area and my grandmother's most trusted worker. She gave the family extra pay when tough times came and, having taught Sargento to read, encouraged his parents to send him to school, covering the cost as she promised. Soon Sargento dreamed of leaving the farm, and my grandmother said that when he graduated from high school, she would pay for the vocational school he hoped to attend. Sargento wanted to become a mechanic and travel the world, working in the United States or Hong Kong or Saudi Arabia, sending back money to his family.

But in 2010, when Sargento was twenty-four and two years away from getting his high school diploma, my grandmother died. He left school and found a second job, enlisting with a private army tasked with guarding the electricity towers from rebel and terrorist attacks. Fire-fights broke out every few weeks. In 2016, seventeen towers in Mindanao were bombed. Sargento worked in fifteen-day shifts, with fifteen days off in between. He made 4,500 pesos, about $90, each month.

By now he had a wife and two kids. His salary was barely enough to provide for them, and certainly not enough to support his parents and siblings. On his days off, he worked on the farm, and during one of those mornings, his father had told him that Rizalina's daughter Lucy was visiting. He remembered my mother, and when he saw the young man next to her, he wondered if this was the same boy he had ridden a carabao with twenty-two years before. He stared hard, trying to match the face before him with the murky image in his memory. He made eye contact, looking for any sign of recognition.

"Is that Albert?"

"Yes."

"I'm Sargento."

My heart damn near burst through my ribcage. Sargento, seeing that I indeed remembered him, smiled. We hugged. Even as we began walk-ing up the trail, we kept patting each other on the back.

On either side of us, thickets of coconut trees forty feet tall seemed to stretch into eternity; it felt like we were ants crawling through tall grass. Sargento and I caught up as we walked far ahead of the rest of the group. After maybe forty minutes, we came to a barren dirt patch. This, Sargento said, was where my grandmother's farm started.

We cut through a thick grove of banana trees, past the pigs feeding in a tub of slop, and came to a wooden shack with an aluminum roof. It was Sargento's family's house. Out front, in a dirt yard encircled by a rickety fence, chickens bumbled around and roosters crowed, their legs leashed to fenceposts so they didn't fight each other.

The vast expanse of the farm surrounded us. Sargento pointed to a patch of yellow grass near the cornfield.

"You used to run around there," he said.

As he showed me around the farm, he recalled the same stories I remembered. He asked me if I still liked coconuts, and when I said I did, he climbed the tree as easily as he had all those years ago. He twisted a coconut off the branch with one hand while his other stayed wrapped around the trunk. I ate at least eight or nine coconuts that afternoon, drinking the juice from the hole he sliced into the top with his machete, scooping the meat with a chunk of husk he'd carved off.

I asked him about Duterte, and he said he liked him, but we didn't talk politics beyond that. There was too much else to discuss. He still hoped to leave the farm. The money was much better overseas.

"I don't want to be a farmer forever," he said as we trudged through the soft dirt along the cornfield. "I want to make my family comfortable."

He planned to go back and finish high school, he said, but he worried about taking time away from working the farm, which would put more strain on his parents and siblings. And anyway, he didn't make enough money to save for vocational school, which he believed he needed in order to get a job overseas. He felt stuck. He had been stuck for years.

After a few hours, it was time to leave. We walked back down the trail slowly, savoring the moment. As we neared the road, he mentioned that he'd felt a heightened responsibility to take care of his family after what happened to his older brother.

Two years earlier, his older brother was killed by thieves who stole his motorcycle. There was no use going to the police, he said. Nobody trusted the police. This part of Mindanao adhered to old traditions of justice. Felix went around the area, talking to people until he learned the names of the three men involved in the murder. He went to the families of the men. Two of the families apologized and offered cash in compensation. A local politician oversaw the settlement. The third suspect, the one whose family did not join the negotiation, was soon found dead, fatally shot. The identity of the gunman is no secret around the area, but I won't be the one to say it out loud.

When Sargento and I parted ways at the farm, we vowed to keep in touch, even though he had no email or Facebook and his early 2000s–model Nokia phone didn't always get reception. I felt guilty as our van rolled down the mountain. The questions I had pondered during my trip—about Duterte, about corruption, about sacrifice—had little bearing on my own life. The farm, whether or not my family sold it, served its purpose for me—as a revenue source for ancestors, a memory to keep, a reminder of what I left long ago. For Sargento and his family, it was a livelihood. A month after my visit, Mindanao again went into red alert. In Marawi, formerly Dansalan, the city of my grandparents, police forces fought militants linked to ISIS. Over the first week of shootouts, at least 129 people were killed. Sargento would be called into battle, survive, then return to the farm.

IN THE YEARS leading up to the revolution against Spain in the 1890s, José Rizal believed so deeply in the power of sacrifice that when he returned to the country after years living in Europe, certain he would face execution, he wrote a letter to a friend, with orders that it be opened only after his death. The letter explained that his death was necessary to spark the uprising, which it did, just as Ninoy Aquino's sparked the revolution that came in 1986. These days, overseas workers are extolled for their willingness to provide for families they almost never see. And Duterte supporters sometimes note that even if they don't condone the drug killings, they see the rising death toll as a necessary antidote to a poison that has long corrupted and stunted the nation.

I can only theorize that the Filipino reverence for sacrifice is rooted in the Catholicism so many of us were raised with, faith that carried the country's people through centuries of oppression and poverty. Blessed are those who suffer.

The Spanish left a deep mark on our people. By the time they relinquished their colony, more than 85 percent of Filipinos were Catholic. Yet over their three centuries in power, the Spanish colonial masters barely made a dent in Mindanao. The farther south they went, the more resistance they met. It was not until 1848, more than three hundred years after Magellan landed on the Islands, that the Spanish finally conquered the Davao region on the southern tip of the country. The people of Davao take great pride in this fact—in the 1960s, officials of the region's biggest city, Davao City, named its highest civic honor after Datu Bato, the Muslim warrior who led the fight against the Spanish.

Rodrigo Duterte, a Davao native, the first president from Mindanao, seemed to embody this spirit of resistance. Unlike the nativist populism sweeping through the West, his truly seemed a populism of the oppressed, a rejection of ancient hierarchies rather than a return to them. In a country whose rulers have, without exception, aimed to appease and impress the United States, Duterte detached from the West. In a county so devoutly Catholic, Duterte, himself a Catholic, accused the church of being "full of shit." In a country where the rules of political engagement encourage corruption, Duterte threatened to kill crooked officials. His popularity reflected "a reaction to the disillusionment in our politics," writer Miguel Syjuco told me. "We see in Duterte a savior who will clean things up. His message is the right thing—not the violence or belligerence, but his message of change as necessary is absolutely right."

Under his rule, business owners said they were no longer paying the bribes that were once customary, and travelers said they stopped worrying about extortion by customs agents. I lost count of all the Filipinos who told me that they saw fewer drug dealers in the streets and felt safer walking outside at night.

It was change built on fear and powered by force of will rather than reform of laws. But in a country where people didn't trust their institutions, where the law's grip was loose and shaky, where the legal system had been used to hide corruption, justify authoritarianism, silence the press, and jail dissidents—in a place like that, who better to turn to than a man who goes out and says what so many have been thinking for years: Fuck your laws. Trust me, Duterte told his people, and hold on for the ride. And so the people placed their faith in a demagogue.

They trusted him not because he was righteous, but because he resisted the old order. Perhaps they were wrong to do so. Duterte admitted that his drug war had spiraled out of control, giving cover to rogue cops, vigilantes, and drug lords who killed to further not public safety but their own interests, targeting rivals and enemies. He announced that he was considering expanding martial law from Mindanao to the whole country—but who even needs nationwide martial law when you have the mandate of overwhelming public support? This was the most troubling aspect of Duterte's rise, the way he reached this popularity even while openly undermining democratic principles. But the more desperate people become, the more they are willing to sacrifice.

BECAUSE EVERYTHING HAPPENED for a reason, my mom resisted the possibility that a sacrifice could be in vain. "Sayang," she'd sadly say whenever anything went to waste—a pity. If we had all this farmland, why not invest in it? I have no doubt she would have if we had had the funds. But walking the long dirt paths to the farm, she couldn't avoid the realization of how costly the renovations would be. She set her sights, instead, on the money her father's old clients owed us. She hung on to the possibility that all those years he spent away from the family didn't have to be a complete loss.

From the farm, we took a van north to the coast, to Cagayan de Oro, the city where my grandfather spent his final years. On the drive, my mom pulled from her backpack the old case files, showing me the names at the top of the page. When we got to our hotel, she went straight for the phone book. Sitting on the bed, my mom dialed the digits matching the names, then turned on her charm, asking politely to speak with so and so, apologizing for wrong numbers, explaining the complicated long-shot situation when she was able to reach the responsible party. After nearly an hour of fruitless attempts to negotiate payments, my mom began to lose steam. She didn't want to spend our only evening in Cagayan inside the hotel room.

"Never mind," she said with a wave of her hand. "It's okay, anyway."

We stepped outside in time for golden hour, when the bustling street shimmered with long shadows and spectral orange beams. For dinner, we sampled food carts, devouring longganisa and chicken gizzard on sticks, fresh lumpia on greasy napkins, steamy balut that nearly singed our fingertips, fluffy white rice wrapped in plastic, ube ice cream sandwiched into hot pandesal, stretching our feast long past sunset, when the city's daytime air of industriousness transformed into a relieved revelry.

On the same streets my grandfather had traversed, we began to debate what he would have thought about Duterte—if he would have seen him as an indulgent despot charging toward his aims no matter the cost, or as an uncompromising force against corruption and disorder. In other words, if he would have seen in Duterte a reflection of Marcos, or of himself.

Our back and forth on the issue carried into the final stretch of our trip. When we spent a day in Davao, we encountered a boisterous reverence for the homegrown president: life-size cardboard cutouts in stores, stickers on cars, placards by roads, posters on walls. His home, a green two-story house in a middle-class subdivision, is something of a pilgrimage site; visitors leave their IDs at a military checkpoint and walk to the end of the block, where a life-size cutout of the president stands at the front door of the house. Nearby, I saw a vendor selling shirts that riffed off Nike catchphrases, perhaps unintentionally morphing them into somewhat dark, cryptic allusions: "Duterte Knows," read one. "Duterte Never Sleeps," read another. Taking it all in like a fangirl, my mom had me snap photos of her next to Duterte cutouts on two occasions, her arm proudly extended with a closed fist, the president's campaign salute.

Davao's city museum honors Duterte no less than the museums in Ilocos honor Marcos. A bust of Duterte's father, the former governor, stands prominently at a second-floor exhibit. There, our tour guide mentioned that the father had stepped down from his seat to accept a cabinet position for the Marcos administration. My mom hadn't known this. She looked bewildered.

She was aware that Duterte was friendly with the Marcos family. He supported Bongbong's recount attempt and deemed the dictator's son a worthy successor. But my mom had chalked this up to political expediency. Ilocos and the regions around it voted as a unit—the "Solid North," people called it—and a Marcos endorsement guaranteed this valuable bloc. She hadn't considered that the ties might run deeper. Was there loyalty there? Reverence, even? A history? Suddenly, my mom was rethinking Duterte.

"I thought he was a man of integrity," she said in the museum. "But what about this?"

I replied that much of Philippine politics seemed to exist within a vast gray area between right and wrong, and nobody's heart was pure, and there were no saviors—only people navigating an entrenched system. While Duterte might be willing to kill in an effort to upend that system, he had still come up through the same old passages to power. "If I grew up here and became a politician, I'd probably be a little bit corrupt," I said, in a tone that suggested I was kidding.

But my mom must have sensed a thread of truth, because her face froze into a mask of shock and disgust. Before she could find the words, I preemptively laid out my defense. "I'd do all I could to help the poor, of course, and make the country better," I said. "But I'd also make sure our family was comfortable and I was comfortable. I wouldn't do that in America, but here it's part of the game, right?"

She shook her head feverishly, and when she finally found the words, she delivered them sternly. "I'm so disappointed you would say that," she said. "I'd be so ashamed if that were the case! I wouldn't want any of that money."

This argument continued the rest of the day and into the next, when we were back in Manila, on our last afternoon in the country. We rode through the city in the open side-carriage of a motorbike, flying through the seams in traffic, exhaust blasting our faces, veering inches from the buses and semis jockeying for position. Over the din of the engine, my mom and I went back and forth.

"What use is righteousness if it adds nothing to the greater good?"

"There is nothing more important than morals. If everybody stood up for their morals, the Philippines wouldn't have these problems."

"But what if some of those problems could be solved by good-willed people who do what they have to do to get things done?"

"God will always know that you sacrifice your morals. You will always have to answer to God."

As the sun dipped, the sky turned pink over the shacks and skyscrapers. The air smelled of fish and fumes. We passed some small boys playing basketball with a rusty hoop perched on a wooden beam fastened with electrical tape to a cinder-block wall. My mom brought up that her father had been very good at basketball and even in middle age had played with men much younger.

"You know, he could have been rich, but he refused to sacrifice his morals," she said. "We could have been millionaires."

I lingered on this alternate reality for a moment, imagining how the world would have unfolded for us, for me. Perhaps my mom and her siblings would have stayed in the Philippines. Perhaps the Concepcion family would have risen to compete with the Aquinos and the Marcoses. Perhaps we would have developed the farm into a lucrative enterprise, built a big house for Sargento and his family, and paid for all of their schooling. Perhaps Sargento and I would have grown up as friends.

"Don't you kinda wish Grandpa had?" I said.

"Of course not!" she said. "All the riches of the Philippines would not have been worth it."

THREE MONTHS after we returned from the Philippines, my mom pawned her jewelry. Some pieces her mother had passed down. A few were gifts from my father. Others, she had found for bargain prices, though they looked no less precious than their expensive companions. She kept her jewelry in a wooden box on the dresser, beside laminated placards of Jesus and Mary that seemed strategically placed to protect her glimmering, prized collection. These were the most valuable things she owned besides her car.

Her return to the real estate game hadn't brought the dividends she expected. After moving into Caridad's duplex four years earlier, she got a job selling newly built houses in San Francisco but managed just a few deals in her first year, not enough to pay the bills, so she picked up more dependable income at an agency filling positions for temporary work. She subbed for city clerks on parental leave, typed out spreadsheets for property management companies, and organized rent checks from Section-8 tenants. She had no health insurance and her hours weren't guaranteed. In her time between the office work, she worked on moving the housing listings that would bring big commissions. Though her rent was low for the area, she made barely enough money to cover it, and often didn't have any left over to pay the minimums on the credit card bills she'd racked up in the leanest years.

Considering alternatives to asking me for more money or borrowing more from her siblings, she remembered that she knew a pawnshop owner in Sacramento from her high-flying years as a realtor—he had been one of her clients. In exchange for the high-interest cash loan, my mom paid a monthly fee to the pawnshop, which could sell the jewelry if she missed a payment. She made all her payments but wasn't getting the income bump she hoped for: four real estate sales she had brewing on the side fizzled out, and a big sale she did manage to close was all for nothing because the real estate company she worked for went bankrupt and was unable to pay her the $20,000 commission she'd earned.

A year after she pawned her jewelry, she met the man who claimed to be an international developer, the man we exposed as a fraud a few nights before Christmas 2018. That situation resolved itself faster than I expected. After my mom and I detected the possible con, I asked her to send me photos of the mystery man, so I'd have a record in case we wanted to go to the police. She copied a couple of photos the man had texted her—apparent selfies in an airplane and at a restaurant—and sent them to me. Or meant to send them to me. Instead, in her harried screen tapping, she accidentally texted the photos back to the man himself.

I wonder what went through his head. I imagine a jolt of confusion chased by a rising tide of anxiety. My mom didn't exactly clarify things when she tried to clean up her error by texting him, simply, "Oops! Sorry, I sent that by mistake!" She was obviously showing his photos to unknown others, and the alleged international developer must have figured nothing good could come from that. Maybe he even read it as a veiled threat. Within weeks, he stopped contacting my mom. We haven't heard from him since.

My mom put the matter behind her—one less thing to worry about—and moved on to the next dilemma. Our deliberations over important financial and professional decisions were often our most relaxing conversations. Burrowing into ground where our interests and desires overlapped, we couldn't afford to waste time veering into the contentious affairs that divided us. Assessing our shared dilemmas, we fell into our old groove, a collaborative partnership since I was old enough to reason. My mom would open by posing a question designed to conjure a sign from the invisible forces: she'd tell me she had to choose between two unstated options, then ask, "One or two?" My answer would affirm her instinctive choice or call it into question. She trusted the mind's capacity to process possibilities in ways we couldn't fully understand, and was a firm believer in the theory that your first guess is your best guess. She'd explain the particulars of her dilemma only after I picked a number. I'd typically favor the safer choice, like the job with better benefits or saving money over investing it, but my mom leaned toward the chance of high commissions or eventual windfalls.

In summer 2019, my mom encountered another crossroads. Down one path: a job opening as a caretaker for elderly people, offering health insurance and guaranteed hours. It was similar to the job she'd had years earlier in San Diego and she didn't think she'd mind it, though it didn't exactly fill her with excitement. "It's not as prestigious as a realtor," she said. Down the other path: more cycles as a temp worker, which paid more per hour and could lead to full-time administrative work if she impressed the right boss. New assignments brought new possibilities, and my optimistic mother couldn't help but believe a promised land lay just around the next bend. Each bend that led only to more barren terrain tested her faith, and I could hear in her voice that she was no longer sure about the prospects of her current path. I voted for the caretaker job, and to my surprise, she agreed. She applied, telling herself that if she was offered the position, it was a sign from God that she should do it, and so it came to be.

With her bright energy and generous heart, she was very good at her new profession. Her shifts pulled her all over the Bay Area, as far as sixty miles away, to the suburban homes of the company's mostly white clients. Some she kept company and made sure they took their medications. Others she fed and bathed. One man was notorious for resisting baths. My mom's supervisor told her not to worry if she couldn't get him to the tub—he had punched the last worker who tried. On my mom's first shift at his house, he hadn't bathed in weeks and smelled it. She studied his report, which listed his fondest memory as the summers he spent on his grandmother's farm in Italy. When it was time to try to coax him into a bath, my mom spoke in a matronly tone, dropping in a few Italian words she knew, thinking that maybe if he thought he was on the farm in Italy, his mind would be at ease. "Bambino, time to take a shower," she said. "Per favore." She raised her eyebrows, pouted her lips, and offered her hand. Without a word, perhaps tranquilized by a spell of nostalgia, he got up. "Molto bene," she said.

Two months in, one client was such a big fan of my mom that she requested her services full-time, five days a week, sometimes six. This was an idyllic development. The woman lived just a ten-minute drive from my mom's place, saving her from long commutes, and she was in decent physical condition, saving my mom from the part of the job she dreaded more than the commutes, the cleaning of human waste. This woman just wanted someone to talk to, accompany her on walks, and prepare her meals. At least once a week, they strolled to the Kabuki theater in Japantown to watch a movie. "I'm really being paid twenty-one dollars an hour for companionship," my mom said. "No stress! No computers!"

A year that began on perilous footing had stabilized by autumn. As Christmas 2019 approached, things were looking up for my mom, though she was no closer to buying back her jewelry. She had a decent job for now, at least. She didn't consider the job permanent—more like a stable state from which to plan her next move. She still checked job listings nearly every day. She preferred the sorts of professions that required formal attire: suits, heels, and jewelry.

The jewelry. Each day the cherished items weren't in her possession, her nerves tightened. She worried somebody would rob the pawnshop. She called the owner every week to confirm her items were still safely locked away. "Oh Lord, please don't let my jewelries be lost," she'd pray.

I learned about the pawned jewelry when she picked me up from the airport a few days before Christmas, much as I'd learned about the international developer's half-million-dollar investment offer the year before. She opened by asking if I could spare $2,500. Assuming this was about some investment opportunity—perhaps involving her interest in renovating Rizalina's farm—I asked what the money was for.

"I pawned my jewelry," she said flatly. "That's how much to get it back."

I was unable to speak for a few seconds. My jaw hung limp before the shock gave way to a torrent of questions.

"When did you do this?"

"A few months ago, four or five maybe."

My mom explained that she'd fallen behind on credit card payments. She didn't want to ask her sisters for money because she'd just recently paid them back and cringed at the thought of opening up another line of credit so soon. She didn't want to ask me because I was already covering a chunk of her monthly bills, and she feared her financial troubles setting me back the way her own parents' middle-age struggles had hindered her.

"I'm embarrassed to ask 'cause I've always been independent and financially capable," she said. "Especially knowing that parents are supposed to financially help their children. I don't want to burden you. I'm not used to asking help from anyone."

"It's okay! You're the reason I'm able to afford it."

"Don't say that. I was just doing my job as a mom. In the hope that I should still be helping you even when you're an adult. I don't like what's happening to my current financial situation. This is just temporary."

I was upset she'd done something so drastic without consulting me. I raised my voice, lecturing as a father might, angry and righteous: Why didn't you ask me first? If I don't have enough I'll tell you but please ask me first! All the money we've been paying on interest!

My mom stared silently at the asphalt ahead, her hands tightly gripping the wheel, as if the empty highway were laced with treachery. Soon I ran out of steam and fell silent. Only then did my mom respond. With the graceful severity of a disappointed nun, she said, softly, "I don't like to be yelled at."

If we'd been sparring, she'd dodged my wild haymakers and countered with a body blow that knocked me to the canvas, curled over and out of wind. I apologized. We didn't raise our voices in anger in our family. Raised voices were for congratulations and punch lines. Anger was icy and brooding, or seared with exasperation.

Our spirits lightened by the time we pulled into the driveway. "Praise the Lord, I can finally have my jewelries back!" my mom said. "I was really so worried!"

The day after Christmas, we headed for Sacramento.

GRASS ACROSS THE CITY had turned a sickly yellow since we last lived in the Central Valley. My mom found a shaded spot beneath trees in the pawnshop parking lot, which sat along a low-slung commercial stretch on a wide boulevard. She drove a black Mercedes-Benz that made me feel self-conscious in a place like this.

I had tried to persuade her to downgrade. To save money, I said, unable to express my more abstract concerns, which had to do with the ethics of presenting a wealth we didn't have. But this was a nonstarter. The car meant a lot to my mom. It represented all the work she'd put in over the years. She'd earned enough money in the past to buy herself a Benz—so what if she wasn't making as much money anymore? She saw no purpose in letting the outside world in on her personal struggles. She preferred to curate an image that accentuated the highlights of her professional life.

After the economy crashed, she held out for as long as she could before parting with her silver Mercedes. She drove a compact Hyundai for four years. But when she decided to get back into the real estate game, she saw no choice but to invest in a luxury car once again, because a salesperson must present an image of success—a whiff of desperation can squander trust. "It's for business," she said when I expressed reservations about the $250 monthly payments.

Needless to say, we wanted to get in and out of the pawnshop as quickly as possible. A squat slab of brick walls and tinted windows barred with iron, the place had the feel of a suburban fort. From the outside, you had no way to know if the shop was open. You had to ring a buzzer to enter. A hunched, white-haired man greeted us, then led us down a hallway lined with as many paintings as could fit—Impressionist landscapes, portraits of anonymous faces, a frowning clown against a black backdrop. Bicycles hung from the ceiling on hooks. Old books filled a pair of shelves. Rounding the corner, we entered a big room that resembled a museum storage warehouse, crammed with thousands of artifacts that spanned time and space. Long glass counters displayed rings, necklaces, watches, and crosses crafted from every precious metal, gem, and pearl I could imagine. One panel was just for rare coins, another for customized knives, another for a helmet and set of armor that looked like the kind worn by warriors in Imperial China. On tables behind the counter stood a dense crowd of inanimate figures, including an ivory carving of a Buddha, an ebony carving of an Egyptian pharaoh, and wooden statuettes with oblong faces and slender frames that I guessed were carved in West Africa. Everything was crammed so tightly together that I got the sense I was seeing only the items that could fit, and that somewhere was a bottomless trove containing the rest of the inventory. Stripped of context beyond these walls, the items were now little more than tokens of hardship, their histories condensed into the single sobering fact that someone, some-where, faced enough trouble to relinquish them.

The pawnshop owner exuded the crusty warmth of a person who believes they've seen it all. He had started the business forty-seven years earlier, after returning from a tour in the navy during the Vietnam War. He was quick to note that he'd been stationed at the Subic Bay base in the Philippines, though his memories were oddly specific and appar-ently limited to the animals he encountered.

"Rats all over the pier, you couldn't walk," he said. "I had monkey over there. I had dog."

"On the ship?" my mom said.

"No, out in the country—you buy it. I ate it."

"Eww, you ate it?"

He nodded proudly, then changed the subject. "You ever see a cockfight?"

Damn it. The ordeal was unpleasant enough without having to reckon with the unwitting racism of some old white war vet. For my own comfort, because anger requires energy I didn't have, I excused his com-ments as innocent blunders. He didn't know any better. His memory was distorted from the fog of war. He was trying to find common ground with us, but he seemed to know little about our ancestral land other than a few semi-shocking anecdotes of exotic adventure.

I wanted to like the man. It's much easier on the soul to like than to dislike. I wanted to blame my discomfort on the wide gap between our perspectives. Maybe I was being too sensitive. He had kept my mom's jewelry safe, at least, and wanted to help. From decades of engaging with hard-luck clientele, he seemed to consider it his duty to dispense the sort of subtle nudges that would keep customers from returning.

"How long have you been in San Francisco?" he asked my mom.

"Almost seven years."

"It's pretty expensive there, isn't it?"

It was at that point I decided: Fuck this dude and his condescension. Fuck him for low-balling her on these six pieces of jewelry, which were definitely worth much more than $2,500. He brought them from his backroom safe and pulled them out of a neatly folded paper bag to confirm they were undamaged. The gold earrings from my grandma, the watch from my dad, the cross inlaid with colorful gems from me, as well as three other pieces I recognized. The items were listed on the side of the bag in blue ink, along with the dates my mom had brought them in. Something strange caught my eye: the dates on the bag were all 2017, which didn't make any sense because my mom told me she'd pawned the jewelry four or five months earlier.

I thought it must be a mistake or misunderstanding. As much as our outlooks diverged, and for all our mutual distrust on worldly affairs, I had never known my mom to lie to me. As soon as we stepped out of the shop, I asked her straight up: "So you first pawned these in 2017?"

"What?"

"That's what it says."

"Noooo! Of course not. Maybe it was just a code or something?"

"You're sure?"

"I'm sure. 2019. That's impossible."

"These say 2017."

I showed her the bag. Her face furrowed in confusion.

"Oh, yeah," she said hesitantly. "I guess. I didn't even realize. I've just been paying interest. I thought it was just within a year."

"But you didn't tell me for two years?"

"Well, because you've been giving me money so I didn't want to bother you more with that," she said, then paused. "Maybe somehow because I was also embarrassed to tell you. I thought I was gonna have the extra money to pay for that. You know, and then I was expecting closed deals. And I was hoping that every time I'll get a deal and I'll get my jewelries, you know. But I told you, I lost four deals."

I dropped the issue. It wasn't worth fighting about. My mom finally had her jewelries back, and I didn't want to spoil the joyous occasion.

THE YEAR ENDED on a good note, though we were too accustomed to unexpected swings to assume any steady rise. We savored the comforts we had and braced ourselves for whatever was to come. At the family Christmas party, at Uncle Bobby's new house in Rio Vista, a growing subdivision on old farmland east of Vallejo, three generations of our barangay repeated age-old patterns: little kids on the living room carpet imagining stories for their action figures and dolls, adults in the kitchen sipping beer and pontificating on serious matters. Auntie Ging had finally retired at seventy-one but found herself restless at home all day, so she'd started volunteering as a teacher's assistant. Uncle Spanky was planning to retire soon, though he hadn't set a date. Lauren was a kindergarten teacher at a Catholic school. Jed had a second child on the way. Roscoe oversaw development planning for a local government, got married, and bought a house in San Francisco, where he lived with Chris, who handled administrative work for a food truck company. Mico was a senior logistics operator with no shortage of competing job offers, and his daughter was a straight-A student who played on a club volleyball team. Mitch was married and building a pension from her civil servant job in Long Beach. My mom had applied for a job selling vacation packages for a hotel company.

The day before New Year's Eve, my dad called to tell me he had finally told his daughters about his son, and they were excited by the news, so we hopped on a video call, giddy and tearful, filled with more questions than the moment could bear. My dad wanted to start the next decade without the weight of the lingering secret, he said, to jump into the 2020s with positive energy. And if that wasn't enough to sway him, his eldest daughter was set to start at college in the United States, a short train ride from me. The revelation he had dreaded unfurled more smoothly than he'd ever imagined. My sisters reacted as I did when I learned about them: with curiosity to catch up on everything we'd missed. We made plans to get together in the spring or summer. Maybe I'd spend my vacation weeks in Beirut, where they lived. Maybe we'd meet in Paris.

In January 2020, my mom interviewed for the hotel sales job. In February, she was hired. She started on March 9, for a week of training, paid at a lower rate, before her full-time benefits kicked in. She had health insurance and vacation time. Her base salary was near minimum wage, but she had a chance at commissions, which she was certain would be high because who better than a former flight attendant, a onetime globe-trotter, a weathered veteran of movement, to pitch prospective customers on luxurious vacation packages at alluring locations across the world?

The week my mom started training was the week the COVID-19 pandemic pulled America into an extended lockdown. Symptomatic patients poured into Jed's hospital in San Francisco. His pregnant wife and two-year-old daughter decamped to her parents' house in Sacramento, in case Jed brought the virus back to the duplex.

The following week, my mom was furloughed. She was one of 80,000 California residents to apply for unemployment coverage on March 18. I worried about how she would handle the crisis. Her information sources weren't going to change suddenly, and I worried she'd think the coronavirus danger was liberal hyperbole, because it had been so long since I'd heard her stray from anything the forty-fifth president said. But my mom took it seriously, which I should have predicted because she was always attuned to avoiding potential threats to the body, such as processed foods, caffeine, and alcohol—though also pharmaceuticals and vaccines. Having read much about the deep state, global conspirators, and imminent plots against Christian civilization, she kept a stash of canned foods and bottled water, and had a small hand-crank generator that could charge electronics and broadcast radio. She was more prepared for dystopia than I was.

While she was upset to lose a job she'd just started, she was grateful to have no choice but to stay home. She kept an eye out for jobs that might allow her to work remotely. The first opportunity that popped up was for a cemetery, selling plots by phone. But when my mom talked to the manager, it turned out remote employees didn't get base pay, only commission, and to get base pay you had to work the counter, ringing up the grieving families coming into the office. My mom and I agreed her top priority should be safety, and praise the Lord, I finally had enough savings to cover her bills for a while, and her landlord, Caridad's daughter-in-law, allowed her to postpone rent payments. She didn't need to do anything right now. For the first time in years, she could sit still, rest, explore new interests. We began to talk about it like a sort of vacation. She deserved a break. She believed in finding blessings in disguise.

That Christmas, our first without a family party, my mom would cook meals for other loved ones to pick up, so that "there's something good you remember. Christmas is supposed to be for enjoying Jesus. It's His day, so why will you allow the Grinch, the evil, to take it away from you. I wanted to bring back the Christmas spirit and make it positive instead of negative because when you're negative, you actually feed the devil with your bad vibes. The devil wants you to be unhappy. God doesn't want you to be unhappy."

MAYBE IN A PARALLEL UNIVERSE my mom buys a guitar, like she often talked about doing, or pores through a collection of Thomas Aquinas essays during her pandemic isolation. But in our reality, the passions she carried through 2020 guided her deeper into the invisible war her sources chronicled. She felt a duty to help the cause. Over my objection, she put up an American flag outside the duplex, a few weeks after racial justice protests swept through the country that summer. She said it was to honor military veterans like Caridad. Uncle Marlon helped her nail the wooden post into a metal stand on the roof. She and Marlon attended Mass outside the closed St. Mary's Cathedral, as well as protests calling on the governor to allow indoor gatherings for worship. She wore her pink MAGA hat to pro-Trump marches in the city, and one Sunday she went on a pro-Trump boat cruise in the Bay. She assured me she always wore a mask, though I expressed alarm that in the photos she sent me most people in the background had not a shred of fabric on their faces. I couldn't dissuade her from attending these events. I felt helpless against the forces guiding her.

Was this the cost of my American comfort? That my mother had on my behalf thrown herself into the ecosystem completely, infiltrating the colonizer class, buying into the terms, and reporting back with zeal? It was in those disorienting moments when I wondered if it was a mistake for her to come to the States. There was no question our investment had benefited me, but was there a road we missed somewhere along the way that would have brought the same sort of benefits without the same sort of sacrifices? It's a hurtful possibility, useless to dwell on except as a reference point for future decisions. Like all immigrants, my mom set dueling examples for her child: to place my faith in the new country like she did and to be willing to depart my homeland for brighter prospects like she did. If there was anything my elders had taught me it was that if things got too bad you could start fresh elsewhere, absorbing the setback in pursuit of long-term peace. There was always someplace else to go if you had the means and will, nations on upward trajectories, or at least less chaotic in some way, or on more stable footing as far as you can tell. Staying one step ahead of the world's turns. A treacherous hopscotch. The next land always has its own problems, and the old problems aren't solved but merely distant, out of sight if you're lucky.

My mom was fully invested in America, for better and worse. Millions of other immigrants were all in, too. Many of them had children who asked themselves the same questions I asked myself, on the front row overlooking a life before the States, birthrights forever tied to the question:

Why did they leave? That my elders willfully landed in the empire partially responsible for their homeland's troubles felt to me like a small measure of unwitting justice, or perhaps the seed of it. For an empire born from anticolonial ideals, what better way to stay in touch with its underdog spirit than welcoming those most intimately familiar with the perils of colonialism? For a country founded on fictions of racial distinction, who better to jump into the mix than people of every complexion under the sun, confusing the old white order, drawing fire, joining the growing ranks of Americans pushing up against the founding caste system, stretching its seams? What story about an empire's rise is more important than the one that tallies the costs accrued? I don't know how to ensure a sacrifice isn't wasted, but the first step must be to appraise it for all it's worth, recording it in full, leaving lessons to bloom in the tales that live on.

"I CALLED THE POLICE," my mom said to me one night on the phone that July.

Her voice was frantic. She didn't know where to begin. My best bet was that she'd either been burgled or had her car stolen.

"Somebody stole my flag."

"What?"

"My flag. Remember, I sent a picture? Somebody stole my flag."

Then she got into the story of how she and Uncle Marlon had tried to put the flag out of reach against just this possibility. "That was the highest we could go with the step stool! So we were thinking the only way to steal it is if they have a step stool too. But it's been taken out, and I don't know, I was just waiting for it to happen really, but I didn't think somebody would really do it. It's only because it's in San Francisco. It just proves how liberal this city is. I hope they didn't step on my car. So anyway I'll need to put it higher somehow."

"What? No, Mom! They shouldn't have stolen it, but please don't put up another flag."

"Oh my gosh, Albert, it's an American flag! In your own country, wow! You can't even put up a flag. No, all the more I have to put it up."

Pulling out my heaviest artillery, I made the case that the flag represented mythologies that have justified oppression without reconciliation, that she was hurting people, deliberately seeking to provoke, and she didn't have to be so loud about what she believed, because why would she knowingly prod at the sore spots of others?

"I'm just proud to be American."

"Put a Filipino flag."

"What? No, I'm an American. I'm a Filipino American. And now somebody stole my flag because I'm a patriot."

There was no doubt this was a reprehensible act. But I imagined the culprit wondering just what sort of resident would put up an American flag in the heart of San Francisco as the country was barreling through such a period of turbulence and reckoning, as divides grew starker and more dangerous, as assumptions faded and democratic transitions were no longer something to take for granted. I wanted to explain all they didn't know about my mother and the house bearing the flag and the history that swirled us into the present; I would have been happy to lay out every twisted detail if I could possibly resist the urge to sock this misguided culprit in the face for infringing on my mom's peace of mind.

My thoughts were racing with fury when my mom called me again, about an hour later.

"Albert, you'll never guess."

She'd just talked to Jed and told him about the flag theft. Jed explained that he'd come home from work that morning to find that the flag had broken off its stand and fallen to the ground, so he'd picked it up and tossed it into our yard for safekeeping.

"Oh my gosh, can you believe?" my mom said. "It just fell! You know, it could be a sign not to have a flag outside the house, di ba?"

I agreed as quickly as my vocal cords could push out the words.

"It's better, I think, not to have it," my mom said. "It must be a sign really."

AT THE TIME, I was about halfway done writing this book. Reading early versions of what I had to say, my mom disagreed with some of my conclusions about our country. She held no doubt that America was the best place for us. She'd calculated every decision on the basis of my well-being, devoted herself full-time to providing me with opportunities available to only the most fortunate, and when she did the math, she was pleased by the results, proud of all we'd accomplished here. "No, it's not a sacrifice," she said. "Those struggles are just temporary. Because in America, you know you can get it back." Seeing the details of our lives laid out in narrative form, she felt rejuvenated, she said. She once again turned her focus to real estate, donning her jewelry and suit jacket to show houses to clients, her enthusiasm beaming through the mask covering half her face. Yet for all her faith in America, she retained the pragmatism that guided our family for centuries. She'd become open to the possibility that maybe the country had served its purpose for her. For the first time since we'd settled in the States, she began to consider the prospects of a future elsewhere. Maybe she'd retire in the Philippines, where our dollars go further. Maybe, she thought, she could plant a new foothold for our barangay on the Islands. She remained joyful, optimistic, trusting in God's plan. "God works in mysterious ways," she said. "It should be a happy ending."

AFTER EXPLOSIVES STORED at the port of Beirut erupted in August 2020, killing hundreds and setting off a near collapse of the government, my dad, his American wife, and their four daughters flew to the States, to stay with some family for a few months and road-trip around the Northeast. It turned out I would meet my sisters for the first time just outside Boston, our faces behind cloth masks when we hugged. They were in their teens, cool as hell in loose sweaters and checkered Vans. They piled into my rental car while our dad and their mom rode ahead in their own vehicle. We would have five days together on New England roads, looping through pine forests and quaint clapboard towns on the way to drop off the eldest of my sisters at her college dorm at the end of the week.

Our route traced the string of energy plants my dad and his wife owned in the region—why not check in on the businesses and close a few deals in between the blueberry fields and lobster shacks? During those work stops, my sisters and I mostly tried to stay out of the way, wandering the offices, briefly sitting in on meetings to show we were a nice wholesome family to do business with. It was all light and playful until one stop, when our aimless exploration of the property led to a discovery that turned my sisters ashen: the man our father was doing business with had a signed photo of Trump and a MAGA hat in his office. This was a scandal to their eyes, and I was touched by their outrage. On meeting us, he'd spoken to us with an ease I hadn't expected in a business meeting, and in doing so did my sisters the favor of exposing them to a side of America they hadn't seen firsthand. In our brief interaction, he'd managed to criticize Colin Kaepernick's protests, advocate for closed borders even though most of the "Hispanics" he knows "are good workers," and declare his intentions to one day build a history museum that properly honors America because "some people wanna tear down our history."

My sisters had kept straight faces inside the office, polite and curious amid their rising dread, but back in the soundproof confines of the car, they burst with questions and observations about this country they knew mostly from afar. "Was he talking about the statues they're taking down?" On the road, with noticeable alarm, they pointed out Trump lawn signs and big campaign flags billowing from the back of trucks. "Why do they have to be so loud about it?" They had aspired to American universities and considered settling in the States at some point, so understanding the country's strange ways was paramount. "How did he still win even though he got fewer votes?" During summer camps they'd attended at American colleges, they'd gotten a sense of our eccentricities. "Nobody ever asks me what my race is except for when I'm here. Why do you care so much about that here?" They were caught off guard by the ritual of saying the Pledge of Allegiance at the start of the day. "It's so weird!" As we drove down a two-lane highway lined with dozens of American flags waving from white columns, they asked why Americans were so obsessed with the flag.

My sisters held no illusions about my country's moral standing, or indulgent habits, or general indifference to the world beyond its borders. Their history teachers in Beirut depicted America as a land that promised more than it delivered. News reports chronicled markers of dysfunction and decline. Yet still America loomed on their horizon, the empire of the age they were born into, the setting of their favorite Netflix shows, home of their favorite TikTok influencers, producer of clothing brands they wore and music they listened to, refuge when they needed to flee the tumult of their homeland.

They wanted to know all about my life in the States, what it was like to grow up here, what it was like to go to an American high school, if it was like in the movies, what my favorite fast-food restaurants were because the ones in Lebanon didn't taste the same, and whether I liked it here, and where my mom was living, and what my cousins and aunties and uncles were like, and where that side of my family came from, and why we ended up in America. We had much to catch up on, and nothing but time on the road ahead. So I began the story . . .

ACKNOWLEDGMENTS

While I can directly trace the facts in this book to specific sources, the ideas
in it evolved with the help of many people.

My editor, Rebecca Saletan, was an enthusiastic collaborator who always
knew what I was trying to say even when my writing lacked clarity, helped me
see the contours of the thoughts I was trying to corral, and guided me through
the narrative challenges tripping me up. My agent, David Patterson, encouraged me to take a reporting trip to the Philippines as soon as I told him about
this book idea back in 2016, served as an invaluable partner in shaping the
book's angle, and advised me to apply for the Whiting Foundation Creative
Nonfiction Grant that provided funding for reporting trips and book leave.
I'm thankful to the Whiting Foundation and their panel of judges for backing
this project and many others.

Nico Medina Mora guided me through art museums in Mexico City, and
our long conversations about the Manila Galleon, the fall of Tenochtitlán, and
the tides of empires helped shape my thoughts on imperialism. Adam Serwer
helped me understand how U.S. policy is designed to uphold white power and
that racist backlash has always followed racial progress in U.S. history. Tracy
Clayton helped me see flaws in my logic and spots of ignorance I failed to
account for, and our many conversations sharpened the book's central arguments. Brian De Los Santos and Pat Del Rosario, fellow children of Filipino
immigrants, helped me understand the overlap in our experiences and the

ways our stories diverged. Jack Feeney and Javier Avalos helped me piece together the details for scenes I wrote about, and helped me understand the lessons we took from our high school years. Anna Roth helped me work through my concerns about structure, and our discussions about the different ways to blend timelines ultimately resulted in the format in these pages. Aemilia Phillips, at the Stuart Krichevsky Literary Agency, and Glory Plata, at Riverhead Books, provided early and insightful feedback on this book's approach to immigrant diasporas and the second-generation experience.

Isaac Fitzgerald, Rachel Sanders, Karolina Waclawiak, and Marisa Carroll edited the BuzzFeed essays that contained my earliest efforts at reporting out my family history, and their thoughts helped me discern the wider themes of the stories I was telling. Anita Badejo, Doug McGray, and Derek Gardner edited and produced a live story I performed for *Pop-Up Magazine* about my uncle Spanky, and helped me untangle my own feelings about the consequences of my family's migration.

My editors at BuzzFeed News have supported this project every step of the way: Steve Kandell, Tina Susman, Ben Smith, and Shani Hilton approved my reporting trip to the Philippines in 2017, and Mark Schoofs, Ariel Kaminer, Jessica Garrison, Heidi Blake, Alex Campbell, and Tom Namako granted me the flexibility I needed to balance writing this book with reporting on the pandemic in 2020.

I aimed for this book to honor my elders who built the foundation I was born onto, and to offer an account of their journeys for the historical record. My elders passed down many of the stories I wrote, and I'm grateful for their willingness to share memories that aren't always fond, and for their teaching me how to confront those shadows with humor and good spirit.

I'm thankful to my dad, Fahim, and his wife, Kimberly, for always helping me see beyond my sightline, and to my sisters Tia, Chloé, Bella, and Maïa for whisking me into their joyful curiosity about the world.

I'm thankful to Rizalina, Manuel, Caridad, Tomas, Ging, Lyn, Mae, Joey, Marlon, Paul, Bobby, Spanky, Ricardo, Donna, Chuck, Alyssa, Mico, Ava, Jed, Angie, Roscoe, Heather, Mitch, Teri, Anton, Chris, Lauren, Ralph, Nicole, Alicia, Sergio, Erin, Kaya, Amelia, Lukas, and Maverick for filling our barangay with love and optimism.

Most of all, I'm thankful to my mom, for teaching me how to tell stories, encouraging my curiosity, and brightening our household with enthusiasm.

AUTHOR'S NOTE

ORIGINS

I first became interested in reporting out my family's history in 2009, when my granduncle Tomas told me about our roots on the southern island of Mindanao. The idea for this book was only a vague aspiration until summer 2016, while I was at work on my first book and visiting California for a nephew's baptism. More than I ever had before, I began asking my elders about their migration journeys, initially out of curiosity rather than any defined project. It was while sitting on the BART on the way to a friend's place in Berkeley, absentmindedly gazing at my reflection in the tunnel-darkened windows, that I felt struck by the desire to turn a journalistic eye to my family's story.

To that point, my reporting career had exclusively focused on the stories of others, with barely an "I" or "me" in sight. So I approached this project using the tools I knew best: interviewing sources, digging into documents, and swimming through an endless pool of historical research. My reporting for this book commenced in December 2016, and I filed my first draft of the manuscript on November 2, 2020.

LANGUAGE

I decided to use the word "Filipino" instead of "Filipinx" because that's how people in the Philippines identify themselves. "Filipinx" traces to the 1960s, when it was popular among activist-minded members of the American-raised diaspora, and in recent years, a growing share of Filipino Americans have adopted the word, just as more people have started using "Latinx" instead of "Latino." Those who use the word argue that it promotes inclusion by avoiding linguistic conventions that falsely define gender as binary, and that it undermines patriarchal norms. Early drafts of this book used "Filipinx," but after consulting with a wide range of Filipinos and Filipino Americans, I ultimately opted for the more common "Filipino." Because Tagalog has no gendered pronouns, Filipinos consider the word gender-neutral and some argue that the campaign to promote "Filipinx" overlooks that fact, applying a Western lens to an ethnic identity rooted across the ocean, and in the process unwittingly excluding Filipinos from the decision. For many Filipinos, the word "Filipinx" refers exclusively to "Filipino Americans." I remain conflicted on the matter, but my opting for "Filipino" in this book is an effort to avoid identifying millions of people by a word with which they don't identify. I keep an open mind over what word we should use to identify our ancestry. There is no *x* in the original Tagalog alphabet, but neither is there an *f.* Some Filipinos propose using a word more deeply rooted in the native tongues, such as "Pilipine," "Pilipini," or "Philippine." I support these calls to update our terminology, but I believe whatever word we use should carry the endorsement of people in the Philippines.

For similar reasons, I decided not to italicize Tagalog words like "tabi apo" and "pwera usog." Language is a constantly evolving pastiche—my own language took in French words like "menu" and German words like "kindergarten." As a child, I didn't consider the word "kawawa" any more foreign than "canyon" or "patio," and I aimed to present that experience as I lived it.

SOURCING

The narrative arcing from my family's years in the Philippines to their immigrant decades in the United States comes from extensive interviews with my mom, my dad, my granduncle Tomas, my grandauntie Caridad, my aunties Ging and Lyn, my uncles Bobby, Spanky, and Marlon, my cousins Mico, Jed, Mitch, and Lauren, as well as interviews with more than a hundred other relatives, friends, and sources in the Philippines, California, Mexico, and Spain. While parts of the story are based on my own recollection, whenever possible I corroborated my memories with those of relatives or classmates who were present.

Tomas's memoir supplied information about our ancestors in Mindanao, including Emilia, Luisa, and Jose, and my interviews with Tomas while helping him translate his memoir into English provided additional details. I also relied on a collection of papers from Tomas's file, which I was able to review because Auntie Lyn and Uncle Bobby traveled to Italy after he died to ship his possessions back to our family in the United States. Roberto Vallangca's book, *Pinoy: The First Wave, 1898–1941* (1977), supplied oral history interviews with Filipino immigrants who arrived in the early twentieth century. Caridad Concepcion Vallangca's books, *The Second Wave: Pinay and Pinoy (1945–1960)* and *The Third Wave: Quo Vadis* (2007), provided oral history interviews of Filipino migrants arriving in the U.S. after World War II. Their books also supplied detailed accounts of their own childhoods and migrations, as did my 2010 interviews with Caridad for an article I wrote about her that appeared on a website that no longer exists.

For my grandmother Rizalina's immigration records, I filed a Freedom of Information Act request through the United States Citizenship and Immigration Services. U.S. immigration statistics are from census records, Pew surveys, and annual data released by the Department of Homeland Security. A National Institutes of Health analysis provided data on how people of various Asian ethnicities classify their race on government forms. U.S. housing sales data are from census records. U.S. economic and workforce data are from the Bureau of Labor Statistics. Global economic data are from the World Bank. U.S. income inequality data are from studies by Emmanuel Saez, an economist at the University of California, Berkeley. Data on racial demographics in football are based on rosters compiled by Pro Football Reference. Philippine economic data are from the Philippine Department of Finance, and statistics on overseas workers are from the Commission on Filipinos Overseas and the Philippine Department of Foreign Affairs. A 1993 study by Philippine army colonel Rolando San Juan provided information on the impact of the U.S. military bases in the Philippines.

I'm grateful for the rigorous research others have done on the subjects I aimed to study. Luis Francia's *A History of the Philippines: From Indios Bravos to Filipinos* (2010) was an essential resource, surveying the archipelago's precolonial society and presenting the Filipino perspective on the succession of colonizing forces that occupied the Islands over the centuries—through, among other things, portraits of José Rizal, Andres Bonifacio, and Emilio Aguinaldo that sharply articulated their ideological distinctions. *History of the Filipino People* (first published in 1960) by Teodoro Agoncillo, Milagros Guerrero, and Oscar Alfonso presented one of the first comprehensive accounts of history from the Filipino perspective, offering insight on the nationalist spirit rising at the time it was written, less than two decades after independence. For the latest research on the archipelago's earliest-known inhabitants, I relied on "Multiple Migrations to the Philippines during the Last 50,000 Years," a 2021 study by Maximilian Larena, Federico Sanchez-Quinto, and more than forty others.

Cesar Adib Majul's *Muslims in the Philippines* (1973) supplied comprehensive details about the dynastic lineages of sultanic families, the region's politics, and the fight against Spain. For additional information on the sultanic years in northern Mindanao, I relied on research by the Universiti Brunei Darussalam, including the papers "The Islamicity of Lanao Sultanate in the Philippines in the 17th Century as a State" (2018) and "The Lanao Sultanate in the 17th Century Zakāt System with Special Reference to the Islamic Perspective of al-Māwardī" (2018), both authored by Sohayle M. Hadji Abdul Racman, among others. I also learned much about the sultanic dynasties of that era from a 2017 visit to Silliman University's anthropology museum in Dumaguete City in the Visayas.

Tamim Ansary's *Destiny Disrupted: A History of the World through Islamic Eyes* (2006) provided historical background on how the conflict between Christian and Muslim kingdoms shaped the modern world. John Darwin's *After Tamerlane: The Global History of Empire since 1405* (2008) supplied historical background on pre-1500 Eurasian empires and the reasons for the rise of western European empires. My knowledge of Congo's precolonial Kongo Kingdom is largely from Adam Hochschild's book *King Leopold's Ghost* (1999), which investigates Belgium's brutal pillaging of the region's resources. Charles Mann's *1491* (2006) presented a glimpse into the civilizations thriving in the Americas before Christopher Columbus and smallpox arrived. Nell Irvin Painter's *The History of White People* (2010) laid out how the concept of European supremacy is a fiction rooted in artificial definitions of race—and how those definitions changed over time to suit those in power.

The journal of Antonio Pigafetta, Ferdinand Magellan's assistant, is the most comprehensive accounting of their famous journey, describing the contents of the ships, the natives they encountered, the expedition's goals, and the horrors that sent the survivors fleeing—I relied on the version translated by

R. A. Skelton (1975). *The Cambridge History of Southeast Asia* (2000) supplied additional details on the political dynamics among precolonial Asian kingdoms. Gilbert Maldonado's *Journey to the Kingdom of New Mexico: Volume One* (2014) and a primary source collection edited by Jon Cowans, *Early Modern Spain: A Documentary History* (2003) provided historical background on how Spain cloaked its conquest in the guise of holy war.

José Rizal's essays, particularly "The Philippines a Century Hence" (1889), and his autobiography (first published in 1918), were instructive for understanding not only the injustices that drove him to call for change but also the colonial influences that kept him from calling for independence. His books *Noli Me Tángere* (first published 1887) and *El Filibusterismo* (first published 1891) provided comprehensive portraits of life under Spanish rule. Ambeth Ocampo's *Rizal without the Overcoat* (1990) framed for me the legacy of the Ilustrados, beneath the sheen of mythology. Stanley Karnow's *In Our Image: America's Empire in the Philippines* (1989) supplied information on U.S. colonial and postcolonial policy in the Philippines, from the Spanish-American War to the Marcos years, including critical details about the decisions and motivations of the highest-ranking U.S. officials. Aguinaldo's memoirs (first published in full in 1967) provided his own version of events, including the promises U.S. officials made and broke. Gregoria de Jesus's memoir, *Mga Tala Ng Aking Buhay*, translated by Leandro H. Fernandez (1930), offered an inside look at the secretive life of the revolutionaries and the fallout from her husband's execution. Lilia Quindoza Santiago's *Tales of Courage & Compassion: Stories of Women in the Philippine Revolution* (1997) provided additional biographical details about Gregoria. Leon Wolff's *Little Brown Brother: How the United States Purchased and Pacified the Philippines* (1960) provided a ground-level view of the military clash between the United States and the Philippines, and the policies that sparked it.

To better understand historical context, I relied on "Pamitinan and Tapusi: Using the Carpio Legend to Reconstruct Lower-Class Consciousness in the Late Spanish Philippines," a 2018 National University of Singapore study authored by Joseph Scalice, "Philippine Culture and the Filipino Identity," an Ateneo de Manila University study authored by Miguel A. Bernard, and "Filipino Identity: The Haunting Question," a 2013 study authored by Niels Mulder. Raul Rafael Ingles's *1908: The Way It Really Was* (2010) provided primary source excerpts of newspaper articles, speeches, and other contemporaneous accounts on life in the Philippines under American rule. William Lytle Schurz's *The Manila Galleon* (first published in 1939) described the experiences of Filipino workers on the ship, and Floro L. Mercene's *Manila Men in the New World* (2007) chronicled the journeys of the earliest Filipino migrants in the Americas.

Carlos Bulosan's memoir, *America Is in the Heart* (first published in 1946), helped me further understand the landscape facing Filipino immigrants in the 1930s. Isabel Wilkerson's *The Warmth of Other Suns* (2010) supplied historical background on the migration of Black Americans from the South to the North and West—as well as the U.S. policies they encountered on both ends of the journey. Maya Angelou's *I Know Why the Caged Bird Sings* (1969) vividly captured the Fillmore District in the years after World War II. Frantz Fanon's *The Wretched of the Earth* (1961) helped me better understand the perspective of the colonized, and the ideas blooming in oppressed lands during the second half of the twentieth century.

John Hersey's *Hiroshima* (1946) supplied a ground-level view of Japanese society before the atom bombs fell and the destruction that followed. Dan Carlin's series on the rise of Japan's empire on the *Hardcore History* podcast also contributed to my understanding of where that country fit into global affairs in the lead-up to World War II. David Halberstam's *The Best and the Brightest* (1969) offered a meticulously reported account of U.S. foreign policy before and during the Vietnam War. Raymond Bonner's *Waltzing with a Dictator* (1987), published a year after Marcos's regime ended, detailed how U.S. support helped him stay in power. I learned additional biographical information about Marcos—and how he is remembered—on my 2017 visits to three museums about him in his home province of Ilocos Norte. *Pork and Other Perks: Corruption and Governance in the Philippines* (1998), a collection of case studies documented by investigative reporters and edited by Sheila Coronel, chronicled corruption in the Philippines in the years after the dictatorship. The 2014 Human Rights Watch report "'I Already Bought You': Abuse and Exploitation of Female Migrant Domestic Workers in the United Arab Emirates" provided information about the treatment of overseas workers.

Details about Mariano Vallejo are from biographical information compiled by the Sonoma County Library and from the court documents in the cases over his land. Details about key U.S. immigration cases are from publicly available court documents, as well as from Mae Ngai's *Impossible Subjects* (2014),

Vivek Bald's *Bengali Harlem and the Lost Histories of South Asian America* (2013), Peggy Pascoe's *What Comes Naturally: Miscegenation Law and the Making of Race in America* (2009), Jia Lynn Yang's *One Mighty and Irresistible Tide* (2020), and two compilations—*Race on Trial: Law and Justice in American History* (2002), edited by Annette Gordon-Reed, and *White Women in Racialized Spaces* (2002), edited by Samina Najmi and Rajini Srikanth. Catherine Ceniza Choy's *Empire of Care* (2003) laid out why the Philippines became the world's primary exporter of nurses, and how that has shaped the diaspora. *Struggling to Be Heard* (1998), an anthology edited by Valerie Ooka Pang and Li-Rong Lilly Cheng, provided background on how young Asian immigrants learn about their history in U.S. schools. The anthology *Reclaiming San Francisco: History, Politics, Culture* (1998), edited by James Brook and Chris Carlsson, provided contextual information on how immigrant waves shaped the city.

I learned about Vallejo's industrial history from reports commissioned by Vallejo's Planning Commission and a visit to the Mare Island Museum, and gained additional insight on life on the city's north side in the 1990s from *My Opinion* (2015), the memoir of Mac Mall, the rapper who had once been Jed's neighbor. Dawn Bohulano Mabalon's *Little Manila Is in the Heart* (2013), Benito Vergara's *Pinoy Capital: The Filipino Nation in Daly City* (1996), Joaquin Jay Gonzalez's *Filipino American Faith in Action: Immigration, Religion, and Civic Engagement* (2009), Yen Le Espiritu's *Filipino American Lives* (1995), and *Positively No Filipinos Allowed: Building Communities and Discourse* (2006), an anthology edited by Antonio T. Tiongson, Jr., Edgardo V. Gutierrez, and Ricardo V. Gutierrez supplied data and anecdotes about the Filipino diaspora's spread in California.

Anthony Christian Ocampo's *The Latinos of Asia: How Filipino Americans Break the Rules of Race* (2016) gave me a framework for understanding why my Filipino friends and I didn't feel comfortable calling ourselves Asian and often felt more kinship with our Mexican classmates than our Chinese ones. E. J. R. David's *Brown Skin, White Minds: Filipino-/American Postcolonial Psychology* (2013), Dylan Rodriguez's *Suspended Apocalypse: White Supremacy, Genocide, and the Filipino Condition* (2010), and *Filipino American Psychology: A Collection of Personal Narratives* (2010), edited by Kevin Nadal, clarified how Filipino colonial mentality frames our perception of racial hierarchy in the United States.

Adam Tooze's *Crashed: How a Decade of Financial Crises Changed the World* (2018) supplied information about the causes of the 2008 economic collapse, including the mortgage bubble. Michael Lewis's *The Big Short: Inside the Doomsday*

Machine (2010) helped me understand how the financial industry exploited the perceived stability of the housing market. Sally Jenkins's *The Real All Americans: The Team That Changed a Game, a People, a Nation* (2007) provided background on football in the early twentieth century, including racist policies that kept the game mostly white. Dale Maharidge's *The Coming White Minority: California, Multiculturalism, and America's Future* (1996) presented evidence of how nativist fears influence policy and alter communities.

The Southern Poverty Law Center's 2018 report *Teaching Hard History: American Slavery* provided information on curriculums around the country from a survey of U.S. schools. Local newspaper archives were critical for tracking down contemporaneous accounts of the events described in this book: the *Petaluma Argus-Courier* and the Santa Rosa *Press Democrat* on Ku Klux Klan rallies in California; the *Yale Daily News, Salt Lake Herald*, and *Los Angeles Times* on old football games; the *Sacramento Bee* on high school sports; the *San Francisco Chronicle* on the city's housing and development policies; and the *New York Times* on Vallejo's demographics, Ferdinand Marcos's suppression tactics, and nationwide "urban renewal" programs. Data on Americans' perceptions of racial gaps are from the 2019 Yale University study "The Misperception of Racial Economic Inequality," authored by Michael W. Kraus, Ivuoma N. Onyeador, Natalie M. Daumeyer, Julian M. Rucker, and Jennifer A. Richeson. Details in this book on racist violence and discriminatory laws in the United States stem from my years reporting on those subjects for local and national news outlets, and from my research for my first book, *Never Ran, Never Will: Boyhood and Football in a Changing American Inner City* (2018), for which I examined the forces shaping American neighborhoods.